N°	Décor	Ext./Int.	Jour/Nuit	Jour de tournage	Scènes	ANTOINE	RENÉ	BERTRAND	CLASSES	RUES	CENTRE	JULIEN	BIGEY	P. FEUILLE	2e PROF	DIRECTEUR	DECASSINE	1 SURVEILLANT	2 SURVEILLANT	GILBERTE	T. BELLE		Figurants
24	PLACE BREDA			S 6	9A, 11, 12, 33	o	+	Δ															2 FEMMES EPICERIE
25	PLACE DE LA TRINITE / RUE DES MARTYRS	EXTERIERS	A J	L 8	47, 9, 35, 19	o	+	Δ														1	
26	MEDRANO - PIGALLE / MOULIN DE LA CHANSON	EXTERIERS	S N	M 9	19A, 29, 42, 65	o	+	Δ															
27	RUE DU CROISSANT / DEVANT BOULANGERIE	EXTERIERS	S	M 10	43, 44, 43A, 43B	o	+															5	
28	RUE MONTMARTRE	EXTERIERS	NUIT	J 11	46	o																	FILLE ET GARCON AU CHIEN
29	RUE St LAZARE / RUES DIVERSES (CAR DE POLICE)	EXTERIERS	NUIT	V 12	46A, 89, 89A	o																4	
				S 13																			
30	TOUR EIFFEL	EXTERIEURS	JOUR	L 15	24	o	+																UN PAYSAN
31	RICHELIEU-DROUOT - CINEMA / BOULANGERIE - BILLARD	EXTERIEURS	JOUR	M 16	20, 22, 21, 23, 23A	o	+			●												15	
32	FÊTE - METRO	EXTERIEURS	JOUR	M 17	25, 26, 27, 43c	o	+																
33	PARLOIR - REFECTOIRE	I	JOUR	J 18	94A, 100	o	+				*							Δ	×	o		20	CONCIERGE / PARENTS
34	ROUTES - PLAGES	EXT	JOUR	V 19	104, 105, 105A, 106, 107, 108	o																	CHAUFFEUR CAMION / 2 GENDARMES
35	DEVANT BUREAU PSYCHOLOGUE	EXT	JOUR	S 20	95, 99	o												Δ					5 GOSSES DU CENTRE
36	COUR (ARRIVÉ PIPEAU) / RUE	EXT	JOUR	L 22	94, 94B, 94c, 99A	o					*							Δ	×			1	
37	STADE - PAYSAGE	EXT	JOUR	M 23	101, 102, 103	o					*							Δ					
				M 24																			
38	DEVANT L'ECOLE (STADE	E	JOUR	V 26	8, 41, 51c, 54c, 54D, 54E	o	+	Δ	×					(Δ)	(×)		(+)			o		10	PARENTS D'ELEVES - VIGNERON / PROF DE GYMNASTIQUE
39	SALLE DE CLASSE	I	JOUR	S 27	1, 2, 3, 4	o	+	Δ	×					Δ									
40	SALLE DE CLASSE	INTERIEUR	JOUR	L 29	7, 38, 39, 50, 51	o	+	Δ	×			o		Δ		o	+			o			LA SECRETAIRE
41	SALLE DE CLASSE	INTERIEUR	JOUR	M 30	54, 54A, 54B	o	+	Δ	×					Δ									PROF. DE CHANT
42	SALLE DE CLASSE	INTERIEUR	JOUR	M 31	56, 58	o	+	Δ	×					Δ									
43	COUR DE RECRÉATION	E	JOUR	V 2	5, 6, 36, 48, 54c	o	+	Δ	×					Δ	×	o	+						
44	COULOIR - BUREAU. LOGE	I	JOUR	S 3	37, 51A, 51B, 58A, 58B	o	+	Δ	×			o		Δ		o				o			SECRETAIRE - CONCIERGE

TRUFFAUT BY TRUFFAUT

TRUFFAUT
BY
TRUFFAUT

Texts and Documents Compiled by
Dominique Rabourdin
Translated from the French
by Robert Erich Wolf

HARRY N. ABRAMS, INC., PUBLISHERS, NEW YORK

Library of Congress Cataloging-in-Publication Data

Truffaut, François.
Truffaut by Truffaut.

Translation of: Truffaut par Truffaut.
Filmography: p.
Bibliography: p.
Includes index.
1. Truffaut, François. I. Rabourdin, Dominique.
II. Title.
PN1998.A3T75813 1986 791.43'0233'0924 86-1247
ISBN 0-8109-1689-4

Published in 1987 by Harry N. Abrams, Incorporated, New York

Times Mirror Books

Printed and bound in France

CONTENTS

ABOUT THIS BOOK

The text of this book consists entirely of writings and remarks by François Truffaut; it is illustrated with photographs of him, scenes from his films, and documents that relate to him or the films. As it stands, in its final form, the book corresponds only in part to my initial project. What I had in mind was a close collaboration with Truffaut himself, taking as my model his book of conversations with Alfred Hitchcock. (Among books on cinema his "Hitch-book" remains an unequaled standard.) Despite his poor health, he encouraged me in my idea and let me consult certain of his private papers as well as the documents, many unpublished, in the files of his production company, Les Films du Carosse. It was he who advised me to start out by assembling, as an indispensable basis for everything else, his most significant published interviews. He made a great point particularly of the ones he regularly granted *Le Monde* at the appearance of each new film, but also of his remarks concerning his childhood and adolescence to Aline Desjardins on the Canadian radio in 1971. Later, he promised, he would take a hand directly in the preparation of the book. Later . . . We should wait, he wrote me in September 1984, for "a more favorable time," mentioning in the same letter his personal projects and future writings, among them the "autobiography" he had begun to dictate to Claude de Givray and which he wished to leave to his daughters.

But François Truffaut was fated never to tell the story of his life and his films with that passion so characteristic of him. Fortunately, though, scattered in newspapers, magazines, books, and press releases are many texts on those themes—the indispensable reflections of a filmmaker on his work, first-person observations, a day-to-day record.

It was never my intention to make this book a kind of rewrite of his own *Les Films de Ma Vie,* nor to gather again the personal testimony of François Truffaut's principal collaborators and friends; that job was done, and done well, in *Cahiers du Cinéma*. As for tributes, plenty of people have written and are writing them, day after day, regularly. So, instead, I have made it my priority to assemble here whatever was truly essential in what Truffaut himself wrote about his own films, beginning with the invaluable prefaces accompanying the complete screenplays published, for the most part, in the magazine *L'Avant-Scène Cinéma*. But there are many other writings, harder to come by: declarations of intention, notes meant for actors or technicians before shooting began, and statements intended for newspaper people before the films opened. Practically every press book (worked out with his participation and with great care) includes a preliminary text, sometimes very short but always stating his personal point of view about the film. The great interest of those writings, besides their beauty (Truffaut was as great a writer as a filmmaker), lies in the fact that they are never abstract, never dryly theoretical. When he wrote these pieces about his films he was their first critic, their first judge, but at the same time he was always speaking about himself, his life, his experiences in making films.

That same approach led me to include in this book texts that Truffaut devoted to a few individuals who were important in his life and who explain much in his work: André Bazin, Jean Cocteau, Jean Renoir, Alfred Hitchcock, Henri-Pierre Roché, Jacques Audiberti, Ernst Lubitsch. They were friends, people who taught him to think, or traveled the same road, and who continually passed on to him, if not their example, at least their experience. Their mark is plain to read in all his work over the years. As in, for example, *Antoine et l'Orpheline* of 1955, a piece of straight writing unconnected with film (something rare) in which the influence of Cocteau is obvious and which already anticipates the "Doinel cycle." Some years after it was written, when Truffaut was shooting *The 400 Blows,* he would call attention to what, in this first real film of his, was "à la Cocteau." And, self-taught but well read, Truffaut could learn also from a Balzac or a Stendhal. Another essay from the same year, *Dessous d'Espoir,* bears traces of his reading at the time; more than twenty years later attitudes similar to those expressed there turn up again in the film *The Man Who Loved Women.*

There remained the task of combining such texts with the interviews Truffaut was always ready to grant. Always in much demand by the press, he was conscientious about everything he said or wrote and often insisted on reading over what he had said and correcting or even reworking it. There are a great many such interviews. Brought together, they would fill several large volumes. I have singled out only the most significant and clearest, abridging them (my apologies to their writers and publishers!) so as to avoid too much repetition. I did let pass, however, because they seemed to me important, certain restatements of things already said—and certain changes of mind—because these are always enriching. For instance, fifteen years after *The Bride Wore Black,* Truffaut's opinion of the film was no longer the same, and he was very good at drawing lessons from his failures and errors with a modesty and lucidity very different from the attitude of some of his colleagues.

Yet, above all, I had to make the book live, to capture the picture of a filmmaker at work, day after day, trying to find his way into the secret of a film. Call it the mechanics of inspiration or his working method, as you will. François Truffaut preserved every last scrap of what had been or could have been of use in writing or shooting his films: handwritten notes, sketches, drafts, the different states of a screenplay, working plans, personnel rosters, correspondence, pages cut out of books and annotated and underlined, like the pages from *Jules et Jim,* Henri-Pierre Roché's novel, cut out and pasted into a large notebook. These materials surely say more about the process of making a film, and say it less abstractly, than long discourses or interviews. Once assembled, the whole lot of these documents can stand without critical commentary, I think. For each film I have tried to track down whatever sparked it off, like this statement of Truffaut's about *Shoot the Piano Player:* "A single image made me decide to make the film. It was in the book. A sloping road in the snow, the car running down it with no noise from the motor. That's all. . . . The rest followed."

François Truffaut, like all filmmakers who interest us, could have said, as Vincente Minnelli did, "I do nothing more than project myself on the screen." By putting together the documents and texts here, like the pieces of a jigsaw puzzle, I wanted to define better what Truffaut projected on the screen and how he projected it. His intentions speak for themselves. The writings take one back to the films, the films to an *auteur* at one and the same time lucid and secretive, with accents of profound truth and zones of shadow. Only a few rare filmmakers have devoted their lives to their films in this way, have been so inseparably bound up with them, have fabricated for themselves a universe so very much like the films they loved, have even found in themselves parallel characters to those populating their films. His films send us back to his life, and his life to the image François Truffaut wanted to give of it. The secret and interest of a work: it all comes full circle.

Dominique Rabourdin

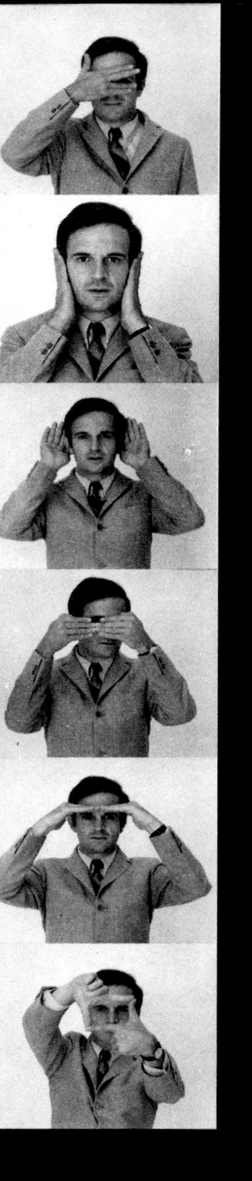

AUTOBIOGRAPHY

François Truffaut at ten

CHILDHOOD

I still retain from that time a great anxiety, and the movies are bound up with an anxiety, with an idea of something clandestine

François Truffaut, you were born in Paris on February 6, 1932, to an architect father and a mother who was a secretary for the magazine L'Illustration, *but where did you spend the first years of your life?*

Oh! sent out for nursing, I think, one place or another, with my grandmothers, maternal and paternal by turns, yes.

Do you think that left its mark on your early years?

I believe so. Especially my maternal grandmother, who had a great love for books. She used to take me to a bookstore where she borrowed books, and I remember that she used to discuss with the owner the novels that had just come out. And then, at my paternal grandmother's it was . . . not out in the country, but at any rate outside Paris, along the main highway where a great many cars went by, before there was the expressway. A lot still go by. Her husband, my grandfather, was a stonecutter, he worked a lot for cemeteries; there was a considerable contrast between my mother's family and my father's.

Were you an only child?

Yes.

One imagines you as solitary and very closed in on yourself. Was it because, at an early age, you had to move around a great deal and became attached to several different persons?

Certainly and, then too, my mother couldn't stand noise. In fact, I ought to say, to be more precise, she couldn't stand me. In any case I had to make myself unnoticed and remain on a chair reading. I didn't have the right to play or make noise. I had to make her forget that I existed.

And how did you react to that?

Ah! you know, I was very submissive, as children always are. They don't discuss things much, they don't raise questions about the education they're given or the way they are being brought up; so I took refuge in reading. I think I very quickly got into the habit of reading enormously. . . .

I lived around Pigalle, Rue Henri-Monnier, that neighborhood a little below Montmartre and Pigalle, and I went to the kindergarten on Rue Clauzel, then to the Lycée Rollin, in the children's classes, and later to different public schools; then with a very bad school record, very much disturbed beginning around twelve or thirteen, I was simply expelled, and consequently changed places often. . . . I can't remember having belonged to any group whatsoever. I think I was always outside things, and quite early on isolated by my tastes, by different things, and if later I had a friend or two it was thanks to the movies, by taking them to the movies, but none of your play groups, no groups. . . . Nor was I one of those children who played in the street, because I wasn't allowed to. . . .

Obviously my childhood wasn't much fun, not that of a martyred child or a child who was beaten, but that of a child unloved or just ignored, which is even then pretty galling.

Patrick Auffay and Jean-Pierre Léaud in *The 400 Blows*

So the cinema entered your life very early?

Yes, in two phases. First, during the Occupation; there were no American films, there were French films and German films, which weren't very good, and I began to take an interest in cinema, I can't say why, but anyway quite early, even to the point of reading reviews in newspapers. I used to run the errands in the morning, and I had to bring back the milk and the newspaper. In the street I was already reading, so I knew the newspaper before my parents; so before hearing them speak about it I knew what shows were on in Paris, principally the movies.

But you say you don't know why you were taking such a special and precocious interest in the cinema. Don't you think it was precisely because you could escape there from the milieu that was rejecting you and that consequently you yourself wished to reject?

Yes, it followed from books. A pretty good escape—anyway, a pretty effective escape—I used to get from novels. I read children's novels but also novels my mother was reading, on the sly from her. And then later there were the films, and the films probably constituted an even greater escape and, in the same way, I began to go to the films secretly. For example, my folks would leave for the theater. After ten minutes had gone by, I was sure they were really and truly gone, and I would go to the movies, with a terrifying anxiety about the schedules, because I was afraid they might get home before me. So the second half of the film was ruined, and sometimes fear would even make me leave before the end, because I had to be in bed when my folks got home. I still retain a great anxiety from that time, and films are tied to an anxiety, an idea of something clandestine, just like the books I used to read clandestinely, but for the films it was even worse. And then they would take me to see a film I had already seen. I couldn't say I had seen it, and I think that that gave me the taste for seeing an enormous lot of the same things again, always the same films.

Interview by Aline Desjardins, Radio-Canada, December 1971; published by Editions Leméac, Ottawa, 1973

Jean-Pierre Léaud in *The 400 Blows*

My first memory of the cinema goes back to 1939

My first memory of the cinema goes back to 1939, a few months before the end of the war.* It was at the Gaieté Rochechouart, a very large movie house facing the Square d'Anvers.

They were showing *Paradis Perdu* with Micheline Presle, with her extraordinary beauty and sweetness, and Fernand Gravey. The house was full of soldiers on leave accompanied by their young wives or mistresses. Perhaps you know that this superb melodrama by Abel Gance takes place between 1914 and 1935, and that a large section of the film is devoted to the war, to the trenches, the munitions factories where the women worked, and so on. There was such a coincidence between the situation of the characters in the film and that of the viewers that the entire house was in tears; hundreds of handkerchiefs perforated the dark hall with points of white. I would never again experience such an emotional unanimity during the showing of a film. We know that periods of war or simply of poverty and destitution favor attendance at movie houses. After the armistice, when the Germans occupied the country, the movie house became a refuge for everybody, and not only in the figurative sense. Later on, it stopped being so, when they took to verifying identities at the exits to find young fellows of an age to join the French workers in Germany. Since that wasn't as yet my problem, my only anxiety watching the film was that the show might be interrupted by an alert; in that case, you had to leave the hall and take an exit ticket and wait in the cellar of the movie house for the end of the alert. Up to 1942 I never went to the cinema by myself, and with the exception of *Paradis Perdu* I have forgotten even the titles of the films I saw. It was beginning in 1942, and particularly when *Les Visiteurs du*

François Truffaut at ten: "I read children's stories. . . ."

*Truffaut's error: *Paradis Perdu* opened in Paris on December 13, 1940.

Jean-Pierre Léaud in *The 400 Blows*

Soir came out, that I got into the habit of going alone, and most times in secret, to see the films of my choice or, more precisely, those shown in the eight or ten houses spread out on either side of Place Pigalle, where I was living. I'll tell elsewhere and on another occasion my memories of playing hookey connected with the cinema. Here I want only to recall the way things were with the cinema under the Occupation, so as to throw Bazin's writings into the right light for the time.

Preface to André Bazin, Le Cinéma de l'Occupation, *Collection 10/18, edited by Christian Bourgeois, Paris, U.G.E., 1975*

I very soon acquired a feeling of solidarity with artistic or "difficult" films. For example, I didn't share my schoolmates' opinion of a film like *Les Visiteurs du Soir,* which struck them as ridiculous, and it even happened that I got hostile toward one of our teachers for whom *Les Dames du Bois de Boulogne* was ridiculous. I remember clearly the sort of scandal that went on over *Les Dames du Bois de Boulogne:* people walked out before the end of the screening. It was then that the name of Cocteau became familiar to me, the fact being that I was always for the artist, the artist made fun of, the artist people sneered at—even sometimes with naïveté, even when the film wasn't worth defending.

Interview by Aline Desjardins, Radio-Canada, 1971

The door was open, I was ready to receive the ideas and images of Jean Vigo, Jean Cocteau, Sacha Guitry, Orson Welles . . .

In 1945 I was thirteen. At that time *Le Roman d'un Tricheur* was already eight years old, but several times a year it was billed at the Cinéma Champollion in the Latin Quarter. I had seen it ten times or so and I knew by heart the commentary, which intoxicated me almost as if it were a musical score. One day a family crisis led me to walk out on my family. I went to a pal's and left a note under his door: "I had to clear out of the house. You have to help me find a place to sleep. Meanwhile I'm going to the Champollion, they're showing *Le Roman d'un Tricheur*. I'll be there all day. Meet me there in the evening." This personal recollection shows how much Guitry's film overwhelmed me, if I could face looking at it three or four times in a row in a single day. The cinema was generally a refuge for me, but when that refuge was inhabited by Chaplin or by Guitry, then I felt myself snug and warm, protected.

The comparison between Chaplin and Guitry will surprise only those who have forgotten that *Le Roman d'un Tricheur* is a story of survival, a eulogy to individualism and to the knack of getting out of scrapes, like many of Chaplin's films.

Preface to Sacha Guitry, Le Cinéma et Moi, *Paris, Ramsay, 1977*

At school: Jean-Pierre Léaud in *The 400 Blows*

I felt a great need to get right into the films I saw, and I managed to do that by moving closer and closer to the screen so as to put the theater itself completely out of my mind. I rejected costume pictures, war films, and westerns because they made total identification more difficult. So, by elimination, there remained only detective films and love films; unlike young viewers of my age I did not identify with the heroic heroes but with the handicapped characters and, more regularly, with all those who found themselves in the wrong.

It's easy to see why Alfred Hitchcock's work, entirely devoted to fear, should have seduced me from the start, and then that of Jean Renoir, aiming at understanding: "What is terrible on this earth is that everybody has his reasons" *(The Rules of the Game).* The door was open, I was ready to accept the ideas and images of Jean Vigo, Jean Cocteau, Sacha Guitry, Orson Welles, Marcel Pagnol, Lubitsch, Charlie Chaplin, of course; of all those who, without being immoral, "question other people's morality" *(Hiroshima Mon Amour).*

Preface to Les Films de Ma Vie

I was fortunate to discover Jean Vigo's films in a single screening, a Saturday afternoon in 1946, at the Sèvres Pathé, thanks to the film club La Chambre Noire, run by André Bazin and other colleagues on *La Revue du Cinéma.* When I went into the theater I didn't even know the name of Jean Vigo, but I was immediately seized by a mad admiration for that body of work, the whole lot of which doesn't come to two hundred minutes of projection.

"1970," Les Films de Ma Vie

Citizen Kane, which existed only in its original language, detoxified us of our fanatical Hollywoodism and turned us into high-principled film lovers. That film was certainly responsible, all over the world, for inspiring countless people to devote their lives to making films. . . .

I was fourteen in 1946 and I had already dropped out of school, so it was through Orson Welles that I discovered Shakespeare, just as it was my taste for Bernard Herrmann's music that led me to listen to that of Stravinsky, from which it often takes its inspiration.

"1967," Les Films de Ma Vie

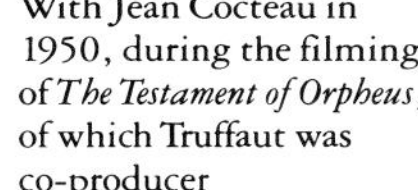

With Jean Cocteau in 1950, during the filming of *The Testament of Orpheus,* of which Truffaut was co-producer

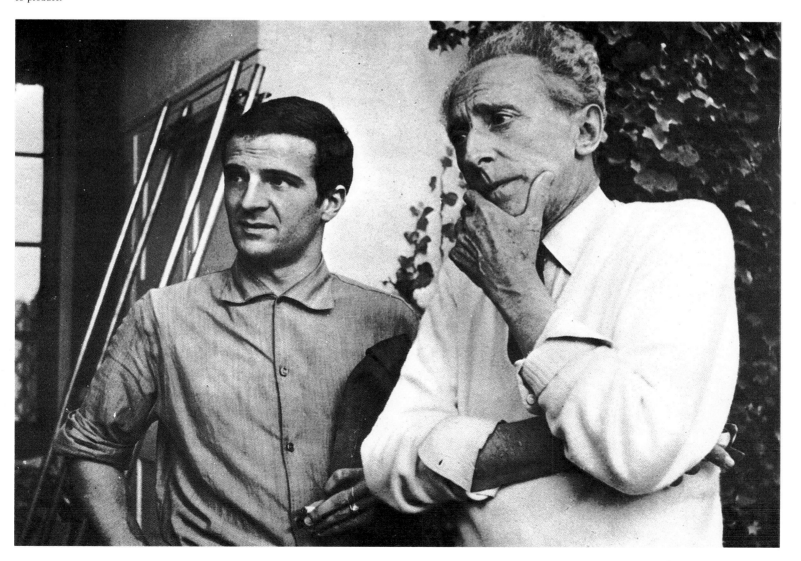

Thursday, June 2nd

Auteur theory (need for)—André Bazin has a great liking for *Citizen Kane* and *The Magnificent Ambersons,* a little for *The Lady from Shanghai* and *Othello,* scarcely any for *Journey into Fear* and *Macbeth,* none at all for *The Stranger.* Cocteau likes *Macbeth* a lot but not *The Stranger.* Sadoul likes *Kane* and *The Magnificent Ambersons* quite a bit but not at all *Journey into Fear* and *Macbeth.* Who is right? Despite my respect for Cocteau, Bazin, and Sadoul, I prefer to go along with the opinion of Astruc, Rivette, Truffaut, and *tutti quanti* who love indiscriminately all of Welles's films just because they are films by Welles and are like absolutely nothing else, for that certain way Orson has which is a Shakespearean dialogue with the sky (the gaze passing above the heads of the extras), for a quality of the image which owes less to plastic form than to a remarkable feeling for the dramaturgy of the scenes, for a perpetual verbal and technical invention, for everything that creates a style, that "Welles style" which one finds in all his films, whether they are luxurious or made on nothing, filmed fast or slowly. I haven't yet seen *Mr. Arkadin* but I know it's a good film because it's by Orson Welles and even if Welles wanted to turn out something like Delannoy, he couldn't. All the rest will only be ushers' gossip.

Signed Robert Lachenay, "Petit Journal Intime du Cinéma," Cahiers du Cinéma, *no. 48, June 1955*

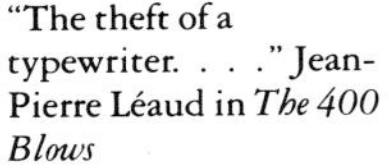

"The theft of a typewriter. . . ." Jean-Pierre Léaud in *The 400 Blows*

When I was fourteen the theft of a typewriter got me into the hands of the cops and I saw what it was all about. One night, for laughs, they jumped on me: "Admit that you jerk off at night, go on, admit it and we'll leave you alone." And the blows, real blows, rained down, and I, already sly: "Jerk off, what's that?" "Ah! You're putting us on," and it began all over again.

Interview by Pierre Ajame, Le Nouvel Adam, *no. 19, February 1968*

ADOLESCENCE

On my part there were truancies, escapes from home, then finally I felt there was a kind of urgency for me to go to work

So you decided to leave your family and go to work?

I don't know to what extent that involved decisions; on my part there were truancies, escapes from home, then finally I felt that there was a kind of urgency for me to go to work. I had my first job when I ran away from home and then I was sent back to my parents again, and what I earned on that job permitted me to place a want ad for another. At that point I was taken on as a stockboy in a concern on the Avenue de l'Opéra that specialized in dealing in seeds, exporting, importing seeds.

You ended up in several different kinds of jobs?

Yes, I did other kinds of jobs and I also worked in a factory during another period, as acetylene welder, and then I began to do a little journalism. . . .

But how did you end up there? Because it's a long way from stockboy for seeds to writing.

Oh well, those are the accidents of life. Actually, when I worked as a laborer it wasn't any kind of fun. It was in a factory that hired women and children so as to pay them less, and the welding turned out wasn't perfect: I often wondered what happened with the materials we welded. Anyway, on Saturdays there was a kind of club in Paris that met in a movie house and that called itself the Club du Faubourg, and I went there because I saw that, from time to time, they talked cinema, and in spite of my mere fifteen years, fifteen and a half, I used to sound off very violently. I used to attack the people who were there, directors, people who had made films I didn't find good. And that made people laugh, considering how young I was. And a man who was the literary director of *Elle,* Pierre-Jean Launay, and who is a novelist, had taken a liking to me and proposed that I come to work for the magazine *Elle,* which would permit me to quit the factory; so I was really happy and I did that for a while, but that didn't continue because "reporting" didn't interest me. For example, to attend a beauty pageant on the Avenue de l'Opéra, that's not much like me. They didn't want to let me write about the cinema; the women who worked there were defending their territory. In short, that couldn't last very long.

Interview by Aline Desjardins, Radio-Canada, 1971

A night at the police station: Jean-Pierre Léaud in *The 400 Blows*

I had quit my job as stockboy without telling my parents. I had opened a film club in the Latin Quarter. I had wanted to open a film club that met on Sunday mornings and it had no success. The truth is, it's more complicated than that. I had used the money from my severance pay for it (because I had given notice to the company I worked for, I had received the Christmas bonus, etc.). I had sunk everything into the film club. I pasted up posters at night to publicize the club's program, but I had fallen in with a swindler, a guy who took all my money while promising films he claimed to own and which at the last minute he didn't bring. Films by Fritz Lang: *Les Trois Lumières* [*Der Müde Tod*], for example. And I found myself facing halls of people who had to be paid back because there wasn't any film! The first time I got by by showing the film that was on that week in the movie house itself, but that wasn't possible every time and finally the whole thing ended badly because, after I had run away again, my father found me, dragged me to the police station, and I found myself in the Center for Observation of Juvenile Delinquents. . . . Just about the way it's shown in the film *The 400 Blows,* except that this was shortly after the war and one felt it in the way things were in that place: there was a lot of poverty, there were young workers who were there because they had stolen lead from the factory, there were boys who were stealing bicycles from cellars, there were still food stamps in that period because, you know, long after the Liberation there was still rationing.

Interview by Aline Desjardins, Radio-Canada, 1971

Up to then, up to when it came to a head in a way, it's pretty black. It was the cinema that was the light in all that?

That's the way it was, really and truly black except for the cinema, and then the meeting . . .

Before going into that Center I had known, had met, André Bazin sort of in passing, three or four times. I had spoken to him about my film club and he was my life buoy because from there, from the Center for Observation, I wrote to him and he helped me a lot. He got in touch with the psychologist of the establishment and he helped me get out because he vouched for me, he said that he would take me on to work with him, at Travail et Culture, finally he gave certain guarantees thanks to which I got out quite quickly.

Cahiers du Cinéma, the first issue, April 1951

You have said something that proves, I think, that André Bazin was your spiritual father. You said: "A reprimand from him was like a sign of affection, what I lacked throughout my childhood." That observation is full of meaning, I find.

Oh yes, certainly.

He was really such a sure guide?

Yes, sure enough, yes . . .

And did he help you subsequently in your work as a critic, which you then took on, for a while at least?

Absolutely yes. He read my first articles. He encouraged me enormously. He published my first articles in *Cahiers du Cinéma* and after that I went to work for *Arts* and then I did film criticism, professionally, for different newspapers. . . .

Bazin rescued you from that center for juveniles. Afterwards, how did that kind of godfather relationship work out?

Bazin was directing the film section of a cultural organization called Travail et Culture and which was responsible to [the ministries of] Tourism and Labor, so I worked under his direction. It was a matter of organizing film showings, in 16 mm, in factories, with Chaplin's films, and different sorts of events that Bazin arranged in the suburbs around Paris: for example, a series of lectures on "How a Film Is Made," with excerpts from *Le Jour Se Lève* with comments by him. So I helped him and that was really a very good period for me. It was at Travail et Culture that I first met Alain Resnais, Remo Forlani, Chris Marker, people like that, friends of Bazin who were getting ready to make films. Then, unfortunately, Bazin fell ill. He had to go into a sanatorium, and they didn't keep me on because I wasn't much use anymore, and in reality it was at that point that I went to work at acetylene welding, then for the magazine *Elle,* thanks to the literary director who had noticed me in that Club du Faubourg where I used to sound off. Then during that part of my life, there was a private thing happened, a sentimental episode that ended badly, that I filmed later in *Love at Twenty.* In the sketch of *Love at Twenty* you see Antoine Doinel falling

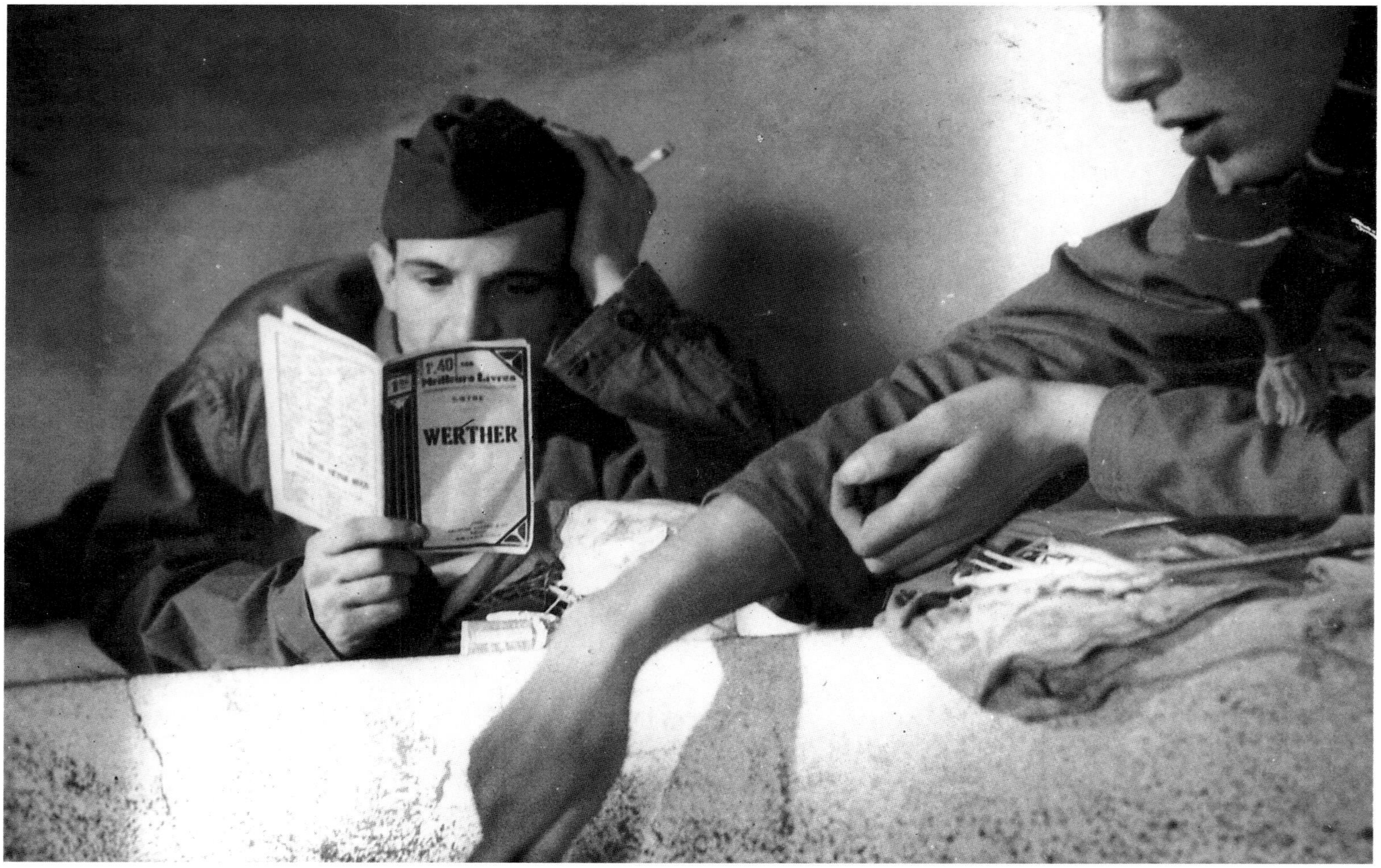

Claude de Givray's film *Tire-au-Flanc,* 1961, produced and acted by François Truffaut, here seen reading Goethe's *Werther* in the economical Classiques Fayard edition

in love with a young girl he meets at the Jeunesses Musicales [young people's concerts], trying to push his way into her life by force, moving away from home and taking a place in her street, opposite her family's place, so as to be closer to her; you see his getting friendly with her parents and becoming so close that, for the girl, he ends up an utter bore, a kind of cousin she can no longer stand. . . .

And he was François Truffaut, that young man?

Right. We can say that that story was really lived; it wasn't the Jeunesses Musicales but, obviously, the Cinémathèque, and the whole thing finally led me to go off into the army.

Interview by Aline Desjardins, Radio-Canada, 1971

Cahiers du Cinéma, no. 91, January 1959, containing Truffaut's homage to Bazin, "Il Faisait Bon Vivre"

André Bazin. . . . Since that day in 1948 when he got me my first job as a fellow film buff, I became his adoptive son and so I owe to him everything good that has happened in my life since

André Bazin, who has just died at the age of forty, was the best writer on cinema in Europe. Since that day in 1948 when he got me my first job as a fellow film buff, I became his adoptive son and so I owe to him everything good that has happened in my life since. He taught me to write about the cinema, he corrected and published my first articles, and it was thanks to him that I was able to get into directing. He died a few hours after the first day of shooting on my film. When I got to his house in Nogent, after a phone call from his friend Father Léger, he looked at me but already couldn't speak anymore and was suffering terribly. The evening before, he was still watching *The Crime of Monsieur Lange* on television, taking notes for the book he was preparing on the work of Jean Renoir.

If I had to draw a portrait of André Bazin, I would have to think of something like the feature in the American magazine, "The Most Unforgettable Character I've Met."

André Bazin, like the characters in Giraudoux's works, was a man "from before original sin." Everybody knew he was honest and good, but his honesty and his goodness always proved surprising because they were offered so abundantly. Speaking with him was like, for a Hindu, bathing in the Ganges. He was so warm-hearted and generous that several times, in conversation, I spoke badly of one or another of our common acquaintances for the sole pleasure of hearing the speech for the defense he would never fail to deliver. . . .

I don't know if the world is wicked or fair, but I'm certain that it is men like Bazin who make it better because, by believing life to be good and by acting as if it were, André did good to everyone who approached him, and you could count on the fingers of one hand the people who behaved badly toward him. Everyone who ever spoke with Bazin, even if only once, can claim to be his "best friend," because in contact with him, overwhelmed by so much purity, it was impossible not to give him the best of yourself.

André Bazin was too warmly alive for anyone to string together hollow phrases such as "still alive," "present among us," etc. He is dead, and that is a veritable desolation, a cruel fact, and an abominable sorrow. One can only weep and reread him. . . .

"Adieux à André Bazin," Arts, *November 19, 1958*

ndré died twenty-four years ago. One might think that the passage of time has assuaged the feeling of his absence. That is not the case.

We miss Bazin.

Preface to Dudley Andrew, "André Bazin," Cahiers du Cinéma, *Paris, Editions de l'Etoile, 1983*

In military prison, 1951

I went AWOL and then I was caught, I broke out of jail, and went from being AWOL to becoming a deserter

I was only eighteen, I still had two years to wait to do my military service and, at the time, there was the war in Indochina, and I signed up. I wanted to sign up for two years only, but the war was going so badly at that point, if I may say so, that enlistments were brought up to a minimum of three years. I said, "That's that, I'm going in for three years." I was a little crazy and I went off for three years, between Christmas and New Year's Day, and I chose that day to sign in in order to pass Christmas Eve as a civilian and New Year's Eve as a soldier, to compare them: I must say, they were both equally gloomy. Then I found myself, having asked to join the army film service (you know people always joke about military logic), I found myself in an artillery regiment in North Germany!

Hard to imagine you . . .

And there, as a gunner, I damaged my ears. I had had one ear damaged ever since childhood, and the other was by the military maneuvers, with the result that today I can't take stereo sound and nightclubs nor too loud noises, evenings especially.

Once again Bazin came to your rescue.

Bazin was appalled, really appalled when he found out I had enlisted. I wrote to him about it; as so often when one does dumb things, one doesn't ask people's opinion, one simply confronts them with the accomplished deed; so I signed up. I filled out all the papers, and I wrote to him, and he said to me: "I feel that had I been in Paris we would have been able to talk together and I would have dissuaded you"; we always called each other *vous,* he always addressed me as *vous,* he had a very great respect for other people, anyway I think it was something pretty intelligent on his part, and so he said to me: "I believe I would have dissuaded you, that we would have talked it over together, but I hope it will go all right." So I did the six-months basic training, then maneuvers in Germany, everything went well. What didn't go well was when I was sent to Paris on leave. I had received all my shots for the Far East, but I was on leave with money, and once again films to be seen and no desire to go back, so I simply didn't go back. I went AWOL and then I was caught, I broke out of jail, and went from being AWOL to becoming a deserter. There was a point where finally they brought me back to Germany in handcuffs, they shaved my skull, and there I was really heading for trouble if it wasn't for Bazin, who took no end of measures in Paris with everyone possible. . . . That took a long time; I was in prison, twice I was locked up in the insane asylum at Andernach, and finally they agreed to discharge me on grounds that didn't strike me as overly sympathetic: for "instability of character."

Interview by Aline Desjardins, Radio-Canada, 1971

3e ANNEE MENSUEL. — N° 5

Ciné-Club du Quartier Latin

BULLETIN INTÉRIEUR DU C.C.Q.L. (ASSOCIATION DÉCLARÉE SOUS LE N° 13.209)
Rédacteur en chef : Francis BOUCHET - **Directeur** : Maurice SCHERER
COURRIER : **Ciné-Club du Quartier Latin**, 16, rue de l'Abbé-de-l'pée, **Paris** (5e)

La Règle du Jeu

Pour ceux qui considèrent la **Règle du Jeu** comme le plus grand film de l'histoire du cinéma, la projection intégrale du chef-d'œuvre de Renoir au C.-C.Q.L. fut un événement. Nous ne connaissions de la **Règle du Jeu** qu'une version plus ou moins atrophiée selon les salles dans lesquelles on pouvait trop rarement la voir.

Cette copie comporte treize scènes ou séquences et quatre plans qui ne figurent plus dans les versions commerciales.

Dès l'ouverture du film, après qu'André Jurieu ait exprimé sa déception au micro, la speakerine annonce « ... mais nous avons à nos côtés un ingénieur de chez Baudron... » ; dans cette version on voit et on entend l'ingénieur. Une scène au cours de laquelle Dalio se jette à plat ventre devant ses domestiques pour récupérer sous un canapé le ressort d'un de ses bibelots mécaniques, scène habituellement marquante est très significative; une troisième scène nous montre les invités dans un couloir, regagnant tumultueusement leurs chambres elle est suivie d'un autre où Octave et Jurieu devisent dans leur chambre commune. De nombreux coups de fusil supplémentaires et la mort du petit lapin qui frétille de la queue dans un dernier spasme, scène célèbre par sa signification mais aussi par sa rituelle absence. Deux scènes intimistes précisent la nature exacte des rapports d'Octave et de Lisette d'une part et de Jurieu et Jackie d'autre part. La scène la plus importante et nécessaire à la bonne compréhension du dénouement du film est la scène de la serre. Octave propose à Christine de partir avec lui, puis étant allé chercher les manteaux, il se laisse convaincre par Lisette et c'est à ce moment là précisément que survient Jurieu.

Très émouvants aussi les adieux de Lisette à Octave et Marceau après la mort d'André, suivis du discours de Dalio, plus long dans cette copie.

Enfin maîtres et valets se confondent en ombres sur le mur, tandis que le film s'achève sur le thème de Mozart par lequel il débute.

Grâce à ces treize scènes, grâce à Renoir, ce fut une très belle soirée.

François TRUFFAUT.

Brève présentation des films du mois

Nous attirons l'attention de nos membres sur :

TILLIES PUNCTURED ROMANCE :
Une utopie se réalise et le C.-C. Q. L. vous présentera ce premier grand film de Charlie Chaplin (Réalisation de Mac Sennet, 1914, avec Mabel Normand, Al St John (Picratt), Chester Conclin et Marie Dressler). Au même programme : « Charlot Dentiste » peu connu lui aussi.

JAMMIN THE BLUES :
Un film de jazz qui est en même temps du très bon cinéma.

Au même programme : courts métrages de Duke Ellington, Lester Young, Illinois Jacquett, Fats Waller, Cab Calloway voire même de Louis Armstrong.

LA GUERRE DES ECUREUILS :
(Inédit en France)
Un sensationnel dessin animé de long métrage en technicolor.
En complément : Cow-Cow Boogie, The Pointer, Woody Nood Pecker diplomate. Il y a chez Walter Lantz moins de poésie que chez Disney mais infiniment plus d'humour et de dynamisme.

PIERRE LE GRAND :
de V. Pétrov.
Un film de la grande époque du parlant soviétique. Celle de Newsky, de la Trilogie de Gorki et des Maxime. Actualités soviétiques en début de programme.

WINTERSET
(Sous les Ponts de New-York)
Présentation exceptionnelle d'un des 10 plus grands films de l'histoire du cinéma et qui a fait école. Rien qu'un cœur solitaire en est étroitement inspiré. Je vous encourage vivement à ne pas manquer l'ultime projection de ce film d'Alfred Santell adapté de Maxwell Anderson, par Burgess Meredith.

FESTIVAL MAX LINDER :
Une parenthèse à notre cycle, Charlie Chaplin. Trois ou quatre films célèbres de celui dont Chaplin dit lui-même qu'il fut son maître.

FESTIVAL 1900 :
Le comique, le mélodrame, le superfilm, le film à épisodes. Accompagnement au piano. (Oranges et Sorbets à l'entr'acte.

LES HORIZONS PERDUS :
Un film de Capra qui n'est pas une comédie américaine et que certains tiennent pour son meilleur film.

Il sera intéressant de comparer ce film dont l'action se déroule dans un monde utopique avec Aubervilliers, d'Elie Lotar, qui sera présenté en fin de programme.

LE PORTRAIT DE DORIAN GRAY
d'Albert Lewin
Le portrait de Dorian Gray, adaption extrêmement fidèle de l'œuvre d'Oscar Wilde. Le film nous révèle Albert Lewin qui sans prétendre au génie nous présente des images où le détail est aussi scrupuleusement observé que chez Carné, Renoir ou Ford son interprète.
« Moana » et « Nanouk » ne sont pas que des documentaires sur les Polynésiens et les Esquimaux. Ce sont les films d'aventures les plus beaux qui soient.

Frédéric C. FROESCHEL.

A la dernière Assemblée Générale ont été élus :
Président du Club : Maurice Scherer.
Secrétaire général : Jean-Marc Aucuy.
Trésorier : Jean Mayeur.
Vice-Président : Francis Ducellier.
Secrétaire administratif : Jean Gruault.
Directeur artistique et programmateur : Frédéric-C. Froeschel.

M. Henri Langlois, Secrétaire Général de la Cinémathèque Française nous prie de signaler qu'aucun des films hors-exploitation que nous projetons ne provient de son organisme.

Ces films proviennent de la collection personnelle de M. Frédéric C. Froeschel et de celles de certains membres du conseil d'Administration du C.-C. Q. L. Nous les tenons à la disposition des Clubs qui nous en feraient la demande.

Nous nous excusons de présenter ce numéro sur une seule feuille. Dès la prochaine parution, et sous le titre de « La Gazette du Cinéma », *dont le service sera fait gratuitement à nos membres, nous vous adresserons un véritable journal du Cinéma.*

François Truffaut's first published article, April 1950 (*Note:* Translations of all illustrated documents appear on pages 230–40.)

FROM FILM FAN TO CRITIC

By encouraging me to write, beginning in 1953, Bazin rendered me a great service

François Truffaut's first contribution to *Cahiers du Cinéma*, March 1953

I have never been able to track down my first article, published in 1950 in the *Bulletin du Ciné-Club du Quartier Latin,* but I recall that it had to do with *The Rules of the Game,* of which a complete version had just been found and screened, with fourteen scenes or sequences we had never seen. I made a detailed list of the differences between the two versions and it was probably that article that led André Bazin to propose that I help him get together the documentation for the Renoir book, for which he had already worked out the basic plan.

By encouraging me to write, beginning in 1953, Bazin rendered me a great service, because I was thus obliged to analyze what I enjoyed and to describe it; and that, while it doesn't make you pass from amateur to professional in one wave of a magic wand, does pin you down to the concrete and does, nonetheless, make you take your stand someplace, at that ill-defined place where the critic holds forth. Obviously, at that juncture, the risk is of losing one's enthusiasm, but happily that wasn't the case.

Preface to Les Films de Ma Vie

Cahiers du Cinéma, no. 31, with Truffaut's most famous polemical article, "Une Certaine Tendance du Cinéma Français"

Opposite
François Truffaut and Jean-Marie Straub in the early fifties

La Parisienne, no. 32, October 1955. François Truffaut's writings were not limited to film reviews

I was no longer excited by anything that did not resemble what I myself would have liked to do, and I was becoming too passionate, too unkind. On the other hand, even today, I've kept something of the critic's attitude

You have just referred to one of your articles. How do you view today your opinions as a onetime critic?

I made known, I spread abroad in *Arts,* the points of view of the *Cahiers.* At the start, especially; because little by little I began to take on a more personal slant, to the extent, no doubt, that I was led to speak of films that didn't interest the *Cahiers.* I likewise learned to submit to certain obligations. In the *Cahiers* you could dispense with telling the story of the film. In a weekly you have to do it, and for me that was a very good exercise. Anyhow, I think that, in the *Cahiers,* you had to try to speak of each film on the plane appropriate to it. In one case you had to speak of the abstraction of the directing; in another, emphasize the screenplay. Every film wants to be grasped in its own fashion.

In any case, the obligation to recount the story every week did me a lot of good. Before then I wasn't even seeing the film. I was so drunk on cinema that I was seeing only the movement, the rhythm. . . . Now I had to make a point of consulting a synopsis (at the beginning, at least), because I had trouble in summing up what took place. This made me aware of all the faults of certain screenplays, of certain principles, of certain ways of telling stories. All the stereotypes hit me smack in the face. That was for me the most rewarding period. It corresponded somewhat, I think, to what the experience of a screenwriter ought to be. It led me to see more clearly, even in my tastes, my choices, my prejudices.

I ended up dissecting films to such an extent that, during my last year at *Arts,* it was no longer criticism, strictly speaking, but already a director's critique that I was doing. I was no longer excited by anything that did not resemble what I myself would have liked to do, and I was becoming too passionate, too unkind. On the other hand, even today, I've kept something of the critic's

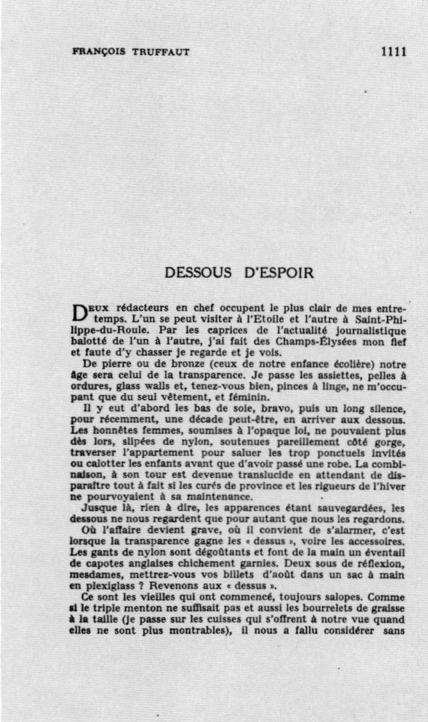

FRANÇOIS TRUFFAUT 1111

DESSOUS D'ESPOIR

Deux rédacteurs en chef occupent le plus clair de mes entretemps. L'un se peut visiter à l'Etoile et l'autre à Saint-Philippe-du-Roule. Par les caprices de l'actualité journalistique balotté de l'un à l'autre, j'ai fait des Champs-Élysées mon fief et faute d'y chasser je regarde et je vois.

De pierre ou de bronze (ceux de notre enfance écolière) notre âge sera celui de la transparence. Je passe les assiettes, pelles à ordures, glass walls et, tenez-vous bien, pinces à linge, ne m'occupant que du seul vêtement, et féminin.

Il y eut d'abord les bas de soie, bravo, puis un long silence, pour récemment, une décade peut-être, en arriver aux dessous. Les honnêtes femmes, soumises à l'opaque loi, ne pouvaient plus dès lors, slipées de nylon, soutenues pareillement côté gorge, traverser l'appartement pour saluer les trop ponctuels invités ou calotter les enfants avant que d'avoir passé une robe. La combinaison, à son tour est devenue translucide en attendant de disparaître tout à fait si les curés de province et les rigueurs de l'hiver ne pourvoyaient à sa maintenance.

Jusque là, rien à dire, les apparences étant sauvegardées, les dessous ne nous regardent que pour autant que nous les regardons.

Où l'affaire devient grave, où il convient de s'alarmer, c'est lorsque la transparence gagne les « dessus », voire les accessoires. Les gants de nylon sont dégoûtants et font de la main un éventail de capotes anglaises chichement garnies. Deux sous de réflexion, mesdames, mettrez-vous vos billets d'août dans un sac à main en plexiglass ? Revenons aux « dessus ».

Ce sont les vieilles qui ont commencé, toujours salopes. Comme si le triple menton ne suffisait pas et aussi les bourrelets de graisse à la taille (je passe sur les cuisses qui s'offrent à notre vue quand elles ne sont plus montrables), il nous a fallu considérer sans

1112 CHRONIQUES

pouffer d'énormes nichons croulant derrière une mauve opacité dentelée. Les jeunes, où ont-elles la tête, à leur tour ont piqué au truc. Que les vierges revêtissent des bas me choquait déjà pour ce qu'ils sont le signe du mystère féminin, instruments de séduction d'après le dépucelage.

1° Mademoiselle X..., 18 ans, vous êtes ridicule avec :

a) votre corsage blanc transparent...
b) ... qui laisse voir votre combinaison transparente...
c) ... sous laquelle je distingue un soutien-gorge transparent.

Impolie ! Vous vous croyez mieux à l'abri derrière trois vitres, dépolies ? Le temps viendra bientôt des lascars dont le regard de salingues percera la triple opacité. Tu es — que tu le veuilles ou non — la jeune fille de Baudelaire !

2° Madame Y..., 30 ans (qu'elle dit), vous êtes non moins ridicule avec :

a) votre corsage rose, transparent...
b) ... sous lequel *aucune combinaison*, mais...
c) ... un soutien-gorge de satin noir !

Et si vous croisez les jambes — celles-là les croisent toujours — je verrais quoi, un jupon que vous pincez à la taille avec l'espoir que l'on vous donnera l'âge de Juliette au lieu que celui de Lady Macbeth. Bientôt nous verrons des communiantes transparentes, des mariées — jolies noces vraiment !

Les bas, sous l'initiative de M. Christian Dior, ont perdu leur couture : *Bas Dior, invisibles mais présents.* Nous y voilà. Se souvient-on qu'avant la dictature du nylon, au moment où la soie n'était peu chère qu'en regard du prix où est le beurre, on avait inventé le bas liquide ; les jolies dames bien blondes s'enduisaient les jambes d'un colorant bronzeux qui imitait le luxueux coup de soleil en hiver, le bas somptuaire en été. Et plus d'une, « la française » est femme de ressources, plus d'une, avec un crayon noir, s'ingéniait à dessiner, ou son amant, la couture depuis le talon, jusque ma foi, un peu au-dessous des fesses. Pour le non prévenu, le déshabillage paraissait mal commode. En somme et selon Christian Dior : si vous n'avez pas de bas feignez d'en avoir et, si vous en avez, feignez de n'en pas avoir.

On m'accusera de généraliser et l'on me citera des femmes qui ne se sont pas soumises à la transparence : toile rugueuse et colorée, jupe entravée. Celles-ci, je les devine impudiques à leur manière, sans dessous dessus comme sans dessus dessous. Sous un tel harnachement, les tissus épousent la forme des chairs qu'ils contiennent, y glisser l'ombre de la main serait impossible et c'est tant mieux pour la morale. Sous ces jupes étriquées, ces corsages haletants mais avec allégresse, il n'y aurait donc rien, aucune lingerie ? Qu'est-ce donc que cet érotisme du dimanche qui ignore les jeux subtils par quoi l'œil exercé apprend les angles convenables à révéler du soutien-gorge le tracé voire la matière, la couleur et partant la vie même de cette gorge ? Le visage sait feindre, la

FRANÇOIS TRUFFAUT 1113

pudeur être fausse, la vertu simulée, le soutien-gorge ne ment pas. Angles vifs, vivement saisis à la faveur d'un bras haussé pour une boucle remise. Dessins en diagonales, ourlets de petites culottes révélés par la démarche, ton orgueil et ton humilité ainsi connus de tous. Sous prétexte de jambes croisées ou décroisées, le joli dentelé d'une combinaison nous ravit. Et les rafistolages compliqués, entrelacs idylliques, le lien mystérieux qui relie tous ces petits losanges de soie, quel est-il ? Stupidement révélé par l'haïssable corsage transparent, d'un ridicule égal à l'homme support-chausseté, nous le préférons deviner par hasard, la connaissance à long terme acquise étant la meilleure récompense.

Sur les Champs-Élysées, une jolie touriste interrogeait un agent de police sur le chemin à prendre. Sa jupe blanche était si fine qu'en dépit du soleil — ou grâce à lui ? — tout le monde guignait au travers deux cuisses fermes comme le roc dont nulle combinaison n'entravait la co-existence moitée. Espérant qu'elle entrerait dans le Passage du Lido, je me précipitai prévoyant la qualité du coup d'œil de cet emplacement ombragé ; la belle étrangère fit comme j'espérais, le soleil sut remplir l'office du projecteur-derrière-fille-en chemise de nuit-dans film froufroutant. Mon seul regret fut de n'être pas seul à jouir d'un spectacle dont cependant j'avais assuré moi-même la mise en scène.

* * *

Nous aurons demain des femmes recouvertes de cellophane comme les pots de confiture. Nous pourrons apprécier avant d'acheter ; le droit d'attouchement viendra pour nos petits-enfants.

Comme le roi de Grimm, victime du rusé tailleur, la femme de demain pourra se promener toute nue sur les Champs-Élysées, ranimer la flamme du soldat inconnu et entendre chuchoter sur son passage : comme le nylon l'habille bien !

FRANÇOIS TRUFFAUT

attitude. Therefore, when I've finished a screenplay, I think I know, if not the defects, at least the dangers from the point of view of clichés and conventions. That guides me, gives me a kind of bias against those dangers during the filming.

The case is different every time. In *The 400 Blows* the danger was the poetry of childhood. In *Piano Player,* the prestige of the man who is always more right than everybody else. In *Jules and Jim,* the character of the woman, who could become an exquisite pain in the neck who gets away with everything. During the shooting I had these dangers well in mind, and part of the work consisted in preventing the film from falling into them.

It happens that this made my three films turn out sadder than foreseen, because seriousness lets one say a lot of things. Something more serious becomes more true. If you read, for example, the initial screenplay of *400 Blows,* you'll be surprised to discover the general plan of a comedy. In *Piano Player,* where the danger lay in having a character who would be too moving, I did so much to bring out the egotistical side of the artist, his wish to cut himself off from the world, his cowardice, that I rendered him not very attractive, very hard, almost antipathetic. That's even, no doubt, one of the reasons why the film failed. The same thing almost happened with *Jules and Jim.* I didn't want people to love Jeanne Moreau's character on principle, so I made it a little too harsh.

In short, improvisation has always worked against the danger I sensed in reading the finished screenplay. That is what survives from my training as critic.

Interview by Jean Collet, Michel Delahaye, Jean-André Fieschi, André S. Labarthe, and Bernard Tavernier, Cahiers du Cinéma, *no. 138, December 1962*

PETIT JOURNAL INTIME DU CINÉMA

par François Truffaut

Mardi 1er Juin

13 heures. — J'accompagne Bazin et son perroquet à la Gare de Lyon. Ils partent à Tourrette-sur-Loup, près de Vence, se reposer trois mois des fatigues de Sao-Paolo et de Cannes. Madame, Bébé et Pluto sont acheminés par la route. Quant au crocodile, il est confié au Musée des Colonies.

21 heures. — Bunuel montre à quelques amis et à quelques amis de ses amis, l'un de ses derniers films : *Robinson Crusoé* où l'auteur de *El* aborde pour la première fois la couleur. (Opérateur Alex Phillips). Bon film, excellent technicolor.

Mercredi 2 Juin

18 heures. — Cocktail au Vendôme pour la sortie de *El*. Je m'ennuie toujours beaucoup à ce genre de manifestation où chacun me fait l'effet d'être ivre... sauf moi. Une grosse dame tient Bunuel par le cou — à la grande confusion de celui-ci — et hurle à la ronde : « C'est un génie, c'est un génie ». Il y a sans doute quelque chose de génial dans ce film : (*El*) dont la phrase-clé risque bien d'être celle-ci : *Le bonheur des sots m'exaspère.*

Jeudi 3 juin

— Une nouvelle qui fera plaisir à quelques-uns : *Notorious et Rebecca* vont être réédités, par les soins de la Colombia.

Vendredi 4 juin

— Le très beau roman d'Audiberti : « Les jardins et les fleuves » est dédié « *à Molière, à Chaplin, à Jouvet* » ; il y est pas mal question de cinéma. Un livre à lire.

Jacques Flaud annonce le résultat de statistiques entreprises tout récemment et portant sur la désaffection des spectateurs de cinéma : 1° *Sur 100 Français, 64 vont au cinéma et 36 n'y vont plus, sur lesquels 30 y allaient avant guerre, 6 n'y sont jamais allé.*

2° *Sur cent Français qui vont au cinéma, 80 choisissent délibérément leur programme.*

3° *Sur cent Français qui vont au cinéma, 80 s'y rendent en compagnie* (combien d'entre ceux-là « en joyeuse compagnie » ? C'est ce que les statistiques dans leur rigueur chiffrée ne disent pas.

— Je dois confesser mon indifférence à l'égard de ce bilan, paraît-il pessimiste. Tout ce que je vois, c'est qu'Autant-Lara tourne 4 films coup sur coup, Becker deux ; que Gance va faire un film après un silence de douze années ; la couleur se généralise ; vraie ou fausse la qualité paye en ce moment et je prétends que tout va pour le mieux dans le meilleur des mondes du cinématographe.

11 heures. — Avec Doniol, rencontrons Bunuel au « Sélect » élyséen. Une enquête que j'effectue auprès de quelques réalisateurs m'amène à leur poser l'indiscrète question portant sur des films improposables parce qu'impossibles à tourner : « *Je puis vous le dire* — nous dit Bunuel — *parce que je sais que je ne pourrai jamais le tourner. Ce serait un film assez réaliste mais dont les personnages se comporteraient suivant les mœurs des insectes : l'héroïne comme l'abeille, le curé comme le scarabée, etc... ce serait le film de l'instinct.* » A Doniol qui l'interroge sur *El*, il déclare : « *On a bien ri en tournant El, on n'arrêtait pas de rire* ». A rapprocher du mot de Renoir : « *Il faut s'amuser en faisant des films, c'est très important* ».

Samedi 5 juin

— Le grand Alfred est arrivé sur la Côte d'Azur où il tourne depuis trois jours son nouveau film : *Catch a thief* avec Gary Grant, Grace Kelly, Charles Vanel, Brigitte Auber, Roland Lesaffre, Georgette Anys, Jean Martinelli, Michel Piccoli, René Blancard, Jean Hebey, Dominique Davray et Gérard Buhr. En Vistavision.

— Jean de Létraz est mort. J'ai toujours pensé qu'il aurait pu être le meilleur scénariste français : je m'explique : ses pièces étaient souvent écœurantes, parfois basses et toujours vulgaires ; à les entendre, le rire se paralysait dans la gorge, on sortait de là humilié et déçu, mais la construction de l'intrigue, l'enchevêtrement des situations, en un mot le travail, étaient irréprochables. Je suis convaincu que rafistolés par lui, les scénarios de *Thérèse Raquin, Les Orgueilleux, La Minute de vérité*, etc... eussent perdu de leur gratuité et surtout de leur maladresse. C'est une opinion...

34

Truffaut's first "Petit Journal Intime" column for *Cahiers du Cinéma,* no. 37, July 1954

François Truffaut and Roberto Rossellini

You used to be very harsh, very severe, right?

Passionate. It is often said that I was a ferocious critic, but in reality I think I was a passionate critic. What people have in mind are the negative articles directed against certain directors, but actually, when I liked a film, I could defend it more energetically than anyone. I think I used to turn out easily five or six articles on the films I liked. It would become practically a real press campaign that went on week after week, for example, to rave about the qualities of *Lola Montes* or *Un Condamné à Mort S'Est Échappé,* like a serial story in the weekly *Arts.* So that, I think, is the reality, but it's true that, in remembering, people recall instead the tough ones.

Was that period to some extent euphoric for you, because you were immersed in what you loved?

Yes, I really had great freedom. I was living alone, I had a tiny room on the Rue des Martyrs, and I was realizing part of my dreams. In any case, I was living in my own way, and it was good. I had always been impatient to be grown up . . . I wasn't that yet, but anyway I was impatient to be independent. I had no nostalgia about childhood. I had the impression that the adult world was one where you could get away with everything, where you have the right to do everything, and where you can laugh at things because nothing is serious. . . .

Interview by Aline Desjardins, Radio-Canada, 1971

François Truffaut in 1956, when he was Rossellini's assistant

Even as a critic I quite certainly dreamed of *400 Blows,* I dreamed of *Piano Player,* I dreamed of *Jules and Jim,* which I had read six years before

What was most spectacular about you as critic was your aggressiveness. When you took to filming a story in the traditional manner, one has the impression that you sobered down from the very moment you laid hands on a camera.

The moment I "laid hands on a camera," as you put it, I quite simply realized the dream of my life. It's perhaps that that sobered me. But I have never dreamed of making films and then given up on making them. Even as a critic I quite certainly dreamed of *400 Blows,* I dreamed of *Piano Player,* I dreamed of *Jules and Jim,* which I had read six years before. And these films, I dreamed them just as I filmed them. I was afraid only of not being capable of making them, but I dreamed them neither more beautiful nor more aggressive.

You know, I think my critical platform was extremely slight. I would write, "This film is a fizzle because it is not sincere." What I reject from my period as a critic are certain general articles in which I said, "Tomorrow's film will be more personal, it will be like a confession or an intimate diary." It is true that the cinema has arrived at that now, but that platform no longer satisfies me. A filmmaker finds himself in filming, and I came to see in the course of work that I did not like direct confession. Let's say that, in spite of *400 Blows*—which was filmed in the first person, though from a perspective of twelve years later—I prefer working in the third person. I prefer telling a story with "he" rather than "I."

Interview by Pierre Ajame, Le Nouvel Adam, *no. 19, February 1968*

I used to see everything in life as competing with the cinema. That is to say, I detested the theater because it was in competition with the cinema, but for the same reason I didn't go in for winter sports, I don't know how to ski, I don't know how to swim, I can't do anything. I will not go to look at a race or a match or whatever it might be, because I would have the impression of cheating on the cinema. I would not even think of going hunting or fishing and such. I've changed my ideas with time, I'm tolerant, I accept the fact that other people go fishing or hunting or skiing, but I myself do not take part, no.

Then what you have is really a "calling"? Because you describe it to me like a real calling . . .

An exclusive calling, yes. The cinema has the absolute exclusivity.

Interview by Aline Desjardins, Radio-Canada, 1971

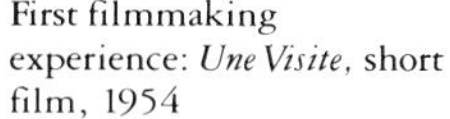

First filmmaking experience: *Une Visite*, short film, 1954

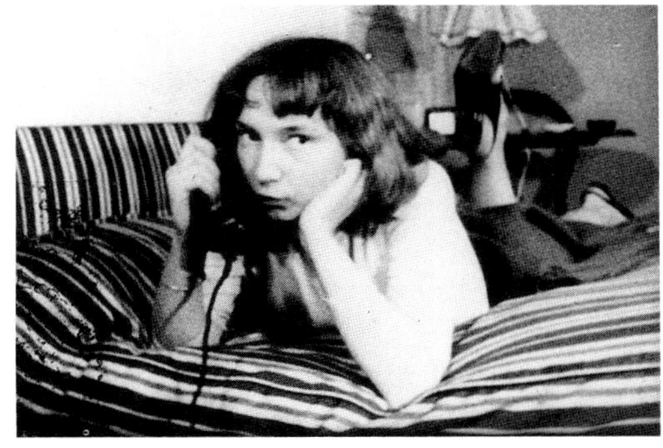

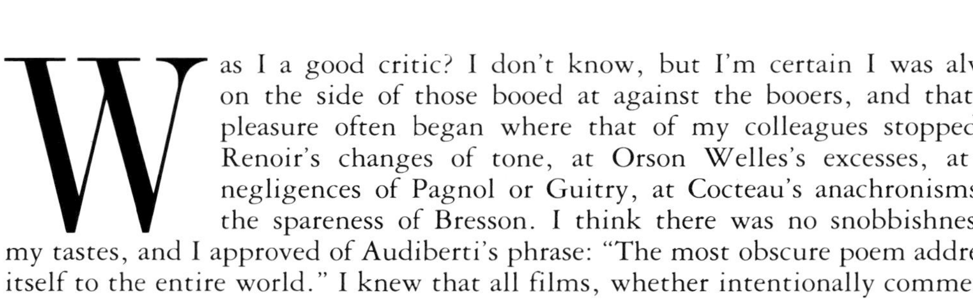

Was I a good critic? I don't know, but I'm certain I was always on the side of those booed at against the booers, and that my pleasure often began where that of my colleagues stopped: at Renoir's changes of tone, at Orson Welles's excesses, at the negligences of Pagnol or Guitry, at Cocteau's anachronisms, at the spareness of Bresson. I think there was no snobbishness in my tastes, and I approved of Audiberti's phrase: "The most obscure poem addresses itself to the entire world." I knew that all films, whether intentionally commercial or not, were subject to commerce, that is to say, were objects to be bought and sold. Between them I saw differences in degree but not in nature, and I brought the same admiration to *Singin' in the Rain* by Kelly-Donen as to Carl Dreyer's *Ordet*. . . .

When I was a critic I thought that a film, to be considered really good, had to express simultaneously an "idea of the world" along with an "idea of cinema": *The Rules of the Game* or *Citizen Kane* fit that definition pretty well. Today I ask of a film I'm watching to express either "the joy of filmmaking" or "the anguish of filmmaking," and I am uninterested in everything between those two, which is to say, in films that don't vibrate.

Preface to Les Films de Ma Vie

How is America going to be for you after the deaths of Renoir and Hitchcock? The same or not?

Let's take up the question of the masters. What masters do you acknowledge? The first is Renoir, I suppose?

Yes, Renoir, because in Jean Renoir's films there is above all the concern with being alive, and yet he has a taste for somewhat enormous things. Renoir has resolved all the problems that face people who are realists and who nonetheless are tempted by things that are a little "heavy." From Renoir I learned to utilize in such cases simple solutions, familiar solutions. Think of *Toni,* for example, which is a kind of an ordinary news item about peasants. There is in it both a very everyday and a very social aspect, yet at the same time it is an extraordinary film, full of pretty strange things like transporting the cadaver in a cart, the revolver, the wallet around the neck, that cousin who sleeps outdoors and who steals the other one's motorcycle. I understand very well what went on in Renoir's head when he made that film. I think he's the filmmaker I understand best, whose motivations I understand best. When I see a film by him, I can very well reconstruct his thinking at the moment he chose the subject, at the moment of shooting, at the moment of editing. Having seen and reseen all his films, I feel on terms of familiarity with him, and I have learned an enormous lot looking at his works. Then, too, there was Rossellini, with whom I worked a little.

Interview by Pierre Billard, Cinéma 64, *no. 89*

How did you become interested in Hitchcock?

Ah! Hitchcock? I was interested in his films from the start. . . .

Hitchcock takes such pains over the notion of plausibility, such pains over getting the story across, such pains over the spellbinding aspect, the harrowing aspect. . . .

Let's say that if one loves cinema as an escape mechanism, well, one escapes ten times more in a Hitchcock film because it's better narrated. He tells modern stories, stories of ordinary people to whom extraordinary things happen. Don't forget that I grew up in fear and that Hitchcock is the filmmaker of fear. You enter into his films as into a dream of great beauty of form, so harmonious, so natural . . . I admired Hitchcock very early and I got into the habit of seeing his films many times, and later, when I made films, I came to realize that, when I had difficulties in directing, it was by thinking of Hitchcock that I could find solutions, and one day I began that book, *Le Cinéma selon Hitchcock.*

Interview by Aline Desjardins, Radio-Canada, 1971

What are your relations with Hitchcock?

I see him when I go to America, less since his wife, Alma, is ill, but I see him. He always recounts his next film in great detail. More for himself than for others, to make sure that he is capable of narrating his next film sequence by sequence. If cinema were a religion, Hitchcock would be the high priest.

Interview by Danièle Heymann and Catherine Laporte, L'Express, *March 13, 1978*

How is America going to be for you after the deaths of Renoir and Hitchcock? The same or not?

No, it won't be the same anymore. I used to go to America regularly, forty-eight hours after shooting every film, to catch my breath, to visit Jean Renoir. He was no longer in a condition to return to France, and even though he was surrounded by warm friends he felt the need to speak French, to get news from Paris. He was very fond of Rivette. Renoir was suffering very much, physically, but he worked every day. Formerly he had no interest in his past work, but Dido, his wife, had nonetheless got all his films together in 16 mm and he was happy to watch them after dinner; sometimes he said very severe things about his films, but he was always full of admiration for Michel Simon or Jean Gabin. Finally it was *French Cancan* that he preferred to watch over and over, for various reasons easy to guess. He never came out with a sour or bitter sentence, he never spoke about death, to the end he had a very great desire to live.

The first time I left him, in 1974, to return to Paris after a long visit, I believed I would never see him again, but then he held out five more years and published four books. Today they are continually discovering projects, manuscripts, summaries of his, and realizing that if he made thirty-five films, he must have planned a hundred or so. Rare as it may be to last out to the age of eighty-four, Jean Renoir's death was truly sad, because of that blend of genius and kindness which impressed everyone.

Interview by Serge Daney, Jean Narboni, and Serge Toubiana, Cahiers du Cinéma, *no. 315, September-October 1980*

THE "NEW WAVE" ENTERS THE SCENE

At the point when we began to want to make films, Rivette was the most active. At that time only Astruc could truly think of himself as a director. We others, we were thinking about films without daring too much to formulate our own ideas. Rivette was the most clearly decided, and he set an example by making films in 16 mm. Rohmer, too, thought of himself as a filmmaker, but he would wait a while yet before he really became one.

Rivette was the first to propose concrete solutions. He made us get together, proposed plans, suggested the idea of filmmakers in association, of groups of directors, and other such ideas.

I remember we approached Resnais—myself and Rivette, Bitsch, and maybe Chabrol (I've forgotten)—to ask him if he would be interested in taking part in this group. On paper it was very fine and simple: Astruc would make a film, Resnais would make a film, in Resnais's film Rivette was an assistant, then Rivette would make a film in which I was an assistant, then I would make a film with Bitsch as an assistant, etc.

In working out the scheme—by no means badly thought through—we had seen that we could make films for twenty-five million very comfortably indeed. We were right. Our idea went on like this: we say to So-and-So, "With a hundred million you make a film without knowing whether it will pay for itself or not; we, with a hundred million, can make four, and we'll be damned if one of them is not a success."

Metteur en scène cinéma cherche 5 garçons 11 à 14 ans pour jouer "Les mistons"

S'adresser à Midi Libre

Après Henri-Georges Clouzot, Robert Hossein et quelques autres, François Truffaut, réalisateur de cinéma, a choisi le Gard comme décor du film qu'il va réaliser : « Avant d'aller à Cannes où j'assurai, pour divers périodiques parisiens (l'hebdomadaire « Arts » entre autres) la chronique du festival, j'ai visité ce département et ce fut pour moi une révélation nous a-t-il déclaré. A St-André-de-Valborgne, j'ai admiré la rudesse, la sauvage beauté de la nature cévenole. A Nimes, j'ai apprécié la splendeur d'une ville qui à non seulement de beaux monuments, mais aussi un « style », une âme.

» C'était plus qu'il n'en fallait pour me décider à venir ici pour mener à bien un projet qui me tient à cœur, mon film : « Les mistons ».

« Les mistons » : un titre prometteur dans ce qu'il recèle d'esprit frondeur, de gouaille, de pittoresque, un titre « accrocheur ». Mais pas un titre seulement, un sujet aussi, et des meilleurs : « J'ai adapté — très librement quant aux péripéties, mais très fidèlement — je l'espère — quant à l'esprit, une nouvelle — excellente — de Maurice Rons. Le scénario est on ne peut plus simple : deux amoureux vivraient la plus douce des idylles si cinq adolescents, inconsciemment épris de la belle, ne venaient, jaloux, jouer les « empêcheurs de roucouler en rond ». C'est tout ».

C'es tout et cela doit suffire à offrir à un auteur de film de talent matière à un court métrage (20 minutes environ) tout en nuances, en fines touches psychologiques...

Du talent, il suffit que François Truffaut en ait autant comme cinéaste qu'en qualité de critique de cinéma pour qu'on ait la certitude que son film s'avère une réussite. En effet, il est considéré à Paris comme le plus représentatif, le plus acerbe, le plus « engagé » des journalistes de cinéma de la « jeune école » moins respectueuse des canons d'une esthétique traditionnelle que des nouvelles tendances, aussi réprouvées par les «ci-devant » qu'elles sont prônées par les enfants terribles du 7me art. L'indulgnce, l'art de ménager la chèvre et le chou ne sont pas dans son rôle d'exécuteur des hautes (?) œuvres cinématographiques. C'est dire que son franc parler lui a valu pas mal d'inimitiés dans les studios et que son premier essai dans la réalisation est guetté par ses adversaires qui ne manqueront pas une occasion, bonne ou mauvaise, de lui rendre avec usure la monnaie de sa pièce.

Mais François Truffaut a confiance, confiance en lui, sans forfanterie, mais sans fausse modestie, confiance aussi en son équipe qui est entièrement dévouée à sa cause : les deux vedettes en sont Bernadette Lafont et Gérard Blain, jeunes premiers aux aptitudes déjà affirmées, et le chef opérateur, notre ami, le Nimois Jean Malige, enfin revenu à Nimes, après qu'il ait réalisé, pour son propre compte, un court métrage humoristique en couleurs sur Palavas-les-Flots : « Je t'enverrai des cartes postales » et un conte de Noël provençal « Le pâtre Nicolas ».

« Il ne me manque plus que «Les mistons » a constaté François Truffaut. C'est dire que tous les jeunes garçons de 11 à 14 ans qui se présenteront demain, à 16 h., dans le hall de « Midi Libre », boulevard Amiral-Courbet, pour prendre contact avec Truffaut et ses camarades seront les bienvenus. Seules aptitudes exigées : une photogénie compatible avec les rôles qui leur seront dévolus à l'exclusion de toute aptitude à jouer la comédie. Avis aux amateurs.

Resnais was interested (at that time he wanted to make *Les Mauvais Coups*). Astruc, too, but he was already in the business, he had loads of appointments and was piling up screenplays two hundred pages long. So we went to see people like Dorfmann and Bérard, with a screenplay that had been written with Rivette and for him, as well as with Chabrol, Bitsch, and me, and which was titled *Les Quatre Jeudis*.

It was a screenplay based on a news item and was influenced by the American cinema, that of Ray, for example. I think that that film would have had the same qualities and the same drawbacks as today, for example, *Le Combat dans l'Île*. It would have been torn between French realism and American reliance on formulas. I think I recall, in fact, that Leenhardt had made quite severe but fair criticisms of it. In short, we proposed that screenplay, but it didn't excite anyone and no producer followed up on it.

The long and short of it is that our mistake was in believing that it was in the producers' interest to make films cheaply. We were ignoring that old law of French cinema that says that the producer is not the one who has the money but the one who finds it and that the only profit he can be sure of is his percentage on the budget for the film, which involves, on the one hand, his salary and, on the other, the general and the unforeseen expenses. That percentage is higher the higher the budget for the film. This explains why films are made for two or three hundred million which could cost half of that and why, deep down, many producers don't give a damn how the film makes out in the long run. I say in the long run because it is nonetheless in their interest that the films be successful, but in the case of big-budget films for which they have found the money by borrowing right and left, they end up in any case with a comfortable salary which, at that point, makes them virtually employees themselves.

François Truffaut and Guy Decomble (The Teacher) during the filming of *The 400 Blows*

That's why it didn't work. It therefore meant that the author of the film had to be the producer as well, so that the interests involved in the film would rest in a single person and wouldn't contradict each other.

Interview by Jean Collet, Michel Delahaye, Jean-André Fieschi, André S. Labarthe, and Bernard Tavernier, Cahiers du Cinéma, *no. 138, December 1962*

It was at the time of the Cannes Festival, in 1959, that we decided, Claude Chabrol and I, to become, as an afterthought, co-producers of *Paris Belongs to Us*. Editing, dubbing, sound track, the film had been finished for several months and was to have its French career in the so-called art and experimental houses. It was to come out shortly in Germany, Belgium, and Canada.

Jacques Rivette was the biggest film fan among us; his film proves him also the most filmmaking-minded. Leaving aside the conditions of filming, *Paris Belongs to Us,* of all the films that came out of the *Cahiers du Cinéma* team, is the most "directed," a film in which the technical difficulties are not bypassed but faced up to with a headstrong pride, a forthrightness from start to finish, and the skill of an old campaigner.

Although he has written little, Jacques Rivette, by the sureness of his judgments, has influenced all the young critics; though having filmed little, he is now offering this film, begun in 1958, the archetype of our efforts.

According to Péguy, Paris belongs to no one, Rivette reminds us at the start of his film, but the cinema belongs to everyone.

"1961," Les Films de Ma Vie

The 400 Blows featured on the cover of *Cahiers du Cinéma*, June 1959

The young filmmakers will express themselves in the first person and will tell us what happened to them themselves

The New Wave, which never was a school or a club, was an important spontaneous movement which rapidly extended beyond our frontiers and for which I feel myself so much the more responsible since I had vigorously urged its coming in my articles, to the point of writing in May 1957, this sort of profession of faith, naïve but full of conviction: "Tomorrow's film therefore appears to me even more personal than an individual and autobiographical novel, more like a confession or like an intimate diary. The young filmmakers will express themselves in the first person and will tell us what happened to them themselves: this might be the story of their first love or their most recent, how they came to take a position with respect to politics, an account of a voyage, an illness, their military service, their marriage, their last vacation; and that will please people, almost necessarily, because it will be true and new. . . . The film of tomorrow will be an act of love."

Les Films de Ma Vie

I think that in life you always end up doing what you want, providing you want only one thing. When a director finally makes his first film at thirty-five, nobody is surprised because they say, that's normal, that makes fifteen years he has been waiting to get into cinema. For my part, I made my first film at twenty-seven, but that also makes a fifteen-year wait to get into cinema, because I decided to do so at the age of twelve. Given the fact that, since the age of twelve, all my efforts tended in that direction, it was perfectly normal that one day or another I should get there. Simply, instead of starting out as an assistant, I did my apprenticeship in journalism and criticism, and I learned by looking at films. But I think there is a way to see films that is just as instructive as collaborating in making them as an assistant; and I made my first film in 16 mm, four years ago, which I didn't edit, but it taught me certain things just the same. The second was a short film, two years ago, *The Mischief Makers,* and if I hadn't had the chance to do *The 400 Blows* as a full-length film, I would certainly have done it at medium length. I would have waited some more, but I was firmly decided not to make documentaries, to make only acted films. Quite simply, it was only a question of length and of chance. Finally, for *The 400 Blows,* from the minute I had the complete screenplay, I was resolved to do it, and if I hadn't been helped I would certainly have made it with less means and I would have sacrificed several passages in the screenplay, but I would have made it. In any case, it would exist this year just the same.

Interview by Pierre Wildenstein, Télé-Ciné, *no. 83, July 1959*

Jean-Pierre Léaud in the final scene of *The 400 Blows*

The first film is so close to you, so personal, that quite naturally, by reaction, out of need also, the second uses borrowed material

During the shooting of *The 400 Blows,* people used to ask me: "What are you going to do after this?" I replied: "I don't know; I hope that I will be making films, but I'm not sure of that." And I came to see that it was very bad to know what you would do afterwards; moreover, it is because of that that I have dropped my projects. . . .

The first film is so close to you, so personal, that quite naturally, by reaction, out of need also, the second uses borrowed material. Before showing something you feel deeply about, you're worried sick: "After all," you say to yourself, "that's of interest only to me, I've made a mistake." And if you make use of someone else's subject: "I've stolen from literature, this story doesn't concern me: can't cinema feed itself on its own?" The two attitudes give rise to the same doubt. But I like to remember that Jean Renoir, the filmmaker I most admire, has to his credit something like six adaptations for ten films.

Interview by Gilbert Salachas, Télé-Ciné, *no. 94, March 1961*

Filming the final sequence of *The 400 Blows*

In fact, there are very few filmmakers of your generation, a fortiori younger, who can turn out a film a year for such a long time and think of what they do as their trade.

Yes, I think it was pure chance at the start. My father-in-law, who headed the Société Cocinor, produced my first film, *The 400 Blows;* he suggested to me that, if I wanted to keep my hands free, I should create my own production firm. So I founded Les Films du Carrosse—the reference is to *The Golden Coach*—and by chance that little company is still in business twenty years later. So everything began with that first film, which made a lot of money, but what I could not have foreseen is the way I would behave in this kind of work. While I had spent my young years in cutting school to go to the movies, as soon as I found myself with Les Films du Carrosse and an office, well, I have never in twenty years missed a day in the office. Even days when a new Bergman or a new Fellini comes out, I wait until seven in the evening to go, probably because I feel myself responsible to those who work with me.

Interview by Serge Daney, Jean Narboni, and Serge Toubiana, Cahiers du Cinéma, *nos. 315–16, September 1980*

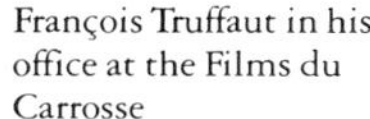

François Truffaut in his office at the Films du Carrosse

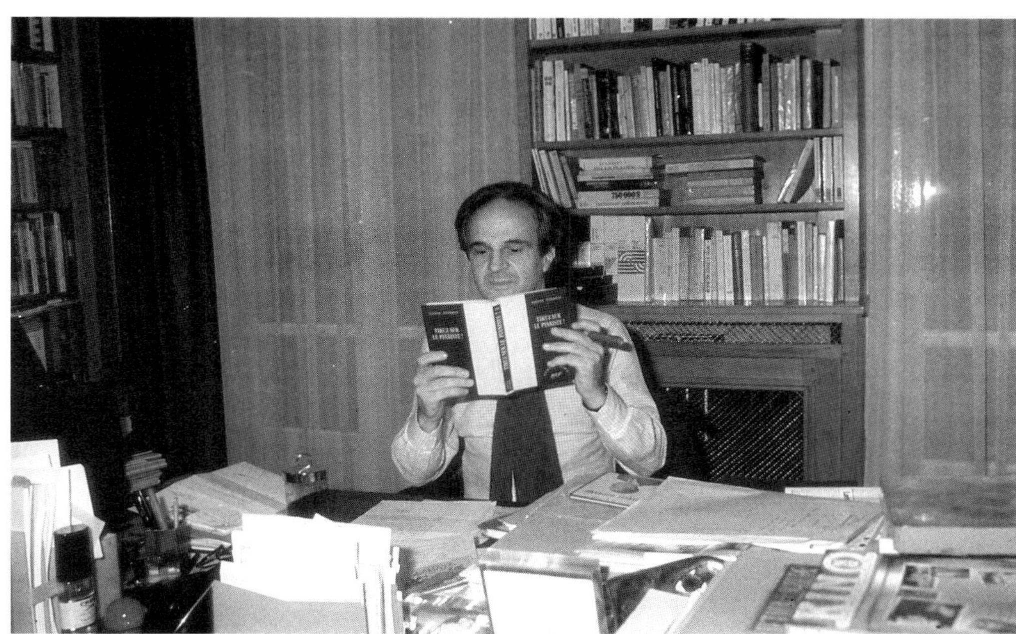

THE CANNES FESTIVAL

You can't talk about cinema with people as different as Mel Ferrer, Sophie Desmarets, Jean Dutourd, Romain Gary

The only thing I regret is having been a member of the jury, because that was a very sad experience. As a journalist I had attacked Cannes, saying: "It's nothing but combines and compromises. It's the realm of political intrigues and advertising mix-ups." It is probably because of that that I was later asked to be on the jury. So I could see how it works. And I saw. It was sad. Honest or dishonest, that was not at all the question. I simply came to realize it was a dialogue among the deaf and that you can't talk about cinema with people as different as Mel Ferrer, Sophie Desmarets, Jean Dutourd, Romain Gary, for whom cinema doesn't mean the same thing, for whom words don't have the same meanings. So you have to end up by compromising. Without being dishonest, you end up with compromising and with stupid blundering, really and truly, and above all with a ridiculous roster of prizes. It is the very notion of a jury that is thrown into question, and

Jean-Pierre Léaud in *The 400 Blows*

Milos Forman, Claude Lelouch, Claude Berri, and François Truffaut at the Cannes Festival, 1968

about that I think Malraux had the last word when he said: "Within every intelligent minority there is a majority of imbeciles." So, all in all, it's the condemnation of the jury as jury.

Interview by Pierre Billard, Christiane Collange, and Claude Veillot, L'Express, *May 20, 1968*

At that precise time, those kinds of brilliant spectacles, the Cannes Festival for example, were attacked vigorously. Yourself . . .

Yes, but that action was understood badly. For me, the shutting down of the Festival was absolutely tied up with what was going on in general: France was shutting up shop, so everything had to stop. That general paralysis was not something I had dreamed of, because I didn't imagine it could be possible. But I found it tremendous. It gave an impression of unanimity (and even if, later on, people realized it was only an impression).

Interview by Gilbert Salachas and Pierre Loubière, Télé-Ciné, *no. 160, March 1970*

Summons to the Prefecture of Police in connection with the Manifesto of the 121

POLITICAL ATTITUDE

The Manifesto of the 121 . . . pleased me . . . because it constituted a call to desert

I receive a great many things to sign, even today still, because at the time I had signed the Manifesto of the 121, and because of that, many people thought I was a man of good will. But I had signed that manifesto for a single, very precise reason: it was the first time that a text, one moreover formidably written by Sartre, was encouraging soldiers to desert. That's what pleased me: the very opposite of a mobilization. Yes, the Manifesto of the 121 moved me, touched me, pleased me; to begin with, because it was insolent and you really felt its weight, its efficacy, and above all because it constituted a call to desert.

Yet you performed another public act in intervening in the La Religieuse *affair.*

Yes, but out of friendship for Rivette. And, then, I consider it was a weakness, because if you've taken the trouble to appoint a Minister of Information, it's certainly in order to filter out information, right? But anyway I was indignant for Rivette's sake. It was revolting but it was comic as well, because Rivette's being mixed up in a scandal—that's well and truly the most paradoxical thing in the world!

Interview by Pierre Ajame, Le Nouvel Adam, *no. 19, February 1968*

Demonstration in defense of the Cinémathèque Française, February 1968

I don't vote. I try to have nothing to do with "officials." A true left-wing filmmaker has to want the cinema to depend on the State, to want culture to be subsidized. I prefer for films to finance themselves on their own, or at least pay their way without help from the State. I prefer the normal game of commerce, making a film and selling it with a profit.

Put another way, if the French cinema has to be nationalized someday, under whatever régime there might be, socialist or "liberal," as we have at present, I think that would be sufficient reason for me to pack up and settle elsewhere, in a country where cinema depends on the capitalist system of expenses and profits.

Interview by Pierre Ajame, Le Nouvel Adam, *no. 19, February 1968*

February 1968: Filming *Stolen Kisses* in Paris

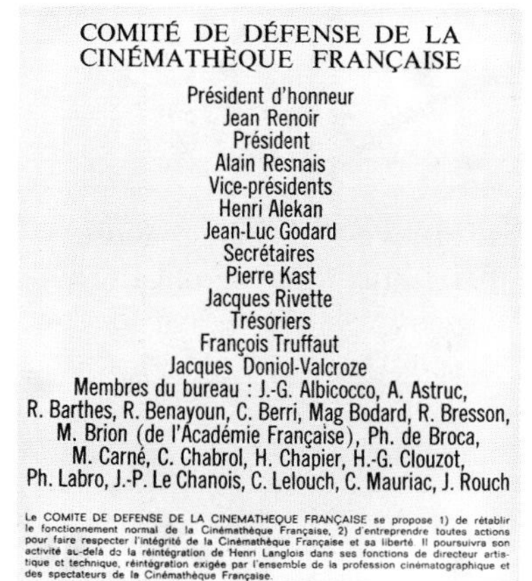

COMITÉ DE DÉFENSE DE LA CINÉMATHÈQUE FRANÇAISE

Président d'honneur
Jean Renoir
Président
Alain Resnais
Vice-présidents
Henri Alekan
Jean-Luc Godard
Secrétaires
Pierre Kast
Jacques Rivette
Trésoriers
François Truffaut
Jacques Doniol-Valcroze
Membres du bureau : J.-G. Albicocco, A. Astruc, R. Barthes, R. Benayoun, C. Berri, Mag Bodard, R. Bresson, M. Brion (de l'Académie Française), Ph. de Broca, M. Carné, C. Chabrol, H. Chapier, H.-G. Clouzot, Ph. Labro, J.-P. Le Chanois, C. Lelouch, C. Mauriac, J. Rouch

Le COMITE DE DEFENSE DE LA CINEMATHEQUE FRANÇAISE se propose 1) de rétablir le fonctionnement normal de la Cinémathèque Française, 2) d'entreprendre toutes actions pour faire respecter l'intégrité de la Cinémathèque Française et sa liberté. Il poursuivra son activité au-delà de la réintégration de Henri Langlois dans ses fonctions de directeur artistique et technique, réintégration exigée par l'ensemble de la profession cinématographique et des spectateurs de la Cinémathèque Française.

February 1968: Pamphlet published by *Cahiers du Cinéma* listing Truffaut as treasurer of the Defense Committee for the Cinémathèque Française

My ideas about life come and go by way of the cinema. And the cinema, one learns its history, its past and its present, at the Cinémathèque!

Your nonparticipation in the life of society has led you to refuse to commit yourself. For example, you did not wish to work on a collective film, Far from Vietnam. *Then, all of a sudden, with the Langlois affair, we saw a Truffaut on a rampage . . .*

Ah, because that was a part of my life, the Cinémathèque! When I say I never had any schooling, well, I did have, there on Avenue de Messine, and I continued it in the hall on the Rue de l'Ulm and at Chaillot. Everything I know I learned through the cinema, out of films. My ideas about life come and go by way of the cinema. And the cinema, one learns its history, its past and its present, at the Cinémathèque! You can learn it only there. It is a perpetual education. I am one of those people who need to see the old films, the silents, the first talkies, over and over again. So I spend my life at the Cinémathèque, except when I'm busy filming on my own.

Listen, I can tell you that I moved into the neighborhood of the Trocadéro just because it's near the Cinémathèque. That's why I reacted in the Langlois affair. It isn't for Langlois, even though I have an immense debt of gratitude to that man, who is naturalness itself, but it's for the survival of the Cinémathèque itself. I reacted because the films I love were going to be endangered. Instead of mucking around with Langlois, you know what Malraux should have done? The Gaumont-Palace is empty every night with their crappy Italian Westerns. Well, it should have been requisitioned for a month for Langlois, to show at last on that screen, which is one of the biggest in Europe, all the great damned-in-advance films you can only see on the tiny screens of the art and experimental houses, from *Greed* to *Lola Montes,* and that only the Cinémathèque has been able to preserve from destruction.

Interview by Pierre Billard, Christiane Collange, and Claude Veillot, L'Express, *March 20, 1968*

François Truffaut, Jean-Pierre Léaud, and Henri Langlois during the filming of *Stolen Kisses*

Did something in particular spark off this tardy interest in politics?

With a universal contempt, I used to think all politicians were gangsters. I would open the paper at the movie page. No problem, I hadn't the slightest idea of what was going on in the world. I was good and angry the day Max Ophuls died, because the papers talked only about the death of Edouard Herriot. I said to myself: "But who is that guy? It's Ophuls who's important!"

Afterwards I woke up a little during the war in Algeria. In *L'Express* there were those white pages, those censored articles. . . . And then I signed the Manifesto of the 121 because it said to the deserters from the Algerian war that they were right and that a part of the population was on their side. Since I had myself signed up in the artillery for very personal reasons, not for ideological reasons, and since I had deserted likewise for very personal reasons, all of a sudden I was touched to see that text making the rounds of the intellectuals, and I signed the Manifesto of the 121. As a consequence a boycott was ordered by Michel Debré. We no longer had the right to appear on television, etc. That didn't last very long, just about a year, a little like a blacklist. . . .

I don't consider myself of the Left, because I am not militant and I have no political activities, but I am leftish, I am not leftist. What I can't take about left-wing intellectuals is that often I have the impression they are on the Left for wrong reasons, that is to say, to make themselves seem youthful, to look revolutionary. For myself, there is only a single, very good reason to be on the Left, that is because it is more just. That's why I vote Socialist.

This is a profession of faith?

Just a piece of information.

Interview by Danièle Heymann and Catherine Laporte, L'Express, *March 13, 1978*

François Truffaut, Marcel Berbert (executive producer), and Henri Langlois with Jean-Pierre Cargol during the filming of *The Wild Child*

DEUX DIFFUSEURS DE « LA CAUSE DU PEUPLE » SONT ÉCROUÉS

Appréhendés samedi après-midi, rue de la Charbonnière, à Paris, alors qu'ils vendaient le numéro 25 de *la Cause du peuple*, Mlle Nicole Prunier, vingt et un ans, étudiante en psychologie, et M. Patrick Weiss, dix-neuf ans, étudiant en histoire, ont été déférés à M. Leloir, juge d'instruction à la Cour de sûreté de l'Etat, qui les a inculpés de maintien ou reconstitution de groupement dissous. Après avoir désigné, tous deux, Mᵉ Revon pour défenseur, ils ont été incarcérés, l'étudiante à La Roquette, son camarade à la Santé.

Rappelons que le jour même où ces jeunes gens étaient arrêtés, M. Jean-Paul Sartre, Mme Simone de Beauvoir et M. François Truffaut avaient pu vendre *la Cause du peuple* dans un autre quartier de la capitale, sans être inquiétés (*le Monde* du 23 juin).

News item cut out by François Truffaut

I put great store in freedom of the press and the independence of justice

Paris, September 8, 1970

Monsieur le Président,

I had made all my arrangements to come and testify on September 8 at the trial of the vendors and distributors of *La Cause du Peuple.* Having postponed until September 10 my departure for the United States, I cannot once again put off that trip, which is why I am addressing my testimony to you in writing.

In the first weeks of June I learned through the press that the newspaper *La Cause du Peuple,* which Jean-Paul Sartre had just agreed to direct, was being systematically confiscated even before the authorities had acquainted themselves with the texts it contained. I learned also that the police were apprehending, arresting, and charging the vendors of those newspapers and sometimes even the readers merely because they had two copies in their pocket or in the saddlebag of a motorbike.

I knew, again thanks to having read it in *Le Monde,* that a court of justice, that of Rennes, I believe, had refused sometime earlier to suspend the publication of this newspaper.

All this showed clearly that the Minister of the Interior was not hesitating, in order to persecute a newspaper, to commit actions that simply had to be termed illegal.

I have never gone in for political activities, and I am no more Maoist than Pompidouist, being incapable of having any feeling for a Chief of State, whoever he might be.

It just so happens that I love books and newspapers, that I put great store in freedom of the press and the independence of justice.

It so happens also that I have made a film titled *Fahrenheit 451* which describes, in order to stigmatize it, an imaginary society in which the authorities systematically burn all the books; I therefore wanted to reconcile my ideas as filmmaker and my ideas as French citizen.

This is why, on Saturday, June 20, I decided to sell the newspaper *La Cause du Peuple* on the public streets. I met there, on the street, other vendors, and among them Jean-Paul Sartre and Simone de Beauvoir. The public, in the street, was interested; my pile of papers dwindled visibly, and when a policeman presented himself before us, I had the pleasure of offering him two copies of *La Cause du Peuple,* which he held in his hand, something which might well have opened him to prosecution. A photo, taken by a passerby, confirms exactly what went on. After having invited us to disperse, the policeman asked Jean-Paul Sartre to follow him to the station, which the writer did very willingly. Naturally I followed the movement, as did Simone de Beauvoir, other vendors, and a few interested pedestrians.

If the police agent asked Jean-Paul Sartre rather than me to follow him, it was obviously because I was wearing a white shirt, a dark suit, and a tie, whereas Sartre was in a rumpled and worn suede windbreaker. Thus there was, already at the level of costume . . . a discrimination between distributors of *La Cause du Peuple:* those who seemed to be selling it to earn their living being more exposed to prosecution than those who were doing it on principle.

What followed confirmed me in that impression, because a passerby, having recognized Sartre, apostrophized the policeman: "But you're not really going to arrest a Nobel Prize winner?" At which point we saw this astonishing thing: the policeman dropped Jean-Paul Sartre's arm, began to walk faster, passed our group, and spun to the right so fast and lively that we would have had to run to catch up with him. We had proof that there was a double standard in the law and that the police were deciding whom to challenge not by the looks of the buyer but by those of the seller.

I cannot conclude this deposition other than by recommending to my colleagues, the vendors of *La Cause du Peuple,* to dress up every day in their Sunday best and to refuse the Nobel Prize if it is ever proposed to them.

Such are, Monsieur le Président, the facts that I would have recounted at the hearing of September 8.

Destruction of books in *Fahrenheit 451*

At the Auberge de la Colombe d'Or, Saint-Paul-de-Vence, with Madeleine and Laura, July 1962

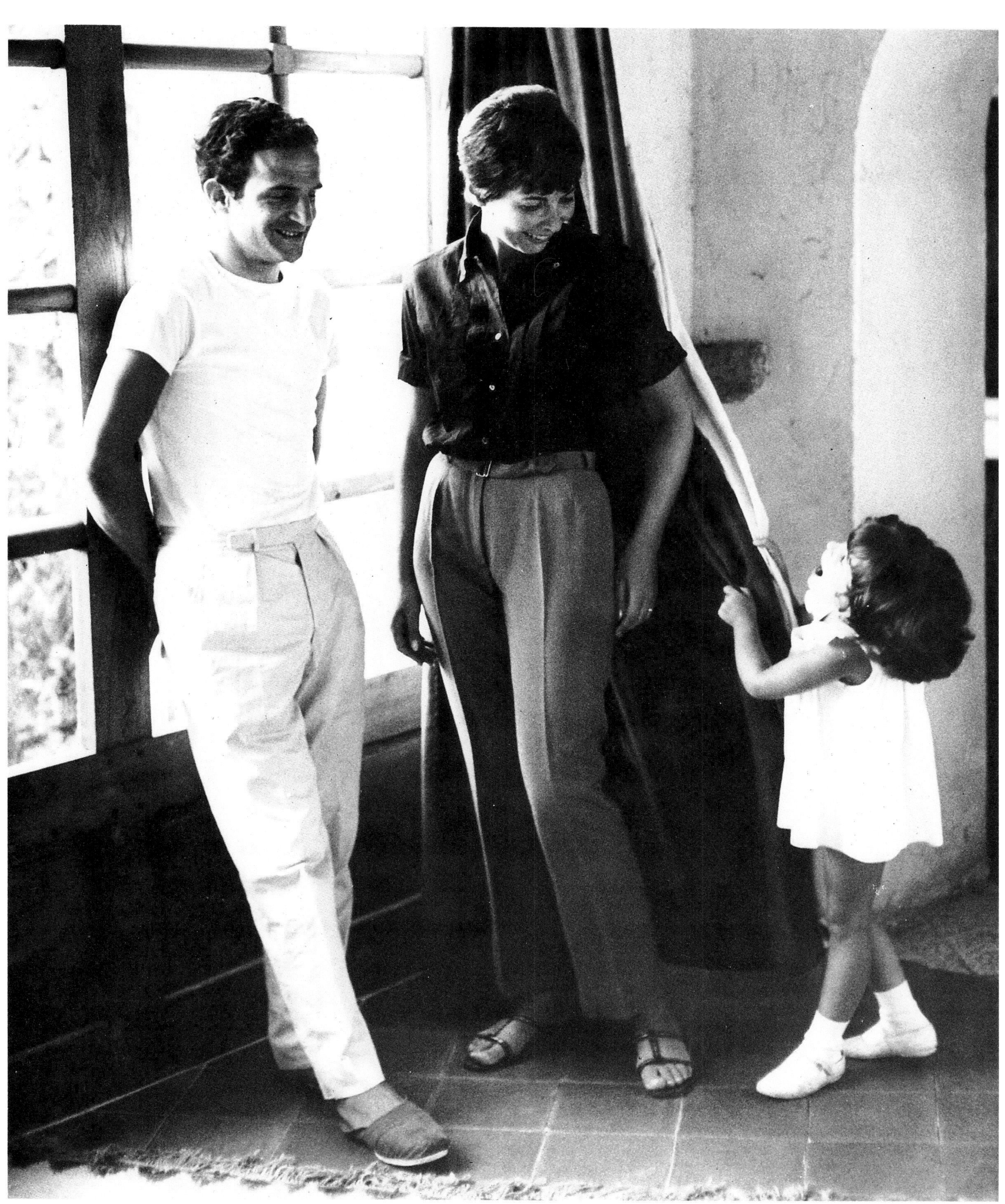

Jean-Pierre Cargol in *The Wild Child*

ELEMENTS FOR A SELF-PORTRAIT

Since the events of May '68, people express ideas in a way that doesn't suit me, no doubt because I am a self-taught man

At present, and especially since the events of May '68, people express ideas in a way that doesn't suit me, no doubt because I am a self-taught man. . . . How can I convey that? . . . Let's just say that, as regards the essential things in life, I lack a feeling for paradox, I don't appreciate it. I have very elementary ideas, very simple and very firm on a certain number of essential points. For example, sometimes people get ironic about paperback books. They speak of them as objects of a consumer society, they criticize their distribution through supermarkets: I find those arguments completely ridiculous and snobbish.

Were I to adopt a similarly sarcastic point of view on that subject, I would be disowning myself, because I began to read with the Classiques Fayard, which were cheap little books, very badly printed, on coarse paper, with very small print, sometimes with pages so gray as to be almost unreadable, and a paper cover that easily came unstitched. . . . But they had an absolutely fantastic catalogue: in alphabetical order it went from Aristophanes to Zola, with a special section for the works of Victor Hugo. They were the ones I read really a lot, because you could pick up those little books for fifty centimes.

That's the way my mind works, just as you see it in *The Wild Child* or in *Fahrenheit.*

Interview by Pierre Loubière and Gilbert Salachas,
Télé-Ciné, *no. 160, March 1970*

On the set of *Fahrenheit 451,* 1966

The way films are going now means that there is more and more co-production with the Americans. You yourself have done it . . .

Yes, *Fahrenheit 451,* I filmed it in London, with Americans and English.

You had no problems?

Oh, yes, because I have a bad . . . How can I explain? I don't have an international turn of mind. I am terribly French. Abnormally, unhealthily French, Parisian. In London, during *Fahrenheit 451,* I lived with the constant feeling that I was on an island. I didn't at all try to fit in with the sixty Englishmen in the crew, though they were very nice. I didn't feel at home. I was bad off.

You find the French superior?

Oh, it's not that! I'm not at all chauvinistic, you know, nor nationalistic, nor flag-waving, nor even proud of being French, as they say. Which doesn't keep me from being very tied to my country, to Paris. I was a little disappointed to discover that side of me.

Opposite
With Jean-Pierre Cargol in *The Wild Child,* 1969

And how does it show itself?

Well, by apprehension, fears . . . One time I went to Rome, I was to film a sketch for Dino de Laurentiis, with Princess Soraya, and I fell ill there. I had drunk an ice-cold tomato juice, I don't know what else, I was sick, and I was terribly afraid of dying in Rome, somewhere else than in France. . . .

In short, I returned home the next day and didn't make the sketch with Soraya.

In London, for *Fahrenheit 451,* I was like under punishment, I lived six months in the Hilton without having a meal outside my room. A car used to come to take me to the studio. When I got back to Paris, everyone said: "So, London, a lot doing, eh?" I didn't dare say, "I've only been in the Hilton." Six months . . .

Interview by Pierre Billard, Christiane Collange, and Claude Veillot, L'Express, *May 20, 1968*

I have only very personal stories, but I don't dare make a film out of them every year. I have to alternate with books

You have often had recourse to novels. You have said that that was, for you, something secure to start out with.

Not a security . . . more a question of lack of imagination. I'd be happy to be like Pagnol, like Guitry, a guy with his head full of stories and characters. I have only very personal stories, but I don't dare make a film out of them every year. I have to alternate with books.

Books that have given me a shock. Chance has no part in it. There is always a long time between the moment when I read them and that when I adapt them. God knows, people have proposed them to me, but I don't want to do anything without due consideration: I will not do *Madame Bovary, Journey to the End of Night,* or *Swann's Way.* . . . Maybe *The Wild Child* opened a new way for me: it's the first time I have been interested in real happenings. Like everyone who gets older, perhaps . . . , I am beginning to break away a little from the novel and to read factual accounts. I've noticed that tendency often—in Hitchcock, for example—in men who have succeeded in ensuring themselves a good life materially: they become readers of "memoirs." In America, this biographical literature has enormous drawing power.

Interview by Pierre Loubière and Gilbert Salachas, Télé-Ciné, *no. 160, March 1970*

Hollywood, 1974: With the Oscar for the Best Foreign Film, *Day for Night*

Do you feel yourself to be a character?

No, no, not at all! I have a retiring personality. Not that I aim at unobtrusiveness . . .

Because it would be affectation to say you aimed at being unobtrusive?

There you are, you don't know how well you've hit it on the head. Yes, that's it. I'm not sufficiently ambitious to aim at total self-effacement, but that attracts me. I am not Monsieur Teste, but I'm fond of him, yes. You know, one always comes back to the same point: nothing interests me outside the cinema. I have no private life, no life of my own outside cinema. That's why I don't feel I am interesting for you. What is interesting for you is an artist who expounds his theories. Me, I don't have any. Robbe-Grillet, yes, he's interesting. He turns up, he has his idea of what a novel should be, what a novel shouldn't be.

Me, I find that all films are films. Therefore, I have no interesting ideas to express for an important magazine.

Then, why did you come?

I came because . . . because for ten years, since television became competition for the cinema, films no longer suffice in themselves. You have to push them. Myself, I'd like it fine if films made their own way, I'd be very glad of it, but no, the cinema needs to be talked about. So I'm perfectly willing to talk about it if that can make it possible for me to continue to turn out films. If someone said to me: "There is a plan for the future: you will make, in the next thirty years, thirty films, thirty films for one hundred million which will earn one hundred twenty," well, I'd accept that contract.

Interview by Pierre Billard, Christiane Collange, and Claude Veillot, L'Express, *May 20, 1968*

Do you already feel like someone who is a success?

No, not at all. But like somebody older than myself, that certainly. I am going to be thirty-eight and have the impression of being fifty. I began to live actively at the age of twelve and, then too, around 1944 or 1945, I saw many films and read many plays from before the war, so that my personal folklore is France between 1930 and 1940. I would have loved to have gone to the dress rehearsals of *Amphitryon, The Trojan War Will Not Take Place, The Satin Slipper.*

I feel that I belong to that generation.

For me, the expression "boulevard comedy" means nothing: it's a good play or a bad one. It cuts no ice with me to hear that Guitry is a good writer of the bourgeoisie: I remember only that he is a wonderful guy for invention and wry fun. The same goes for Giraudoux ("flowery," "decorative," etc.), for Claudel, for Zola, whom I loved very much. I remain very solid in my tastes, and words like populist, naturalist, melodramatic, boulevardier, unanimist, or others do not have any a priori pejorative meaning for me. First I ask to see for myself, and I don't give a damn about the label.

Interview by Pierre Loubière and Gilbert Salachas, Télé-Ciné, *no. 160, March 1970*

With Isabelle Adjani during the filming of *The Story of Adele H.*

I have always preferred the reflection of life to life itself. If I opted for books and films from the age of eleven or twelve, it was certainly because I preferred seeing life through books and films

You alluded, a little while ago, to the ideas in vogue since May '68. Don't they include, precisely, the desire for a sort of return to the savage or, in any case, natural state?

Maybe so, but I can't adopt that point of view. I have always preferred the reflection of life to life itself. If I opted for books and films from the age of eleven or twelve, it was certainly because I preferred seeing life through books and films. I have absolutely no feeling for nature. When I filmed *Jules and Jim,* I chose one chalet out of twenty or so others, but before then I had never looked at a chalet or a meadow or a forest. As a filmmaker, I know I have to have the most beautiful chalet, but only for the good of the film. If someone asked me what were the places I loved most in my life, I would say the countryside in Murnau's *Sunrise* or the town in the same film, but I would not cite a place I had really visited because I never visit anything. I'm aware that that's a little abnormal, but that's how it is. I don't like landscapes or things; I like people, I'm interested in ideas, in feelings.

Interview by Pierre Loubière and Gilbert Salachas,
Télé-Ciné, *no. 160, March 1970*

With Jean Desailly and Françoise Dorléac on the set of *The Soft Skin*

What interests you, you said, are people and feelings. The critics often make a point of this, asserting that Truffaut is a vulnerable, sensitive person. Don't you get a little annoyed when you hear that?

Having been a journalist myself, I am less sensitive than others to that sort of comment. I am not contemptuous or skeptical about what is said or written, but I don't attach much importance to it. I know that people who know me or who look attentively at my films see very well what there is of toughness in them, and when people say, "Once again Truffaut-the-tender," I know perfectly well that that's false, because my films are not sentimental, even if they are built on sentiments. Note that sometimes, on the contrary, people say, "It's cold, dry" (for example, about *Fahrenheit* or *The Soft Skin*). For me, the adjective "sentimental" is pretty derogatory, but seeing as how I work most often in the domain of sentiments, I understand that misunderstanding. In fact, it doesn't bother me.

Interview by Pierre Loubière and Gilbert Salachas,
Télé-Ciné, *no. 160, March 1970*

The refusal to conform to fashion runs so deep in me that sometimes it even makes me turn my back on themes that might otherwise interest me

Would I dare film *Jules and Jim* today? I would feel as if I were paying court to fashion, making a feminist film. At the time, I had been struck by the fact that, in all films, even good ones, if you showed one character loved by two others you let the public make its choice of one over the other. There was never the idea of the "impossible choice." And I liked that, the idea of showing that sometimes nobody's right, that a woman can love two men and that the two might get along with each other. That idea motivated me. Now, it would be "taken up": feminism, independence, the woman's choice. . . . The way things are now would more likely make me want to chuck it all.

I know that this attitude may appear offensive. Let's say that the refusal to conform to fashion runs so deep in me that sometimes it even makes me turn my back on themes that might otherwise interest me. But I can't work under pressure, under threat. And one of the greatest threats in 1978 is fashion.

Interview by Danièle Heymann and Catherine Laporte,
L'Express, *March 13, 1978*

With Jeanne Moreau between takes of *Jules and Jim*

Does the François Truffaut of today, whom some find more sober, feel he has denied the Truffaut of twelve years ago, the leader of a virulent opposition to the conventional structures of the French cinema?

No. At that time I was living only for the cinema. Today also. So, for that reason, I feel faithful. Sure, if you want to say that having been poor, then no longer being so, or having found oneself on one side of the barricade and then on the other, is disowning oneself, then maybe you're right . . . although, you know, the material question . . . When I was poor, I wasn't aware of it; I no longer am, and I'm not one bit more aware of it. I am cinema-cinema. There you are, I feel like a pure

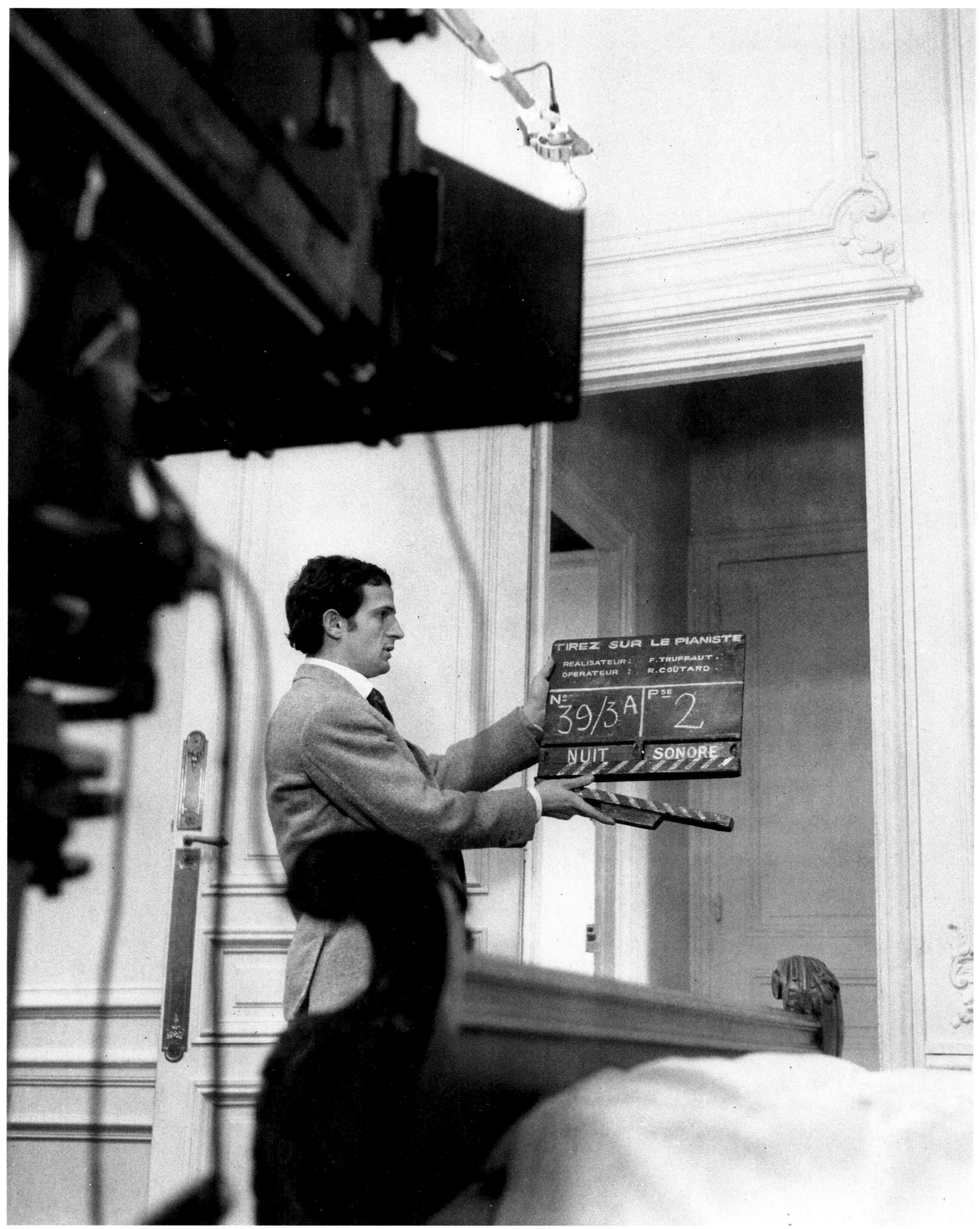
TIREZ SUR LE PIANISTE
REALISATEUR : F.TRUFFAUT.
OPERATEUR : R.COUTARD.
N° 39/3A
P^SE 2
NUIT
SONORE

product of cinema. When I'm asked: "What has happened to you in these nine years?" I reply: "Nothing, I've made seven films, that's all."

You don't feel yourself aging?

Not really, no, except perhaps by way of certain exterior signs. Other people, the way they speak to you . . . I took part in a radio broadcast, not long ago, with Sylvie Vartan, and I said to myself: "Myself, I don't want to *tutoyer* anyone, I don't like the 'chum' style and everything that goes with it." Well, I was wrong to fuss over it because . . .

It never entered their heads to address you as tu . . .

Yes, that's it. Everyone said to me, "Monsieur Truffaut." Monsieur! That day I really became aware of the generation gap.

Your enthusiasm of ten years back for the cinema has been affected by this?

I didn't feel like an enthusiast ten years back, and I don't feel myself an enthusiast today. It's my life. I don't know how to say it any better: it's my life. Ah, all the same, I await films made by others with less impatience than in the past. There is, let's say, a film lover's purity you can't help but lose when you take to making films yourself.

For example, in '47 or '48 I knew in advance that Orson Welles had shot in twenty-one days a film called *Macbeth* and that he was going to present it at Venice. I lived for that film. When they announced that Laurence Olivier's *Henry V* would show at the same festival, I was heart and soul for Welles. When they then announced that Welles was withdrawing his film from the competition, I thought: "Ah! the scum! That has to be a put-up job." . . . There you are. Today I no longer live like that for somebody else's film, it's impossible.

Interview by Pierre Billard, Christiane Collange, and Claude Veillot, L'Express, *May 20, 1968*

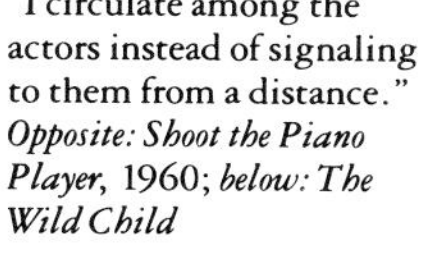

"I circulate among the actors instead of signaling to them from a distance." *Opposite: Shoot the Piano Player,* 1960; *below: The Wild Child*

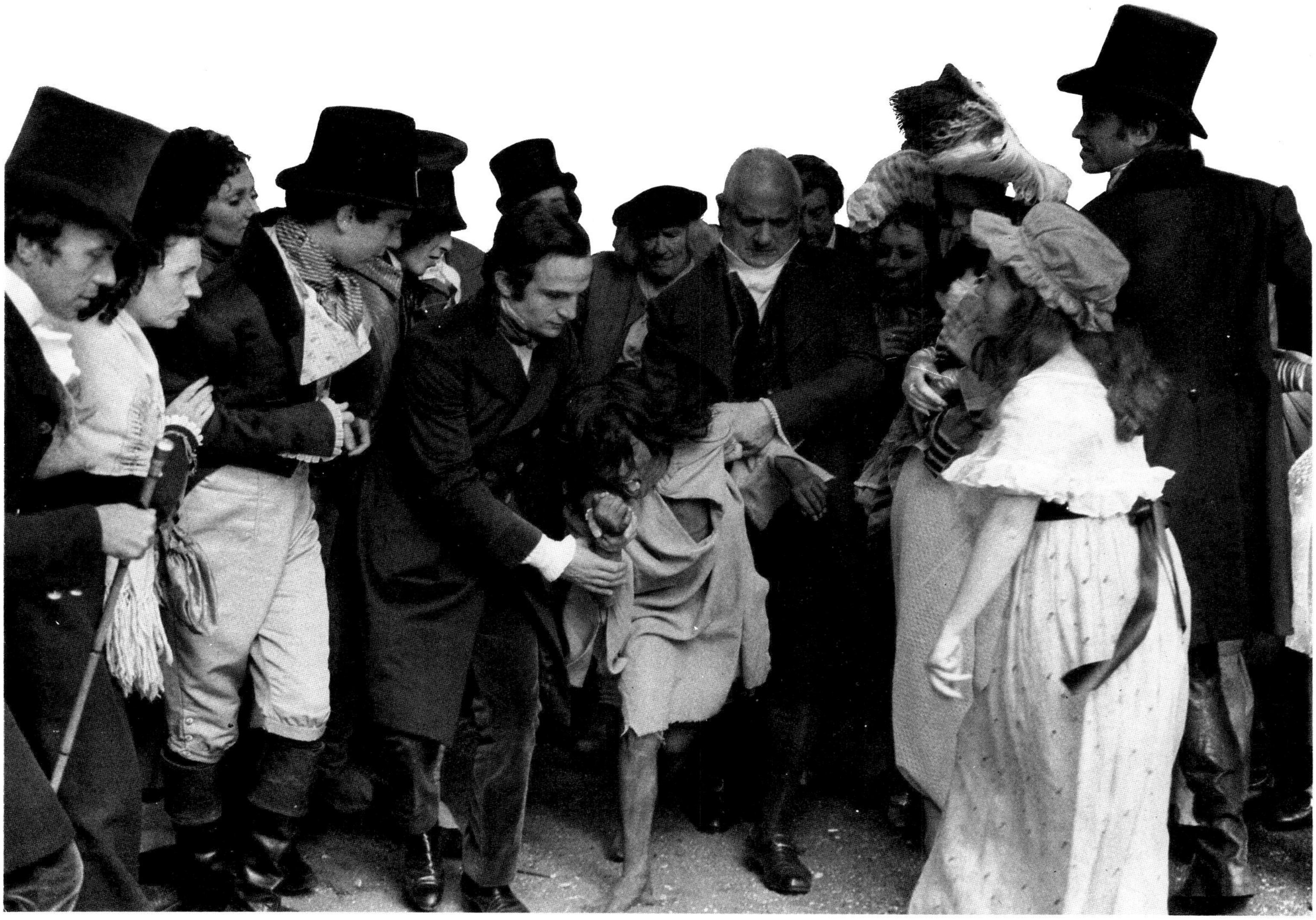

"For you, death represents what?" It is something very logical that scandalizes me when it touches children, when it is out of chronology

You're obliged to think of it when you're filming because that is a job involving a beginning and an end, a job that has a limit in time; so one thinks about death, one thinks also about the actors in an egoistical fashion, in a falsely friendly fashion. . . . For example, if I'm shooting in the mountains I don't want the actors to go off skiing; what can you do, a film is a baby you protect all the way. There is a kind of feeling of relief when the film is finished.

Is it in order to avoid that image of death that you always have in mind two films? Is it so as to push back its limits?

Yes, whenever one of my films comes out I am always in the process of working on another; I have already fixed the dates, already hired the main characters; I think it's for emotional reasons, to endure less anguish, to attach less importance to how the release of that film will go, and everything connected with it, that's it.

Interview by Aline Desjardins, Radio-Canada, 1971

The Green Room

Kika Markham and Stacey Tendeter in *Two English Girls*

For you, death represents what?

It is something very logical that scandalizes me when it touches children, when it is out of chronology. The scandal, I think, is when one does not die in his right order, when children die before their parents. From another viewpoint, if it really was chronological, if it was never paradoxical, then life would probably become even more monstrous. If we knew we were all going to die at the age of eighty-five, for example, I think that life would no longer be an adventure, or . . . it would perhaps be an adventure of great bitterness. Probably there has to be that kind of crazy "odds," of risk, of the unknown, of paradox, of mystery, for life to be interesting.

"T.D.C.," 1982, in connection with showing The Green Room *on television*

Claude: "I could write pages and pages about them every day. I prefer looking at them."

I believe that the cinema is an improvement on life because it is extraordinary

I believe that the cinema is an improvement on life because it is extraordinary: consider what power you have, when you make a film, organizing an entire life, an entire life in itself, a life without bottlenecks, without hindrances, an intense life, and that brings us back to our friend Hitchcock. I think the director's power is something very beautiful. . . . One senses it, for example, while improvising a scene. In *Two English Girls,* there was a moment out in the country in England when I felt I wanted a character to come on who wasn't called for in the story. I said: "He's going to arrive just there, it will be the first time a car is seen in the film, because it's a costume film," and in this setting we've been seeing for an hour by then in the film, one suddenly sees a car driven across the landscape: the character Diurka, whom we've seen in Paris, is arriving and is going to be present at the death of one of the two girls. All that episode, which was improvised, gave me enormous joy because I felt in making it an extraordinary power, the power of creating life really, ultimately, one life alongside another, obviously.

Interview by Aline Desjardins, Radio-Canada, 1971

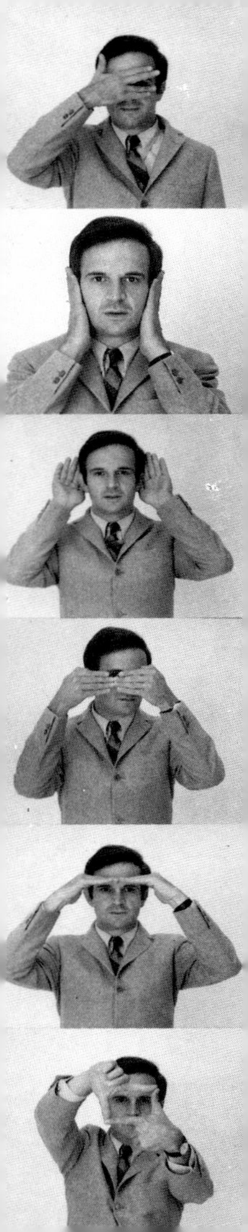

THE FILMS IN MY LIFE

1954 UNE VISITE

I was improvising, which is something absolutely senseless for an amateur

Jean-José Richer (The Brother-in-Law) blowing smoke

Laura Mauri (The Girl) laughs at the young man's blunder

Far right
Florence Doniol-Valcroze (The Little Girl) falling asleep

I had nevertheless made films in 16 mm, one at least. I shot a film a very long time ago in the apartment of Doniol-Valcroze, with his little girl who acts in *L'Eau à la Bouche* and who was a good deal smaller at the time. I was improvising, which is something absolutely senseless for an amateur: you can, even then, put in a little work before shooting. I had no story but three actors: two boys and a girl, without counting Doniol's little girl. I came to realize that half the shots done in a day were strictly useless. I had no feeling for ellipsis. When the film was finished, I borrowed a viewer and a moviola to edit it, and I put in an enormous lot of time at that. It was by doing that that I learned most; I had blasted open doors that would have opened by themselves, all that superfluous stuff. In any case there was no story, it was incomprehensible and unshowable. So much so that I didn't really know much more when it came time for *The Mischief Makers;* but I had made up my mind not to be boring and I had an obsession about blank places. I suffer physically when I sense people being bored in a movie theater, even if the film isn't by me. There are directors who don't care one bit about the public, and in a certain sense they're right.

Interview by Gilbert Salachas,
Télé-Ciné, *no. 94, March 1961*

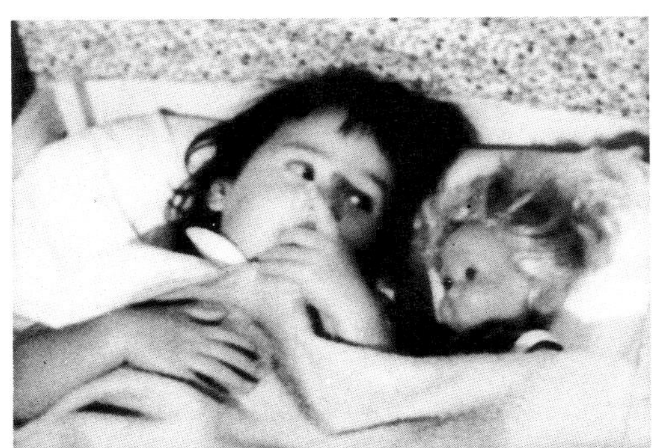

Laura Mauri opens the door and smiles

Jean-José Richer furtively embraces Laura Mauri

THE MISCHIEF MAKERS

How can you make excuses for a "first film," and above all how can you get by without excusing yourself?

1957

The Mischief Makers is not really a film but a quarter of a film illustrating different aspects of childhood, with all the other sketches remaining to be shot. The episode takes off from a short story by Maurice Pons published in the collection *Virginales*.

From reading *Virginales* and particularly *Les Mistons* I acquired a store of images—the word "profusion" wouldn't be too strong—of such precision, and naturally of such beauty, that the desire to "fix" that dream immediately became imperative. For me, an apprentice-filmmaker, as for Maurice Pons, the story of those two lovers made the butt of persecution by a handful of spiteful kids constituted essentially a pretext for showing, on the one hand, children free on their own and, on the other, impatient lovers.

Making a film presupposes that you take yourself for an artist, consists in trying to impose on others your own view of things, a view that, for convenience, is called "truth." Presenting my first film—even if the gap between the intentions and the result makes it something like a game of hide-and-seek among Martians—I am tempted to proclaim: "Here you are, Ladies, Young Ladies, Gentlemen: REAL children and REAL lovers!" But I don't forget that Pirandello wrote: *To each his truth.* Anybody can set himself up as a filmmaker, and a "second film" can be excused by the precedent created. But how can you make excuses for a "first film," and above all how can you get by without excusing yourself? Still and all, if—thanks to the images of Jean Malige, the words of Maurice Pons, the music of Maurice Le Roux, the presence of Gérard Blain, Bernadette Lafont, and five kids from Nîmes—"my" stammered truth becomes a little "your" truth, then I'll repeat the offense soon and without too much embarrassment.

"Mon Premier Film," press book, November 24, 1957

Bernadette Lafont (Bernadette) and Gérard Blain (Gérard) at the arena in Nîmes

100 *VIRGINALES*

amoureux notre surveillance. Nous ne devions plus compter sur des rencontres de hasard, mais organiser un réseau d'informations minutieuses. Chacun de nous à tour de rôle fut tenu de monter la garde, soit devant la villa des Jouve, soit à l'entrée du foyer universitaire. Notre filature s'exerçait ensuite à travers toute la ville. Jamais Yvette ne put se rendre au Prisunic, jamais Etienne ne put manquer un cours, sans que cela ne fût noté avec soin dans nos carnets de poche. Chaque semaine, nous confrontions nos observations et dressions dans un grand cahier, l'emploi du temps présumé de nos deux suspects. Pour combler les blancs, nous prenions plaisir à imaginer des horreurs :

« mardi 24. 19 h. 30. Y. pas rentrée. Couchera évidemment chez E. »

« samedi 28. 9 h. E. sorti seul à bicyclette. Se renseigner à la Brigade fluviale. »

Le jeudi matin, ils jouaient ensemble au tennis, sur une grande place herbeuse, ombragée de platanes. Nous nous retrouvions tous derrière les grillages du court. Qu'est-ce qui nous [illegible] là, [illegible] par ces matinées claires, tandis que volaient les balles sur le sable [illegible] L'amour du sport ? Ou la courte jupe plissée, les jambes nues d'Yvette ? Lorsqu'elle se baissait pour

VIRGINALES 101

ramasser une balle, nous nous poussions du coude. Qu'une autre s'envolât par-dessus les grillages et roulât dans l'herbe à nos pieds, Etienne avait beau crier, comme c'était l'usage sur le court :

— balle, s'il vous plait !

aucun de nous ne bougeait. Mais qu'Yvette s'approchât de nous, transpirant légèrement, légèrement essoufflée sous son tricot de coton, et qu'à travers le grillage, elle nous dit de sa voix précieuse, en souriant, simplement :

— je vous en prie !

nous nous bousculions, tels de jeunes chiens, pour lui renvoyer sa balle. C'est Etienne qui nous remerciait. De rage, nous tournions le dos, jurant de ne jamais reparaitre sur le court. Le jeudi suivant, nous étions tous là.

Deux ou trois fois, nous réussimes à les surprendre au cinéma. Les films qu'ils avaient choisis ne nous intéressaient guère. Des vedettes américaines s'y embrassaient à pleines bouches. Mais du fond de la salle obscure, nous ne perdions pas de vue, un seul instant, le couple détesté, redoutant et souhaitant tout à la fois le moindre écart aux convenances. Lorsque, par mégarde, le visage d'Etienne se rapprochait tendrement de celui d'Yvette, il se trouvait toujours l'un de nous pour crier d'une voix fabriquée :

— A la tienne, Etienne !

et tous, nous pouffions de rire, insoucieux des

Far right
Pages of the book by Maurice Pons cut out and annotated by François Truffaut

Gérard Blain chasing Bernadette Lafont: "What do you feel for me?"

EVERYTHING TOOK PLACE OUTDOORS, IN SUNLIGHT

Before making *The Mischief Makers,* I had been a film fan, had been a critic, I loved the cinema. I had no idea if I wanted to make one kind of film or another. I hadn't thought about that, I knew vaguely that I wanted to make films, that's all. *Les Mistons* was a short story by Maurice Pons that I picked out because it was easy to film. Everything took place outdoors, in sunlight, and there was no need of a producer, it was enough to have the film and I knew someone in Montpellier who had the equipment. . . .

It was really and truly while filming *The Mischief Makers* that I came to realize that there were things I liked and things I didn't and that the choice of story for a film is more important than one thinks and that you cannot simply jump into things. I realized, for example, that the story in itself did not please me, that there was no connection between the lives of those five children and the pair of lovers. Every time I had to shoot things that were truly connected with the subject, like the pestering pranks played on the pair by the five children, I was ill at ease. Whereas every time I did things with the children that were almost documentary, I was happy and everything went well. We were making a kind of investigation into truth, if you will, using the children, because they have a terrific feeling for realism, and because that interested me.

It was thanks to the mistakes of *The Mischief Makers* that I came to realize, for *The 400 Blows,* that this time I had to stick close to childhood and, above all, very close to what is documentary, working with the minimum of fiction. At the start of the New Wave it was said by people against us, young filmmakers, they said: "After all, it's not so different from what was done before," and I myself believe that the platform—after all I don't know if we had a platform—but in any case, as concerns myself, I had never thought that if I made films I would revolutionize the cinema or that I would express myself any differently from the people who made films before me. I always thought that the cinema was something very good, except it was lacking in sincerity, and that what had to be done was the same thing only better. . . . There's no enormous difference between *Chiens Perdus sans Collier* and *The 400 Blows.* It's the same thing, only myself I wanted to make my own because I didn't like the other. That's all.

Interview by Jean-Pierre Chartier, "Cinéastes de Notre Temps," French radio, December 1, 1965

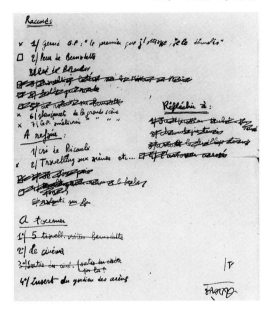

Notes made by François Truffaut during the filming of *The Mischief Makers*

RIGOROUS BERNADETTE

It is always with emotion that I encounter Bernadette Lafont, her name or her face, her image fixed in a magazine or her undulating body in a film, because even though I am older than she we made our debuts on the same summer day of 1957, she in front, I behind the camera. The title of the film written on the clapper board was *Les Mistons.* The films got hold of Bernadette Lafont and never again let go. Twenty, thirty times I've seen her on the screen, a whimsical and at the same time rigorous artist, never demagogical, an upright candle never vacillating, always valiant, never running down. When I think of Bernadette Lafont, French actress, I see a symbol in motion, the symbol of vitality and therefore of life.

For Studio 43, *1984*

Bernadette Lafont and Gérard Blain with the five "mischief makers" between hostilities

1958

HISTOIRE D'EAU

It's neither Godard's best film nor Truffaut's

The film is signed Jean-Luc Godard and François Truffaut. I think you will agree with me that it's neither Godard's best film nor Truffaut's. It was made in an unforeseen way, like an experiment in improvisation. There had been floods in the Paris region. I had gone to see the producer Pierre Braunberger who is as charming as the Mayerboum in *Schpountz* [a film presented by Truffaut at Annecy] and I said to him that seeing the flooding I thought it was a shame it should survive only in documentary. When you see a documentary, and you're a real film addict, more a cinemaniac than a cinephiliac, you say to yourself: those deserts, those mountains, those pipelines—it would be real good if two characters, right there, were chasing each other. That is, you love cinema so much in its conventional form that you become incapable of admiring it just as a record of beauty. It's because of that, I think, that real film fans don't like documentaries.

If you visit a factory you say to yourself: Hold on, somebody could stage a film chase in this factory. It's the permanent warp you get from an apprenticeship with the American cinema. So I said to Braunberger: "Give me a little film," not even having a story to show him. "Jean-Claude Brialy [who was still scarcely known at the time] is willing to come with us, Chabrol is lending his car, and we'll go right to the heart of the floods with a girl who's also willing to work." We simply took off one weekend, and I must say that when we got there, there wasn't much water to be seen already. And the little water there was didn't inspire us, because we saw people looking for boats to get their belongings out. In the middle of all that, to rent a boat and carry on like crazy struck us all of a sudden as pretty indecent. Well, I had brought along six hundred meters of film and I brought back six hundred meters of exposed film but it didn't impress anyone but us and not even us. I said to Braunberger: "You've lost six hundred meters of film. Keep it around." Jean-Luc Godard wanted to see those six hundred meters and said: "I can have fun making a montage." He made a montage of the film in his fashion, a commentary. It was obvious, once the film was finished, that it wasn't his or mine and that it would be logical for both to sign and to make a present of it to the producer who never made a fortune out of it.

Interview by the Fédération Française des Ciné-clubs, Cinéma 67, *no. 112*

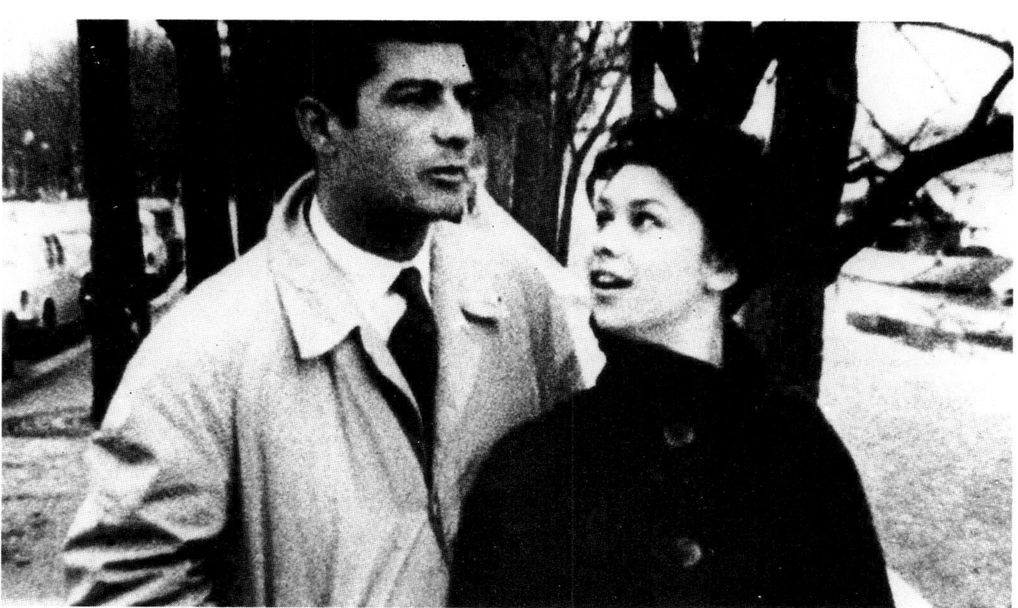

Jean-Claude Brialy and Caroline Dim: "We decided to proceed on foot."

les
Quatre Cents
coups
UN FILM DE
FRANÇOIS TRUFFAUT

THE 400 BLOWS

1959

Adolescence leaves pleasant memories only for adults who can't remember

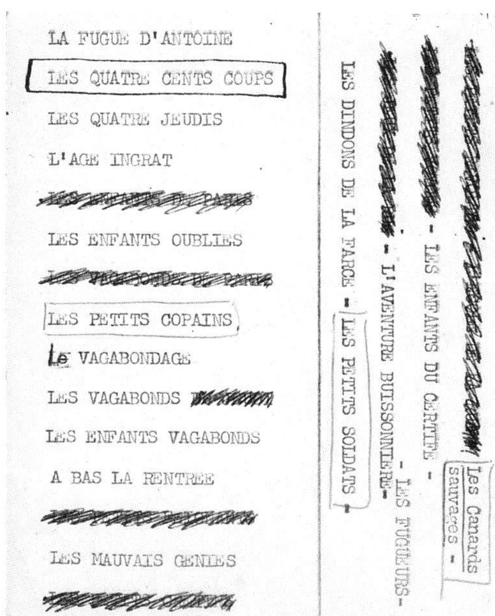

LA FUGUE D'ANTOINE
LES QUATRE CENTS COUPS
LES QUATRE JEUDIS
L'AGE INGRAT
LES ENFANTS OUBLIES
LES PETITS COPAINS
Le VAGABONDAGE
LES VAGABONDS
LES ENFANTS VAGABONDS
A BAS LA RENTREE
LES MAUVAIS GENIES
LES DINDONS DE LA FARCE - LES PETITS SOLDATS -
- L'AVENTURE BUISSONNIERE - - LES FUGUEURS-
- LES ENFANTS DU CERTIFE -
Les Canards sauvages -

Different titles considered for *The 400 Blows*

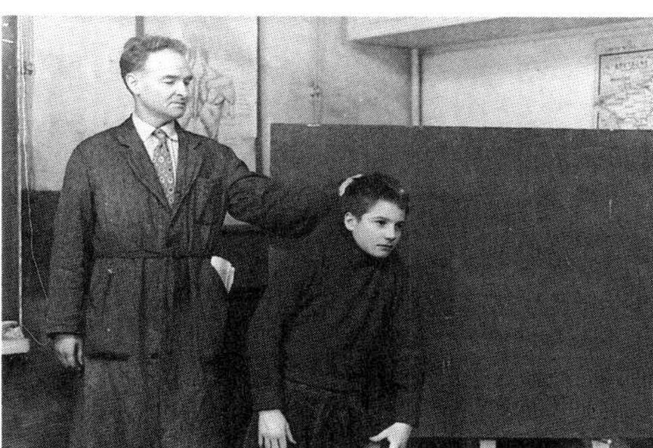

Guy Decomble (The Teacher) and Jean-Pierre Léaud (Antoine)

Letter to Jean-Pierre Léaud's father

Paris, le 20 Octobre 1958

Monsieur P. LEAUD
12, avenue George V
PARIS 8°

Monsieur,

Je suis bien décidé à confier un rôle important des "400 COUPS" à votre fils Jean-Pierre, sans savoir lequel encore.
Je désire lui faire passer plusieurs scènes du film cette fois sans caméra, le

JEUDI 23 OCTOBRE 1958, à 15 H

à mon domicile : 27, rue Saint-Ferdinand - Paris 17°
Métro : ARGENTINE ou TERNES
Immeuble D - 6ème Etage à gauche en sortant de l'ascenseur.

Votre fils Jean-Pierre m'a semblé très intelligent et assez précoce pour que les quelques semaines pendant lesquelles nous lui ferons manquer la classe, ne constituent pas un handicap insurmontable pour sa scolarité.

Avec mes remerciements, veuillez agréer, Monsieur, l'assurance de mes sentiments distingués.

François TRUFFAUT

Opposite
Publicity poster for *The 400 Blows* made for the Cannes Festival

Contrary to what has been often published in the papers since the Cannes Festival, *The 400 Blows* is not an autobiographical film. A film is not made all alone, and if I had wanted only to put my adolescence into images, I would not have asked Marcel Moussy to come and collaborate on the screenplay and to write the dialogue. If the young Antoine Doinel sometimes resembles the turbulent adolescent I was, his parents are absolutely unlike mine, who were excellent, but, on the contrary, are more like the families who confronted each other on the TV program *Si C'Etait Vous,* which Marcel Moussy was writing for Marcel Bluwal. It was not only the television writer I admired in Marcel Moussy but also the novelist of *Sang chaud,* which is the story of a little Algerian boy.

Our intention, from the start, was to draw the portrait of a child who would not be an unhappy child nor a spoiled child but simply an adolescent. For parents, the word "adolescent" has scarcely any meaning; it only acquires one in the eyes of schoolteachers. For Papa and Mama you're a "child" until you go off for your military service from which you return a "man," and moustached if you please.

If there was a thesis behind our film, it would be this: adolescence leaves pleasant memories only for adults who can't remember. When you're in that difficult age, the thirteenth year is your bad luck time: discovery of injustice, first sexual curiosity left unsatisfied, too early desire for social independence, and often lack of family affection.

The appalling gap between the universe of adolescents and that of adults is admirably expressed in Cocteau's sentence in *Les Enfants Terribles:* "The death penalty not existing in the schools, Dargelos was sent home." Thus, when I was thirteen, I was extremely impatient to become an adult in order to be able to commit all sorts of errors "with impunity." It seemed to me that a child's life was made up only of "crimes" and that of an adult of "accidents." I used to throw the pieces of a broken plate down the drain, whereas today I can entertain my crowd telling how I ran my car into a tree.

In her book on adolescent sexual problems, Maryse Choisy recounts the curious experiment tried by Emperor Frederick II. He asked himself

Claire Maurier (The Mother), Jean-Pierre Léaud (Antoine), and Albert Rémy (The Father)

what language children would express themselves in if they had never heard a single spoken word. Would it be Latin, Greek, Hebrew? He turned over a certain number of newborn babies to nurses assigned to feed and bathe them, but he rigorously forbade anyone to speak to them or caress them. Well, all the children died at a very early age: "They could not live without encouragement, friendly faces and attitudes, without the caresses of their nurses and wet nurses. That is why the songs a woman sings rocking a baby are called nursing magic."

Writing the screenplay of *The 400 Blows* we had in mind Emperor Frederick's experiment. We tried to imagine the behavior of a child who had survived such treatment when he approached his thirteenth year, on the brink of revolt.

Antoine Doinel is the opposite of a mistreated child; he simply is not "treated" at all. His mother never calls him by his first name: "Child, if you please, you can clear the table," and while he is doing that his father speaks as if he weren't present: "What's to be done with the kid during vacation?"

An unwanted child, Antoine never or scarcely ever "opens up" at home, he is terrorized by his mother, whom in a vague way he admires. He makes up for it outside, where he boasts and swaggers: it can be taken for granted that he has an opinion about everything and that his classmates keep away from him a bit because he is as supercilious and insolent as, at home, he is humble, sensitive, and sneaky. Fear of his mother has made him a little cowardly with her, clumsily servile, which works against him in turn.

His behavior when he is alone is significant: a mixture of good and bad actions. He puts coal on the fire but then wipes his hands on the curtains, takes what is doubtless stolen money out of his secret hiding place, sets the table, uses his mother's toilet articles, her eyelash curler. . . .

He is already a perpetual anxiety case, because he no sooner gets out of one complicated

Roger PEYREFITTE. Les Clés de Saint Pierre........
François TRUFFAUT. Imitation de J.-C. ....
Bonheur d'expression ....

Paul MORAND. Mai 1920.........................
Paul LÉAUTAUD. Journal littéraire (1927)..........
Thomas PLATTER. Mémoires (Suite) (*traduit par* JEAN CARRIVE *et* PIERRE LEYRIS)...............

Andrée TÉTRY. La protection de la nature..........
Michel MOHRT. Le roman des nouveaux émigrés......
Paul SÉRANT. Quelques non-conformistes..........
Les Livres par JACQUES LAURENT................
Le Théâtre, par PIERRE MARCABRU..............
Le Cinéma, par CLAUDE MARTINE...............
René GEORGIN. La langue des affaires..............

Le Galant adventureux (*nouvelle*)....................
FAYARD-JARDIN. Paprika ....
Notes de PHILIPPE JULLIAN, FRANÇOIS SENTEIN, HENRI JAUNE, G.-J. GROS.

First appearance of the character Antoine in Truffaut's short story published in *La Parisienne*, no. 28, May 1955, with an introduction "Imitation de J.-C." (Jean Cocteau), signed J.S.

FRANÇOIS TRUFFAUT 515

*

ANTOINE ET L'ORPHELINE

Antoine aimait la pénombre. Au réveil, elle nous fait prendre les objets anciens pour des jouets nouveaux. Les rideaux tirés, les volets ouverts révélaient l'imposture. Ce jouet nouveau était le vieux chandelier, cette panoplie, la culotte de laine.

Etre le fils d'une admiratrice d'Alfred de Vigny n'est pas facile. Il était criminel d'être malade, tousser interdit. La main sur la bouche pour refouler la toux, Antoine entendait hurler sa mère : « *Souffre et meurs sans parler* ». Dans la baignoire elle criait à travers la porte : « *J'aime la majesté des souffrauces humaines* ».

Cloîtré dans la chambre nommée la chambre du fond parce qu'elle était au bout de l'appartement et que le soleil n'y parvenait guère. Antoine préférait prolonger sa nuit jusqu'au soir. C'est pourquoi Antoine ne cessait de rêver.

Eveillé, il dormait encore.

Agir en dormant est le somnambulisme. Antoine conservait au-delà qu'il est convenable, intacte, son enfance.

Les petits enfants charment. Les grands enfants importunent et font honte.

Antoine obéissait aux mystérieuses et absurdes disciplines qu'à force de respect et de patience l'enfance pousse jusqu'au rite. Construire des équilibres de fourchettes et de couteaux sur un verre surmonté d'un bouchon ; tenir serré un clou dans la flamme de la bougie jusqu'à la brûlure intolérable. Le repas fini, une peau de banane rigoureusement écartelée devenait vite dans l'assiette une étoile de mer en tissu éponge ou, retournée, une pieuvre en peau de femme.

On comprendra Antoine si je le montre aux bains de mer.

Il se croyait incapable de nager, comme écrire une lettre ou conduire une automobile. La volonté de faire-comme-les-autres le jetait à l'eau. Il faisait alors les mouvements de natation qui conviennent, puis étonné d'avoir nagé, se posait la question : « Ai-je pied ? » — L'interrogation devenait si impérieuse

516 ANTOINE ET L'ORPHELINE

qu'il se mettait debout ; ses pieds ne touchaient pas le fond ; alors il renonçait et ses gestes devenaient ceux de l'assoupissement.

Ainsi on repêcha Antoine d'un Centre d'observation de mineurs délinquants, puis de l'Armée où il avait devancé l'appel croyant que les somnambules deviennent officiers. Accoutumé aux miracles il ne remerciait pas ses sauveteurs, c'était naturel.

* * *

Un jour la mère d'Antoine mourut.

Ce jour-là Antoine eut vingt ans.

Cette mort fut la mort du loup et le silence qui désinfecta la maison la fit inhabitable.

Antoine n'avait jamais usé de quoi que ce soit qui lui appartînt. D'aussi loin que remontaient ses souvenirs, il avait habité chez les autres, fumant leurs cigarettes, portant leurs vêtements.

Faisant l'amour avec la femme des autres, l'idée ne lui était jamais venue qu'il pût en avoir une à soi. On l'eût fait s'esclaffer en lui suggérant qu'il aurait peut-être un jour des enfants.

Impénétrable en ses projets, la destinée fit Antoine rencontrer, au sortir d'un concert de musique italienne, une jeune fille rose et blonde : Henriette avait vingt ans, vivait seule et n'avait pas d'amant.

De longs silences entrecoupés de maximes sur la faillite des arts au XXe siècle firent d'Antoine étonné l'amant de cette charmante fille.

Ils s'installèrent dans l'appartement dont le père d'Antoine, explorateur lointain, avait vendu le mobilier pour financer une expédition. Quelques lits et canapés demeuraient qui brisaient la nudité des neuf pièces.

Antoine et Henriette s'aimèrent dans un théâtre vide. Le jour ni la nuit n'existèrent plus pour eux, ils faisaient sonner le réveille-matin toutes les deux heures pour faire l'amour.

Ai-je fait comprendre qu'avec Henriette Antoine ne vivait pas sa première aventure ?

Affligé d'une apparence insignifiante, il ne possédait aucune qualité morale mais plutôt quelques uns de ces agréments qui font les jeunes filles se moquer, mais par quoi l'on s'acquiert aisément les faveurs des femmes, qu'un usage des hommes a faites moins exigeantes et tout à la fois davantage.

Antoine, on le pense, ne se faisait guère d'illusion sur ses conquêtes forcées. Il n'était point la dupe de ces nouvelles et éternelles Bovary. Elles lui offraient le divertissement et non le plaisir.

L'inconstance de ces femmes, leur indécence, leur immodestie, leur peu de retenue enfin, blessaient sa pudeur qui était grande.

Jean-Pierre Léaud and Jeanne Moreau

Patrick Auffay (René), Jacques Dufilho, and Jean-Pierre Léaud in a scene omitted from the final version

situation than he falls into another. Caught up in a network of lies, one after the other, he lives in fear and anxiety. He is trapped in a stupid tangle and would kill himself rather than admit anything. The man who steals an egg ends up having to steal a cow. Antoine Doinel is a difficult child. And as Marcel Moussy would say: *"Si C'Etait Vous,* if it were you."

"Je N'ai Pas Ecrit Ma Biographie en Quatre Cents Coups," Arts, *June 3, 1959*

IT IS NOT AN AUTOBIOGRAPHICAL FILM

When I was shooting *The Mischief Makers, The 400 Blows* already existed in the form of a short film, which was titled *Antoine's Flight* and was simply a portion of the film, the middle of the film: nighttime in Paris, a boy who, having lied at school, does not dare go home and spends the night outdoors. It was only those twenty minutes or quarter of an hour in the middle of the film.

May one know what impelled you to lengthen the story and to make your film longer?

Yes, it was because I was disappointed by *The Mischief Makers.* By and large I had rejected the style of films made up of short skits. I knew that the other skits would be too different from *The Mischief Makers,* so I preferred to leave *The Mischief Makers* as a short and to take my chances with full length by spinning out the story. Among the seven or eight stories I had entirely ready, I preferred *Antoine's Flight,* which became *The 400 Blows.*

Does the screenplay of The 400 Blows *constitute in some way an autobiography?*

No, very partially. All I can say is that nothing is invented. What didn't happen to me personally happened to people I know, to boys my age and even to people I read about in the papers. Nothing comes from pure fiction, but it is not an autobiographical film completely.

Interview by Pierre Wildenstein, Télé-Ciné, *no. 83, July 1959*

"À LA COCTEAU"

As for Jean Cocteau, we knew when we filmed in that apartment, Claude Vermorel's, we knew that it was "à la Cocteau." We were well aware of it and I even cut from the film passages which were not very successful and which reflected even more that atmosphere à la Jean Cocteau. I believe moreover that it was from that moment on that Jean Cocteau really loved the film, which was close to him in the oddness of the décor and a little in the situation as well.

Interview by Pierre Wildenstein, Télé-Ciné, *no. 83, July 1959*

I have a great fidelity to admirations I once had and to death in general. So there are periods when I miss Cocteau so much that, eight days in a row, I go and listen to the records he made and reread his books. And that "Cocteau week" does me good because among living writers there are no authors who interest me as much as he does. Distance in time does not exist for me.

In connection with The Green Room, Unifrance Film, *1977*

FRANÇOIS TRUFFAUT 517

Il ne sut le bonheur qu'avec Henriette ; avec Henriette il connaîtrait plus tard qu'il n'y a pas d'amour, qu'il n'y a que des obstacles à l'amour.

Ce bonheur, pour le mériter mieux, il convenait, pensa Antoine, de rompre les aventures en cours. Il écrivit donc deux lettres dont voici la première :

Madame,

Après que Monsieur votre mari m'a fait l'honneur de me présenter à vous, vous m'avez fait celui de vouloir être ma mère, puis ma sœur ; plus ample connaissance faite, nous pensâmes être bons amis, vous devîntes ma maîtresse. Je propose aujourd'hui que vous redeveniez la femme de votre mari car j'avoue que je suis un peu las d'être votre sujet et le complément de ce brave Gérard.

Je caresse vos enfants et pose mes lèvres sur vos doigts.

ANTOINE

... et la seconde :

Chère Amie,

Voilà bientôt six mois que vous me laissez espérer que vous serez ma maîtresse ; puis vous me faites faire antichambre sous prétexte que « nous sommes de la race de ceux qui s'estiment et non de ceux qui couchent ».

Quittons-nous donc « bons amis ». Je regrette seulement votre obstination à vouloir être aimée non pour vous même mais pour ce qui en vous appartient le plus aux autres : votre conversation.

Amitié

ANTOINE

* * *

Antoine aimait regarder dormir Henriette. Sur ces paupières au repos se peignait un regard triste qu'Antoine ne lui connaissait pas. Henriette était pure jusque dans le sommeil, les rêves lui étaient inconnus.

Au bout de cinq à six semaines ils furent à court d'argent. Antoine fit le projet d'emprunter à son grand-père. Il fallait un prétexte. Ce fut Henriette. Il importait que les apparences fussent sauves et les convenances observées. Antoine présenterait Henriette comme sa fiancée.

Les grands-parents habitaient J... ; on s'y rendait en train.

Antoine avait la passion des trains mais à la condition de voyager seul ; il savait la valeur des sourires aux portières, l'ins-

518 ANTOINE ET L'ORPHELINE

tallation des valises, le frôlement des visages s'effaçant dans le couloir. Il rêvait d'express internationaux, de départs pour la neige, de pantalons fuseaux bien tendus, de chandails blancs. Le ravissaient aussi la chute d'une bretelle de combinaison, les bas qui tournent et que l'on replace, la jupe tirée sur le genou, les baisers qui s'envolent des fenêtres.

Tout à sa déception de voyager vers la banlieue, il négligeait un peu Henriette, mais lorsqu'il s'en rendit compte son empressement ne fut que plus vif et sa tendresse s'en accrut.

Ils arrivèrent enfin chez les grands-parents ; la grand'mère était sèche : un jour qu'elle pleurait au cimetière, son visage s'était figé et les larmes avaient durci comme le suif tombé de la bougie ; sa face était un instantané de pleurs ; avec cela, méchante comme savent l'être celles qui ont souffert plus qu'à une femme n'appartient. Sur chacun inventant le pire, elle tombait parfois juste, c'est le secret de l'intuition provinciale. Le grand-père était à principes ; il complimenta la fiancée. Il crut à propos de raconter ses fiançailles et, mis en verve par ces souvenirs qui faisaient la grand-mère hausser les épaules, il fut intarissable.

Henriette descendait les escaliers en fredonnant *Mon père m'a donné un mari.* Cette chanson familière à Antoine depuis l'enfance, lui apparut alors monstrueuse, terrifiante : *Mon Dieu quel homme, quel petit homme, mon Dieu quel homme, qu'il est petit* ! Ce petit homme qui disparait dans le lit de sa jeune femme devait, ne pouvait être, pensait-il, que le Diable.

Le piano : une méthode apprend à poser les doigts ; la meilleure — allemande — enseigne à les ôter. Ainsi, pour une femme, il est cent manières de se déshabiller. L'une d'elles révèle l'innocence ; Henriette se déshabillait comme s'épluche un fruit. Chiffons de soie jetés sur la chaise, jupes enjambées. Les femmes coupables ne savent que s'habiller.

Antoine aidait Henriette à s'habiller. Il aimait qu'elle fût boutonnée par côté plutôt que par devant ou par derrière. Les hanches sont un endroit plus rare que la gorge ou le cou et Antoine ne manquait jamais, avant de clore la robe, de passer sa main sur le ventre — mouvant à travers la combinaison — d'Henriette. Son indiscrète main, main de voleur, revenait nue ; un voleur qui restituerait les objets, bouclerait les bracelets, voleur de préséances.

L'épilation des jambes d'Henriette était une autre cérémonie aux rites immuables. Antoine plaçait son bras gauche dans le prolongement d'un mollet d'Henriette, la main se coquillant sur un genou. De l'autre main il appliquait en le faisant tourner sur lui-même un petit ovale noir. La jambe épilée était blanche, et heureuse Henriette. Une application de lavande précédait la mise en place des bas.

FRANÇOIS TRUFFAUT 519

Les bas ne sont pour les femmes qu'un accessoire parmi tant d'autres. Aux yeux d'Antoine ils étaient le signe du mystère féminin. Il lui semblait que les bas étaient la connaissance même de ce mystère et cela l'irritait que les vierges en revêtissent.

La famille d'Henriette la réclamait en province. Une vieille tante était morte. Antoine et Henriette délibérèrent ; elle s'absenterait huit jours. Il l'accompagna à la gare. Il était jaloux qu'elle partît et non lui. Jaloux aussi d'un monsieur seul dont les sourcils épais s'animèrent quand il comprit qu'Antoine qui installait les bagages dans le filet laisserait Henriette seule avec lui dans le compartiment. Henriette feignait de rien voir et promit d'écrire souvent.

* * *

Antoine avait assez peu envie de rentrer. Il était déshabitué de vivre seul. Il prit le parti de traîner à Pigalle. C'était le soir.

Pigalle. Le jour : un village où la vie se vit au ralenti. Des musiciens cherchent des engagements. Pigalle, le soir : la vie s'y vit à l'accéléré, les musiciens sont embauchés, le village devient forêt, forêt de Bondy qu'une fée transforme en forêt de Charles Perrault. Les soldats américains se font voler leur montre par des magiciens arabes qui les revendent aux garçons de café. Les femmes invitent, promettent, et le refus transforme en jurons ces promesses.

Pigalle c'est le milieu. Le milieu ainsi nommé parce que les extrêmes s'y confondent.

N'ayant pas le cœur de retrouver la maison vide, Antoine prit dans un hôtel non loin de la place Pigalle une chambre pour la nuit. Il fut longtemps avant de s'endormir.

Les hôtels sont des temples à l'amour. Quand rêvent les enfants, ronflent les maris, soupirent les bourgeoises, quand les immeubles dorment, les hôtels sont des ruches où viennent et vont des serviettes nid d'abeilles portées avec de doux messages par des bonnes discrètes, aveugles et diligentes qui parcourent les couloirs à pas feutrés, d'une démarche de crêpe, infirmières d'une clinique où l'on ne guérit guère que les maux d'amour.

Adoucie, l'électricité fait sa journée ne s'éteignant que pour étreindre.

D'épais rideaux laissent s'évader un rais de lumière suffisant à intriguer le promeneur nocturne. Il imagine des accouplements idéaux, l'acteur et l'actrice préférés, en couleurs et beaucoup de formes : billets sous les portes, valets soudoyés.

Demain, les hôtels borgnes ne dormiront que du demi de leur œil pour abriter les amours illégales, celles qu'interrompent

Claire Maurier and Albert Rémy

HAS ROSSELLINI INFLUENCED ME?

Ah! There is certainly a very great faculty of admiration in me, a need to admire, which sometimes is directed to literature, sometimes to the cinema. Some of those men I've admired at a distance, like Orson Welles, whom I only met once or twice and who has played no role in my life . . . or very indirectly and without his knowing it. But someone like Rossellini was important because I worked with him for several years; I was his assistant during a period when he didn't make a film, but I worked with him, we traveled. I learned a lot from him, I believe; he took over from Bazin a little, the transition between the phase of criticism and the phase of creation. About Rossellini I would say that he cleared up my ideas, he put me wise in a certain way. Rossellini was very anti-American and he was against sophistication. He was for clarity, simplicity, coherent and logical discourse. I think that if *The 400 Blows* was, for a first film, something fairly clear-cut and fairly straightforward, coherent, and logical, I owe it to Rossellini, certainly.

Interview by Aline Desjardins, Radio-Canada, 1977

Rossellini became, as Jacques Flaud put it, the "father of the French New Wave." It is a fact that every time he arrived in Paris he got together with us and had us show him our amateur films, read our first screenplays. All those new names which, in 1959, surprised the French producers when they came across them every week in the listing of films in preparation were known to Rossellini for a long time: Rouch, Reichenbach, Godard, Rohmer, Rivette, Aurel. In fact Rossellini was the first to read the screenplays of *Le Beau Serge* and *The 400 Blows*. It was he who inspired *Moi, un Noir* by Jean Rouch, after having seen *Les Maîtres Fous*.

Did Rossellini influence me? Yes. His rigorousness, his seriousness, his logic helped a bit in getting me over my complacent enthusiasm for the American cinema. Rossellini detested clever tricks for titles and credits, scenes preceding the title, flashbacks, and in general everything decorative, everything that doesn't serve the idea of the film and the nature of the characters.

If in certain of my films I have tried to follow simply and honestly a single character, and in an almost documentary manner, it's to him I owe that. Vigo aside, Rossellini is the only filmmaker to have filmed adolescence without going sentimental, and *The 400 Blows* owes much to his *Germany, Year Zero*.

Written for Mario Verdone, Roberto Rossellini, *Paris, Seghers, 1963; reprinted in* Les Films de Ma Vie

520 ANTOINE ET L'ORPHELINE

une lettre dictée, une alliance ôtée, les reproches, les questions d'argent, les voilettes qui ne masquent pas la rougeur, voilettes qui se refusent à être complices, voilettes qui multiplient la honte.

Amours coupables qui se font et se défont le jour.

A l'amour qu'il se fait dans le monde les hôtels prennent une part extrême.

Quand l'aube fut venue Antoine quitta la chambre comme un voleur solitaire.

Il revint chez lui et se jeta tout habillé sur le lit.

Quelques jours passèrent, qu'il meubla à traîner les milk-bars et les salles de cinématographe. Un film le laissa dans le ravissement. Une actrice américaine y allait et venait sans parler, mais promenant un buste superbe que laissaient deviner de nombreux corsages. Il retourna le lendemain voir ce film et compta quatorze corsages différents, plus une robe. Une troisième vision lui inspira un article dans lequel il faisait remarquer qu'au contraire des gravures égyptiennes qui montrent les femmes, le visage et les membres de profil et la poitrine de face, cette actrice se montrait le visage de face et la poitrine de profil. Il détaillait les corsages, les tissus dont ils étaient faits. Il confia cet article à une gazette cinématographique.

Dans un bar aux Champs-Elysées, Antoine retrouva un ami, René qu'il avait perdu de vue depuis qu'Henriette emplissait sa vie. René était un grand garçon au visage émacié et à la diction saccadée. Sa maîtresse, une jeune femme américaine dont le mari parcourait le monde des affaires, venait de le quitter, lui préférant un grand blond au charme slave. Ils devisèrent en célibataires qu'ils étaient, firent le serment mutuel de ne se quitter qu'ils ne fussent de nouveau en ménage et médirent des femmes puisque se réconforter est cela. Quelle inconséquence est la leur, ne mettent-elles pas aux fenêtres leurs petites culottes à sécher ? Vieilles filles, elles racontent leurs coliques; mariées, elles pouffent aux histoires inconvenantes. Sont-elles enceintes ? Elles exhibent jusque dans les transports en commun leur face hilare à l'air béat et repu. Ils convinrent que le mérite que l'on a d'être vertueux se mesure au pouvoir que l'on a de ne l'être pas ; que savoir faire l'amour, c'est savoir à quel moment il convient d'ôter sa cravate. Ils moquèrent les gens qui font l'amour le samedi soir parce que le dimanche est jour férié, et les femmes qui le font comme le le matin le petit déjeuner : par devoir.

Enfin, ils firent tous deux l'éloge des fantaisies et des raffinements que les sots rassemblent sous le nom de vices, et qui les invente, convinrent-ils, est poète.

Puis vint le jour où Antoine calcula qu'il devait recevoir une lettre d'Henriette. Elle n'avait point laissé d'adresse où lui écrire, promettant de le faire la première. La boîte aux lettres resta vide.

FRANÇOIS TRUFFAUT 521

Le lendemain, Antoine, certain d'avoir une lettre, se précipita à la loge du concierge. Il n'y avait rien qu'un prospectus. Il oublia le courrier du soir et s'en aperçut le lendemain matin, heureux de penser que ses chances s'en trouvaient doublées. Hélas ! rien encore. Il prit alors le parti de souhaiter que la lettre n'arrivât point et comme rien ne venait il feignit de souhaiter qu'elle arrive pour brouiller le jeu. Un grain de sable enraye la machine, plusieurs grains s'annulent, et ce fut le jour où Henriette devait revenir. Antoine pensait qu'elle n'avait pas voulu écrire pour se faire désirer et que son retour fût une plus grande joie. Il la désarmerait en jouant son jeu : il s'enquit des heures du train pour aller l'attendre à la gare. Vainement ; elle n'y était pas.

Le dépit, dès lors, s'installa dans le cœur d'Antoine, dépit qu'il fallait transformer en tristesse, la mauvaise humeur en chagrin, la jalousie en douleur d'estomac.

Une fois encore il revint seul mais pour trouver une lettre. Henriette écrivait que le décès de sa tante posait des problèmes qu'elle ne pouvait résoudre qu'en prolongeant son séjour d'une huitaine. Elle parlait aussi du temps qu'il faisait et qui était mauvais, de nouveaux tissus acquis et d'un cousin dont elle avait fait connaissance. Elle ne s'excusait pas de n'avoir point écrit plus tôt. Cela et la légèreté de sa lettre indisposèrent Antoine, qui résolut de faire attendre quelques jours sa réponse. Pour mieux se prouver qu'Henriette lui manquait, il installa le désordre dans l'appartement sans savoir que l'ordre et le désordre ne sont qu'une même chose. Henriette, un mois plus tard, épousa son cousin ; Antoine n'entendit plus parler d'elle et l'oublia.

FRANÇOIS TRUFFAUT

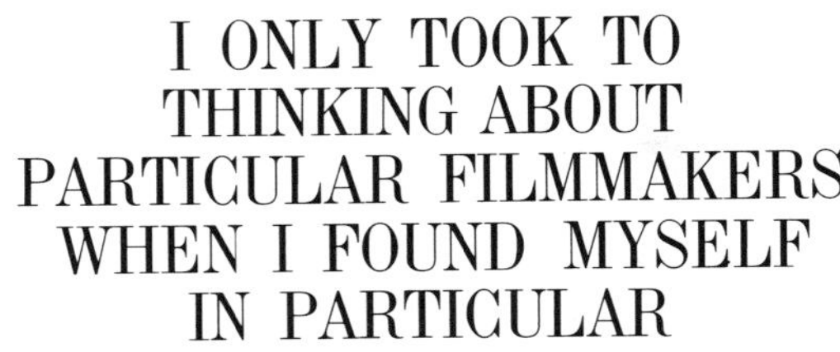

I ONLY TOOK TO THINKING ABOUT PARTICULAR FILMMAKERS WHEN I FOUND MYSELF IN PARTICULAR SITUATIONS

In my film *The 400 Blows* there was—everyone saw it—the influence of Jean Vigo, which is obvious, but there was another, and no one thought of it: it was that of *Germany, Year Zero,* which was the only film where a child was followed in documentary fashion and was shown as more serious than the adults around him. It was the first time that that was done on the principle that seriousness is found in children and frivolity in adults. Rossellini reinforced something already present in Renoir, a taste for getting right up close to life, for being very documentary. And Rossellini thinks you shouldn't write screenplays, that only louses write screenplays, that a cinematic conflict comes solely from facts on hand: such a character at such an epoch and in such a country set up against such a character who, himself, is from that other country, and then! the natural conflict between them is all there, and now you take off from it and there's nothing to be invented.

So when I began work on *The 400 Blows* I made up file cards: "at school," all sorts of gags at school; "at home"; "in the street." I think everyone does something like that; for many films that's what you do, for comic films, you can even do it for dramatic films. And that material is even based on memories, and I came to realize that you can make your memory work for you: I had found a class photo, the classical class photo with all the pupils lined up, and one morning it occurred to me that I could remember the names of only two friends. By looking at the photo every morning, for an hour, I got back the names, the parents' professions, where they lived. It was then that I met

Production "LES FILMS DU CARROSSE"
10, rue Hamelin – Paris 16°
Tél. KLE 54-60 – Poste 62

Film "LES QUATRE CENTS COUPS"

FEUILLE DE SERVICE

LUNDI 10 NOVEMBRE 1958

1er jour de tournage

HORAIRE : 9 H – 18 H (1 H pour déjeuner)

RENDEZ-VOUS : 9 H – 82, rue Marcadet – Paris 18° – 6ème étage au fond de la cour

Décor : chez Loinod – Jour

Nos à Tourner : 18 – 34 – 49

réserve : 52 53

Acteurs	Rôles	Costumes	Prêt à Tourner
Claire MAURIER	Gilberte Loinod	0 – 1 – tablier manteau I	9 H
Albert REMY	Julien Loinod	0	9 H
Jean-Pierre LEAUD	Antoine Loinod	0 – 2	9 H
Daniel COUTURIER	Bertrand Mauricet	prévu	10 H

Accessoires

lit d'Antoine praticable (draps teintés)
cartable Antoine – Le Ponin –
1 paire de chaussettes trouées – café chaud – bol – pain – beurre – cuillère –
chemise sale – glace – œuf brouillard – cartable Mauricet – 1 poste de radio –
lit des parents praticable – 1 tub – serviettes – savon – torchon.

MACHINISTES – ELECTRICIENS

Rendez-vous à 8 H

RAPPORT PRODUCTION

LUNDI 10 NOVEMBRE 1958 – 1er jour de tournage 9 H – 18 H

Immeuble 82, rue Marcadet – Paris 18° – 6ème étage au fond de la cour

Décor : chez Julien Loinod

8 H – Installation et montage du matériel au 6ème étage.
9 H à 9 H 30 – Mise en place du plan N° 18
9 H 30 – Répétition avec les acteurs – tirage des lignes – montage matériel lumière
10 H 30 – Suite réglage lumière
11 H – Répétition en lumière – avec acteurs.
11 H 30 – On tourne le 18/1 – son témoin
11 H 40 – Fin du plan 18/1
Changement décor pour cuisine – 18/2 – réglage
12 H – Départ déjeuner
13 H 15 – Reprise réglage dans cuisine – suite
13 H 25 – Répétition avec les acteurs.
13 H 35 – on tourne le 18/2
13 H 50 – Fin du plan – son seul
et préparation contre-champ
14 H – Répétition du 18/3 – et suite réglage
14 H 25 – Répétition pour le jeu
14 H 35 – On tourne le 18/3
15 H – Fin du plan 18/3 – plan rapproché sur Antoine
15 H 20 – On tourne le 18/4
15 H 25 – Fin du plan 18/4
Changement axe et séquence – préparation du 34^{A}
16 H 15 – Fin du plan 34^{A1} – et mise en place plan rapproché
16 H 35 – Répétition du 34^{A2}
16 H 45 – On tourne le 34^{A2} (boucles cassent à la caméra pour la 2ème fois)
16 H 50 – Fin du plan 34^{A2}
changement axe pour le 34^{A3}
17 H 15 – On tourne le plan 34^{A3}
17 H 20 – fin du plan 34^{A3}
préparation du plan 34^{A4}
pose d'un rail – réglage lumière
17 H 50 – suite réglage lumière – plombs sautent sur l'étage.
Obligation prévenir E.d.F.
Répétition jeu pour le lendemain
18 H – Fin du tournage

Shooting roster and production report of the first day on the set. Antoine not yet called Doinel

Moussy and that I asked him if it interested him to work with me on this.

I cut school a lot, so all those problems of phony excuse notes, signed notebooks, I knew all that by heart, you can be sure. Including hiding the schoolbag behind the entrance gate.

At that time there were two movie houses facing each other on the boulevards: the New York and the Cinéac Italiens, both opening at ten in the morning. They had a clientele composed almost exclusively of elementary and high school kids. And we couldn't all turn up carrying our schoolbags because that would have looked just too funny. And every morning there was a group there of fifty or sixty youngsters, all waiting, and the first theater to open its doors got the whole clientele because we were in a hurry to hide, we felt terribly guilty, especially, in the midst of all that.

In *The 400 Blows* I have an episode where the boy goes to school, without a note of excuse because he was absent three days, and where he decides to say his mother died. Good. We don't know that he's decided that. We only know that he has decided to say something enormous. And that dodge of "my mother died," he could say it thirty-six different ways: it could be shifty, it could be plaintive, it could even be I don't know what, and I decided that it had to seem as if he had given up on saying it and that it would therefore be the teacher who would oblige him to say it. So when the teacher says to him: "Where is your note of excuse?" the boy says: "It's my mother, M'sieur, it's my mother . . ." So the teacher says to him: "Your mother, your mother, what's wrong with your mother?" And it's just because the teacher puts the pressure on him like that that he says to himself: "OK, if he wants a fight, he's going to get it," and the boy says to his teacher: "My mother, she's dead." I told him to think at that moment, to himself: "*You* don't

Patrick Auffay (René) and Jean-Pierre Léaud (Antoine)

Remarques sur le scénario

1°) Le comportement des parents d'Antoine et plus généralement de tous les adultes mis en cause dans ce film sera nuancé, clarifié, humanisé dans le prochain traitement.

2°) L'idée première de la révélation de la "batardise" sera abandonnée comme trop évidente au profit de celle-ci, plus visuelle : Antoine, en faisant l'école buissonnière, rencontre sa mère au bras d'un homme. Comme elle ne dit rien le soir à la maison, il imagine une complicité totale, et, partant, une impunité systématique, vite démentie par les faits. Sa mère sera présente à l'école quand il recevra la gifle paternelle. Cette déception constitue un moteur assez puissant pour entraîner la première fugue.

3°) Certains petits gags ou scénettes n'ont guère de rapport avec l'intrigue proprement dite; on s'efforcera de les conserver en les intégrant plus adroitement à l'action, de manière à brosser un tableau de l'enfance en général : joyeuse, triste, brimée, gâtée. Interviendront donc, épisodiquement, des petites filles et des petits garçons d'âges différents.

4°) La fin n'est pas définitive mais son principe devra être sauvegardé : liberté mais avec une ombre, juste révolte récompensée à demi ... Nul doute qu'un meilleur agencement final reste à trouver.

Remarks on one of the first stages of the script

"My mother, she's dead."

A night at the police station

give a shit she's dead, eh? *You* don't give a shit." He thought just that, that gave him the intonation I wanted and even the right look on his face.

I only took to thinking about particular filmmakers when I found myself in particular situations. And even more when editing than when shooting. In the classroom scene, when the father turns up to slap his son, I had problems in crosscutting. I knew I couldn't get out of it without cutting back and forth a lot—because it was a rapid action—whereas in the film as a whole it was simply recording how things stood. And there I knew I was obliged to "make cinema," and I thought of Hitchcock, because I had nothing to go by, I couldn't see how to crosscut the scene. So, I knew—things with Hitchcock being really felt deep down—I knew that we had to see the principal, we hear a noise at the door, the principal goes to it, the boy feels worried, and we cut to the mother. For example, that made me say to Claire Maurier looking for her son in the classroom: "Look straight at him, directly at the boy's table," because I knew that it was that that would be dramatic and not the reality, where she would seek out her son among all the other pupils.

The boy doesn't want to go home anymore, because he has told such a lie and it made so much trouble at school. Those were pretty enormous things and for me, realist that I am, it bothered me to do that. And I got through by recalling Renoir and a particular scene in *The Human Beast* where Jean Gabin, after having killed Simone Simon, came back the next morning and said to Carette, with an enormous simplicity, and it was simplicity that put it all across at that particular point, he said: "All right, there you are, I won't see her anymore, I killed her."

Interview by Jean-Pierre Chartier,
"Cinéastes de Notre Temps,"
French radio, December 2, 1965

François TRUFFAUT

27, rue St Ferdinand

PARIS (17)

ETO:81-59

LES FILMS DU CARROSSE

Les Quatre cents coups.

LA FUGUE D'ANTOINE. Premier traitement.

(titre provisoire)

On devine un corps d'enfant sous les draps de ce divan qui bloque la petite entrée d'un minuscule appartement; quelques cheveux dépassent peut être sur l'oreiller; c'est la pénombre. On entend des portes claquer; une belle jeune femme vient reveiller trés brusquement son antoine. Elle empoigne le dessus du lit, couvertures et draps et agite le tout violemment: "Allez mon petit, lève toi et en vitesse s'il te plait". A toute vitesse, nous voyons Antoine faire un simulacre de toilette, s'habiller, replier son divan, dé- -crocher le pot à lait et sortir en courant; nous le retrouvons dans la rue courant d'une boutique à l'autre. Il est bientôt de retour avec le lait, le pain et le journal. Comme il revient doucement, il attend dans l'entrée que ses parents aient fini de s'engueuler dans la chambre à coucher; en tendant l'oreille, il comprend qu'on parle de lui, peut-etre pour l'envoyer en pension si ce n'était pas si couteux. Bruits de pas. Antoine feint une activité quelconque; sa mère entre: "Ah, tu es là?"

Petit déjeuner trés rapide; mauvaise humeur géné- -rale; Antoine demande à son père de lui donner l'argent pour payer la cantine de la semaine: "Demande à ta mère!". La mère: "Ah, pardon, je n'ai plus d'argent, moi!" Nouvelle engueulade entre le père et la mère dont Antoine fait les frais. Finalement le père donne l'argent à Antoine: "En échange tu mettras cette lettre recommandée à la poste." Antoine répond qu'il est déja en retard. Le père: "C'est tout de même pas parceque tu arrives quelquefois en retard qu'on te colle des zéros de conduite toutes les semaines, n'est-ce pas ? Alors

---

1 : Intérieur salle de classe – Jour

Le Générique défile.

Le pupitre se soulève, un élève en sort la photo d'une starlette en maillot. La photo circule de table en table, ce qui permet de voir l'aspect apparemment studieux de la classe : élèves qui mordent leur porte-plume ou qui tirent la langue avec application. Le professeur surveille.

Commentaire.- Le paradis perdu de l'enfance est une invention de vieux messieurs. Comment y croire à dix huit ans quand le souvenir de l'âge ingrat reste aussi vif qu'une démangeaison ? Nous le re- prochait-on assez de ne pas tenir en place et d'avoir le diable au corps ? A la maison comme à l'école, nous n'en finissions pas d'avoir treize ans. Antoine Loinod s'en souvient bien : c'était pour lui le temps de l'injustice.

La photo est arrivée entre les mains d'Antoine qui y ajoute des moustaches.

LE PROF. – Loinod ! Apportez moi ce que vous avez là.

Antoine se lève à contre-coeur.

LE PROF. – Ah! c'est du joli ! (regardant toujours la photo) Au piquet ! (La mettant dans sa poche) Bien entendu, c'est largement suffisant pour faire sauter votre tableau d'honneur.

Il regarde sa montre et s'adresse à l'ensemble de la classe.

LE PROF. – Plus qu'une minute !

LA CLASSE – Oh!

LE PROF. – Silence !

The first two pages of the script, still titled *Antoine Runs Away*

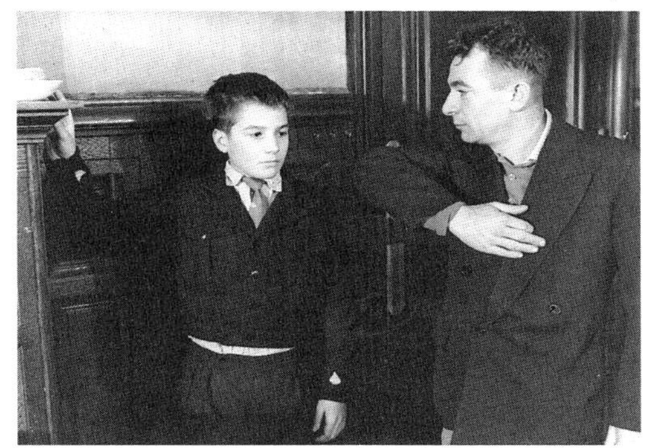

At the Center for Observation of Juvenile Delinquents

ANTOINE DOINEL MOVED AWAY FROM ME TO BECOME MORE LIKE JEAN-PIERRE

Where did I find the name of Antoine Doinel? I thought at first of using something like a name that I found pleasant to the ear, that of Etienne Loinod, a contributor to *Cahiers du Cinéma* (in reality, the anagram-pseudonym of Jacques Doniol-Valcroze). I sincerely believed I had invented the name of Antoine Doinel until the day someone called to my attention that I had simply borrowed the name of Jean Renoir's secretary, Ginette Doinel!

It was Jean Renoir himself who taught me that the actor playing a character is more important than that character, or, if you prefer, that you always have to sacrifice the abstract for the concrete. No wonder then that Antoine Doinel, from the first day of shooting of *The 400 Blows,* moved away from me to become more like Jean-Pierre. On the screen, Antoine Doinel showed more courage than expected and was of such great apparent sincerity that the public forgave him even to the point where the parents and other adult characters, whose behavior Marcel Moussy and I had wanted to put across less black and white, finally appeared almost odious on the screen.

In the other films of the Doinel cycle, I readjusted my sights and took into account the extraordinary phenomenon of the sympathy that Jean-Pierre Léaud always elicits from the public, and so there are scarcely any displeasing characters in *Stolen Kisses* or *Bed and Board,* which were written in collaboration with my friends Claude de Givray and Bernard Revon and where we aimed at a good balance between all the forces involved. Antoine Doinel is not what you would call a model of behavior. He is tricky, he has charm and takes unfair advantage of it, he lies a lot and covers up even more, he demands more love than he himself has to offer, he is not man in general, he is a particular man.

Preface, "Qui Est . . . Antoine Doinel,"
Les Aventures d'Antoine Doinel,
Paris, Mercure de France, 1970

In uniform: Antoine is the smallest of the juvenile delinquents

ANTOINE (ému) - Non

GENDARME - Ca veut dire que ton père et moi, nous n'aurons sans doute plus droit de te reprendre à la maison même si nous le désirons. Ca veut dire que tu seras bon pour le Centre d'apprentissage. Ah! tu voulais gagner ta vie. Tu verras, le fer comme c'est dur.

---

101 SORTIE DU CENTRE - JOUR - EXT

Les "mineurs délinquants, en rang, se rendent au stade en chantant une chanson de marche (à trouver avec Constantin. Eventuellement, ils ne chanteront pas réellement mais on entendrait la chanson au film) Deux surveillants les encadrent.

---

102 STADE MUNICIPAL - Jour.

C'est un match de foot-ball. Quelques échanges. Le ballon sort des limites: "Sortie". Un gosse se précipite pour récuperer le ballon; Antoine l'évince: laisse-le moi et sort. L'autre gosse reste sur la touche. Echange de regards. Antoine envoie le ballon et file à toutes jambes. (Musique ininterrompue jusqu'au mot FIN)

---

103 ALENTOURS STADE MUNICIPAL - JOUR.

Antoine se faufile à travers les haies. On entend des coups de sifflets et des cris de poursuite. Selon la disposition des lieux, on rendra logique la réussite d'Antoine, poursuivi par un seul surveillant, l'autre devant garder le reste de la bande.

---

104 DIVERS.

Paysages successifs. Antoine court toujours, de plus en plus essouflé. Le panorama est tour à tour plat, valonné, accidenté, monotone, morne, pittoresque. Plans rapides, rapidement enchainés.

---

105 UNE ROUTE DE CAMPAGNE- SORTIE AUBERGE-FIN d'APRES-MIDI.

Antoine s'approche d'un camion et lit sur la plque arrière: Fourcroy sur Mer. Il fait le tour du camion, personne à l'avant; il monte à l'arrière et se couche sous des baches. Le camion démarre.

---

106 INTERIEUR CAMION-JOUR.

Antoine aperçoit quelque chose qui pourrait bien être la mer; le camion longe effec-tivement une route qui longe la mer, disparaissant et reapparaissant tour à tour. Dans un virage, comme le chauffeur rétrograde sa vitesse, Antoine saute du camion en marche et tombe, assez brutalement sur le sol.

---

107 SUR LA PLAGE-JOUR.

C'est la marée basse. Antoine avance en courant, puis trés lentement vers la ligne, trés mince, des flots. Il s'arrètera seulement quand ~~[illegible]~~ l'écume viendra mouil-ler les semelles de ses chaussures. Il soulève délicatement un pied, recroqueville l'autre, recule, avance et recule à nouveau, se baisse pour ramasser un coquillage.

---

108 La dernière image de ce plan, Antoine au bord de la mer, devient fixe et se fond trés lentement en "enchainé" sur une autre en mouvement: Antoine et Robert qui marche dans les rues de Paris (on aura déja vu cette image d'école buissonnière). Cette image se fixe à nouveau /nous rappellant qu'ellé est prise par un photographe des rues/ tandisque l'on entend les dernières phrases du commentaire:" C'est ainsi que je reçus une carte de Fourcroy sur Mer ou je réussis à rejoindre Antoine...

Comment allons-nous ? Trés bien, merci...et vous ? Nous sommes libres ~~[illegible]~~ et loin des tourments de l'adolescence mais quand nous marchons dans les rues nous ne pouvons nous empecher de regarder comme des complices nos successeurs de la treizième année recommencer LES QUATRE CENTS COUPS !

FIN

Antoine discovers the sea in the final scene of *The 400 Blows*

1960

SHOOT THE PIANO PLAYER

You shouldn't look for reality in *Piano Player*

I couldn't get a film out of a book I detest, and even if I didn't like a book's style, I could say to myself: the style doesn't matter, it's the facts that matter. But no. Because the irritation the style arouses in me rebounded so much that every time a producer gave me a book to read, even if it was only in résumé, I was obliged to say no because the summary someone had made seemed to me to have no flesh on it and I believe a book can be adapted purely on its qualities of style. It's a little dangerous to speak of equivalence to the image, but just the same. . . . In Goodis I like a lot of things: characters, action, and also the way it's written. For example, Thérésa's confession before committing suicide is something I would be incapable not only of writing but of imagining, and even if a screenwriter who was a friend brought it to me I would refuse it . . . yet it's good as it stands. It's as it is in the book. But sometimes influences pile up . . . I remember I wanted to do this book because I admired it.

Charles Aznavour (Charlie Kohler)

With Charles Aznavour

June 29, 1962

Monsieur Francois Truffaut
Films Du Carosse
25 Rue Quentin Bauchart
Paris 8eme arr.
France

Dear Francois--

Today I received a letter from Helen Scott, requesting that I inform you as to whether the motion picture rights for a re-make of THE BURGLAR are available. The motion picture rights are owned by Columbia Pictures Corp., Hollywood, California, and they released the film in 1957. The film was produced by Samson Productions, Philadelphia., Pa., and was sold to Columbia. Therefore, if you decide that you would like to re-make the picture, it would be necessary for you to negotiate directly with Columbia Pictures.

Astor Pictures invited me to a screening of SHOOT THE PIANO PLAYER (with English sub-titles) and my reactions to the sub-titles were mixed. There were instances when I felt that the sub-titles harmonized brilliantly with the rhythm of the film, but at other instances the effect was sometimes superfluous, sometimes ambiguous. Also, I felt that there was an over-usage of slang expressions, especially in the scenes involving the two gunmen. Aside from that, the title-writer was precise and got the meaning across, and I would say that in total the sub-titles are better than adequate.

I'm glad that you received the film-viewer and are pleased with it.

Grove Press is bringing out a movie edition of SHOOT THE PIANO PLAYER and I will see to it that you receive a copy when the book is published here.

Your friend,

David Goodis
6305 North 11th Street,
Philadelphia 41, Pa.

Nicole Berger (Thérésa) and Charles Aznavour (Charlie)

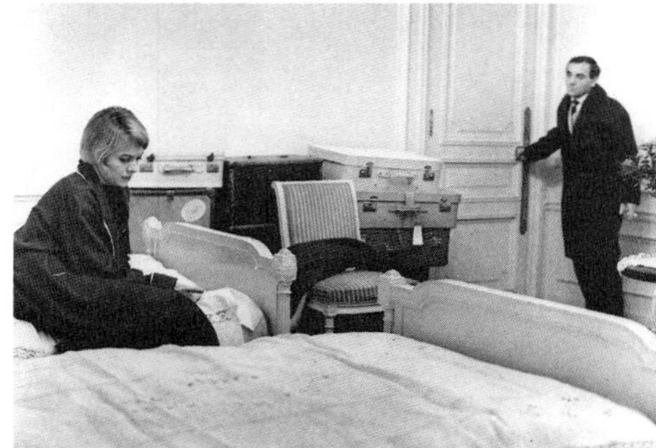

At the time of *The 400 Blows* and the euphoria of Cannes, I said to Braunberger there's a book I want very much to do, which I liked very much when I read it a few years back; on the other hand I very much liked Aznavour also, so if we can put those two things together, let's do it. Braunberger bought the rights and made a contract with Aznavour. And afterwards, rereading the book, I realized I hadn't been at all scrupulous, the book calling for a character who's very robust, someone corpulent in the style of Sterling Hayden, and the famous scene where he kills Plyne in the bar is a scene based on the principle of the strong guy who is sitting on his prey and doesn't want to take advantage of him, but the other guy has a knife and he's obliged to kill him despite himself.

All that collapsed because of the choice of Aznavour. That tormented me for a few days until I pulled up short and shifted gears. That's why I called in Marie Dubois for the role of Elena, because I said to myself: we're going to do the contrary, we're going to take a girl who will be the stronger of the two, who'll almost carry him on her back, and then a guy who will be practically a dishrag and we'll work it out that way. And we did make out. Sometimes other influences came in. Seeing the film again, I remembered that there was a whole part in the relationship with Nicole Berger that was influenced by Moravia's *Lo Sdegno.* Part of that story got in, about the woman who encourages her husband's success; in the first scenes with Nicole Berger, he thinks she has contempt for him. That's why you can say that this kind of film is made out of an amalgam, with a lot of quotations besides, with the American films I liked. The strongest influence was from Nicholas Ray's *Johnny Guitar.*

The adaptation was made in a free and easy manner. We worked out for ourselves the ending in the snow. Albert Rémy, Daniel Boulanger, and I sat around a table asking one another who was going to shoot whom. On top of it, the cold got some of us and we decided to film with those who weren't sick. Finally we liquidated earlier those who had to get back to Paris. All the ending was done just like that, with the slight reservation that, in spite of Braunberger's amicable insistence, I had had it in mind to make Marie Dubois die, so I had filmed that little bit of final scene involving a new waitress.

Another influence, that of Audiberti. I was quite distressed that he did not like *The 400 Blows,* and he hadn't dared tell me. As a rule he liked everything, never rejected anything. One day he said to me, "There's something of Simenon in it that bothers me. It lacks a second thing, the idea that it's simply a story." I thought of Audiberti while filming *Piano Player* and one aspect of the character of Plyne is clearly influenced by that. I said to myself: "It has to be a character like Audiberti who has a completely magical idea of young people." At that precise moment the whole film turned around, you get the point that the sympathetic and timid little guy is not so timid and makes out pretty well by himself, and that the real victim of society is someone who places women too high, like Audiberti and like the owner of the bar. It's more influenced by the personality of Audiberti himself than by his books.

Marie Dubois (Léna) hides Charles Aznavour (Charlie)

You shouldn't look for reality in *Piano Player*—neither in that family of Armenians in the snow near Grenoble nor in the bar at Levallois-Perret (you don't dance in real bars)—but simply for the pleasure of mixing things around to see if they're mixable or not, and I believe a lot in that idea of mixing which, I think, presides over everything.

Interview by the Fédération Française des Ciné-clubs, Cinéma 67, *no. 112*

by Paul Wendkos under the title *The Burglar.* There was a sentence in it that I found fantastic. A boy running away from a reformatory was taken in by an old man, and the boy's comment was: "I asked that old man what his trade was. He answered me: 'I go into houses, I'm a burglar.'" Well, there I found something in front of me that accords exactly with *Shoot the Piano Player.* It's an admirable intersection between crime story and fairy tale. Here you have material which could be sordid; we're dealing with gangsterism, criminal matters, and it's handled in a purely fairy-tale tone. That sentence, "I go into houses, I'm a burglar," is truly sublime.

Interview by Pierre Billard, Cinéma 64, *no. 86*

CHARLES AZNAVOUR, A POETICAL CHARACTER

It was seeing Charles Aznavour in *La Tête contre les Murs* that made me want to make a film with him.

What struck me about him? His fragility, his vulnerability, his graceful figure that makes him look like Saint Francis of Assisi.

In films I don't much like the tough guys, the guys who smash things up, characters who are simply terrific a priori, those who dominate the action and whom nothing can get at. It's not a question of build because the immense Sterling Hayden, for example, is as fragile as the little Aznavour: their most conspicuous muscle is the heart. Someone can be frail and vulnerable without being a victim. That's why I wanted the character of the *Piano Player* to be quite complete: rich, poor, courageous, easily frightened, timid, impulsive, sentimental, authoritarian, egotistical, tender, gentle, and also lucky in love, even while never taking the first steps. Charlie is timid all right, but women adore timid men and throw themselves at them. I never suspected how easy it would be to work with Aznavour. He brings with him such truthfulness that little by little he becomes the entire film all by himself. One finds in him a harmonious dosage of audacity, humility, aggressiveness, and resignation. I see in Charles Aznavour, above all, a poetical character.

Press book, Shoot the Piano Player, *1960*

With Charles Aznavour and Marie Dubois

Far right
Charles Aznavour (Charlie) and Michèle Mercier (Clarisse)

THAT IMAGE OF A CAR GLIDING THROUGH THE SNOW WITH NO NOISE FROM THE MOTOR

For *Shoot the Piano Player,* which is adapted from a novel by David Goodis, a single image made me decide to make the film. It was in the book. A sloping road in the snow, the car running down it with no noise from the motor. That's all. That image of a car gliding through the snow with no noise from the motor, that was something I wanted terribly to visualize, and all the rest followed. There is another novel by Goodis that I wanted to adapt just because of a single sentence. In France it appeared under the title *Le Casse,* but it was filmed in America

Marie Dubois flees with Charles Aznavour

MARIE DUBOIS: VEHEMENT AND PASSIONATE

The French cinema has at its disposal a batch of young actresses under thirty whose lack of genuineness seems to me dismaying. Those Mylènes, those Pascales, those Danys, those Pierrettes, those Luciles, those Danicks are neither "true" young girls nor "true" women but "baby dolls," "chicks," pin-ups. You have the feeling that they were created by the movies for the movies and that they wouldn't exist if the movies didn't exist. They're the rage for one year, two years sometimes, and disappear as they came. For three seasons the distributors and producers force them upon films as if they were stars, whereas they don't bring in a single customer and their sophistication, nine times out of ten, makes a mess out of the dramatic probability of the role they're given.

That's why I wanted to use an unknown for the principal feminine role in *Shoot the Piano Player.* Marie Dubois (that stage name is the title of a novel by Jacques Audiberti) is neither a "chick" nor a "baby doll," she is neither "piquant" nor "saucy," but she is a decent and worthy young girl whom it is within the bounds of verisimilitude to fall in love with and have it recipro-

The death of Léna in the snow

Daniel Boulanger (Ernest) and Claude Mansard (Momo)

cated. You wouldn't turn around to look at her in the street, but she's fresh and affable, a little tomboyish and very juvenile; she is vehement and passionate, chaste and tender.

Press book, Shoot the Piano Player, *1960*

BOBY LAPOINTE, THE SUBTITLED SINGER

It was in 1959 that I saw and heard Boby Lapointe for the first time at the Cheval d'Or. One of his first songs was inspired by Léon, the director of the cabaret:

Il a du bobo, Léon,
Il va peut-être canner, Léon.

And the hall went into rapture when Boby sailed into "Framboise":

Pour sûr qu'elle était d'Antibes,
C'est plus près que les Caraïbes,
Et malgré ses yeux de braise
Ça ne mettait pas à l'aise
De la savoir Antibaise
Moi qui serait plutôt pour!!!

At the table next to mine was Jacques Audiberti who, when the name "Antibes" was pronounced, looked at me as if to make me a witness, with a jovial and proud expression as if to say right out: "You see how we are, we, in Antibes."

With Charles Aznavour and Marie Dubois

Because of that unforgotten moment I have always paired in my memory those two timid giants, Boby Lapointe and Audiberti: each one—in a mess when it came to practical living—had refused the adult state, each of them remained a colossal child.

Just before beginning a film, *Shoot the Piano Player,* in which Charles Aznavour would play—but not sing—I asked Boby Lapointe to come and sing "Framboise" in front of the camera. In those years the playback was practically never used and, moreover, I believe that Boby had not yet made a recording. So he played and sang "live," just as he did every evening at the Cheval d'Or, solidly planted on his legs, bending his torso in time, his head swinging back and forth to the rhythm of the music, his face remaining completely serious with a sort of stubborn sadness in his look.

My producer, Pierre Braunberger, didn't like that scene with Boby singing "Framboise" and he said to me: "One can't get the words, the song will have to be cut out. Your singer needs to learn to pronounce well, or if not he'll have to be subtitled!" I took that observation literally and had subtitling prepared, each line of the song appearing below the image, syllable by syllable, in perfect synchrony. The result was excellent, the effect ten times funnier. Aznavour, who had liked the way Boby worked, had him hired for the first part of his recital at the Alhambra and he was announced as "Boby Lapointe, the subtitled singer." His first record was brought out at that same time.

Later Boby became an actor, and I saw him in *Les Choses de la Vie,* then I ran into him one evening at Orly airport. He was waiting for a plane for Rome, where he was going to act in a film. He still had his good Provençal accent, contradicting the anxiety in his face. I asked him what was the film he was going to act in:

"I don't know. It's called *Chabagua.*"

"Do you have a good part, are you happy with it?"

"I don't know, I don't understand anything about my contract. Take a look."

I looked at the contract and I saw that Boby Lapointe was engaged to play the role of . . . Chabagua: he had the leading role and didn't know it!

Often in the studios, in the editing rooms, I hear young people singing Boby Lapointe's songs, "not knowing the name of the author, not knowing for whom his heart beat"—and not even knowing that the author has left us. That's why when I think of Boby it's not as a dead performer but as an affectionate, modest, apprehensive, and gentle comrade who has disappeared, skipped out on us.

Quoted in Huguette Lapointe,
Boby Lapointe, *Paris, Encre, 1982;*
reprinted in the press book for the rerelease of
Shoot the Piano Player, *1983*

GEORGES DELERUE, THE MOST FILM-LOVING OF MUSICIANS

Georges Delerue is a very interesting man because he is the most film-loving of musicians. He is one of the few who understands perfectly well what we had wanted to do in a film. I am very grateful to him because, for *Shoot the Piano Player,* all the musicians I asked to do the music turned me down after being shown the film. It was a thankless film to do. Georges Delerue saw the film and he was the first to see what it was really about; he caught the reference to American films, saw it wasn't a parody but rather a pastiche, that there were, successively, ironical things and then others that had to be moving; and at top speed he wrote music I find stunning. So then I owed him a film in more comfortable conditions, *Jules and Jim,* which he did very well and now he has just done *The Soft Skin.*

Interview by Pierre Billard,
Cinéma 64, *no. 86*

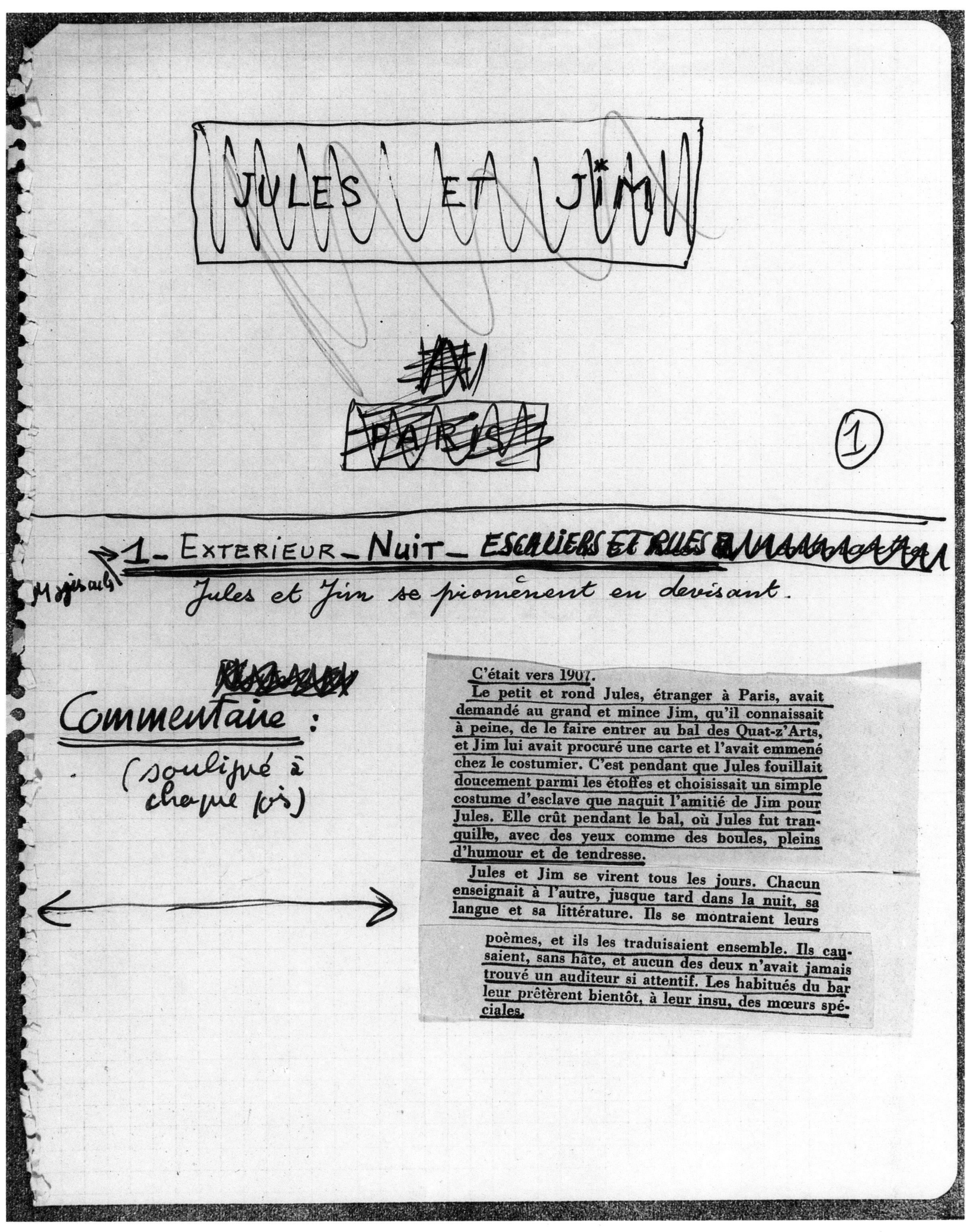

JULES ET JIM
PARIS
1
1 - EXTERIEUR - NUIT - ESCALIERS ET RUES
Jules et Jim se promènent en devisant.
Commentaire :
(souligné à chaque fois)

C'était vers 1907.

Le petit et rond Jules, étranger à Paris, avait demandé au grand et mince Jim, qu'il connaissait à peine, de le faire entrer au bal des Quat-z'Arts, et Jim lui avait procuré une carte et l'avait emmené chez le costumier. C'est pendant que Jules fouillait doucement parmi les étoffes et choisissait un simple costume d'esclave que naquit l'amitié de Jim pour Jules. Elle crût pendant le bal, où Jules fut tranquille, avec des yeux comme des boules, pleins d'humour et de tendresse.

Jules et Jim se virent tous les jours. Chacun enseignait à l'autre, jusque tard dans la nuit, sa langue et sa littérature. Ils se montraient leurs poèmes, et ils les traduisaient ensemble. Ils causaient, sans hâte, et aucun des deux n'avait jamais trouvé un auditeur si attentif. Les habitués du bar leur prêtèrent bientôt, à leur insu, des mœurs spéciales.

JULES AND JIM

1962

When at times fiction takes us far from real life, all of a sudden we say what we think, we rescue ourselves by sincerity

Opposite
First page of Henri-Pierre Roché's novel cut out and annotated by François Truffaut

Friendship: Oskar Werner (Jules) and Henri Serre (Jim). "Neither had ever found such an attentive listener." *Right:* The visit to Greece; *below:* The nights in Paris

I can say that my reading, in 1953, of *Jules et Jim,* the first novel by an old gentleman of seventy-four, once and for all settled my vocation as filmmaker. I was twenty-one and was a film critic. It was love at first sight for that book and I thought, "If I ever succeed in making films I will film *Jules et Jim.*"

Shortly afterward, reviewing an American film, *The Naked Dawn* by Edgar Ulmer, in the weekly *Arts,* I devoted a few lines to *Jules et Jim:* "This film, *Naked Dawn,* proves that the cinema can express everything and that a film could be made even out of one of the finest modern French novels, *Jules et Jim* by Henri-Pierre Roché, in which a woman loves two men equally during almost an entire lifetime, thanks to an aesthetic and new morality incessantly reconsidered."

Someone passed on that article to Henri-Pierre Roché, who then wrote me: "Dear François Truffaut, I was very touched by your few words about *Jules et Jim* in *Arts,* notably by 'thanks to an aesthetic and new morality incessantly reconsidered.'"

Soon afterward I met the author of the book, who was enchanted at the idea of a first contact with the cinema, and since he wasn't living in Paris, we launched a long correspondence exchanging ideas about how to adapt the novel.

But I felt that *Jules and Jim* would be a difficult and ambitious film, and I didn't as yet feel sure enough of myself to venture on it. So I made two films before this one.

In *The 400 Blows,* Jeanne Moreau, to bring us luck, came along with her friend Jean-Claude Brialy to film a short, improvised scene at night in the street: she was asking Jean-Pierre Léaud to help her catch her dog. Jean-Claude Brialy turned up, got rid of Jean-Pierre Léaud, accosted Jeanne Moreau, and left with her to look for the little dog.

It was on that occasion that I got Jeanne Moreau to read *Jules et Jim.* She was enthusiastic and accepted the role of Catherine right away.

I then wrote to Henri-Pierre Roché, sending him several photos of Jeanne Moreau. He replied on April 3, 1959: "Many thanks for the photos of Jeanne Moreau. She pleases me. I am happy that she likes Kathe. I hope to know her someday."

It was four days after writing me that letter that Henri-Pierre Roché died.

At the start of '61 I thought that the time had come to concretize this old dream. I tried

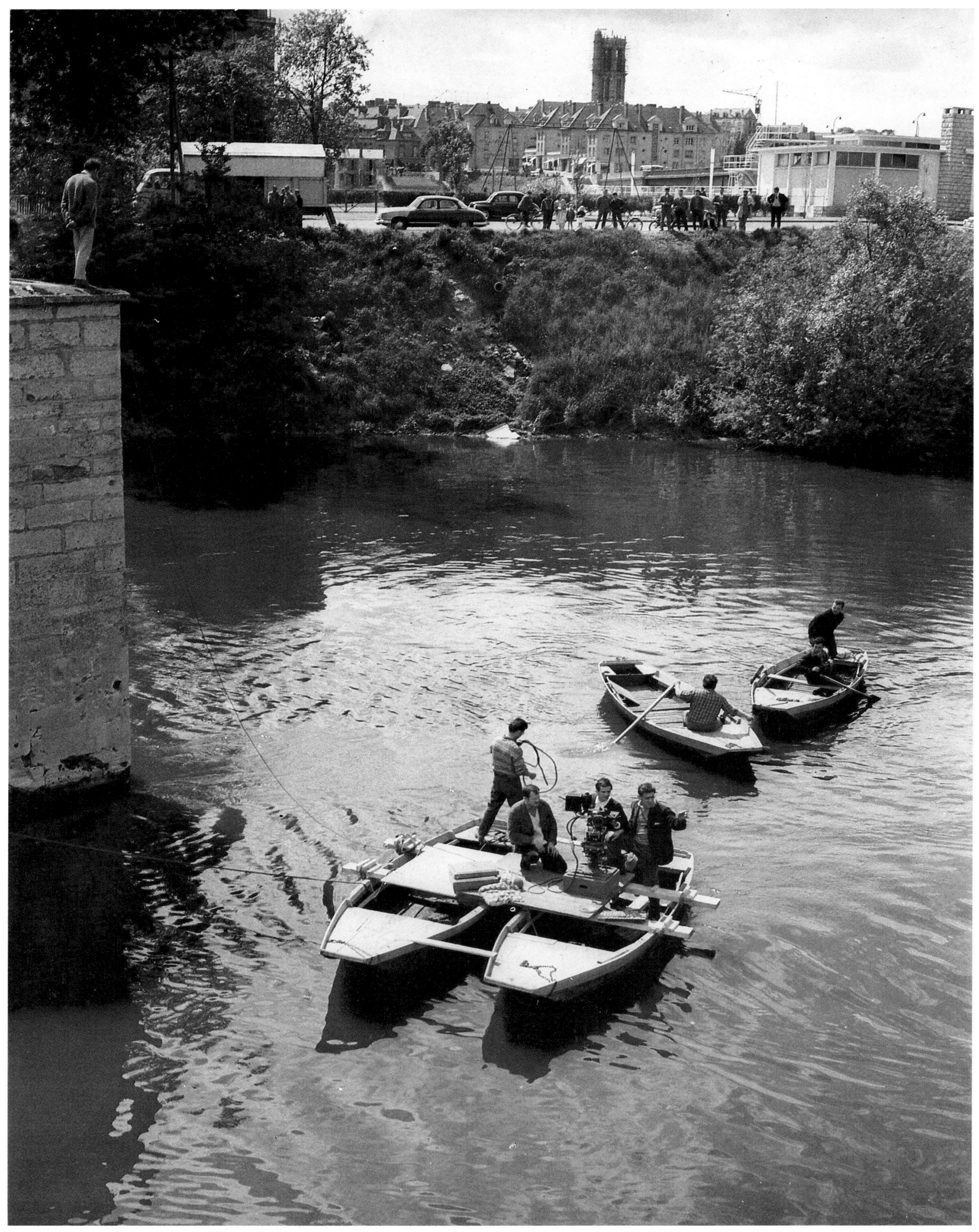

Opposite
François Truffaut and Raoul Coutard at the camera during the shooting of *Jules and Jim*

Boris Bassiak (Albert) and Sabine Haudepin (Sabine)

Jeanne Moreau (Catherine) meets Henri Serre (Jim)

to transpose faithfully that beautiful book, which the publisher Gallimard presented as: "A pure three-sided love."

Starting out with the most scandalous situation there can be—two men and a woman living together through a whole lifetime—one had to bring off a film about love that would be as "pure" as possible, and to do that through the innocence of the three characters, their moral integrity, their tenderness, and above all their sense of decency, also through the kind of friendship between the two masculine characters.

Jean Gruault and I adapted this little-known book with no less love and no less respect than if it had been Stendhal's *The Red and the Black* because, for us, Henri-Pierre Roché's novel is a masterpiece on the level of the finest classical works.

With this film I wanted to get back to the "tone" of *The 400 Blows:* a story recounted in half-tints, sad in its line but droll in its details.

If this film is successful, it must resemble the book that inspired it and thus constitute a hymn to love, perhaps even a hymn to life.

"Un Pur Amour à Trois," foreword to the press book of Jules and Jim, *1962*

Marie Dubois (Thérèse) imitates a locomotive

Right
Catherine and Jim in the chalet in Germany

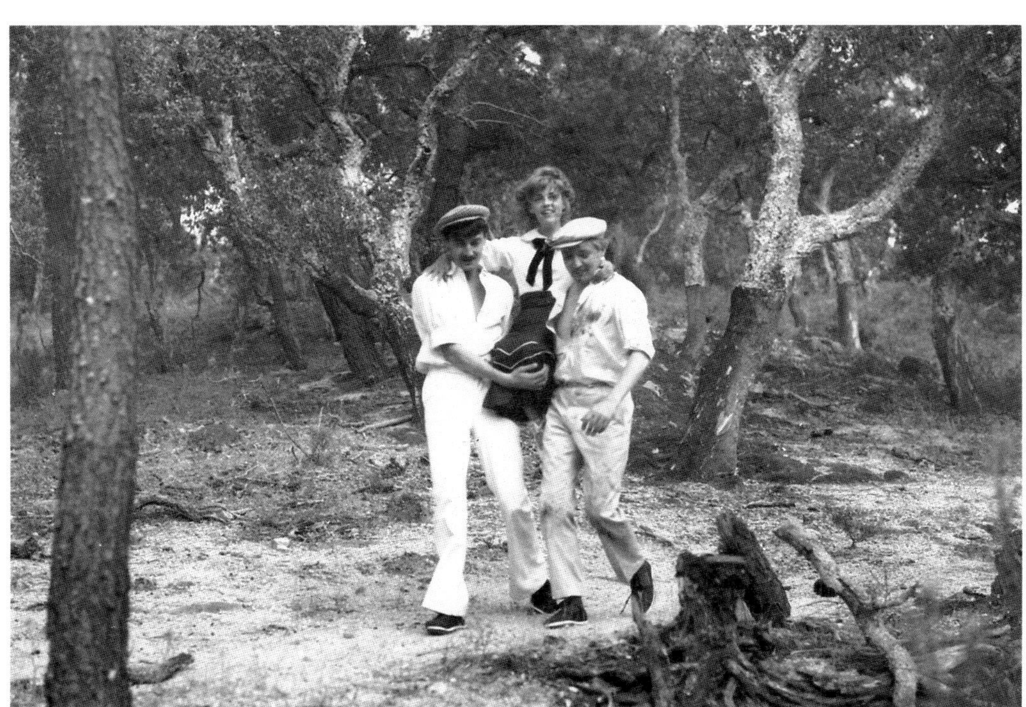

"A pure three-sided love." Henri Serre, Jeanne Moreau, Oskar Werner

HENRI-PIERRE ROCHÉ REVISITED

From the first lines I fell in love with the prose of Henri-Pierre Roché. At that period my favorite writer was Jean Cocteau because of the swiftness of his sentences, their apparent dryness, and the precision of his images. I discovered in Henri-Pierre Roché a writer who seemed to me stronger than Cocteau, because he obtained the same sort of poetical prose by using a less extensive vocabulary, forming ultrashort sentences made up of everyday words. In Henri-Pierre Roché's style emotion is born out of the lacunae, the blanks, out of all the words rejected, is born out of the ellipsis itself. Later, examining manuscript pages by Henri-Pierre Roché, I saw that his style, falsely naïve, was a result of the enormous percentage of words and sentences crossed out: from an entire page covered in his round schoolboy hand he finally let stand only seven or eight sentences, themselves two-thirds crossed out. *Jules et Jim* is a love story in telegraphic style, written by a poet who tries very hard to make you forget his culture and who lines up words and thoughts like a laconic and factual-minded peasant.

For the German edition of Jules et Jim, *1983*

MORE A CINEMATIC BOOK

How did you go about adapting it?

On the book, which I knew by heart, I marked with one or several crosses whatever pleased me most, I wrote in a few comments, and I gave the lot to Jean Gruault, co-adapter and dialogue man for the film. He wrote a text of two hundred pages which I went over, working with paste and scissors and leaving myself the option of improvising while shooting the scenes, which seemed to me indispensable at the last minute. For example, I read the letters Apollinaire wrote in the collection *Tendre comme le Souvenir*. As I read along they became more intimate for me, more familiar, I spoke about them, I made a monologue out of them which I gave to the actor and which, little by little, became a scene. Thus, when at times fiction takes us far from real life, all of a sudden we say what we think, we rescue ourselves by sincerity.

I kept an off-screen commentary throughout the film every time the text seemed to me impossible to transform into dialogue or too beautiful to be amputated. I prefer, over the classical adaptation, which willy-nilly transforms a book into a theater piece, an intermediate form which alternates dialogue with reading aloud, which corresponds in a way to a filmed novel. I think in any case that *Jules and Jim* is more a cinematic book than the pretext for a literary film.

Interview by Yvonne Baby,
Le Monde, *January 24, 1962*

Jeanne Moreau

"The Whirlwind of Life." Henri Serre, Sabine Haudepin, Jeanne Moreau, Boris Bassiak and his guitar

Oskar Werner and Jeanne Moreau

Catherine and Jim cannot have a child

Paris, le 22 Décembre 1961

Monsieur Oscar WERNER
Triesen
Liechtenstein

Mon cher Oscar,

Tout d'abord reçois mes remerciements pour le superbe calendrier théâtral que j'ai bien reçu et le gros livre en deux volumes que je n'ai pas encore eu le temps de lire.

Le film est terminé et les premières projections sont fort chaleureuses en général (et chaleureuses pour toi à 100%). Bref, tout va assez bien malgré quelques petits ennuis de censure.

Jeanne qui est venu passer 24 heures à Paris serait très heureuse et moi aussi si tu pouvais venir à la première du film, le Mardi 23 Janvier (par coïncidence le jour anniversaire de Jeanne).

Moi aussi je suis étonné par le comportement de la BETA-Film qui avait d'abord accepté que le doublage fut supervisé par Marcel Ophuls, pui qui, indirectement, l'a évincé tout récemment. En ce qui te concerne, je sais qu'ils sont réticents et qu'ils invoquent parfois ton accent autrichien (ce qui est stupide étant donné la nationalité du personnage dans le film), parfois les dédits financiers que tu leur réclames.

En tous cas il y a quelques semaines, je les ai prévenus par lettre que je n'irais présenter le film en Allemagne que :

1) si tu faisais toi-même le doublage de Jules;
2) si Marcel Ophuls choisissait et dirigeait les autres comédions;
3) si le titre demeurait "Jules et Jim".

Etant donné que nous avons vendu le film à forfait pour l'Allemagne, ils en seront les seules victimes si le sabotage de la version allemande nuit commercialement au film.

...

Aux dernières nouvelles, on me dit qu'ils se décideraient pour le titre "Jules, Jim et Catherine", ce qui vaut mieux tout de même que "Oh toi, adorable sorcière".

Je vais leur envoyer une dernière lettre demain, après quoi j'abandonne toute idée de surveiller cette version.

Réponds-moi vite au sujet de la première du film à Paris le 23 Janvier

Letter to Oskar Werner

JEANNE MOREAU: A LUMINOUS MEMORY

The woman is passionate, the actress is passionately enthralling. If I imagine her at a distance, I do not see her reading a newspaper but a book.

Jeanne Moreau doesn't make you think of a flirtation but of love.

Unlike so many actors and actresses who can't manage to act except by means of conflicts and tensions, to the point of sometimes confusing "concentration" with those camps of sinister memory, Jeanne Moreau is at her best in a merry and tender working environment, which she does her bit to create and which she helps preserve even when there are powerful emotions to be projected. Generosity, ardor, complicity, comprehension of human fragility: all of that can be read on the screen when Jeanne Moreau is acting.

In all my twenty years of cinema, the filming of *Jules and Jim,* thanks to Jeanne Moreau, remains a luminous memory, the most luminous.

1979

Jules at Père-Lachaise cemetery

Next page
The last page of the book cut out and annotated for filming

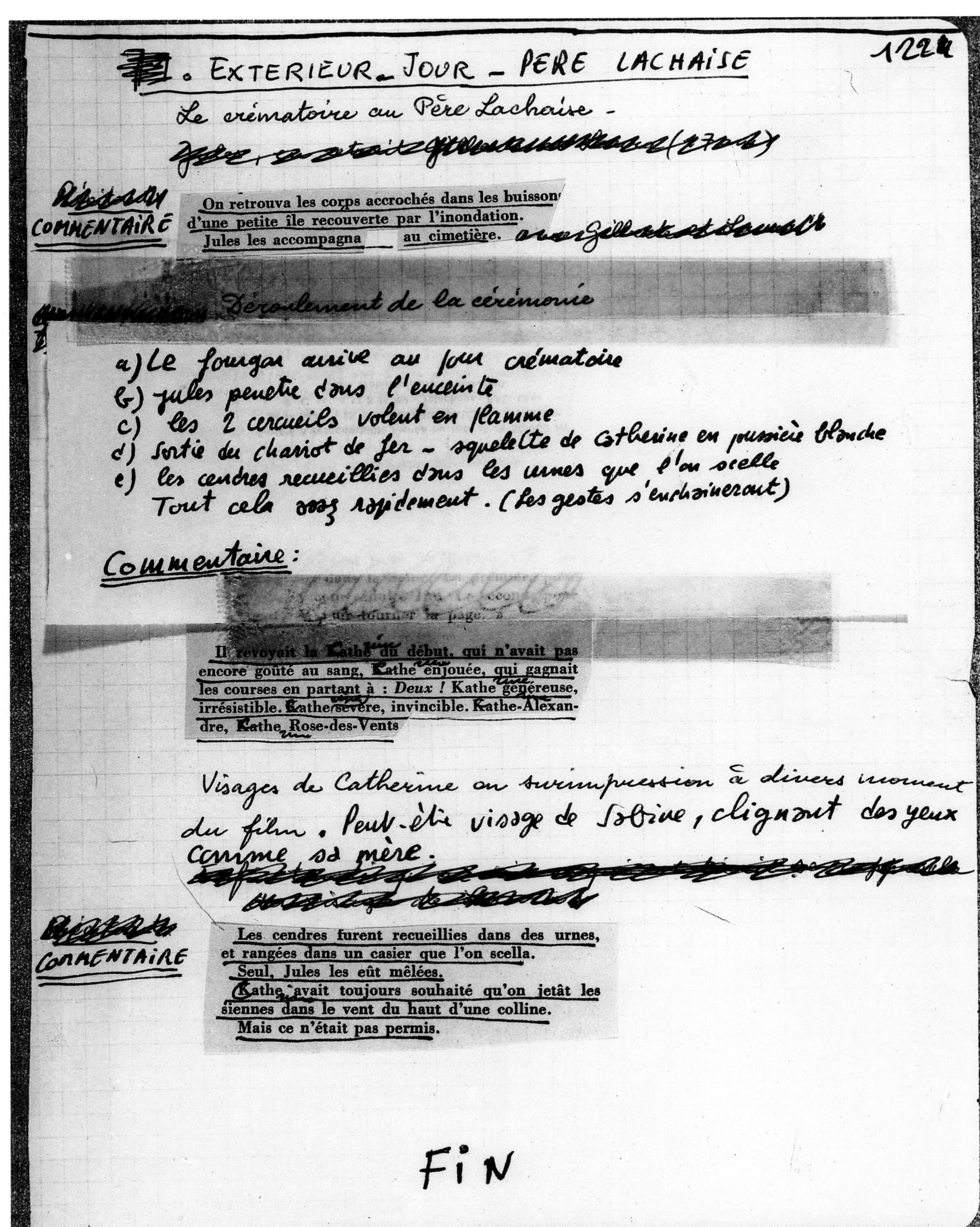

122

. EXTERIEUR – JOUR – PERE LACHAISE

Le crématoire au Père Lachaise -

COMMENTAIRE

On retrouva les corps accrochés dans les buissons d'une petite île recouverte par l'inondation.
Jules les accompagna au cimetière.

Déroulement de la cérémonie

a) Le fourgon arrive au four crématoire
b) Jules pénètre dans l'enceinte
c) les 2 cercueils volent en flamme
d) sortie du chariot de fer – squelette de Catherine en poussière blanche
e) les cendres recueillies dans les urnes que l'on scelle
Tout cela rapidement. (les gestes s'enchaîneront)

Commentaire:

Il revoyait la Kathe du début, qui n'avait pas encore goûté au sang, Kathe enjouée, qui gagnait les courses en partant à : *Deux !* Kathe généreuse, irrésistible. Kathe sévère, invincible. Kathe-Alexandre, Kathe Rose-des-Vents

Visages de Catherine en surimpression à divers moment du film. Peut-être visage de Sabine, clignant des yeux comme sa mère.

COMMENTAIRE

Les cendres furent recueillies dans des urnes, et rangées dans un casier que l'on scella.
Seul, Jules les eût mêlées.
Kathe avait toujours souhaité qu'on jetât les siennes dans le vent du haut d'une colline.
Mais ce n'était pas permis.

FIN

1962

LOVE AT TWENTY: ANTOINE AND COLETTE

I don't like my films, except for the sketch in *Love at Twenty*

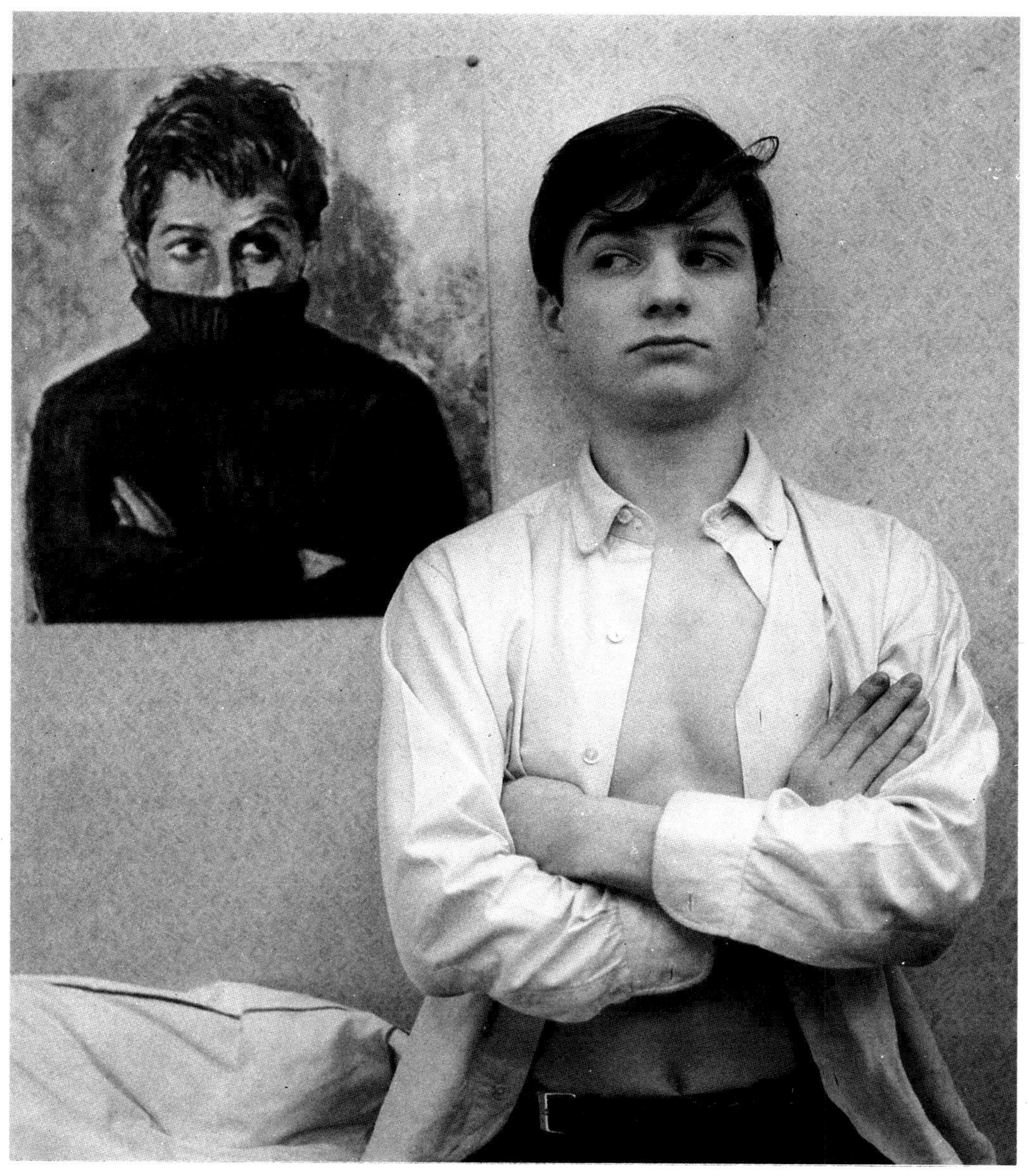

Antoine Doinel three years later (Léaud in front of Léaud)

When I offered to make the French episode in *Love at Twenty* for him, Pierre Roustang not only gave me a free hand but also proposed that I make the choice, with him, of the young foreign directors who would do the other stories.

Each of four directors was invited to write an original screenplay illustrating love at the age of twenty, then to film it, each in his own studio and with actors and technicians of his choice.

Pierre Roustang never tried to influence any of those directors. He didn't try, on the pretext of balancing the film, to get a skit that would be funnier or more sensual or longer or shorter. He gave free rein to chance and luck but also to the taste, intelligence, intuition, and sensibility of each of us. . . .

For my part, the French episode gave me the occasion to realize a project I hadn't dared to launch on my own, a short sequel to my first film, *The 400 Blows,* in which we would meet up with the young Antoine Doinel three years later having his first sentimental adventure, one that would illustrate the moral: you risk losing everything by wanting too much.

"Le Film Vu par François Truffaut,"
press book, 1962

Synopsis of *Antoine's Passion*, which will become *Antoine and Colette*

LA FOUGUE d'ANTOINE

(court-métrage)

Antoine DOINEL, cela était prévisible, serait violemment amoureux à la première occasion.

Il a maintenant seize ans et demi. Ses quatre cents coups d'adolescent l'ont conduit jusque devant le juge pour enfants. Evadé d'un Centre d'Observation des Mineurs Délinquants, il a été repris cinq jours après sa fuite et transféré dans un Centre plus surveillé. La "psychologue" attachée à l'établissement s'étant intéressée à lui, il a finalement été remis en liberté surveillée. Ses parents ont été déchus de leur autorité.

Antoine a une chambre en ville près de la place Clichy. Il travaille comme magasinier dans une maison de disques et il s'est passionné pour la musique. Il s'est inscrit aux Jeunesses Musicales de France et ne rate pas un concert d'initiation à la musique classique. Il sort souvent avec son labadens René BIGEY. Lorsqu'ils ne parlent pas haute fidélité et stéréophonie, ils parlent des filles qu'ils ont connues, connaissent ou connaitront.

C'est en assistant à un Récital Berlioz qu'Antoine devient fou d'amour pour une jeune fille, Colette qui se trouve là, ce dimanche matin dans le Théâtre du Chatelet quelques rangées devant lui. Il la suit des yeux à la sortie, elle dit bonjour à ses amies.

A d'autres concerts, Antoine la remarque et un jour il parvient à s'asseoir à côté d'elle; connaissance.

Une autre fois, il réussit à la raccompagner chez elle. Par ses employeurs, Antoine obtient parfois des places pour des grands concerts (non réservés aux Jeunesses Musicales) grâce à quoi Antoine réussit à sortir seul avec Colette.

- 2 -

Par bribes, il apprend qu'elle est la fille d'une polonaise, que son père est mort mais que son beau-père, très gentil possède un garage près de la gare Saint-Lazare; sa mère tient une petite boutique de tissus au dessous de l'appartement.

Colette décourage plutôt les élans amoureux d'Antoine mais celui-ci n'en tient pas compte. Sous prétexte de rapporter des livres prêtés, il se rend chez Colette; elle n'est pas là mais sa mère le reçoit; elle est très jolie et elle parle avec un très fort accent.

Le lendemain, Colette dira à Antoine : "Ma mère vous a trouvé très romantique."

Plus tard, la mère de Colette, plus familièrement dira à Antoine : "Vos cheveux, vous allez les laisser pousser jusqu'où ?"

Bref, Antoine têtu, ayant remarqué un petit hôtel en face de la boutique de la mère, déménage et vient s'y installer.

~~Comme tous les jeudis midi, il va déjeuner chez ses parents. Son père lui rappelle les difficultés qu'il a eues à l'élever, ses incartades; sa mère dit : "C'est fini, tout cela est oublié, parlons d'autres choses."~~
~~Le père d'Antoine fait rougir son fils en lui parlant filles, acné juvénile, etc ...~~

Antoine, qui surveille depuis la fenêtre de sa chambre d'hôtel, les allées et venues de Colette, est maintenant tout à fait accepté chez les parents de la jeune fille au point même de manger chez eux parfois en l'absence de leur fille. Le principe de ce sketch est le suivant : Antoine, à

- 3 -

force de vouloir se rapprocher de son idole est devenu quelqu'un de la famille, donc un empêcheur de danser en rond, et notre histoire se termine un soir, alors qu'Antoine dîne chez les parents de Colette.

Un garçon vient chercher Liliane pour l'emmener au cinéma et Antoine reste avec les parents à regarder la télévision.

François Truffaut

Jean-Pierre Léaud (Antoine) with Marie-France Pisier (Colette) in her first role

"Mornings I wake up singing." Jean-Pierre Léaud

Antoine works in a record shop

Truffaut's specifications for the role of Colette

Le role de Colette, héroïne aux coté de Jean-Pierre Léaud, du sketch français de "L'amour à vingt ans" n'est toujours pas distribué.

Nous recherchons donc non pas une petite jeune femme mais une petite jeune fille agée de quatorze ans au moins et de quinze ans et demi au plus, l'essentiel étant d'en paraître tout juste quinze.

Elle ne doit être ni mutine, ni piquante, ni pimpante, ni aguichante, ni froufroutante ni sexy mais bien plutôt simple, bien élevée, fraiche, jolie et tout à la fois un peu grave et assez rieuse. De taille moyenne, elle devrait avoir une chevelure de teinte indifferente mais naturelle et elle sera si possible, spirituelle, mélomane et de bonne culture moyenne.

Antoine and Colette at the Jeunesses Musicales

I DID IT IN A CAREFREE MOMENT

I don't like my films, except for the sketch in *Love at Twenty.*

That sketch gave me the occasion to work with Jean-Pierre Léaud again and to realize a project that I had given up like a fool and regretfully. I had thought at a certain point of making a sequel to *The 400 Blows,* to go back to the same character a little later in his life, no longer in his adolescent life but in his working life, and I didn't do it for a stupid reason. *The 400 Blows* having been very successful, I was afraid to look as if I were taking advantage of that success. Well, since then I've learned that you should never give up an idea for such exterior and secondary reasons as reasons of outward appearances. You have to do exactly and intensely whatever you really want to do. If you make frivolous films and serious people tell you you have to make serious films, refuse: if you're frivolous, make frivolous films. You need to doubt in matters pertaining to your choices and your work, but not when it comes to your vocation. So I thought of going back to the same character, Antoine Doinel, and following him in the same way as in *The 400 Blows,* that is, in a documentary manner, in his first romance, his first sentimental affair.

That film really was improvised. We had only the outline. I knew that I would make him a music lover who would meet a girl, likewise a music lover, and who would have an adventure with her that would come to nought.

Keeping along that slender thread, we invented every day with Jean-Pierre Léaud, Marie-France Pisier, and two actors I like a lot: Rosy Varte and François Darbon. To compensate for *The 400 Blows,* I had very sympathetic grown-ups—no more talk about the boy or his family, but we show the girl's parents—and this time I showed a different family, a family that gets along all right. That's the reason I probably like that film more. It's because it's lighter and at the same time more simple, I think even closer to life. I did it in a carefree moment: *Jules and Jim* had just come out and had been very well received, which was why I went to work on *Love at Twenty* in a really cheerful mood.

Interview by the Fédération Française des Ciné-clubs, Cinéma 67, *no. 112*

Antoine visiting Colette's parents

A MELANCHOLY FILM

When *Love at Twenty* was finished, we realized that it was a melancholy film, sometimes even desperate, and was so without our having sought it, simply because love at twenty is something sad in the way it's out of sync with the adult style of life.

"Le Film Vu par François Truffaut," press book, 1962

La Mère : Qu'est-ce que c'est
Colette : Décidément, c'est le vrai défilé
Colette se lève pour aller ouvrir. Les autres regardent vers la porte. Colette revient, accompagnée d'un jeune homme un peu plus âgé qu'Antoine.

	COLETTE	
286		Maman, j'te présente Albert. J't'en ai déjà parlé. Voilà
287		Antoine, vous vous connaissez déjà, je crois..
288	ALBERT	Oui, on s'est vu. Salut !
289	COLETTE	Une minute Albert. Je vais chercher mon manteau
290	La MERE (à son mari)	Donne-moi une cigarette, s'il te plaît.
291	COLETTE	Bon, ça y est hein ! je suis prête. On se tire, Salut !

Et Colette s'en va avec son copain laissant Antoine attablé avec les parents. Le Père et la Mère se regardent gênés. le beau-père : Bon, eh bien si on regardait cette émission...

Tous les trois s'installent devant le poste de télévision sur lequel apparaît le visage du présentateur de la soirée musicale, Bernard Gavoty.

FIN.

Last page of the script of *Antoine and Colette*

Rosy Varte (Colette's mother), Jean-Pierre Léaud (Antoine), and Jean-François Adam (Albert): "Sure, I've seen you around. . . . Hi!"

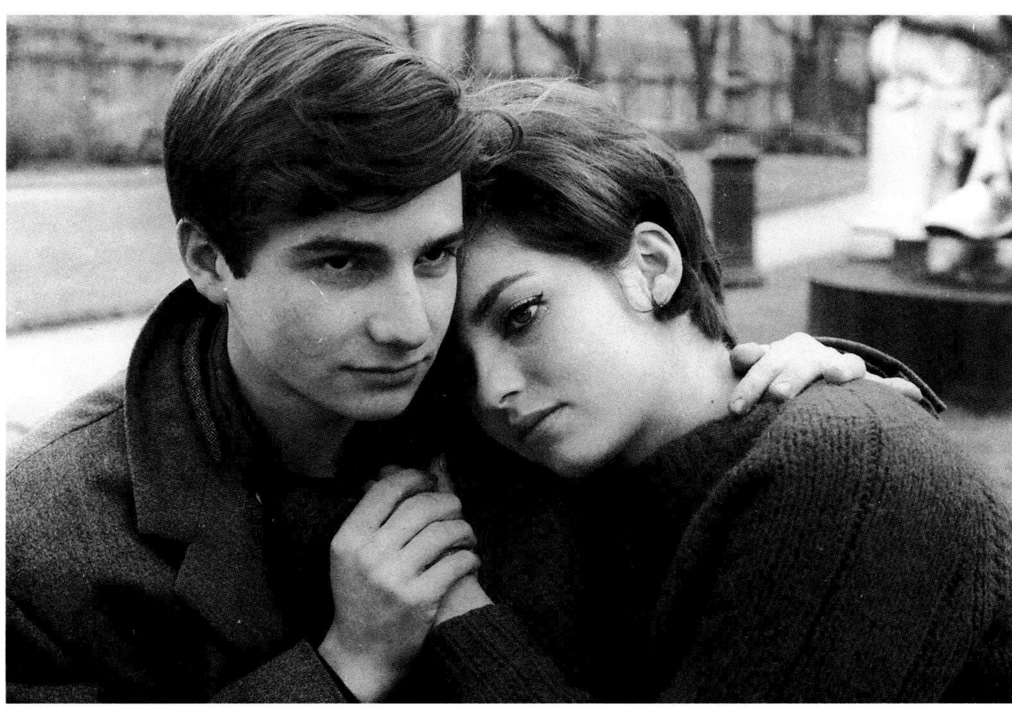

Jean-Pierre Léaud and Marie-France Pisier

Opposite
Antoine takes a room facing Colette's house: Jean-Pierre Léaud and Marie-France Pisier

News clipping about the crime that inspired *The Soft Skin*

Le fait divers qui fut à l'origine du film de Truffaut "La peau douce" évoqué devant les Assises de la Seine

PARIS. — **M. Buisse, juge d'instruction au tribunal de la Seine, a signé hier une ordonnance renvoyant Nicole Gérard, 41 ans, meurtrière de son mari, le Dr Guy Gérard, devant la cour d'assises de la Seine.**

Le 26 juin 1963, au restaurant « le Petit Chevreau », rue de la Huchette, Nicole Gérard avait abattu son mari de deux coups de fusil de chasse à chevrotines, l'un atteignant le médecin à l'épaule droite, l'autre à la tempe droite.

Ce fait divers avait inspiré le metteur en scène François Truffaut qui en fit un film, « la Peau douce », interprété par Françoise Dorléac et Jean Dessailly.

Il s'agissait là d'un drame supplémentaire dans la vie de la jeune femme, trois fois divorcée et qui avait survécu à deux tentatives de suicide.

En 1948, déjà, elle avait tenté de mettre fin à ses jours parce qu'un médecin militaire avait refusé de l'épouser.

Son mariage avec Guy Gérard remontait à 1951. Trois ans auparavant, les deux jeunes gens s'étaient rencontrés à Paris, au cours d'une soirée. De cette liaison était né un enfant, Franck, en 1950.

Pour légitimer l'enfant, le docteur Gérard s'était décidé à épouser sa maîtresse l'année suivante. Mais, n'éprouvant plus aucun sentiment pour sa femme, il n'avait pas tardé à la détester et les difficultés de la vie commune les avaient encore plus séparés.

Les incidents s'étaient succédé et avaient dégénéré plus d'une fois en scènes de violence.

En 1959, las de cette existence, le médecin avait quitté le domicile conjugal, laissant la garde de l'enfant, ainsi que leur appartement, à sa femme. Il lui laissa également une pension mensuelle de 1 400 francs.

Cette situation désespéra Nicole Gérard qui aimait toujours son époux. Elle tenta de se suicider en absorbant des comprimés de phénergan, mais elle fut sauvée « in extremis », en même temps que le petit Frank qui avait suivi l'exemple de sa mère.

Après ce drame, le docteur Gérard prit son fils auprès de lui et, tirant définitivement un trait sur le passé, il se fiança à une jeune fille qu'il se promit d'épouser dès que la procédure en divorce introduite contre sa femme se trouverait à son terme.

UNE LONGUE CRISE

En juin 1962, le jugement en divorce fut prononcé en sa faveur, mais Nicole Gérard fit appel de cette décision.

Cependant, elle n'attendit pas le résultat de cet appel et, un an plus tard, désespérée d'avoir perdu son fils, elle prit sa funeste résolution. Aux policiers qui l'arrêtèrent, elle expliqua qu'elle avait voulu se venger de toutes les « tracasseries » que son mari lui avait fait subir.

« L'acte qui lui est reproché, déclare le rapport des experts psychiatres, est typiquement une réaction passionnelle motivée par la rancœur et la crainte de subir un nouvel échec. Il est l'aboutissement d'une longue crise en tension alimentée par de multiples incidents, comme la seule issue qui s'offrait à une véritable impasse... »

Devant les jurés de la Seine, Nicole Gérard sera défendue par Me Germaine Sénéchal. Me Jacqueline Trouvat, pour sa part, assistera la sœur de la victime, Mme Ribac, qui s'est constituée partie civile.

L'ESPOIR - NICE - 27 JUILLET 1965

Jean Desailly (Pierre) and Françoise Dorléac (Nicole)

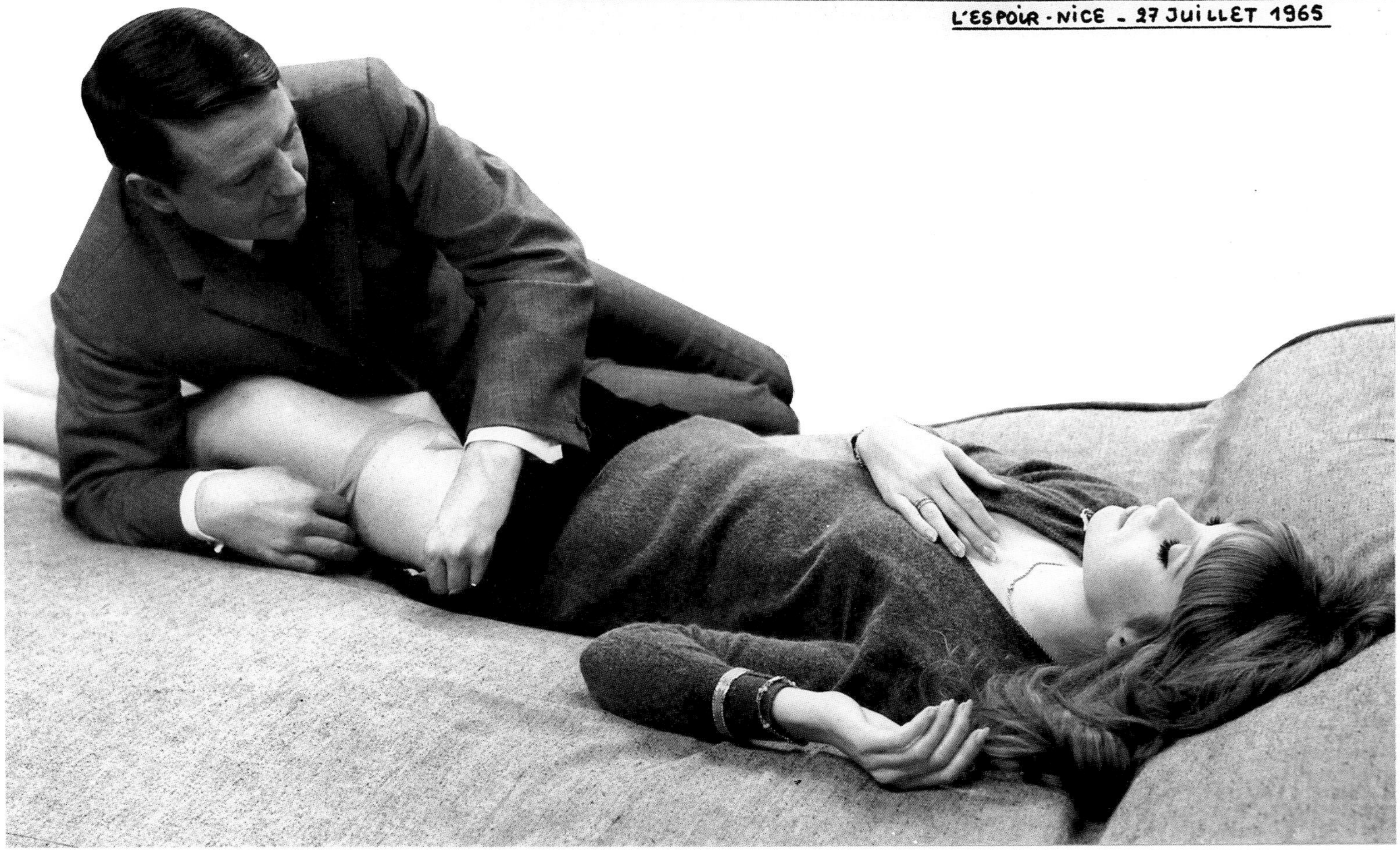

1964

THE SOFT SKIN

I would like my fourth film not to be a sinking ship any longer but a train running across the countryside

When I was a film critic I was inclined to make fun of film directors who declare: "The cinema is very difficult," and I preferred those who claim, "It's very easy."

Once I became a filmmaker I saw that I was forbidden to join up with those of the second tendency. Misgivings, anxiety, doubt, skepticism, pessimism, and, if I dared, I would add anguish, are my daily lot from the first day of writing the script to the last evening spent mixing the sound.

I have already made three films, *The Soft Skin* is the fourth. Up to now I have always had the feeling, on each first day of shooting, of launching a boat onto the sea, and then the work consisted of adjusting the tiller day after day to forestall the shipwreck which errors in calculation in the preparatory work could fatally cause.

Righting a boat in a storm is very fatiguing, and it is also very elating. If you have to bring a wreck into port, you should at least want the wreck to be a fine one.

With Françoise Dorléac

Right
Entrance of a theater showing a film by Jean Cocteau

At present I'm tired of those maritime images, and I would like my fourth film not to be a sinking ship any longer but a train running across the countryside.

I'd like to have a fine, regular, harmonious trip, without chaos and without mistakes in switching tracks. I'd like for the improvisation, instead of hurriedly covering up weaknesses, to be limited to oiling the wheels, to hitching on a car without diverting or slowing down the run.

Then the travelers, who are eventually the spectators, will have a good trip and, so much the better if they're all content, women and children first.

Unifrance Film, *no. 59, first quarter, 1964*

THE STORY, HIGHLY DETAILED, OF AN ADULTERY

Why so long a delay between Jules and Jim *and* Soft Skin?

Because I prepared *Fahrenheit 451,* from Bradbury's novel, for which I had bought the rights during the euphoria of *The 400 Blows* success. I did not manage to make that film in France: I had to have color, as the subject called for. On the other hand, I couldn't have a female star: I had two women's roles and I didn't want one to be more important than the other. Nor, in a science fiction film, could I have a foreign accent. I didn't want a known actress and, with only one name actor—I had thought of Charles Aznavour and of Belmondo—and a subject that was a little baffling, I wasn't able to make the film, the first European science fiction film. I then had some good luck in my misery (the rights cost me really a lot, and we had done three scripts . . .), I found an American producer who bought everything, script, rights to the novel, and who signed a contract with me to make the film the next year in New York. So before making *Fahrenheit* in America I wanted to do a film in France, whence *The Soft Skin.*

What is it, then?

It's the story, highly detailed, of an adultery. It's written by mixing together a good many authentic news stories from these last years. I am very partial to true stories and I have a big file full of them. On the basis of stories that intrigued me, with Jean-Louis Richard (with whom I had done the script of *Fahrenheit* and, for whom, that of *Mata Hari*), we wrote *The Soft Skin.*

Interview by Guy Allombert,
La Cinématographie Française, *October 19, 1963*

THE SCRIPT IS BUILT OUT OF SEVERAL NEWS ITEMS

Did you find the subject of The Soft Skin *in* Detective *magazine?*

The script is built out of several news items concerning love stories that turned out badly and from which we made a single story. It will be less original than *Jules and Jim,* the story is more traditional, it is closer to *The 400 Blows* in the sense that Audiberti, who didn't like *The 400 Blows,* said that it was like Simenon. *The Soft Skin* is a story of adultery, very realistic, which will give an antipoetic idea of love, the reverse in a way of *Jules and Jim,* like a polemical reply. What interests me most is the character of the betrayed woman: she is always made the unattractive character, but here she will be considered in the most anticonventional way possible, she will be the equivalent of Jules in *Jules and Jim.*

Interview by Raymond Bellour and Jean Michaud, Lettres Françaises, *no. 1,000, October 30, 1963*

Françoise Dorléac with Jean Desailly, choosing a book by Jean Cocteau

IF SOMEDAY I DIRECT A FILM ABOUT LOVE, THE INFLUENCE OF BALZAC WILL APPEAR MORE DIRECTLY

I am not cultivated. I am not even a self-educated man. As a matter of fact, I have never learned anything by myself—outside of what the cinema has brought me.

Still, when I was thirteen or fourteen I bought, at fifty centimes each, 450 little volumes very badly printed on grayish paper, Les Classiques Fayard. And I set out to read them, in alphabetical order, without skipping a single title, a single volume, a single page.

I was very much impressed by Alphonse Daudet *(Jack, Les Contes du Lundi, Le Nabab).* But the great revelation for me was Balzac, and it's not by chance that the youngster in *The 400 Blows* sets up an altar to him. What I preferred was *La Peau de Chagrin* because of the kind of madness that occurs in it. Now I'm fonder of *Le Lys dans la Vallée, Les Illusions Perdues, Eugénie Grandet.* If someday I direct a film about love, the influence of Balzac will appear in it more directly.

Interview by Georges Sadoul, Lettres Françaises, *no. 775, May 28, 1959*

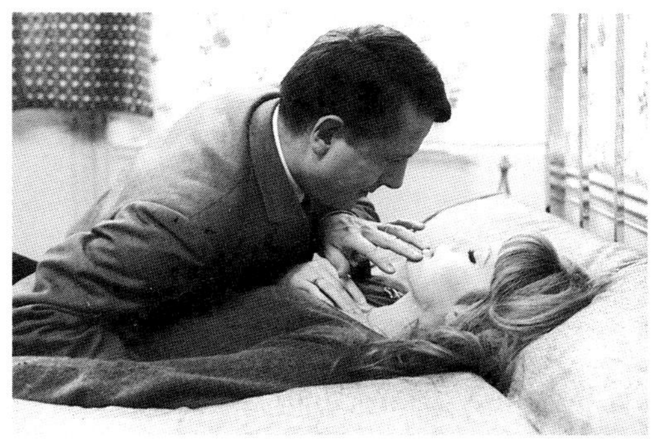

"In that second-class hotel"

AN ANACHRONISTIC CHARACTER

What interested me in *The Soft Skin* was to show an anachronistic character. I really kept thinking: I have to show a character of the nineteenth century, and what is furthest from a nineteenth-century character is an air hostess, because she rides Boeings. It's that opposition which pleased me. Because of that, when he talks about Balzac in the restaurant, he speaks of him in the present tense. He says: "We are in Tours, Honoré does this. . . ." I took my inspiration from a man one sees from time to time on television who is passionate and is obsessed by his passion: it's Henri Guillemin, who has done books on Benjamin Constant, on Rousseau. I was inspired by a man more at his ease with the dead, the onetime glories, than with the world of today. The other idea is that of Duvivier in *The Rules of the Game* of whom it is said: "He is capable of going across the Atlantic by airplane but not the Champs-Elysées at the pedestrian crossing." We have that in this character, who lives in his books. Something happens to him that happens to others but has never happened to him. From that moment on, everything he does is the worst. He goes off on a trip, he takes her with him, he puts her up in that second-class hotel, he makes gaffes all the way, that's the idea. The film has been condemned for one thing I profoundly desired: he doesn't say to Ceccaldi, "I've come with a girl." Now, like Jaccoud, Desailly is a man who can't do that. When Jaccoud went to a restaurant with Linda Baud, he left her in the car, went into the restaurant, and began looking to see if there was anyone he knew. If there was, he got back in the car, he went to another restaurant, where he chose a table at the back and had her sit facing the door. Every time the door opened, he asked her: "Who is it?" That character pleased me, as an emotional person and as a man who, every time he encounters a difficulty, chooses the worst solution. He's a blunderer.

"The story, highly detailed, of an adultery"

What we weren't able to choose, Jean-Louis Richard and I, was between the story of a madman or that of a man like you, me, other people. When you write a script, you should never hesitate over an important point without finding a solution for it. What we never worked out was precisely that temptation. We should have made a choice. For example, for a time at Rheims I wanted to make him faint when he saw the girl through the window. Ceccaldi drinks his beer; he would have got up and would have fallen backward. And then we said to ourselves: that's going to make a film about a nut, people will say it's the story of a sick man, and we dropped the idea, which ended up instead in *Fahrenheit*. The story of a madman could have been enthralling; as the story of a normal man it was another film. Finally we did neither one nor the other.

Interview by the Fédération Française des Ciné-clubs, Cinéma 67, *no. 112*

SHE WAS CALLED FRANÇOISE . . .

Two hundred numbers of the *Cahiers* have come and gone and, along with them, Bazin, Ophuls, Becker, Cocteau, Little Biesse. When Jean-Pierre Léaud talked to me about him [Biesse], I asked: "He's the one who looks like an Italian bicycle racer?" He was the one.

Films disappear and also those who make them and those who judge them and those who watch them. Those who act in them also, and even if the *Cahiers* has less interest in those, I ask permission to publish one or two photos of Françoise Dorléac who died, on June 26 of last year, in a car accident on the way to the Nice airport. For the public, it was a news item, the more cruel because it struck down a very beautiful girl of twenty-five, an actress who hadn't yet had time to become a star. For all those who knew her, Françoise Dorléac represented even more, a person such as one meets rarely in one's lifetime, an incomparable young woman whose charm, femininity, intelligence, grace, and unbelievable moral force made her unforgettable to anyone who had spoken with her for an hour.

A strong personality, on occasion authoritarian, contrasting with a fragile and romantic physique of the seaweed or greyhound type, Françoise Dorléac, to my mind an insufficiently appreciated actress, would certainly in her thirties have made true contact with the broad public, who would have then adored her as all those who had the luck to work with her adored her.

The difficult thing, for young actresses, is to carry through harmoniously the transition from young girl to woman, to drop juvenile roles in favor of adult roles. I believe that Françoise Dorléac, precocious and premature woman, with her face and her body already constructed and, as they say in the studios, built to last and in order to last, was the only young actress of whom one could think that with time she would please more and more. Ever since her adolescence she took two ice-cold showers a day, explaining: "It's at twenty that you prepare for your forties." When she showed herself impatient to find roles and to make

Franca (Nelly Benedetti) shoots without aiming, and Pierre (Jean Desailly) collapses

Opposite
The last version of the screenplay of *The Soft Skin:* the final scene

films, I tried to convince her that she had nothing to fear from the years that pile up one after the other and that time was working for her. I told her we would make a film together every six years, and I made dates with her for 1970, 1976, 1982. Every time I wrote her, I put on the envelope "Mademoiselle Framboise Dorléac" to be sure she would read my letter smiling.

Françoise Dorléac was intransigent, on the edge of intolerance; she was a moralist, her interviews were rich in high-principled aphorisms about life and about love. She could look at anyone she mistrusted with a suddenly very hard look. Life had not yet given her a beating; indulgence would have come later.

Until then, so many smiles, laughs, and uncontrollable laughter, and that's what makes June 26th of last year unacceptable, those great rounds of laughter cut short.

Cahiers du Cinéma,
no. 200–201, April-May 1968

DISAGREEABLE TO WATCH

The Soft Skin: I knew right away it would be a flop, as soon as I had done the mixing. I looked at the film very lucidly, as if someone else had made it, and I saw that it was depressing, that it was a film that "ran downhill." I understood then that it would be disagreeable to watch.

A film that "runs downhill" is rarely liked. I mean a film presenting a situation that gets worse and worse; it's the very opposite of the idea of "exaltation" that one expects from a "show." That's a law rarely proved wrong.

Failure gets you down a lot?

No. It's pretty stimulating, on the contrary. I've gone through more periods of feeling empty and sad after successes than after failures. I had violent spells of the blues after *The 400 Blows* and *Jules and Jim,* for example.

I think there's something exciting about failure. It makes you want to work fast, to start again, to say: "Come on, in three months I'll be doing another one." Whereas after a success . . . the expression "to rest on one's laurels" was not invented for nothing.

Interview by Pierre Ajame,
Le Nouvel Adam, *no. 9, February 1968*

166 INTERIEUR RESTAURANT.

Franca entre. Un serveur la reconnaît: "Bonjour Madame Lachenay."

— Elle avance (dans la salle) et nous la précédons en gros plan - travelling-arrière; elle regarde droit devant elle.

— Ce qu'elle voit: Pierre en train de lire, en fumant.

— Travelling avant subjectif vers Pierre

— On repose sur Franca qui avance

— Pierre lève la tête et voit Franca. Il est surpris

— Franca le regarde et met la main dans la poche droite de son imperméable.

— Pierre esquisse un mouvement de la main et peut-être même un sourire

— Franca sort la main de sa poche d'imperméable et en retire les photos, qu'elle jette devant elle, comme à la figure de Pierre, en vrac

— Pierre voit les photos voleter devant lui

— Franca ouvre son imperméable et saisit le fusil

— Pierre voit le fusil; il se lève

— Franca, le fusil à la taille, tire sans viser

— Pierre s'écroule.

— Franca regarde vers Pierre

— Il s'effondre entre la table et la banquette

— Plan général de tout le restaurant. Les gens se lèvent.

— Retour sur Franca qui laisse tomber le fusil et s'assoit sur une chaise. On entend "off": il faut appeler (vaguement) un médecin, la police!...

— En gros plan, Franca qui respire (à pleins poumons) et souffle comme au sortir de l'eau. Un grand soulagement.

On entend "off" le patron composer le numéro de la police sur le téléphone du bar.

FIN.

451
05003-2

FAHRENHEIT 451

Why not popularize, with the help of the cinema, fine literary texts?

1966

Why *Fahrenheit 451?* Because for a long time I had wanted to make a film that is read aloud. Why not popularize, with the help of the cinema, fine literary texts? Then, too, I wanted to talk about books. Already I had in mind filming *Le Bleu d'Outre-tombe* by R.-J. Clot. This was the story of a schoolteacher. So inevitably she read books aloud in class, but the subject couldn't be shaped into anything. What decides me on making a film is when I manage to combine everything, the subject, the characters, the form. Cinema has to hold people's attention in every way possible. It's circus, music hall. But not at all theater. *Fahrenheit* is a book about the future, the story of a civilization in which all books are burned because books are useless, contradict each other, and serve only to trouble people. A team of firemen exists only for that job. But one day one of the firemen begins to read a book and to ask himself why he's burning it. That's the whole film.

When I was told that story, I knew immediately that I would film it. That was over a year ago. Since then, I've been thinking. I myself think a long time in advance about the films I want to make, and if I have one idea per month, that's terrific. It's enough to have six or seven big ideas in a film, but they do have to be there. *Fahrenheit* I wanted to film in English.

Films for me are born while driving. Look, last week I had a little idea. I don't really take sides politically. If I signed the Manifesto of the 121, it was because I had been a deserter and because I wanted to express my solidarity with those who were deserting. That's all. *Fahrenheit* looks like a left-wing film, and that gripes me. Well, the other day I decided that the firemen would conspicuously burn *Mein Kampf.* If they burn *Mein Kampf* too, then I correct their aspect as "filthy fascist firemen." That's an idea. Films get born like that, slowly, from idea to idea.

"Une Idée per Mois,"
L'Express, *September 27, 1962*

After discovering books, Montag will turn his flame-thrower against his own captain

NOTE CONCERNANT LA POST-SYNCHRONIZATION DU ROLE DE MONTAG

Independamment des questions de la qualite du synchronisme, de la prononciation anglaise pour ce role, et des variantes possibles dans le vocabulaire, toutes questions pour lesquelles je ne suis pas competent, et m'en remets definitivement a Norman Wanstall et Helen Scott, je souhaite qu'Oscar Werner puisse rapporter des ameliorations dans sept scenes du film:

Nos. 21 a 27: Premiere scene de Montag rentrant chez lui et retrouvant Linda. Dans cette scene, Montag parle trop fort. Bien qu'il soit a une certaine distance de Linda, il ne doit pas donner l'impression d'hostilite, mais de vie normale.

No. 70 : Au lendemain de l'evanouissement de Linda. Meme reproche, mais cette fois, plus serieux, car Montag doit chercher a obliger Linda a se rappeller ce qui s'est passe la veille, mais sans animosite -- plutot sur un ton fatigue, sans quoi, nous sommes dans le contre-sens absolu.

No. 79 : Pour la premiere fois, Montag lit un livre, la nuit devant la television. Effectivement, il doit lire comme un enfant qui commence a apprendre. puisque c'est

Montag (Oskar Werner), Linda Montag (Julie Christie), and their friends in the Montags' living room

The firemen ready to intervene

The Captain (Cyril Cusack) and Montag (Oskar Werner)

A FABLE OF OUR EPOCH

Many science fiction works can be considered fairy tales for adults and that is why *Fahrenheit 451* can be considered a fable of our epoch and looked at as such.

Two aspects of science fiction alternate in the futurist literary production: one dealing with the earth and its inhabitants, one that brings on stage extraterrestrial beings such as Martians, Venusians, robots, monsters, etc. Ray Bradbury's novel *Fahrenheit 451* belongs to the first category. The action, in fact, takes place on our planet, but with a slight leap ahead in time, and in a way one could say to the viewers: this story takes place "where" you wish, "when" you wish. Bathed in an atmosphere more strange than resolutely extravagant, the narrative keeps to a quite simple postulate: we are in a society where it is strictly forbidden to read and to own books. In that society the firemen's function is not to extinguish fires but the contrary, to track down book owners and to burn their books publicly.

With the story taking place in an unspecified country, the film can be said to be make-believe, but within that make-believe a certain reality has been respected, so the story resembles what we know of the resistance that several countries put up against Nazi oppression, but with the difference that here the persecuted men are only booklovers.

One of the principal themes in *Fahrenheit 451* is love of books. Certain people feel for books a purely intellectual love: what interests them is the "contents" of the book. Other readers, however, feel a sentimental, almost physical attachment for books as objects. That feeling is frequent, for example, in someone whose early years were spent in the country or in a place where books were rare objects, or then again in someone whose childhood was punctuated by the annual offering of books as awards for high marks in school or to celebrate birthdays.

In the minds of the latter, the book exists almost completely apart from its contents and becomes a cult object. With time, its bindings, its jacket, even its smell take on a particular sentimental significance for the person who owns it.

In making a film on *Fahrenheit 451,* my first aim was to bring out the qualities of visual invention in Ray Bradbury's novel. My second aim was to attempt this dosage: to film fantastic things as if they were everyday, everyday things as if they were fantastic, and to mingle one with the other. When you dream, you don't see an extraordinary world, you see our everyday world curiously deformed. It is that deformation I have tried to show in *Fahrenheit 451.* The authors of science fiction being the fable writers of our time, and their works often resembling fairy tales for grownups, this film can be thought of as both a tale by Andersen and a fable by Jean de La Fontaine, or then again, thanks to Bernard Herrmann's music, as an opera about literary censorship.

Fahrenheit 451 is the temperature at which a book catches fire and burns up. In all countries of the world, today still, books are put on the Index, seized, or even burned in the street, as for example on May 2, 1964, at Djakarta. Literary censorship appeared at the same time as the invention of printing and probably will only disappear with it. Wouldn't the strongest protest we could make be to learn all the books by heart? That is the program of action suggested to us by *Fahrenheit 451,* whose story does not necessarily take place in the future but "when you will" and "where you will."

Sketch for a text in the press book of Fahrenheit 451, *1966*

Montag shows how to find hidden books

If someone were to make up, on the basis of your film, a game of people-books, which would you like to be?

Marie Dubois by Audiberti.

"A Propos de Fahrenheit 451,"
Arts-loisirs, *September 14, 1966*

BERNARD HERRMANN: IF PEOPLE ARE BORED, AT LEAST IT WILL BE TO MUSIC

FRIDAY, MAY 27: Second session with Bernard Herrmann, who is busy afternoons directing his opera *Wuthering Heights.* We look at the second half of the film, then go back to the beginning. There will be thirty-seven musical numbers for a total of fifty-five minutes, thus half the film. Since we have practically chosen to have music only for scenes without dialogue, that means that half the film is strictly visual, something that really pleases me. In almost all films, the acting and dialogue time increases in shooting, while the silent part (scenes of action, violence, or love scenes, or facial closeups) diminishes for lack of time to shoot all the takes planned. Stimulated by all the silent films from between 1920 and 1930 seen or reseen in the past two years, I have hung on to my "privileged moments" so that they would not shrink. This does not mean that the film will be less boring than any other but that, if people are bored, at least it will be to music, and when it's that of Bernard Herrmann. . . . No one gets tired of listening to numbers two or three minutes long, for example those in *Vertigo* or *Psycho,* not to mention the sound track of *Citizen Kane,* which made it the best musical and radio film ever made in Hollywood.

"Journal de Fahrenheit 451,"
Cahiers du Cinéma, *no. 180, 1966; published with* La Nuit Américaine, *Paris, Seghers, 1974*

The Monorail: Oskar Werner and Julie Christie

Arrest of the "Book Woman" (Bee Duffell)

IN MAKING A FILM, WE ARE ABNORMALS SAYING SOMETHING TO NORMAL PEOPLE

TUESDAY, JUNE 21: I am stopping this diary today, giving up carrying it on until the mixing is finished, because I don't want to go on any longer about the problems of detail that will be my sole concern to the end of July. Here is what my appointment book has:

Recording music: July 6 and 7.
Premixing (to get all the voice tracks on one): July 8 and 9.
Mixing: from July 11 to 22.

After that will come the color correction of the print (with the cameraman Nick Roeg) at Technicolor and, in Paris, the work of subtitling and dubbing in French with the help of Suzanne Schiffman. We obviously have to turn over two good copies to Venice and that will be the end of this adventure, in which I gained many white hairs and lost a good many others. Everybody who works by fits and starts knows that phenomenon of speeded-up aging, which compresses two years into seven months by making us age by work rather than by year. A finished work leaves us dazed, with the impression of having got a hard blow on the head.

Preparation of the book-burning at the house of the "Book Woman"

Montag (Oskar Werner) and Linda (Julie Christie) in front of their home screen

The adaptation of *Fahrenheit 451* having been written a year before the script of *The Soft Skin,* there are, curiously enough, points in common in the two films, and if Montag's wife is named Linda—and not Mildred as in Bradbury—it's probably because the Jaccoud affair was already on my mind. For the rest, *Fahrenheit 451* would be more like *Shoot the Piano Player*—perhaps because it involves in both cases an American novel, built up with American material? I don't know how the film will turn out. I know it will be only remotely like all this I've written here, because it's pretty clear that I've spoken only about what surprised or astonished me and not about what was well settled for a long time in my head or Bradbury's. Now, on the screen, you'll see only that, what was in our heads, Bradbury's fantasy and then mine, and if they mix well. My films, like those of many filmmakers, are born out of an idea of *mélange,* of the desire to attempt a new dosage of preexisting elements:

The "Book Men" in the snow (Oskar Werner and Julie Christie)

"Well, well, it would be interesting to tell a story like that but treating it in a different way from the usual one." Here, in the case of *Fahrenheit 451,* it was a matter of treating a fantastic story with familiarity, making themes that were too strange banal and everyday scenes abnormal. I don't know yet if the result will give the impression of a normal film made by a crazy man or a crazy film made by a normal man, but I am convinced that in writing a book or making a film, we are abnormals saying something to normal people. Sometimes our madness is accepted, sometimes it's rejected. Ever since I came to understand that, the question of knowing if a film of mine will be a success or not really worries me less and less, and I will never again know the fear I felt shooting *The 400 Blows* of not interesting anyone. I think Sartre is right in calling all those who think their existence is indispensable "louses," but I approve of Renoir when he rejects the usual formula "no one is irreplaceable." My slowness obliges me to film only a third of my projects and to reject two films each time I begin one, but I believe I still have a lot of *mélanges* to make, new dosages to experiment with. I am a French filmmaker who has thirty films to shoot in the years to come: some will succeed, others not, and it's just about all the same to me, as long as I can make them.

"Journal de Fahrenheit 451,*"*
Cahiers du Cinéma, *no. 180, 1966;*
published with La Nuit Américaine,
Paris, Seghers, 1974

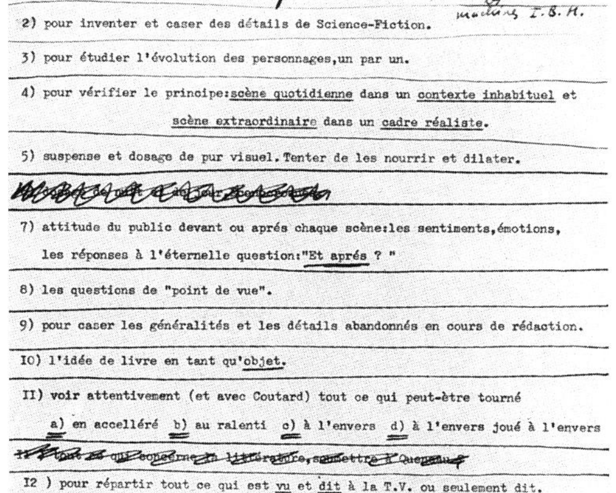

RELIRE LE SCENARIO POUR:

I) condenser le dialogue au maximum; le remplacer par du visuel

2) pour inventer et caser des détails de Science-Fiction.

3) pour étudier l'évolution des personnages, un par un.

4) pour vérifier le principe: scène quotidienne dans un contexte inhabituel et scène extraordinaire dans un cadre réaliste.

5) suspense et dosage de pur visuel. Tenter de les nourrir et dilater.

7) attitude du public devant ou aprés chaque scène: les sentiments, émotions, les réponses à l'éternelle question: "Et aprés ? "

8) les questions de "point de vue".

9) pour caser les généralités et les détails abandonnés en cours de rédaction.

IO) l'idée de livre en tant qu'objet.

II) voir attentivement (et avec Coutard) tout ce qui peut-être tourné a) en accelléré b) au ralenti c) à l'envers d) à l'envers joué à l'envers

I2) pour répartir tout ce qui est vu et dit à la T.V. ou seulement dit.

13) pour caser quelques détails drôles pour soulager aprés tension

I4) pour relier les scènes entre elles intimement (crochet, maillons)

15) du point de vue Montag, [illegible] (Est-ce qu'il agit? est-ce qu'il aime Clarisse.)

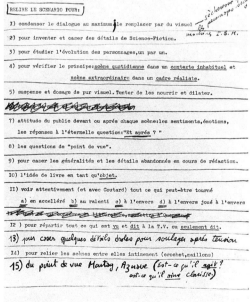

Notes on the script (1962)

The Captain (Cyril Cusack) destroyed in his turn by the flame-thrower

With Julie Christie during the filming of *Fahrenheit 451*

1967

THE BRIDE WORE BLACK

One thing intrigued me: to make a film about love without a single love scene

EDGAR ALLAN POE
SPECIAL
AWARD
presented to
François Truffaut
for his screenplay
The Bride Wore Black
M.W.A. Award
by Mystery Writers of America

The Mystery Writers of America Award for the screenplay of *The Bride Wore Black*

The Bride Wore Black

You have perhaps noticed that your copy of the script mentions on the front page: "In order that the plot of *The Bride Wore Black* not be spoiled before the film comes out, we ask you not to divulge it and not to let anyone read this script, which is only a working tool."

We think in fact that rumors or written or photographic reports devoted to Jeanne Moreau, "murderess of five men," would rob the film of a lot of its freshness. That is why the film, while in the making, will be generally presented to the press as a police "investigation" led by Jeanne Moreau "to find the person responsible for killing her husband on her wedding day."

The various murders and the finale will be shot with no persons unconnected with the production authorized to follow the filming and, as far as publicity is concerned, will pass by in silence.

Note to collaborators, actors, and technicians of The Bride Wore Black, *1967*

TO GIVE LIFE TO A GREAT DEAL OF DRAMA

At the origin of *The Bride Wore Black* are my admiration for William Irish, author of crime stories that read like dreams, my desire to make another film with Jeanne Moreau, and finally my wanting to try the experiment of filming a superdramatic story studded with extreme situations but depending on a great many realistic details.

Since it's a foreign novel and not localized, I saw to it that no place should be recognizable. Rather than Frenchify the book, I preferred suggesting a kind of imaginary country. With its four hundred takes, *The Bride* is my least crosscut film. I felt it like that. The form of a film comes to one's mind generally at the same time as the idea. If there are numerous takes in sequence, it's because each of the six male characters has only a quarter hour of film to exist before our eyes. Now, one's existence is much more real within a sequence of takes comprising a few calculated dead spots than in a broken-up piece of crosscutting.

In fact, what I had to do was to give life to a great deal of drama.

The real action of *The Bride Wore Black* is over when the film begins! Julie Kohler has loved only one man in her life, and he was killed on their wedding day. Everything important has therefore happened before the story starts. This is a narrative principle found more often in the theater than in films. For example, one could cite a great many plays in which the characters comment on the death of a child, from *The Cherry Orchard* to *Virginia Woolf*. Here, it is through the heroine's contact with the five men she will meet, and who will speak to her of love, that we will find out the mechanism of the preceding drama.

In fact, one thing intrigued me: to make a film about love without a single love scene. There is not one kiss to be found in the film. The action on the screen is virtually that of a crime film, yet the dialogue never concerns that action. The dialogue deals only with the relations between men and women. By being systematically out of phase, I can have two completely different films that move ahead simultaneously. Each man represents a different way of looking at women. For Michel Bouquet, a romantic provincial, they are magical, inaccessible: I thought a lot about Audiberti. For Michel Lonsdale, concerned above all with winning the elections, they are brainless: I thought of Jean Dutourd. For Charles Denner they are collection pieces, but a collector can cave in occasionally. There are also Jean-Claude Brialy, Claude Rich, and Daniel Boulanger, because *The Bride* let me make use of six actors I had been dreaming of working with for years: "six at a blow," as Grimm's little tailor put it. To accompany those six men, to differentiate them, to color them, a great musician was needed. Bernard Herrmann came from California to give a certain air of opera to our fairy tale for grown-ups.

As for Jeanne Moreau, after *Jules and Jim,* in which her role was extremely well rounded, I felt the need to make her do something very different, so no love on screen and something quite hard about her. In *The Bride* she is not really a character but more a goddess, a symbol. After seeing the film, people can guess what goddess is meant and what symbol. Mysterious but human and fragile, she conveys us from one man to the other, she becomes a sort of mediator between the male characters in the film (who put themselves in her hands) and the viewer sitting in the dark.

Jeanne Moreau speaks very little in *The*

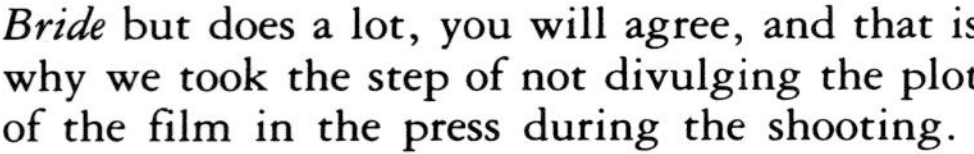

Bride but does a lot, you will agree, and that is why we took the step of not divulging the plot of the film in the press during the shooting.

At present, nothing hinders us from telling the true story of *The Bride Wore Black;* nonetheless we hope that the final outcome of the plot will not be made known, remaining the privilege and secret of the film's viewers exclusively.

"La Vie et le Drame," 1968, text by Truffaut for the press book of the film. Compiled on the basis of his statements in Le Nouvel Adam, Cinéma 68, Cahiers du Cinéma, *and* Lettres Françaises

Daniel Boulanger, Michel Bouquet, Charles Denner, Michel Lonsdale, and Claude Rich

Upper right
Michel Lonsdale and Daniel Boulanger

The exit from the church and the death of David Kohler (Serge Rousseau)

Opposite:
Jeanne Moreau in a publicity photo for *The Bride Wore Black*

YOU CAN'T FILM DEATH FOR FIFTY-SIX DAYS WITHOUT BEING AFFECTED BY IT

The Bride could seem oversimple and mechanical to anyone who refuses to have a film for adults begin with "once upon a time." For me, and for my actors as well, *The Bride* is nonetheless a serious film. Because you can't film death for fifty-six days without being affected by it. I am convinced, moreover, that the first death scene a filmmaker shoots marks a stage in his career. That struck me when I passed from *The 400 Blows* to *Shoot the Piano Player,* in which I deliberately forced myself to film material very remote from my biography: those American novels I love so much and of which *The Bride* is one of the classics.

I should like to say finally that the five men Julie comes across on her way take us back to that principle of enumeration which makes reading fairy tales so fascinating: "Goldilocks and the Three Bears," "The Three Little Pigs and the Big Bad Wolf," "Snow White and the Seven Dwarfs."

How do you put across that fairy-tale atmosphere?

By a constant effort at simplification and visual stylization. For example, at the end of the only scene bringing together the five men, the text says: "They decide to separate and never again to try to see each other." And the image shows, with disregard for all verisimilitude, the five friends walking down an iron stairway and, once at the bottom, going off in all directions. On the other hand, in this color film Julie never wears anything but black and white, and rather than entering a scene or leaving it one can say that she appears and disappears. This dreamlike character is considerably reinforced by the music of Bernard Herrmann (the composer of Welles's *Citizen Kane* and Hitchcock's *Vertigo*), which draws the film more toward opera. Which suits me fine: it's one mask more.

You cite Hitchcock and you love him. Did he influence you in this film?

Certainly for the construction of the story because, unlike the novel, we give the solution of the enigma well before the end. Thus the public doesn't have to wait so long for an explanation which, even if ingenious, rarely deserves to make up the finale of a film.

Contrariwise, the desire to make the characters speak of everything else but the intrigue

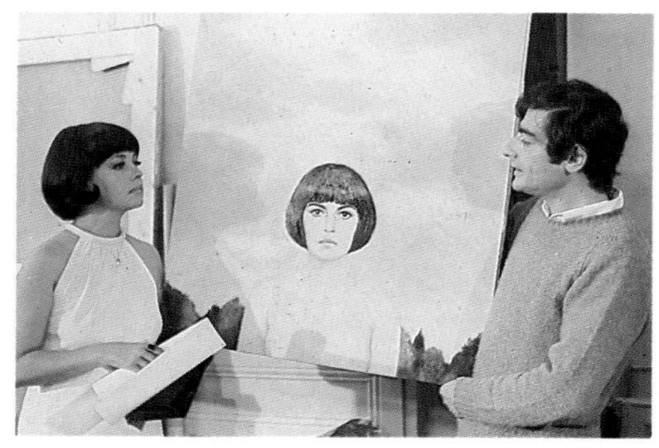

itself is decidedly not very Hitchcockian and more characteristic of a European turn of mind. Between Renoir and Hitchcock I have always thought that a bridge was established by Cocteau. Long before *The Bride,* wasn't he speaking of "filming death at work"?

Interview by Yvonne Baby,
Le Monde, *April 18, 1968*

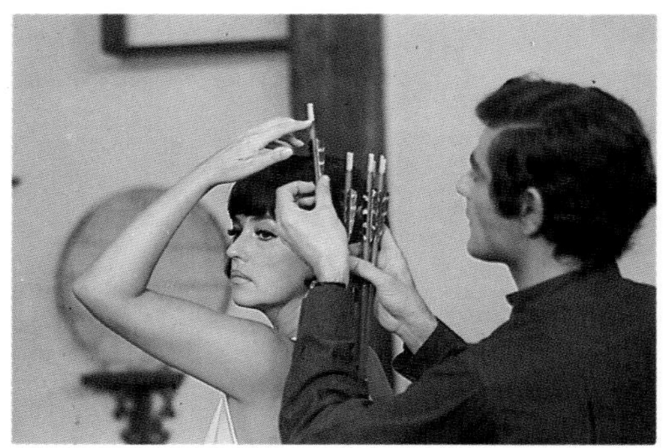

The painter and his model: Fergus (Charles Denner) and Julie Kohler (Jeanne Moreau)

Julie Kohler (Jeanne Moreau) at David's grave

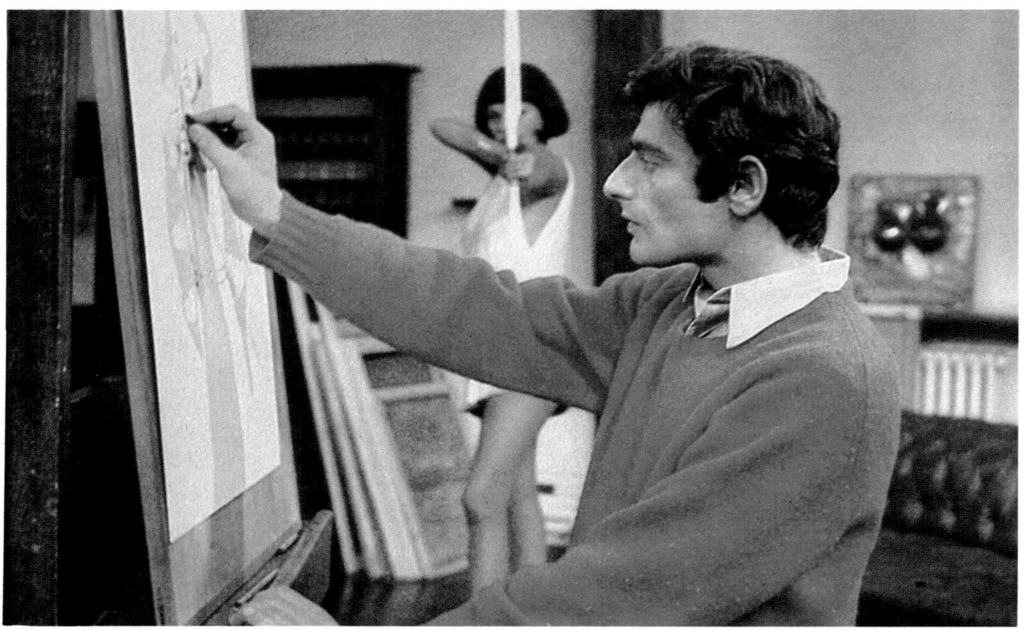

THE SCREEN IS OCCUPIED BY SOMEONE WHO FINDS HIMSELF IN THE WRONG

I think that *The Bride* to some extent resembles my other films. *The Soft Skin* went back to certain themes in *Piano Player* and *The 400 Blows; Fahrenheit 451* connected up with the other films.

In *The Bride* we get back a little to the imaginary country of *Fahrenheit 451,* and also to the principle of American themes, as in *Piano Player,* treated in a French spirit. Recently it came to me that *The Bride* even resembles *The Mischief Makers:* the five men Jeanne Moreau meets are the kids grown up.

If there is a common bond in all my films, it is that in the long run the screen is occupied by someone who finds himself in the wrong.

Interview by Gérard Langlois,
Lettres Françaises, *April 10, 1968*

Do some of your films-objects, with the passing of the years, inspire in you affection or repulsion?

The only one I regret having made is *The Bride Wore Black.* I wanted to offer Jeanne Moreau something like none of her other films, but it was badly thought out. That was a film to which color did an enormous lot of harm. The theme is lacking in interest: to make excuses for an idealistic vengeance, that really shocks me. When I saw *The Old Gun* I felt a certain discomfort, yet I had done the same thing! One should not avenge oneself, vengeance is not noble. One betrays something in oneself when one glorifies that.

Interview by Danièle Heymann and Catherine Laporte,
L'Express, *March 13, 1978*

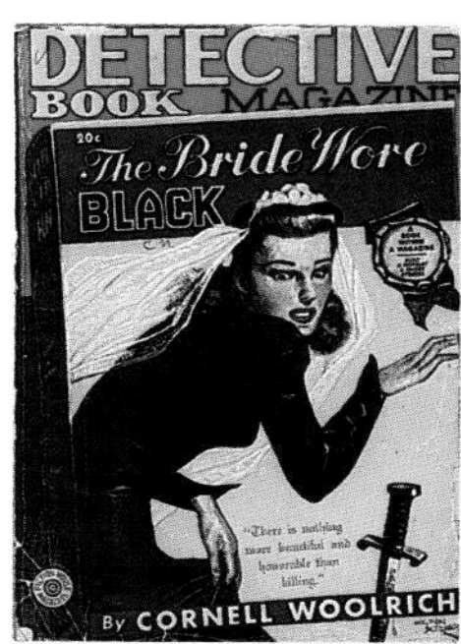

Cover of the American edition of *The Bride Wore Black* by Cornell Woolrich (pen name of William Irish)

Below
Julie Kohler pursues her vengeance: Jeanne Moreau with, respectively, Michel Lonsdale, Michel Bouquet, and Daniel Boulanger

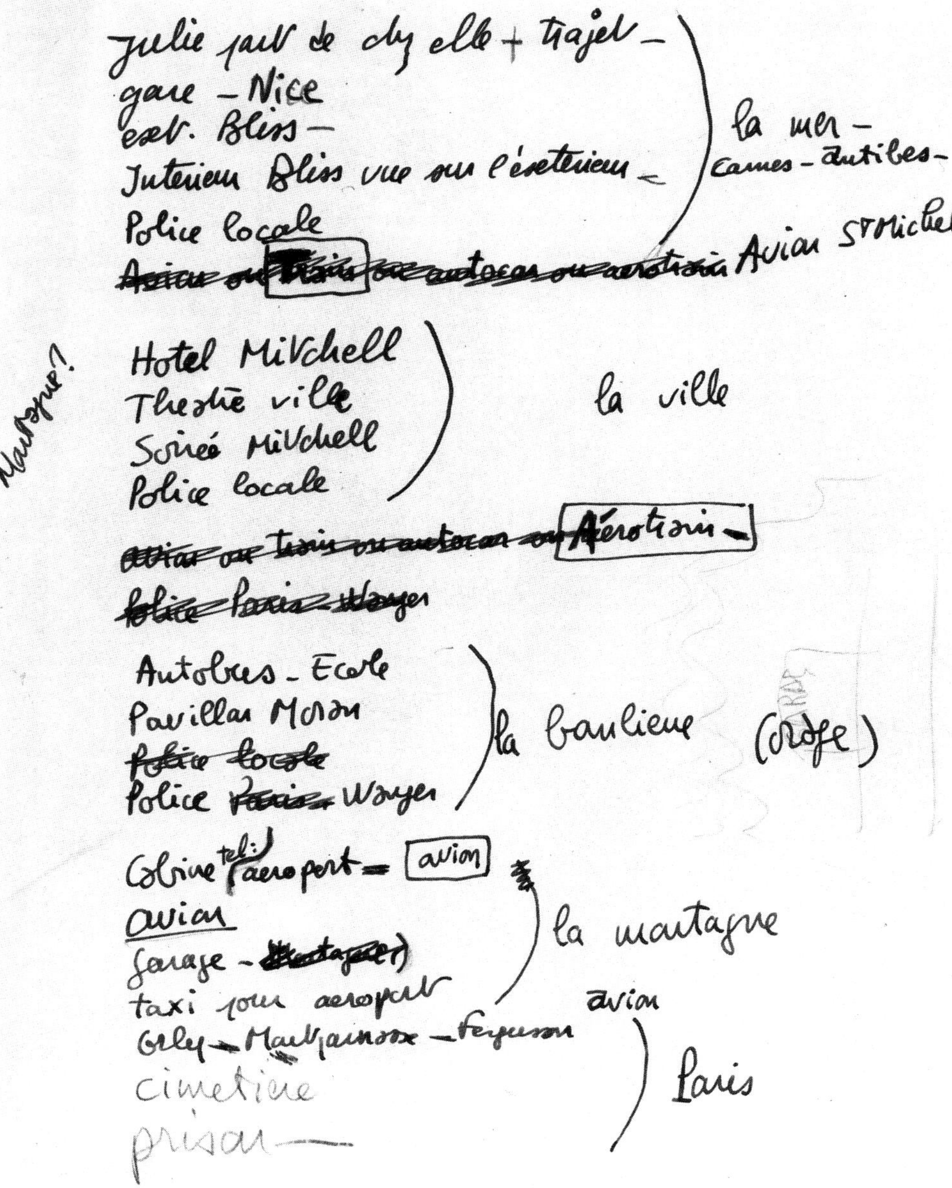
Julie part de chez elle + trajet –
gare – Nice
ext. Bliss –
Intérieur Bliss vue sur l'extérieur –
Police locale
Avion St Michel
la mer – Cannes – Antibes –

Montagne?
Hotel Mitchell
Théâtre ville
Soirée Mitchell
Police locale
la ville

Aérotrain –

Autobus – Ecole
Pavillon Moran
Police Wayer
la banlieue

Coline tel: aeroport – avion
avion
Garage –
taxi pour aeroport
la montagne

avion
Gely – Ferguson
cimetière
prison –
Paris

The itinerary and victims of Julie Kohler

Corey (Jean-Claude Brialy) on Julie's trail

1968

STOLEN KISSES

Stolen Kisses is quite simply a film that hopes to resemble a song

Christine (Claude Jade) and Antoine (Jean-Pierre Léaud)

At the end of *The 400 Blows* (1959), Antoine Doinel was running away from a reformatory and we left him at the edge of the sea on a beach in Normandy. In the episode for *Love at Twenty* (1962), we found him a stockboy at Philips, enrolled in the Jeunesses Musicales, and meeting his first love (Marie-France Pisier) at a concert. To get close to her he goes to live in the same street, in the building exactly opposite hers, but he succeeds only in annoying her and he becomes the protégé of the girl's parents, a sort of sponging cousin, the opposite of a happy lover.

In *Stolen Kisses,* we find Antoine Doinel five years later, finishing his military service and trying to get used to civilian life again. I asked my friends Claude de Givray and Bernard Revon to think up and write with me these new adventures of Antoine. We had decided that Antoine Doinel would do all sorts of jobs and find himself in a number of environments, but we wanted to avoid the drawbacks of the episodic film. It was while looking at the cover of a telephone book that the solution came to us: "Dubly Agency: investigations, shadowing, inquiries." In point of fact, the job of private detective, something much closer to life than that of a secret agent, offered us a framework into which we could cram all the ideas we had in mind. But fantasy, if it is not to bore the public with its overly arbitrary elements, must have a realistic point of departure. Which is why Claude de Givray and Bernard Revon spent a lot of time asking around at various hotels, emergency mechanics, shoe stores, garages, and most of all at the Dubly Agency, whose technical advice was invaluable to us.

Then, together, we built up the story like a chronicle, yet loosely enough to leave the last word to improvisation. In my last two films the choice of subject had scarcely encouraged improvisation. With *Fahrenheit 451* and *The Bride Wore Black* I had ended up being interested in abstractions, and I felt the need to return to the concrete, to the small happenings of life, even if I never lost sight of Renoir's very true saying: "Reality is always like a fairy tale."

In a film like *Stolen Kisses,* the characters take priority over the situations, the settings, the theme. They are more important than the construction, more important than everything, whence the importance of a good choice of actors. I feel more and more now the need for hiring intelligent actors for my films, even if I have them play roles in which that is not the chief characteristic. So I chose all the interpreters of *Stolen Kisses* a few days before shooting by going to the theater. That's how I got the Théâtre Antoine team, Delphine Seyrig and Michel Lonsdale; the trio from the Théâtre Moderne, Claude Jade, André Falcon, and Harry Max; a deserter from the play *La Puce à l'Oreille,* Daniel Ceccaldi; from the Théâtre Lutèce, Jacques Robiolles; and from the Théâtre de Paris, Jacques Rispal. Claire Duhamel came from the Centre Dramatique in Aix-en-Provence, François Darbon from the Athénée, Martine Ferrière from the Théâtre National Populaire, and the conjurer Delord from the Galerie 55!

But the pivot of the film, its raison d'être, is obviously Jean-Pierre Léaud. If from a film made with him people expect something telling about modern youth, they will be disappointed, because Jean-Pierre interests me precisely because of his anachronism and his romanticism: he is a nineteenth-century young man. As for myself, I am a nostalgic type, my inspiration is constantly turned toward the past. I have no antenna to tune in on what is modern, I function only through my sensations. That is why my films—and more particularly *Stolen Kisses*—are full of memories and make a real effort to revive memories of their youth in the people watching them.

When my films are finished, I realize that they are always sadder than I would have liked. This one, *Stolen Kisses,* I wanted to be funny. I don't know if it is, but in any case we ourselves had fun making it. When I began to make films—it's already ten years ago now—I thought at first that there were funny things and sad things. Then I tried to pass abruptly from a sad thing to a funny thing. Today what strikes me as most interesting is to work in such a way that the same thing can be funny and sad all at once. That is one of the reasons why I asked Charles Trenet's authorization to use as the title the two words, *baisers volés,* that he had used in his song "Que reste-t-il de nos amours," whose chorus is heard during the credits. I think Trenet is the one who has found the truest poetical equilibrium, who has best managed to mingle gravity and frivolity in his songs. *Stolen Kisses* is quite simply a film that hopes to resemble a song.

Press book for Stolen Kisses, *1968*

Antoine Doinel (Jean-Pierre Léaud) trying to readjust to civilian life

IF *STOLEN KISSES* IS A GOOD FILM IT WILL BE THANKS TO LANGLOIS

The joys of military service

I began shooting *Stolen Kisses* on Monday, February 5, and on February 9 I arrived on the set two hours late because I had just left the board meeting of the Cinémathèque in which Henri Langlois was replaced by Pierre Barbin. From then on, I led a double life of filmmaker and militant, making phone calls between every shot, giving interviews to the foreign radio stations to try to make up for the silence of the French radio, writing hasty and vengeful articles for *Combat,* and attending all the meetings of the defense committee, for which, having become treasurer, I had to endorse fifty or so checks from supporters every evening, even if I had to miss the projection of that day's rushes!

The film, I think, did not suffer because of all that, perhaps even the contrary. . . . The actors improvised their dialogue, everyone stood back somewhat from the film, which turned into a game played when there was time. Fortunately the principle of the screenplay lent itself to that state of mind, and in any case we quite quickly arrived at the slogan for this film dedicated to the Cinémathèque: "If *Stolen Kisses* is a good film it will be thanks to Langlois, and if it's bad it will be because of Barbin."

Interview by Gérard Langlois,
Lettres Françaises, *April 10, 1968*

The sergeant-major (François Darbon) comments on Antoine's military record

LIKE AN AMATEUR FILM

Compared with other films, let's say with adaptations of novels in general, Stolen Kisses *gives an impression of a very great freedom in construction, a little like an amateur film.*

Still and all, I believe *Stolen Kisses* hangs together only because of its craftsmanship. The screenplay is so slender. . . . If it had been my first film I think it wouldn't have stood up. In the direction there is a lot of trickery; while shooting, we constantly caught up with certain things, put together two or three elements, strengthened a scene in which nothing happened. . . .

That was improvisation then?

Improvisation, but with professional skill. But it's true the success of *Stolen Kisses* lies in its unpredictable aspect: one never knows what scene is going to follow the one on the screen. That success is due also, I believe, to the actors. Because of them, the curve of interest never sags. Here, after an hour of film, we have the chance to have Michel Lonsdale come on, a terrific character, and ten minutes later, his wife, Delphine Seyrig. The admirable interpretations of all those actors strengthened the line of interest.

So we began with almost nothing. For Jean-Pierre Léaud's various jobs I chose only occupations I had not practiced myself, because I wanted the autobiographical aspect to be very much masked over, very indirect: night watchman (I have always dreamed about that job because I think you would have time to read a lot), private detective (who, like a journalist, meets up with an enormous lot of people from different circles).

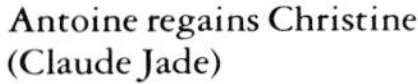

Antoine regains Christine (Claude Jade)

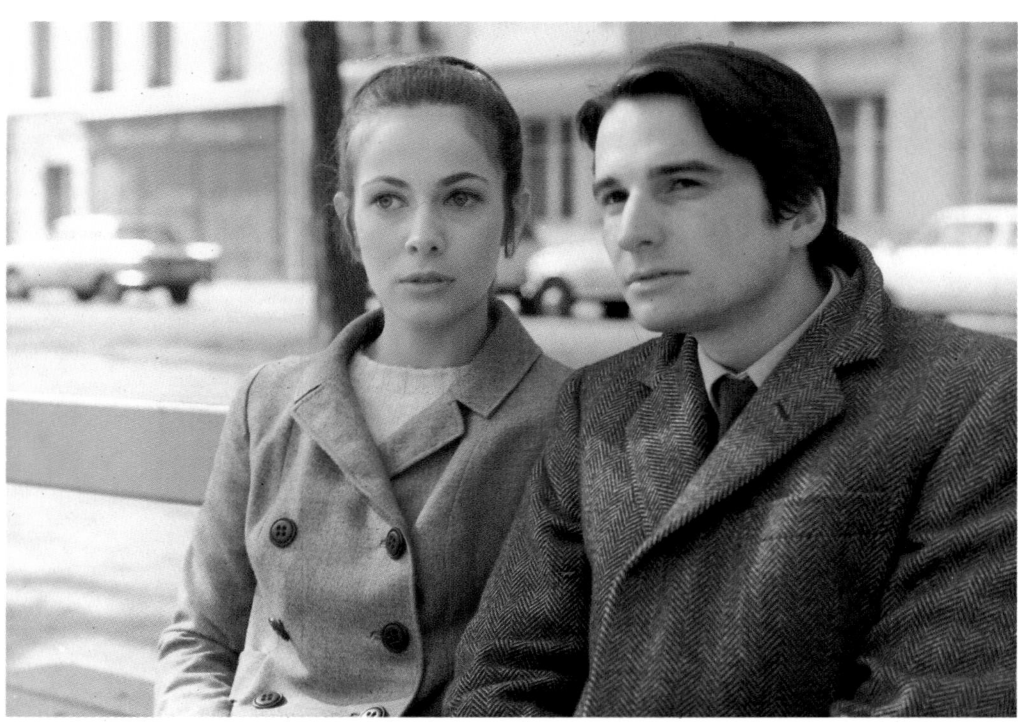

Then I had to make him encounter people. I had been very satisfied with Lonsdale in *The Bride,* and I put together for him the same sort of character: a guy detested by everyone and who doesn't know why (I absolutely didn't want a jealous husband asking that his wife be trailed). I then proceeded by cutting things out and by little touches one after the other, but I wasn't very proud of myself. What's strange, you see, is that, making *Stolen Kisses,* I seem to be expending the best of myself while waiting to make *Mississippi Mermaid* as a commercial concession. Well, the truth is, I filmed *Stolen Kisses* in order to make the money that would enable me to acquire the rights to adapt the *Mermaid!* In the course of filming I became more sure of myself. Perhaps it's the absence of a single, very evident goal for Jean-Pierre that has given the impression of a rich, teeming film, the themes all registering on their own, naturally.

Interview by Pierre Loubière and Gilbert Salachas,
Télé-Ciné, *no. 160, March 1970*

Right
The beautiful Madame Tabard (Delphine Seyrig)

Monsieur Henri (Harry Max) teaching Antoine Doinel the job of private detective

THE IDEAL WOULD BE TO HAVE ALWAYS AS MUCH GAIETY AS SADNESS

In my previous films I had from the start, in the screenplay, funny elements and sad elements. . . . For me, the ideal would be to have always as much gaiety as sadness, but I realized that, with the things improvisation introduces along the way, my films ended up in general sadder than foreseen. I think that *Jules and Jim* shouldn't have been so sad, nor *The 400 Blows.* That idea influenced me in *Stolen Kisses:* the screenplay was purely comic and the sad things got added in the shooting, so we arrived at the fifty-fifty dosage I had been trying for for so long.

Interview by Jean-Pierre Chartier,
"Cinéastes de Notre Temps," French radio, 1970

Dialogue in *Stolen Kisses* rewritten by Truffaut during the filming

1 (1

Madame D: Regarde qui est là..
Monsieur D: Antoine... ça fait plaisir de vous voir après tout ce temps... vous êtes en permission?
Antoine: Non non je suis réformé, mon engagement a été cassé..
Madame D: Vous avez dîné...
Antoine: Oui oui.. ne vous dérangez pas pour moi..
Monsieur: Non je suis sûr que vous n'avez pas dîné... ~~vous~~ asseyez-vous..
Madame: Christine va être désolée.. elle n'est pas là...
Monsieur: Heu... Vous n'êtes pas malade au moins.. on vous a donné une réforme provisoire?

CHARLES TRENET, MY FAVORITE SINGER

In *Combat,* thirty years ago, I read a very violent article against Charles Trenet: "That gentleman who was already around before the war with his carnation in his buttonhole. . . . There has been the war, millions of dead, but here he is, back on stage with his hat and his carnation in the buttonhole. . . ." That made me adore Charles Trenet, he's my favorite singer. . . . People stubbornly want everyone to change; me, I'm for the pig-headed guys. I like people who are faithful.

Interview by Danièle Heymann and Catherine Laporte,
L'Express, *March 13, 1978*

If I love Charles Trenet's songs, it's not only because they're the work of one and the same person—words and music—but also because it's impossible to guess if the music was composed before the words, or the contrary. Like John Ford's films, his songs make the old quarrel over form and content obsolete, because they are at one and the same time a form and a content.

One can't say: there is a vase and then there are flowers. The melodies are of an unbelievable simplicity, and yet it is really rare to confuse two tunes by Trenet (out of the four hundred we know). The words constantly give the impression of spontaneity, even if that's not the case, and I see, in all that way of being and of doing, something more than elegance, grace, lightness, something that resembles the peak of politeness; yes, for me, Charles Trenet is fantastically polite.

Since he has decided to make his farewell to the music hall, we shall go say goodbye to him often.

Le Point, *April 21, 1975*

François Truffaut at 37, between two takes of *Mississippi Mermaid*

MISSISSIPPI MERMAID

1969

The *Mermaid* is above all else the tale of a degradation through love, of a passion

I read *La Sirène du Mississippi* when I was doing the adaptation of *The Bride Wore Black*. At that time, I actually read everything William Irish wrote in order to steep myself in his work and to keep as close as possible to the novel, despite the unfaithfulness necessary in films. I like to know thoroughly any writer whose book I transpose to the screen. Thus, when I had to face an "Irish problem," I had good chances of finding an "Irish solution." I had proceeded in that manner with David Goodis for *Shoot the Piano Player* and with Ray Bradbury for *Fahrenheit 451*.

In *La Sirène,* I admired above all the distribution of incidents, the appearances, disappearances, and reappearances of the main characters. I therefore respected that construction in the film, and I tried to preserve all the proportions.

20 CIGARETTES
MAHÉ
AKWON-LAWSON-St-DENIS
RÉUNION
20 CIGARETTES

Louis Mahé, the chief character of *Mississippi Mermaid*, owns a tobacco factory on Réunion Island

Irish is one of those American writers who have been influenced by films. That influence appeared to me more tangible while I was adapting the *Mermaid* and was working with the book in hand as if it were already the screenplay. In the novel, Irish says of the detective that he had the most direct gaze that anyone ever met up with. That was the only indication I gave to the interpreter of the role, Michel Bouquet, and it was enough for him to build his character.

My final screenplay was less an adaptation in the traditional sense than a choice of scenes. With this film, I was finally able to realize every director's dream: to shoot in chronological order a chronological story that represents an itinerary.

And what is that itinerary?

Like the story, shooting began on Réunion Island, continued in Nice, Antibes, Aix-en-Provence, Lyons, to finish in the snow near Grenoble.

The fact of respecting the chronology permitted me to "build" the couple with precision. The story being at its source full of the romanticism of the last century, I thought that the sentimental journey of the novel (which we followed) had to be doubled by a physical journey. That means that at each stage the viewer must know exactly where the characters are in their physical relations as well as their sentimental relations. It is perhaps in this that the film, which might belong to the category of "love and adventure films," can be said to describe a couple of our day. The situation remains quite exceptional, but the characters are close to us.

Why did you pick Catherine Deneuve and Jean-Paul Belmondo?

Jean-Paul Belmondo is, with Jean-Pierre Léaud, my favorite actor, and as for Catherine Deneuve, it was impossible not to think of her. The fact is, her role as the *Mermaid* brings together various sides of her we have been able to see lately: for example, her romantic side in *Benjamin* and her "secret life" side in *Belle de Jour*. Then too, in a film linked with a certain American tradition, it was a good thing to have two actors of equal celebrity. But while I myself find the Deneuve-Belmondo couple superb, I certainly feel there exists in Paris a prejudice against stars and, even more, when they come in pairs. In New York the point of view is very different: I was there last year and when I spoke about the *Mermaid* to some American newspaper people, they said to me: "Catherine Deneuve and Jean-Paul Belmondo are charming, they're going to make a pretty little couple."

Finally, and because he is the most complete actor in Europe, Belmondo alternates in his career three characters: one who descends from Sganarelle, one who patterns himself after the heroes in American gangster films, and one who would be Gabin's son in *The Human Beast*. It's that third possibility that I asked him to explore by making use of his grave manner, which permits him to do love dialogues so well.

Because once again you have made a film about love?

Yes. But even if I have the reputation of making many love stories, here I felt very clearly that for the first time I was making a film about a couple. In the *Mermaid* there is

The cover of *Waltz into Darkness*, the novel on which *Mississippi Mermaid* is based.

no second man or second woman, and I could concentrate entirely on the intimacy of one couple: the shift from formal address as *vous* . . . to intimate use of *tu,* with dips back into *vous,* the confidences, the long silences, and what, through trials and setbacks, leads two people to make themselves indispensable to each other.

In *The Bride* there are five crimes and here only one. The *Mermaid* is above all else the tale of a degradation through love, of a passion. I think most of my films are built on the principle of a complication in which the protagonist, always weaker than his partner, gets caught. As usual, it's the heroine who takes the initiatives; as usual also, the story is, if not told outright by the hero, at least visibly lived through by him.

Why did you refer in your film to Johnny Guitar?

Because *Johnny Guitar* is a false Western, just as the *Mermaid* is a false adventure story. My taste leads me to pretend to submit to the laws of the Hollywood genres (melodramas, thrillers, comedies, etc.). Within a constraint of this type, I feel a great freedom of action throughout my filming. For example, during the shooting of this film, which was almost that of a superproduction, I could permit myself to write the dialogues for the next day every evening, in order to profit even more from the psychological advantages offered me by chronological shooting. The actors had just time enough to learn the texts they were handed at the last moment; their surprise then passed immediately into the scene and they could verify its intensity in observing the reactions of the technical crew, who were discovering the changing situations along with them.

In this profession you have to try to make progress, and in standing back and considering my most recent films, I had the impression that I had neglected a little the visual aspect, which is so much more grave now that color is almost obligatory. I have therefore forced myself to take more care with the photography, aided in this by the extraordinarily photogenic character of the sky on Réunion and by the sensitivity of my cameraman, Denys Clerval. Moreover, since *Jules and Jim,* I have never had such good conditions for filming, and it seems to me that for *Mermaid* the various talents all added up particularly well, whether it was Antoine Duhamel, the person responsible for the music, or Yves Saint-Laurent, to my knowledge the most film-loving of couturiers. Yves Saint-Laurent has a real grasp of what movie costumes need to be, and he has conceived them at one and the same time for movement and for stylization. That last little coat, whose making really worried me, became thanks to him a character in the film.

You have dedicated Mermaid *to Jean Renoir . . .*

Stolen Kisses was dedicated to Henri Langlois because I shot it during the Cinémathèque affair; this one goes to Renoir because, in my work of improvisation, it was of him that I was always thinking. With each difficulty I asked myself: "How would Renoir get out of this?" For I think a director doesn't ever have to feel alone if he knows well the thirty-five films by the author of *The Rules of the Game* and *Grand Illusion.*

Interview by Yvonne Baby,
Le Monde, *June 21, 1969*

The illusion of happiness: Jean-Paul Belmondo (Louis Mahé) and Catherine Deneuve (Marion)

The time of suspicion (Catherine Deneuve and Jean-Paul Belmondo)

WORKING WITH CATHERINE DENEUVE

I defy anyone to close William Irish's fine novel *La Sirène du Mississippi* without thinking: "Ah! Catherine Deneuve would be terrific in that role!"

Sure enough, in 1967 when the producers suggested I film *Mississippi Mermaid,* Catherine was the star they envisaged and everyone hoped for. I finally didn't come to terms with those producers because they wanted to hold on, by contract, to the right to change the film right up to its final editing. After our discussions broke off, the producers went to a lot of trouble to convince Catherine Deneuve to make *Mississippi Mermaid* with other, more "understanding" directors, and she refused, pretty courageously, because she was risking losing the role altogether.

Weeks passed and then months, options were dropped or changed hands, and I found myself the following year with the adaptation rights to *Mermaid* in my pocket: "Hello, Catherine? What will you be doing in January 1969?" In short, our initial failure to get together was followed by a rendezvous in mutual faith.

"The tale of a degradation through love, of a passion"

Catherine Deneuve's career rose steadily from *Belle de Jour* to *Benjamin* and from *Chamade* to *Mayerling,* all of it given a terrific kick-off by Jacques Demy with *The Umbrellas of Cherbourg.* Last year Catherine Deneuve was described in the American magazine *Look* as "the most beautiful woman in the world." Beautiful Catherine Deneuve is indeed, and to such an extent that a film of which she is the heroine could almost dispense with a story. I am convinced that the viewer is happy simply looking at Catherine, and that that contemplation is worth the price of the ticket! When you shoot scenes with her in the street, you are struck by the demonstrations of respect and sympathy she elicits. It is not uncommon that famous actresses have to put up with all sorts of insults from passers-by. That is never the case with her, and I suppose that apart from the sympathy she arouses, people never associate Catherine with the memory of a mediocre film and, thus, with an evening wasted.

To what can I compare Catherine? If you have to liken her to something, you shouldn't compare her to a flower or a bouquet, because there is a certain neutrality about her that leads me to compare her instead with the vase into which all kinds of flowers can be put. Her behavior, her allure, her reserve permit the viewers to project onto her face whatever feelings they themselves would like to imagine. Despite her rather romantic and frail appearance, Catherine has the utter naturalness of girls born after the war, the same imperturbable side to her, and a modesty which, in her work, makes her never give herself over entirely. That reserve makes you dream, heightens the mystery, and permits the viewers themselves to "fill the vase."

Catherine adds a note of ambiguity to any and every situation, to every script, because she gives the impression of holding back a great number of secret thoughts that can be guessed at in the background; then little by little they become the main point and create the whole atmosphere of the film. That impression of a "double life" perhaps comes also from a kind of severity you sense in her gaze. If Catherine's face is very sweet, her gaze is sometimes quite hard: it judges, and then it expresses great lucidity.

From that point of view, her most exemplary film is *Belle de Jour.* In it she plays her role a little differently from what Buñuel expected. Not that she went against his directions, but she kept herself just this side of the situations he wanted to put her into. She got around anything risqué, kept it down to mere suggestion, at the most, sketched it in. I am convinced that her holding back that way—something dictated by an excess of modesty rather than by artistic reasons—contributed notably to the film's success. With a more exhibitionistic actress or one who let herself go more easily, *Belle de Jour* would have been less spellbinding. All the women watching it went along with her, full of emotion, to those curious afternoon rendezvous. . . .

Greta Garbo? I don't go in much for comparing Catherine with Greta Garbo; I have never "read" secret thoughts in Garbo's face, but Catherine is, like her, a "slow-motion" actress. Certain actresses move too much and upset the rhythm of the film. Catherine instead is slow; sometimes I asked her to liven up more, but generally I appreciated her tranquility, which gave each scene its own density. Note that the majority of actresses who have been elevated to myth are hieratic actresses like Greta Garbo, Marlene Dietrich, Carole Lombard, Grace Kelly, and not the frenetic actresses, of whom some can nonetheless be wonderful, like Kay Kendall or Paula Prentiss, whose names are scarcely known to the public. Julie Christie, with whom I've worked, hardly ever stands still, and she hides behind her hair because she's so afraid of being found out. She gets around that difficulty by adopting the point of view of the person observing her. If, as Louis-Ferdinand Céline thought, people are divided into voyeurs and exhibitionists, Catherine is a *voyeuse* and, because of that, she gets closer to life than most actresses who preceded her.

The detective Comolli (Michel Bouquet) and Mahé (Jean-Paul Belmondo)

We will never again see, in today's films, a man who goes "cockadoodledoo" as in *The Blue Angel,* a man who gets down on all fours to sit up and beg as in *Nana,* women who are altogether bitches or altogether victims, as in prewar films. From now on, if the roles that film directors offer actresses are less beautiful, they are more true and get further away from the theater.

Catherine Deneuve is an actress who is straight "cinema." She has a sure sense of interest in everything to do with her physical appearance, and she never makes a blunder in taste when it comes to hairdo, makeup, clothes. That's why so many women copy her way of dressing and doing her hair. However, she doesn't always have a sense of what's best for her as regards the character she is playing. She can say the key sentence in a scene with her back turned and walking away from the camera. It is the most difficult physical scenes—like changes of voice, a real rage, a fit of hysterics—that she does best, as we saw in *Repulsion* and in *Mississippi Mermaid.*

I had formed a certain idea of Catherine Deneuve before shooting *Mississippi Mermaid.* I imagined that she had an exaggerated idea of what was in her own interest as an actress and that it took precedence over the film. I suspected her of being a perfectionist and therefore forever disappointed. I did not think she was won over to the film in advance, and because of that I mistrusted her a little. I thought she would be too preoccupied with details, and that she would often demand explanations, justifications. In short, despite my desire to make a film with her, I set out on this film with certain reservations which she guessed right away. While she was making *April Fools* in America, I wrote to her in Hollywood and sent her more or less sneaky warnings like: "In my films we work in good humor," or "It is forbidden to think that we will make a masterpiece; we will try to make a living film."

The last refuge: a chalet in the Alps

Because of that, in the first days of shooting, we were both on guard. Then I discovered soon enough that we were thinking the same thing and were in agreement right down the line.

Catherine, in reality, does not fuss over questions of detail. She sees things in the broad view and never quibbles. In fact she calculates very little and prefers to let herself go. She possesses a very strong instinct that whispers to her that, in some venture, she will be very much at ease and, in some other, unhappy. She is very little the actress in real life. She possesses also a decency that I appreciate a lot. Nothing that happens to her astonishes her, her successes please her but don't bowl her over. This is a feminine quality that actually underlines women's superiority over men. Men tend to believe too much in their own merits, they twist and squirm like monkeys on the rungs of the social ladder, while women know it's chiefly a matter of luck. They're not vain about their talent. For a woman, only happiness matters. All the rest is a laughing matter. Catherine is like that.

Unifrance Film, *1969*

LETTER TO ROBERT HAKIM

Paris, November 16, 1966

My dear Robert,

Well, I did go to see Jean-Paul Belmondo this morning and we talked a long time about *Mississippi Mermaid.*

He very much liked the novel, the characters, and the story.

The only reservation he wished to express to me concerned the character's age, which is in fact rather more in the book. I think I managed to reassure him completely on that point, explaining to him how I saw things, and so he expressed his desire to make this film with me. I told him how very important it is that shooting begin in January or in any case before February 15, and that seemed to suit him.

Having mentioned several details in the book, I could see for myself that Jean-Paul had read it very thoroughly. I told him the adaptation would follow the book quite closely, and he manifested no wish to subordinate his agreement to an examination of the screenplay, which would in any case be materially impossible because preparation for shooting has to begin in two weeks and I expect to write the major part of the dialogue as we go along in the shooting, as I have almost always done in my films in French.

I've been wanting to make a film with Jean-Paul Belmondo for a long time now, and I believe the wish is mutual. That's why I'm persuaded that everything will go well if you can come to an understanding with him on the material questions.

I will phone you tomorrow to hear the news, and I beg you to believe me yours faithfully.

JEAN-PAUL'S GRAVITY

We had never had occasion to work together, but I had known Jean-Paul for several years. In the course of a trip to Brazil in 1962 we had planned to work together, on Audiberti's novel *Monorail* or on Bradbury's *Fahrenheit 451,* but things worked out differently.

For my part, I have no doubt that Jean-Paul Belmondo is the best young male lead of the day, the best and the most complete. Belmondo can act with the same verisimilitude an aristocrat or a common man, an intellectual or a gangster, a priest or a clown. That versatility is such that Jean-Paul could even play a man whom women love, a seducer, or on the contrary a man they turn down, and he would be capable of carrying those two contradictory roles either toward drama or toward comedy on request.

His voice—superb, not in the least "Comédie-Française" but clear, low, and natural—permits him to speak ultimately sad dialogue without ever becoming boring or banal. In *Mississippi Mermaid* it is precisely Jean-Paul's gravity that interests me most, that gravity which never slides over into heaviness and which gives the full weight of intensity to the feelings to be expressed. Belmondo has an admirable gift for making himself listened to, looked at; like Jean-Pierre Léaud, he is always interesting. Those two are my favorite actors. I like to think of them while writing dialogue, I am never disappointed when they speak it, and evenings after work I find myself thinking that, because of them, the film is coming out better than the script. That is the best stimulant, the real criterion.

"A Propos de Jean-Paul Belmondo," press book for Mississippi Mermaid, *1969*

Truffaut with Catherine Deneuve and Jean-Paul Belmondo

"If I were blind, I'd pass my time caressing your face."

THE LOVE SCENE IN FRONT OF THE FIRE

HE: If I ask you questions, will you answer?

SHE: Yes.

HE: You've loved a lot of guys?

SHE: Yes.

HE: Why did you break up?

SHE: Sometimes I walked out, other times it was they who walked out.

HE: You never had children?

SHE: No, but . . .

HE: You almost did?

SHE: Yes, but I didn't want any, no . . .

HE: Several times?

SHE: Yes.

HE: Was it sad?

SHE: Sad and deplorable. It doesn't always end up well, and sometimes I would say to myself I would never make love again, that I wouldn't let anyone else touch me, and then one forgets . . . luckily!

(*A silence falls between them.*)

SHE: Ask me some more questions.

HE: No.

SHE: You, you're more serious than me, and then too you haven't suffered . . . well, not the same way. You've loved girls?

HE: Only one.

SHE: Only one; then it was important. How old was she?

HE: Twenty-three, and I twenty-six.

SHE: It didn't work out . . . Why? Surely you wanted to marry her, and she didn't want to?

HE: Listen, we're going to talk about something else. The person is dead . . . That's why afterwards I couldn't go out with other girls, so I had that idea of looking for a wife by correspondence . . .

SHE: Obviously . . . That girl you were in love with, it's easy to see she was better than me . . .

HE: She was different . . . We said we were going to talk about something else . . . Don't be sad . . . Tomorrow we have to go to the dressmaker's for your dress.

SHE: I don't want that dress anymore . . .

HE: Don't be like that, you wanted that dress and anyway it's been ordered, so we'll go.

SHE: It was for you I wanted to dress myself up, to please you better, so that you would want me all the time . . . And then now . . . at this moment . . .

HE: That doesn't matter, I told you so, I want you to be pretty . . . Well, even more . . . Yes, I know you don't like me to tell you you're pretty, you think I'm exaggerating. Wait, I'll explain it to you, wait . . .

SHE: I'm waiting for you.

HE: You'll see. I'm not going to talk to you anymore about your beauty and, if you prefer, I'm even willing to say you're a mess; I'm going to describe you as if you were a photo or a painting . . . Be quiet . . . Your face . . . Your face is a landscape; you see, I'm being neutral and impartial . . . Yes, a landscape. To start with, there are the two eyes, they are two little lakes . . . brown . . .

SHE: Greenish brown . . .

HE: Two little greenish brown lakes, the forehead is a plain, and the nose . . . There . . . It's a little mountain . . . Little. The mouth is a volcano . . . Open up a little because I like to see the teeth . . . No, not so much . . . Just a little . . . There . . . When you're bad, do you know what comes out of your mouth? Toads, nothing less, and necklaces of pearls when you're nice. Wait . . .

SHE: I'm waiting.

HE: Let's say something about your smile now . . . Let me see it . . . No, that one's not the stupendous one, that's the one you wear in the street or in the shops, give me the other one, your true smile, that of happiness . . . There . . . Terrific . . .

No, that's too much . . . It hurts my eyes to look at you . . . (*He closes his eyes.*) Wait . . . Wait . . .

SHE: I'm waiting.

HE: I've got my eyes closed and yet I see you perfectly . . . I'm checking now . . . If I were blind, I'd pass my time caressing your face . . . Like this . . . Your body too . . . And then, if I were deaf, I'd learn to read your lips with my fingers . . . Like this.

(*She leans toward him, she puts her head on his shoulder, she snuggles close.*)

HE: Even if all this has to end badly, I am delighted to make your acquaintance, Madame.

From the screenplay

1970

THE WILD CHILD

From this experience I don't retain the impression of having played a role, but simply of having directed the film "in front of" the camera

I waited three years to make *The Wild Child.* I had read in *Le Monde* in 1966 a review of a thesis by Lucien Malson on "wild children," children who were deprived from the start of all contacts with human beings and who, for one reason or another, grew up in isolation. Among the fifty-two "serious" cases Lucien Malson cited, between the wolf-child of Hesse (1344) and little Yves Cheneau of Saint-Brévin . . . , the clearest and most instructive example of isolation seems to have been that of Victor de l'Aveyron, studied at length and minutely by Doctor Jean Itard, who became interested in the boy immediately after his capture by hunters in the middle of a forest in the summer of 1798.

The "savage" was hirsute and moved like an animal, sometimes on all fours, sometimes standing. Naturally he lived entirely naked, his body was covered with scars, he had nails like claws and expressed himself only in grunts and growls. In the forest he ate only chestnuts, acorns, and roots, and it was thought that he must have spent seven or eight years in total solitude, from the moment of his abandonment to that of his capture. The wounds that Victor de l'Aveyron (the name given him) had on his body were traces of struggle, probably bites from fighting with animals, but on his throat, near the tracheal artery, a deeper scar than the others seems to have been made by a knife cut. He was perhaps a child someone wanted to kill, to get rid of, when he was three or four years old, and who was abandoned in the forest in the belief that he was already dead. It is supposed that dust and leaves stuck to the wound, and so it healed by itself. The truth, however, is that all this is hypothesis, because the mystery of how and why the wild child of the Aveyron was abandoned has never been explained.

Victor de l'Aveyron (Jean-Pierre Cargol) in the forest before he comes under Dr. Itard's care

At the start of the film, Victor walks on all fours

Transferred to the gendarmerie at Rodez, the "wild child" rapidly became such an object of public curiosity that he was spoken of in the newspapers of the time, in the gazettes, for example *Le Journal des Débats,* and so, quite soon, the Parisian scientists asked to examine him. He was therefore transferred from the Rodez gendarmerie to the institute for the deaf-and-dumb in Paris, the Institut des Sourds-Muets, a large building that still stands on Rue Saint-Jacques. The doctors who examined the "wild child" in Paris thought that he was feeble-minded or an idiot, that that was why he had been abandoned, and that it was no use bothering with him. According to them, he should be sent to Bicêtre with the madmen and incurables. That was not the opinion of Jean Itard, a young doctor engaged in research on deafness. He thought that the wild boy of Aveyron was deserving of education, and he asked to be allowed to take charge of him in his own house near Paris. He thereupon undertook to educate Victor by inventing and utilizing all sorts of procedures still used today to reeducate deaf-mutes or retarded children.

This film subject corresponded to themes of interest to me, and now I can see that *The Wild Child* has something of both *The 400 Blows* and *Fahrenheit 451.* In *The 400 Blows* I showed a child who lacks for love and who is growing up without tenderness. In *Fahrenheit 451* it's a grown man who lacks for books, that is, culture. With Victor de l'Aveyron, the "lack" is even more deep-rooted: it is language itself. These three films are therefore based on a major frustration. Even in my other films, I have tried to describe characters who are outside society: they don't refuse society, society refuses them.

When I set about writing the screenplay of *The Wild Child* with my friend Jean Gruault, the main difficulty was in transposing a text actually consisting of two reports drawn up by Dr. Jean Itard. The first, dated 1801, was probably intended for the Académie de Médecine; the second, written in 1806, was designed to convince the Ministry of the Interior to renew the pension of Madame Guérin, the child's caretaker. To extract a screenplay from those two texts, we imagined that Dr. Itard, instead of writing these reports, had kept a daily diary. This gives the story the allure of a personal chronicle and preserves the author's style, which

The Gendarmerie transfers the Wild Child to the Institute for Deaf-Mutes in Paris

"He is settled on a large branch, a bit curled up like a cat in its lair" (from the screenplay)

is simultaneously scientific, philosophical, moralistic, humanistic, in turns lyrical and familiar. In this way I remained faithful to Dr. Itard's reports, whose style I liked very much and which I reread repeatedly in the course of shooting so as to salvage one idea or another or simply also to steep myself in them.

I collected some documents, but not systematically. I simply read a few works on deaf-mutes as well as Maria Montessori's book. I am always afraid that an excess of documentation might make me drop an idea, by making the subject appear too vast; I like to limit myself from the start. To begin with, the film had to be kept to an hour and thirty minutes, though obviously, in treating such a subject, one could go on piling up details for a full three hours of projection.

Nor did I want to call in a medical consultant during the shooting; I didn't want anyone to prevent me from doing certain things. I was satisfied just to get particular bits of information, sometimes even in the course of shooting. For example, having to manipulate tuning forks, I didn't want to use them just any old way. I invited an "eye and ear" specialist to dinner, and he gave me two or three precise instructions on the question. With that to go on, I was able to improvise two short scenes on ear training that I could not have thought up without that information, but I didn't want anything more systematic when it came to technical advice.

Before shooting, I had several medical films on autistic children run for me, and I realized that there exists a very great variety of behaviors: you have children who are very sweet, very slow, who do something heartrending, who tap on a table all day long; you have others who are very frenetic; you have others whose gaze is really that of an animal and others whose gaze is directed nowhere. You have some who live in slow motion. So I thought I had every right to invent.

The film includes a series of exercises that Itard has the child do in order to educate his ear, his eye, his senses. Evidently you have a documentary aspect there, and our working criterion was consequently the same as for a documentary: is it clear? Is it understandable? The public had to be able to follow those exercises, to know from the start of each exercise just what Dr. Itard is trying to get from the child, so as to follow its progress straight through and with unflagging interest. I applied myself rigorously to this, with the help of an off-screen commentary in which Jean Itard keeps up his diary.

Now I come to the choice of actors. *The Wild Child* is a two-character film. It seemed to me that the essential job in this film was not to manage the action but to concern oneself with the child. I therefore wanted to play the role of Dr. Itard myself in order to deal with him myself and thus avoid going through an intermediary. But I didn't come to that decision right away, and the choice of the actor began by causing me some headaches.

At first I thought of movie actors, then of television actors, but it occurred to me that people would be bothered by having seen them before: the European cinema demands more in the way of plausibility than the American. Dr.

Itard existed: he was one of the pioneers of otorhinolaryngology, a man not famous like Pasteur but nonetheless known, perhaps more in America than in France. The film itself has a quite strong savor of authenticity, because it is a true story scarcely at all fictionalized.

Generally for a film of that kind one hires little-known actors. So I looked for an unknown for the role of the doctor, especially among journalists, then among my friends. Then, given that the child never speaks because he is, to all intents and purposes, a deaf-mute and that he has to be directed by and in images, I came to realize that I had to try to do it myself.

I don't know if I was right or not to act, I don't know if I am a good actor or a bad actor, but I don't regret my decision: I feel that if I had turned over the role of Dr. Itard to an actor this would have been, of all my films, the one that gave me the least satisfaction, because I would have had no more than a technical job. I would have been saying all day to some gentleman: "Now take the child, make him do that, lead him there," and that was what I wanted to do on my own. I am glad I did it myself. From the day I decided to play Itard the film took on for me a truly complete and definitive raison d'être.

From this experience I don't retain the impression of having played a role, but simply of having directed the film "in front of" the camera and not "behind," as usual.

As for the choice of the boy for the principal role, I thought of two kinds of children: at first of extremely well-educated children, sons of famous dancers or boys attending the dance classes at the Opéra. What had led me to that idea was seeing photos of Nureyev. I often think of Nureyev as someone who would be terrific in a film where he wouldn't be a dancer but some sort of savage.

So I started off with the idea of finding a child Nureyev, and then I dropped that idea because the little dancers I saw were really just too sweet. In the next phase, I went to the opposite idea, which was to go back a little to *The Mischief Makers,* my first film, where I directed five boys from Nîmes, of whom one or two really had something savage about them. Now, of course, they were married and fathers of families, because I had filmed *The Mischief Makers* back in 1957. But I should have liked to find a little boy along those lines. I sent my assistant to watch when school let out, at Arles, Nîmes, Marseilles, etc. It was in a street in Montpellier that she noticed, questioned, and photographed among others a little gypsy boy, Jean-Pierre Cargol.

Jean-Pierre, the little gypsy I finally chose to play the role, is a very handsome child, but I think he really does look as if he just came out of the woods. The role of Victor is a role that might seem difficult for a child. To direct Jean-Pierre, I was always looking for comparisons. For the eyes I would say to him: "like a horse." I mimed Harpo Marx for him when he had to express the idea of amazement with round eyes. But nervous laughs or sickly laughs were difficult for him because he's a very gentle child, very happy and well balanced, who could only do quiet things. The difficult scenes such as the nosebleeds and hysterics were only sketched out. We stopped quite quickly. We avoided anything spectacular: in this film what matters is not to frighten or impress people, but to tell the story.

In that connection, I know that making a child act in the films or theater generally has a bad reputation. Personally I don't at all believe that children's personalities are massacred when they become actors. On the contrary. And anyway, they are now very well protected by quite severe rules governing their employment. A commission studies the script, doctors examine the child, the director of the school has his say. The "case" goes before a commission of the prefecture. The parents pocket no more than twenty percent of the child's pay, the rest being deposited in a savings account. If the film is made during the school period, a teacher has to take care of educating him, etc. In the particular case of *The Wild Child,* the commission decided, moreover, to make the film a test case for several reasons: it is a film in which the child does nothing shocking, he is not mixed up in gangster stories or sex stories; he was filming with a team that had the reputation of taking good care of children. I had chosen to shoot the film in July and August precisely so as not to disrupt the schooling of the child chosen. Naturally it's a tiring role, so he had to pass more searching psychological tests than usual. Then, when the film was finished, we saw that the cinema had done a lot for his development. To my mind, the difference between Jean-Pierre Cargol before and after the filming is astounding.

The film crew gave him a little 8-mm camera at the end of the shooting, and he said: "I will be the first gypsy director."

At the start of the film, Victor walks on all fours, he can't manage to stand, he can't bear clothes, he eats like an animal. He starts with nothing and little by little comes to adapt himself. Because he never became a normal man, a man like others, it can be argued that

Right
Dr. Itard (François Truffaut) personally takes Victor in his charge at his house near Paris, with the aid of his housekeeper Mme Guérin (Françoise Seigner)

Far right
"The stage of the mirror": Jean Dasté (M. Pinel), Jean-Pierre Cargol, and François Truffaut

Educating Victor: "Thanks to Jean Itard, Victor made very great progress in his behavior."

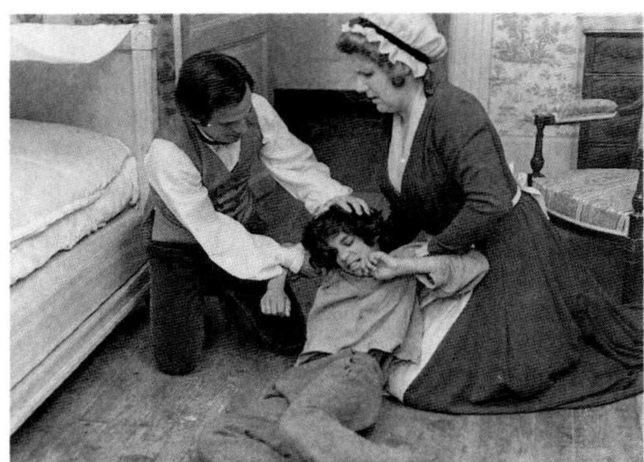

"I remained faithful to Dr. Itard's reports, whose style I liked very much."

"The light, where everything takes place"

it would have been better to leave him in the forest. I think however, like Itard, that the life he was living was miserable, and the fifteen or so scar marks on his body are proof that he had to fight and perhaps even kill to survive.

Thanks to Jean Itard, Victor made very great progress in his behavior. He came to walk normally, he put up with clothing, he could do certain jobs and render small services, but he never succeeded in speaking, because, of all the vital functions, the use of speech is the most profoundly tied up with earliest childhood.

It was Jean Itard who chose the name of Victor for the "wild boy," because he had noticed that the child was particularly sensitive to the sound "O" and that he never failed to turn around when he heard it spoken behind him.

I think that the strength of this story lies in the situation. The child has grown outside civilization, so much so that everything he does in the film he does for the first time: when he consents to sleep in a bed, it is for the first time; when he wears clothes, it's for the first time; when he eats at table, it's the first time. He sneezes for the first time, he weeps for the first time. To my mind, each step forward already constitutes a terrific piece of luck, and the film draws its force from the accumulation of all those forward steps.

People may wish to know the end of the true story, which the film doesn't tell: Victor lived to the age of forty, always in the care of Madame Guérin, Jean Itard's housekeeper, in a little house on the Rue des Feuillantines, which was an annex to the Institut des Sourds-Muets, doing little jobs and living in peace.

As for the moral of the story, Malson's study insists on it and I think the film brings it out: what is natural comes to us as a heritage, but what is cultural can come only through education. Whence the importance of that education and the beauty of this theme.

"Comment J'ai Tourné L'Enfant Sauvage," *in* L'Avant-Scène du Cinéma, *no. 107, October 1970*

FOR THE FIRST TIME I IDENTIFIED WITH THE ADULT, WITH THE FATHER

Opposite
"I felt it was a more important role than the director's."

One senses—you will tell me if it is so—that in a way you come full circle with The 400 Blows *and* The Wild Child.

Probably yes. I wasn't aware of it while doing it, but it's a film that responds, ten years later, to *The 400 Blows*. We have on the screen, as we said a while back, someone who lacks something essential, but this time some people are going to try to help. It's a true story down to its slightest details. Only, the choice of this story is more revealing than I myself thought, and I realized it afterwards: while I was shooting the film, I relived a little the shooting of *The 400 Blows* during which I initiated Jean-Pierre Léaud into the cinema, during which I taught him what cinema basically is. And so the decision to play the role of Dr. Itard myself was a profounder choice than I thought at the time. I saw it at first as a practical convenience, because I didn't want to hire a star. I would in any case have taken a little-known actor, but that little-known actor would have considered it a big chance for him to play Dr. Itard, so he would never have consented to take a back seat to the child, he would have pushed him aside so as to be seen better himself. I don't know . . . I felt it was a more important role than the director's, because Dr. Itard maneuvered that child and I wanted to do that myself, but it's probable that it all had deeper meanings. Until *The Wild Child,* when I had had children in my films I identified with them, and here, for the first time, I identified with the adult, the father, so much so that when the editing was finished I dedicated the film to Jean-Pierre Léaud because that changeover, that shift, became completely clear for me, obvious. It is a film whose significance was brought home to me from the outside, by friends, by people who spoke to me about the film.

Interview by Aline Desjardins, Radio-Canada, 1971

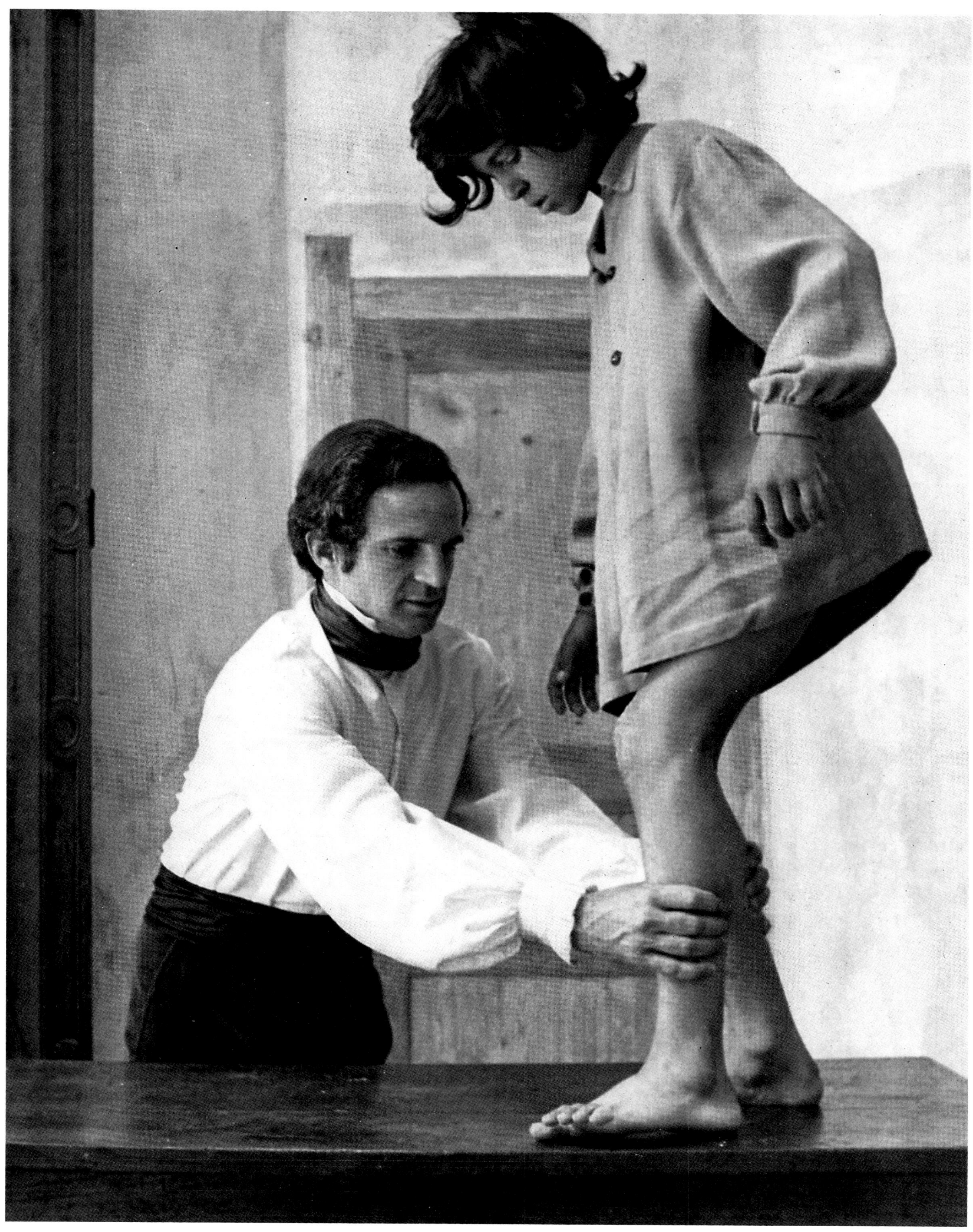

NNNN ZCZC PSW948
FRPA HL UWNX 063
BEL AIR CALIF 63 29 210P

LT
FRANCOIS TRUFFAUT
NUMBER 5 RUE ROBERTESTISNNE PARIS8 (VIA WUI)

MON CHER FRANCOIS
JAI VISIONE LENFAND SAUVAGE QUE JE TROUVE MAGNIFIQUE JE TE
PRIE DE MENVOYER UN AUTOGAPH DE ACTEUR QUI JOUE LE DOCTEUR
IL EST FORMIDABLE JE DESIRE CET AUTOGRAPH POUR ALMA HITCHCOCK
FES YEUX ETAIENG INONDES DE LAMES CE FILM

CFM 5 8

PAGE 2/13

DIT ELLE EST LE MIELLEUR DE TOUS CHEUX CE TRUFFAUD AFFECTION
PROFONDE

HITCHCOCK

Telegram of congratulations from Alfred Hitchcock

At the Institute for Deaf-Mutes in Paris, before Dr. Itard takes charge of him, Victor is treated like some curious beast

1970

BED AND BOARD

I classify myself in that family of directors for whom the cinema is a prolongation of youth

"DOMICILE CONJUGAL"

Notes (dictées par F.T.) pour servir à

~~Note pour~~ l'établissement du premier script de Domicile Conjugal. (à l'intention de Claude de Givray et Bernard Revon).

1er ACTE - Ils sont mariés !

1/ - Nous éviterons une exposition au sens traditionnel du mot, c'est-à-dire ~~au sens~~ (documentaire et) anti-dramatique. Nous chercherons ~~au contraire~~ plutot à faire savoir au public d'une façon amusante :

a) que ~~Jean-Pierre~~ Antoine est marié;

b) que son métier consiste à teindre des fleurs.

2/ - ~~Claude Jade~~ Christine donne des cours de violon soit à domicile, soit au domicile conjugal (il ne s'agit pas de choisir, mais de prendre les avantages des deux situations si nous en avons besoin).

First difference from *Stolen Kisses:* in this new film Claude Jade plays a role which is not really her type. Moreover, I had asked her as well as Jean-Pierre Léaud to act as "adults": I wanted her to look twenty-five and to dominate her husband. You know one never works really well with actors before a second film! It was when I saw *Stolen Kisses* again that I recognized an error I had made in not giving Claude Jade sufficient guidance: during his military service the relations between Doinel and Christine had changed, and Doinel then says something abominable to her that makes her leave him: "Love goes along with admiration, and I just don't admire you." Claude Jade, it appears, had not quite got the point of the scene and, taking that phrase as harmless talk, she didn't flinch when she heard it. It was because of that error that I decided to control everything she had to say phrase by phrase, because, for her to be indulgent, as she is in *Bed and Board,* one has to suppose she has a formidable superiority! . . . And because she is well brought up, her words have to be chosen carefully. For example, the scene on the staircase where she says of her virginity: "Virgin at twenty! . . . A real creep. A living anachronism!" There you have a first, very free feeling for language, and then a second, more "educated."

All such choices are in the end negative choices, that is to say, obtained by elimination, of unpleasant situations for example. To avoid dragging Doinel into a tale of bourgeois adultery, I didn't have the luck, as in *Stolen Kisses,* of being able to count on a Delphine Seyrig, at one and the same time a fairy-tale personage and an adolescent's dream woman. So I looked for her equivalent in exoticism. But choosing a Japanese woman—which would have inspired a lot of American scriptwriters—I had to avoid cliché. That's why, after having introduced her in a kimono, I preferred showing her very soon in Western dress. With a Japanese I spared myself also overdoing words and conversations, rendered impossible by the obstacle of the language. Thus I could tell a love story quite swiftly with a maximum of idealization and, subsequently, the maximum of disillusion for the partners.

I have always been afraid of the second halves of films. The viewer has accepted many things in the first half hour, where one can

Antoine (Jean-Pierre Léaud) dyes flowers for a living

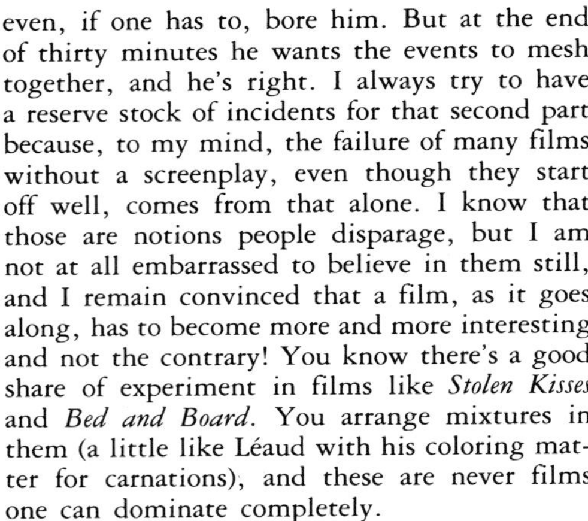

even, if one has to, bore him. But at the end of thirty minutes he wants the events to mesh together, and he's right. I always try to have a reserve stock of incidents for that second part because, to my mind, the failure of many films without a screenplay, even though they start off well, comes from that alone. I know that those are notions people disparage, but I am not at all embarrassed to believe in them still, and I remain convinced that a film, as it goes along, has to become more and more interesting and not the contrary! You know there's a good share of experiment in films like *Stolen Kisses* and *Bed and Board.* You arrange mixtures in them (a little like Léaud with his coloring matter for carnations), and these are never films one can dominate completely.

Interview by Gérard Langlois,
Cinéma Pratique, *nos. 103–4, 1970*

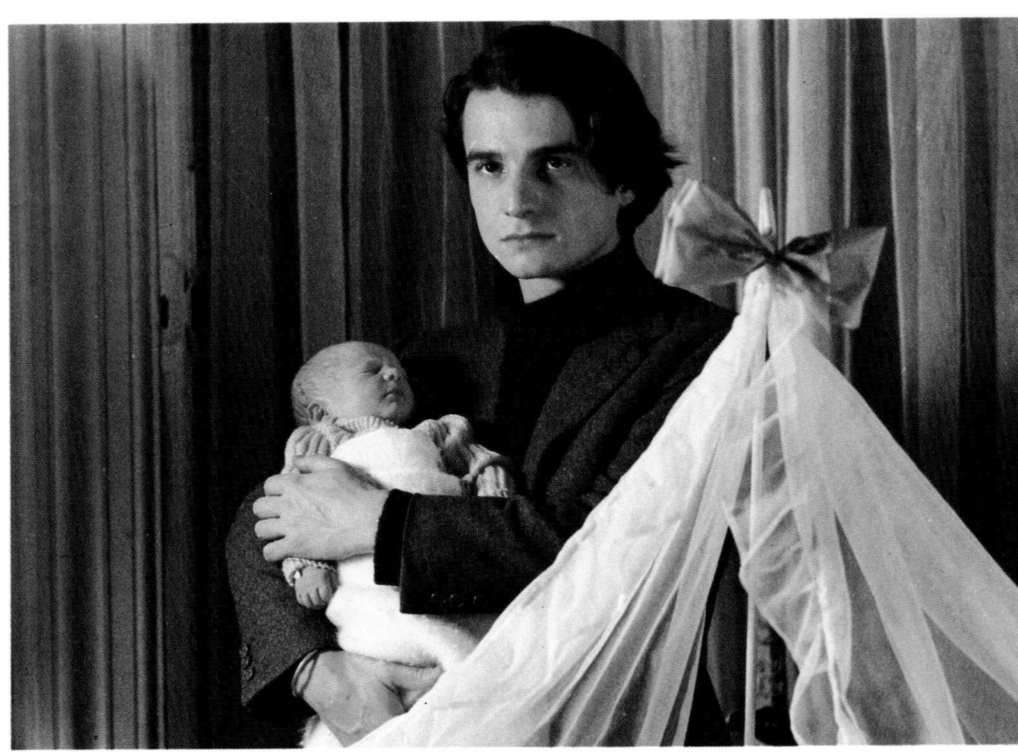

Jean-Pierre Léaud holding the "newborn Alphonse Doinel" in his arms: publicity photo for *Bed and Board*

I'M DONE WITH DOINEL

The critics, and perhaps also the public, persist in making a distinction between the "intimist" Truffaut of the Doinel cycle and the "novelistic" Truffaut, who adapts Goodis, Bradbury, Irish; between the Truffaut influenced by Renoir or Rossellini and the one who takes Hitchcock as a model . . .

That misunderstanding is not serious, but it comes about because the critics don't see, in *Stolen Kisses,* what comes from *The Bride* or was possible for me thanks to *Fahrenheit,* and because they too often look at influences from outside, comparing or differentiating the subjects although it's obviously on the style that influences are truly exerted. Take the example of Hitchcock: I know that his lesson is as present in *The Wild Child* as in *The Bride,* because if the material of *The Wild Child* is very remote from Hitchcock, by deciding to place a commentary at the start or the end of a scene, to end a phrase by one word rather than another,

On the set of *Bed and Board* with Claude Jade

I am doing nothing more than applying the laws of that science of which he is the master and which consists of making yourself really listened to. I constantly think of that film *Dial M for Murder,* which is not a major item in his production because it's a play filmed almost as it was, but which I consider as one of the strongest examples of authority in the cinema: how to make people listen to a text that is neither poetic nor full of feeling, whose aim is purely informative, utilitarian, and that would be just chatter if filmed otherwise by other directors! There is a secret there which I try never to lose sight of and which perhaps explains in part why such an unrewarding subject as *The Wild Child* could interest the public. In addition, for the past few years I have been influenced by Lubitsch, whose very special twist of mind fascinates me, the more so since he has been gradually forgotten after having exerted an enormous influence at the time, on Leo McCarey certainly, in another way on Hitchcock, and in yet another way on the old films about marriage by Ingmar Bergman! This consists in arriving at things roundabout, in asking oneself: "Given that you have a particular situation to get across to the public, what will be the most indirect, most intriguing way of presenting it?" This roundabout way of working (which is also Hitchcock's, but directed toward malaise, suspense, toward the problem of how to make a scene dramatic) is what showed me in *Bed and Board* how to treat the intrigue with the Japanese girl: the idea of the flowers to make the wife discover the truth, then the disguise as a Japanese, which permitted me to avoid the outburst of a family quarrel and not to drop back into the sordid moments of *The Soft Skin*. But for that last sequence we knew that the big moment comes when Doinel opens the door and sees his wife as a Japanese, that after that the scene was not interesting to carry further, or rather that it would be, but in the spirit of the American comedy of the thirties, showing the wife serving the meal in Japanese fashion and his not knowing what to do or say. But I think that would ring false today, because the public has a greater need of plausibility. I found myself stuck at that point, and I had to end very quickly with the only thing that could come as a surprise at that moment: the tears of little Claude Jade in disguise, while the spectator was still in the act of laughing.

Bed and Board seems to me really a film about language with, on the one side, the utilization of the banalities, clichés, wisecracks of everyday life, on the other the difficulties of communication with foreigners (American boss and Japanese mistress).

I wasn't at all conscious of that, but it so happens that I really do enjoy writing dialogue ever since *Fahrenheit,* where I suffered with having to keep to what was written in English without being able to verify if it rang true or not. And I became aware because of that experience that the sound track is the most satisfying element in a film. Before then, for all of two or three years, I was under the somewhat Hitchcockian influence of the idea of the silent film: the less dialogue in a film, the better it was, whence the long, purely visual stretches in *The Soft Skin* and *Fahrenheit*. But afterwards, when I had come back to France, I took my revenge with *The Bride,* where I had the men talk a lot, and since then I take great pleasure in making the characters express themselves, no longer afraid to be long-winded when it's called for. . . .

How to "arrive at things roundabout." Claude Jade (Christine) and Jean-Pierre Léaud (Antoine)

Hiroko Berghauer (Kyoko) and Jean-Pierre Léaud (Antoine): "A maximum of idealization and, subsequently, the maximum of disillusion for the partners"

The discomfort of dining Japanese-style

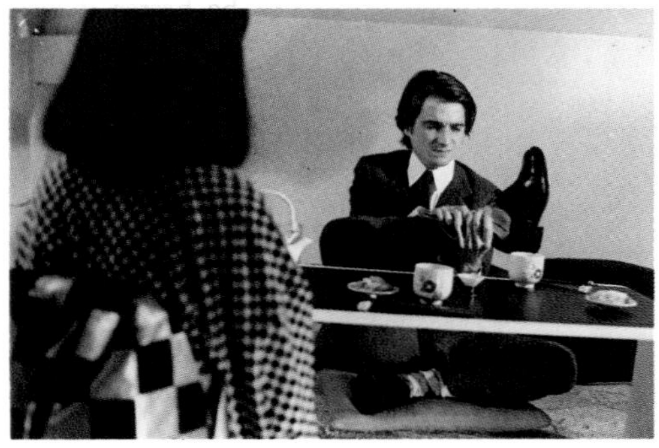

What are your relations with reality, in both the preparation and filming phases, in films like Stolen Kisses *and* Bed and Board?

There are, to begin with, a certain number of elements that come from personal memories, like dyeing flowers in the courtyard and the opera singer who doesn't like to wait. But mostly we have Claude de Givray and Bernard Revon arrange interviews (here with concierges, florists, bistro patrons, individuals working for the Americans), which enable us to cover just about all aspects of the film. It's a reassuring way of working for me, because I'm afraid of original screenplays and feel in those cases the need to base myself on real life. But from that point on, the question of realism doesn't mean much, because a film is made from a seesaw between the real and the stylized. Thus, when I ask Jean-Pierre Léaud to act the discomfort of a Japanese-style meal, we are tending toward a stylization of the American comedy type, with simplified gestures that suggest drawings. On the other hand, when the couple talk to each other in the apartment, I insist that that has to be as truthful as possible, that such and such a word not be forgotten, that one silence come on the heels of another. . . . I classify myself in that family of directors for whom the cinema is a prolongation of youth, that of the children sent to amuse themselves in a corner who remake the world with toys and who continue those games in adult years by means of films. That's what I call "backroom cinema," with a rejection of life as it is, of the world in its real state, and, as a reaction, the need to recreate something which has partly to do with the fairy tale, partly with those American movies that set us dreaming when we were young. But if, until *The Wild Child,* I was not very open to reality, not even in my reading because I used to read only novels, the fact of becoming enthusiastic over Dr. Itard's report and of succeeding in overcoming my scruples with respect to a historical and scientific reality encouraged me to take another path if I wished.

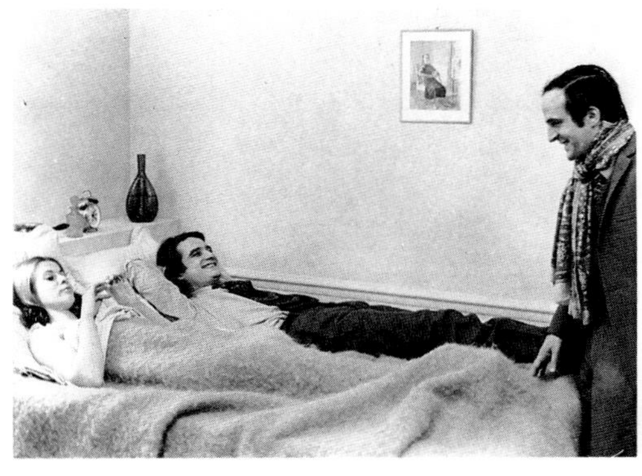

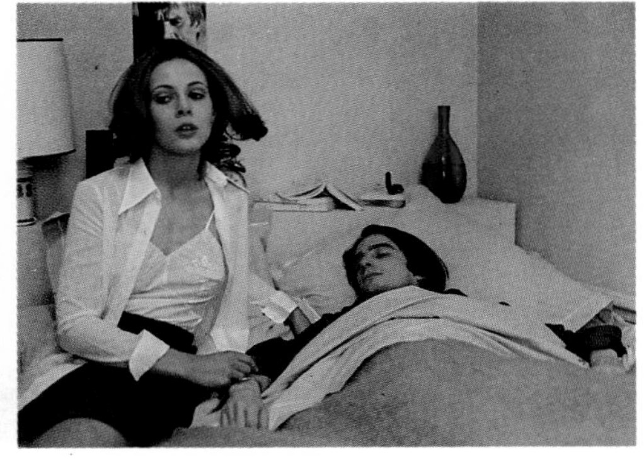

There is both a Renoir side and an American comedy side in Bed and Board.

Renoir for sure, with that courtyard that might recall *The Crime of Monsieur Lange*. But I don't really see Renoir resorting to trick shots for a gag, like the flowers that open and let Japanese words of love come out: that's more like Leo McCarey. I like the end of *The Awful Truth* very much, and the use of the Tyrolian cuckoo clock to bring the couple together again: on the hour a little woman comes out and bows, while every half hour it's a little man, and at the end McCarey makes the little man and the little woman come out together. That's the Lubitsch turn of mind I was referring to a while back.

What's to become of Antoine Doinel and what are you going to do now?

I don't know exactly, but I think I'm done with Doinel for several reasons. First of all, because there would be between him and Jean-Pierre or between him and me too great a divergence: he would have to be given an ambition, an aim, something he hasn't had so far because it's not in his nature, or I'd have to do the portrait of an asocial being or an artist. . . . And then, and above all, because I consider that I've already done the sequel to *Bed and Board,* though in a very different style, in my other films, and not only *The Soft Skin;* if I continued with Doinel I would fall back on scenes from *Jules and Jim,* the *Mermaid,* the *Piano Player* especially. My present concern is therefore with finding other directions for working with Jean-Pierre, perhaps a historical film that would let me show him in costume and get him once and for all away from Doinel. . . . Meanwhile I have no immediate project and I'm busy with books: André Bazin's on Renoir, which I am putting into shape, and *Les Aventures d'Antoine Doinel,* which is coming out in the *Mercure de France* and brings together the four screenplays involving him. I feel, after ten full-length films, the need to take a break and step back from what I'm doing. It's a little like what happens with books in a library: after a certain time you can't lay hands on them when you want them, and then you know you've got to arrange them properly.

Interview by Guy Brancourt,
Cinéma 70, *no. 150, November 1970*

"Stylization of the American-comedy type." *Top:* Jean-Pierre Léaud with, respectively, Hiroko Berghauer and Claude Jade; *above:* Jean-Pierre Léaud and Claude Jade

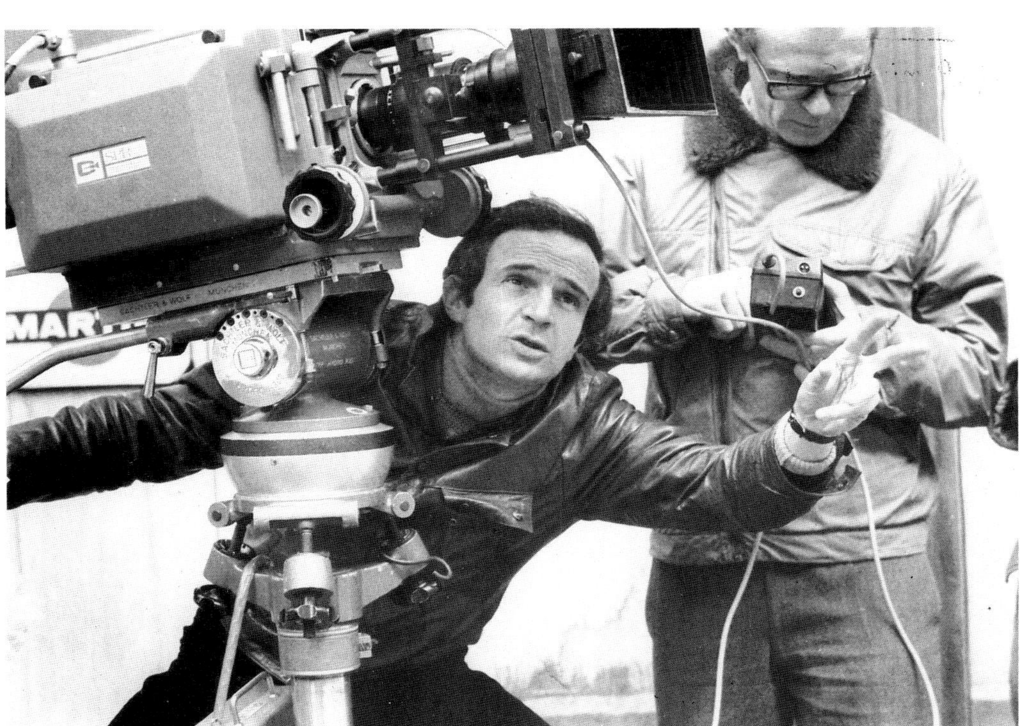

"I take great pleasure in making the characters express themselves."

TWO ENGLISH GIRLS

1971

Two English Girls will not be an erotic film but a film of feelings

The reasons that lead a filmmaker to choose one subject rather than another are often mysterious, even to himself, and they don't become evident until after the shooting, when the film turns up in the form of a long celluloid ribbon running behind the little polished glass screen of the moviola in the editing room.

The starting point for *Two English Girls* was my admiration for the author of the novel, Henri-Pierre Roché, and my intimate acquaintance with his work.

One day in 1955 I bought his first novel *Jules et Jim,* wrapped in cellophane, among a whole batch of bargain books in the bin of a bookshop on the Place du Palais-Royal. What attracted me was the title *Jules et Jim,* the sweet music made by those two Js. When I read on the back of the book that it was the first novel by a seventy-four-year-old man, my curiosity peaked. Reading *Jules et Jim* made me really enthusiastic, and I understood that it was a false novel, composed of memories reconstituted at a distance of fifty years, whence this very rare mixture of folly and wisdom.

I love true stories, tales of real experience, memoirs, reminiscences: I love people recounting their lives.

Three years after *Jules et Jim,* Henri-Pierre Roché, with whom I had begun a correspondence, sent me his second novel, *Deux Anglaises et le Continent,* in which I found once more the almost shocking nature of the situations purified by the innocence of the characters.

Henri-Pierre Roché died in 1959, just as I was making my first film, *The 400 Blows.* He had given me his consent for a film of *Jules et Jim,* which I therefore embarked on two years after his death, in 1961.

Jules and Jim is the story of two friends who love the same woman for a large part of their lives. *Two English Girls* is that of two English sisters who love the same man for some twenty years.

The young Frenchman Claude (Jean-Pierre Léaud) makes the acquaintance first of the older sister, Anne, who has come to Paris to study sculpture. Anne secretly intends her young sister, Muriel, for Claude.

And it so happens that the two young people fall in love during a vacation in England. They will be prevented from marrying, however, by Claude's mother, who has been a widow for twenty years and loves her son utterly

Opposite
Anne (Kika Markham) and Muriel (Stacey Tendeter) "sick with grief"

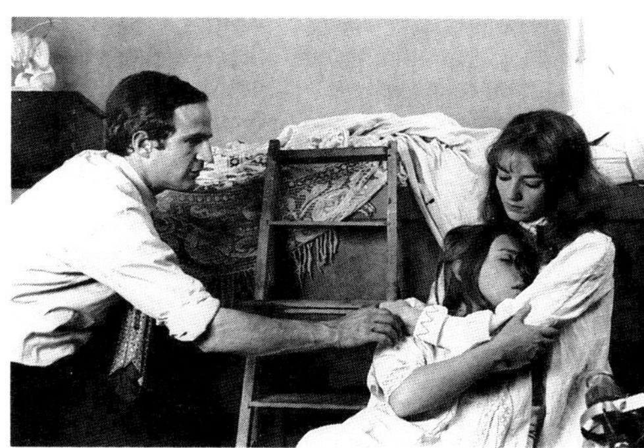

Right
The same scene being staged by François Truffaut

Pages of *Jules et Jim* annotated for the filming of *Two English Girls*

Anne (Kika Markham) and Claude (Jean-Pierre Léaud): "I understood that with this film I wanted to squeeze love like a lemon."

selfishly. Later, in France, Anne will have her first experience of love with Claude, then life will separate them. Muriel still loves Claude, they will come together again but never succeed in becoming a couple, because Muriel has too absolute a conception of love while Claude's is purely relative.

The story of *Two English Girls* cannot be summed up. It has us follow the emotions of three romantic and rather literary-minded young people who experience a passion over many years.

To adapt *Les Deux Anglaises* for the screen, I proceeded in the same way as for *Jules et Jim.* I read and reread the book (several times each year) until I knew certain pages by heart, then I annotated it in the margins and I marked passages with one, two, or three crosses according to the importance I attached to them. I gave the whole of it to Jean Gruault (who had been my associate on *Jules and Jim*), and a few months later he handed me a script of five hundred pages whose length so frightened me that I let it sleep for two years in a drawer.

At the start of this year, I went back to work on it with scissors and Scotch (tape, not bottled) and reduced the script to two hundred pages, while asking Jean Gruault to work it over again after me. We collaborated in a way at a distance, by correspondence, as we had done also for *The Wild Child.*

For the same reasons that impel us to make people we care for meet each other, I think there exists between books the possibilities of fascinating rapprochements. That is why, at the same time we were writing the adaptation of *Two English Girls,* we undertook to read biographies of the admirable Brontë sisters, also puritanical, romantic, and rather impassioned English girls, as well as Marcel Proust's memories of his earlier years. The hero of *Two English Girls,* Claude (in reality the young Henri-Pierre Roché), would be something like a young Proust who had fallen in love with Charlotte and Emily Brontë and had loved both of them for over ten years without being able to make up his mind about one or the other.

Two English Girls will not be an erotic film but a film of feelings, and behind the plot, sometimes amusing, sometimes distressing, which will extend across several periods separated by long gaps in time (say, from 1908 to 1923), we propose, through images, to sing the praises of life.

"Pourquoi Les Deux Anglaises?"
first press book, before filming, 1971

MY *TWO ENGLISH GIRLS,* MY ELEVENTH FILM

Two English Girls is my eleventh film, but I prefer considering it the first . . . Well . . . the first of a new series of ten!

Actually, for the fifty days of shooting *Two English Girls,* I felt as if I were tackling something new for me, perhaps because I had never worked so much with the actors nor given so much thought to the use of color, perhaps also because the screenplay of this film was rather special. . . . We drew the screenplay, Jean Gruault and I, from the second novel by Henri-Pierre Roché (the first was *Jules et Jim*), but that novel already constituted a kind of adaptation since the author wrote it between 1954 and 1957, making use of his memorandum books from the years 1900 to 1920 as well as private diaries and letters. Thus it was literary material but real, lived through, suffered through, and felt.

I don't take to the idea that the cinema addresses itself to people who don't read. Films like *The Golden Coach, Citizen Kane, Summer Interlude* induced me to become a director, but before that, novels like *La Peau de Chagrin, Thérèse Raquin, Froment Jeune et Risler Aîné* had given me the desire and the hope of becoming a novelist. The films I've made from books—*Shoot the Piano Player, Jules and Jim, The Bride Wore Black,* the report on the wild boy of Aveyron—did not constitute in my thinking "adaptations" of literary stories in the playwriting sense of the expression but rather, and deliberately, "filmed homages" to books I loved.

That twin love for books and films led me in 1966 to make *Fahrenheit 451* after Ray Bradbury. That book, in its theme itself, represents nothing less than a homage to all the books published since the invention of printing. Because of that, the films I make are addressed to people who love books, and that is even truer of *Two English Girls,* a romantic story that I wanted to be equally like a novel.

The most embarrassing question of all

Right
The game of the pressed lemon played by Anne, Muriel, and Claude

those usually posed to a director who has just finished a film is: "What were you trying to do?" As concerns *Two English Girls,* the reply came to me suddenly during the work of mixing, as a consequence of having watched the film run back and forth, and I understood that with this film I had wanted to squeeze love like a lemon.

Like almost all tales of feelings, *Two English Girls* deals with loves hindered and thwarted, but the obstacles—even if the most important of them is made concrete in the attitude of an ever-possessive mother—are moral, inward, I would even say mental. I felt the need to go even further in describing feelings of love, a little further than one usually goes. Sometimes in love there exists a real violence of feeling, and that's what I wanted to film. I'm not speaking only of embraces, which I attempted to treat objectively and plainly, without music, but also of avowals, confessions, breakups that can lead characters to vomit or faint. To sum up that attempt in one sentence, I tried to make not a film of physical love but a physical film about love.

"I was twenty and I permitted no one to say that that is the best age to be." Nizan's phrase applies well to the three characters in this film, perhaps the most serious I have made.

The story of *Two English Girls* takes place over a long time, punctuated by separations, voyages, rediscoveries, and deaths. It suggests the whole course of an existence. It shows two English sisters both in love with a Frenchman they call "the Continent" and greet with "Bonjour la France." He is a young man who plans to go into literature but becomes only an art-lover. Fatherless, he has been brought up by a mother who regards him as her work: "When you were born I called you my monument and I raised you stone by stone." The two Brown sisters illustrate two aspects of love, two feminine characters one can encounter in life: Anne who will become a beautiful, radiant young woman and Muriel, the puritan in love, who will never attain her ideal because she seeks only the absolute.

At the start of the story Claude has made the acquaintance of Anne, who secretly intends him for her younger sister, Muriel, whom she adores passionately. At first Claude has scarcely noticed Muriel, so little that Anne can say: "The expected bolt from the blue hasn't taken place." Then suddenly Claude has had the reve-

Muriel's blindfolded eyes: "Don't look at her yet," Anne had asked.

Muriel faints after reading Claude's letter breaking off with her

lation of his love for Muriel and he wants to marry her. Claude's mother objects. She has obliged the two young people to separate for a year, and that first missed rendezvous will be followed by a number of others in this chronicle of three young existences that we rush through: "Fifteen years passed like a breath," because it is indeed a race taking place here, obviously an obstacle race, the obstacles of love.

It is difficult for me to analyze a film I have only barely finished. I can only express my gratitude to those who made it come alive. In the first place, the actors: Jean-Pierre Léaud, who made a considerable effort to come close to Henri-Pierre Roché, once and for all saying goodbye to his adolescence, in the role of Claude Roc, a young dilettante led by an intellectual curiosity to the limits of cruelty and who will discover, late, the sufferings of love. Jean-Pierre Léaud, in this work as an actor so new to him, gave proof of possibilities of emotion one would never expect in his half-brother, Antoine Doinel.

Kika Markham, down-to-earth heroine, gentle and realistic, with her great, moving look, became Anne, the devoted sister of Muriel, who is played with all the verve of her deep and throaty voice by the young Stacey Tendeter. These two English actresses had done a little theater, some radio and television, but had never acted in films and above all had never acted anything at all in French. I guided them scene by scene, giving them instructions inspired by my reading of all the available biographies of the admirable Brontë sisters, also passionate, puritanical Englishwomen.

Claude encounters Anne again when she comes to Paris to study sculpture

Anne and Claude spend a week in a cabin on a little island

Claude, fifteen years later, at the Rodin Museum

Thanks to Nestor Almendros, the chief cameraman, this is the first of my six films in color that I am satisfied with visually from the first frame to the word End. It was logical, too, that I should ask Georges Delerue, the most cinematic of musicians, to write and direct his most violent and most lyrical score.

One should not feel alone when shooting a film. I had around me throughout this new filming Jean-Pierre Léaud, Kika Markham, Stacey Tendeter, Nestor Almendros, Jean Gruault, Georges Delerue, not to forget the memory of Henri-Pierre Roché: no, I was not alone while digging that first tunnel under the Channel that, I hope, *Two English Girls* will become.

Interview by Pascal Thomas, used as preface to the complete screenplay published in L'Avant-Scène Cinéma, *no. 121, 1972*

I DON'T DESPISE MONEY, I JUST DON'T LOVE IT

Since I gave up criticism for directing, I have never replied to an unfavorable article and I have never attacked the press. I'm not going to start that today, but I have something to say about the screenplay you are about to read.

A film is something intimate like a letter, but it is also two hundred million old francs invested by different persons.

I don't despise money, I just don't love it, but the idea of making others lose it is unbearable to me.

I love my work enough to believe it interesting, not enough to believe it indispensable or beyond reproach.

The Paris critics as a whole did not like *Two English Girls,* and one of them, Jean-Louis Bory, declared on the radio that he had found himself bored from the first frame to the last. Because of that, I was asked to reduce this film of two hours and twelve minutes to a more customary length, and I therefore agreed to cut fourteen minutes.

I had already had such misadventures with *Shoot the Piano Player, The Soft Skin, Mississippi Mermaid,* but thanks to the faithfulness of the American, Scandinavian, and Japanese public, none of those films finally ran at a loss.

Those fourteen minutes of cuts are clearly indicated in the text reproduced in *L'Avant-Scène.* I sincerely think that they make the narration more vigorous and do not harm the story, which is that of three lives. Naturally, a copy of the original state will be deposited with the Cinémathèque Française for lovers of complete versions.

L'Avánt-Scène Cinéma,
December 14, 1971

A few years after Anne's death, Claude rejoins Muriel at Calais: "It was done . . . there was red upon her gold."

SUCH A GORGEOUS KID LIKE ME

1972

All of a sudden I chose to make fun of myself

As soon as I finish a sad film, I have only one wish: to make a gay one. Generally speaking, the desire not to repeat oneself incites most filmmakers to go in opposite directions from one film to the next: calm after the storm, tenderness after violence, the lyrical after the everyday, etc. And still I am regularly asked: "Which of your past films will the next one be like?" And since a reply is expected, I can say that *Such a Gorgeous Kid Like Me,* my twelfth film, will be a mixed salad of *Shoot the Piano Player* and *The Bride Wore Black* with a sprinkling of *The Mischief Makers.*

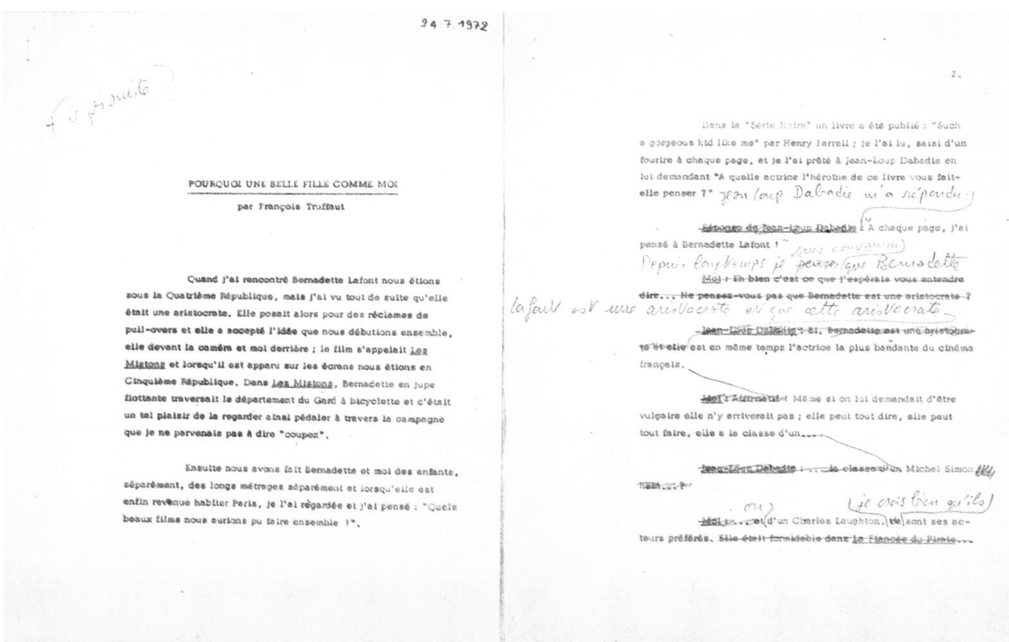

24.7.1972

POURQUOI UNE BELLE FILLE COMME MOI

par François Truffaut

Quand j'ai rencontré Bernadette Lafont nous étions sous la Quatrième République, mais j'ai vu tout de suite qu'elle était une aristocrate. Elle posait alors pour des réclames de pull-overs et elle a accepté l'idée que nous débutions ensemble, elle devant la caméra et moi derrière ; le film s'appelait Les Mistons et lorsqu'il est apparu sur les écrans nous étions en Cinquième République. Dans Les Mistons, Bernadette en jupe flottante traversait le département du Gard à bicyclette et c'était un tel plaisir de la regarder ainsi pédaler à travers la campagne que je ne parvenais pas à dire "coupez".

Ensuite nous avons fait Bernadette et moi des enfants, séparément, des longs métrages séparément et lorsqu'elle est enfin revenue habiter Paris, je l'ai regardée et j'ai pensé : "Quels beaux films nous aurions pu faire ensemble !".

2.

Dans la "Série Noire" un livre a été publié : "Such a gorgeous kid like me" par Henry Farrell ; je l'ai lu, saisi d'un fourire à chaque page, et je l'ai prêté à Jean-Loup Dabadie en lui demandant "A quelle actrice l'héroïne de ce livre vous fait-elle penser ?"

A chaque page, j'ai pensé à Bernadette Lafont !

Eh bien c'est ce que j'espérais vous entendre dire... Ne pensez-vous pas que Bernadette est une aristocrate ?

Si, Bernadette est une aristocrate et elle est en même temps l'actrice la plus bandante du cinéma français.

Même si on lui demandait d'être vulgaire elle n'y arriverait pas ; elle peut tout dire, elle peut tout faire, elle a la classe d'un....

... la classe d'un Michel Simon

... et d'un Charles Laughton, sont ses acteurs préférés. Elle était formidable dans La Fiancée du Pirate...

Beginning of François Truffaut and Jean-Loup Dabadie's presentation in dialogue of Bernadette Lafont

"If I had had a happy childhood, in a happy home with parents who smooch over each other and all like that, well, I wouldn't be here today!"

One day, on the Paris-Madrid plane, I opened an American novel titled *Such a Gorgeous Kid Like Me* and, hearing me howling with laughter at each page, the hostess went and informed the pilot that a passenger was going crazy and that it might be wise to alert the control tower. . . .

At the same time as laughter was provoking sharp physical pains in me, I was seeing Bernadette Lafont superimposed over the deeds and gestures of the heroine of the novel, Camille Bliss, as if the author Henry Farrell had had her in mind while writing his book.

Back in Paris, I wanted to buy the rights to the novel, and I learned that they were already owned by Columbia Pictures and that that great company, whose trademark is the Statue of Liberty, had already spent two hundred thousand dollars on the project before giving it up; the rights, therefore, were to be had on condition of reimbursing those two hundred thousand dollars. Shaking at the knees, I left the Columbia offices and the following Sunday, for the first time in my life, I laid a triple pari-mutuel bet: the 8, the 1, and the 3 (out of admiration for Maurice Leblanc's novel titled precisely *813*).

At the same time as twelve million Frenchmen, I learned from the newscaster Léon Zitrone that I would have done better with the 4, the 5, and the 1, and I found myself poorer by one hundred thousand francs. I went back to Columbia where Jack Wiener, his heart wrenched by seeing me thinned down by twelve pounds in one week, proposed this time that I should make the film for his company. If *Such a Gorgeous Kid Like Me* is a flop, the guy in the uniform who opens the elevator doors for you in the Columbia Pictures building in Paris next year will be me.

With a Columbia contract in my pocket, I still had to convince Bernadette Lafont: it took no more than making her listen over the phone to my riffling the pages of the book. I should say we had both got a lot of fun out of filming *The Mischief Makers,* the film of our respective debuts. In those days I used to get my feet tangled in all the cables and I confused camera and spotlight; as for Bernadette, not yet turned twenty, it was enough for her to walk into a room and say hello for three floodlights to blow out.

I needed a partner for the adaptation and dialogue of *Such a Gorgeous Kid Like Me.* I recruited Jean-Loup Dabadie because he was the one who said the best things to me about my films, even about those withdrawn after the third day of first-run showing. We began to work together during vacation, at Antibes, and I saw right away that we were going to form a two-man team like Noël Noël and Fernandel in *Adémaï-Aviateur* when they each board a plane under the impression that the other knows how to fly it. We would know on the evening of the premiere if we had managed a happy landing.

As a rule I always ask the actors in my films to act with moderation and "plausibility." That only half-rouses them to enthusiasm and gets me later criticisms like: "Truffaut, as always in half-tints . . . the sweet and tender Truffaut, etc." With *Such a Gorgeous Kid Like Me,* I had the chance to film a story whose characters are all crazy, which let the actors play it to the hilt, "as if their life depended on it," as Audiberti said of Joan Crawford in *Johnny Guitar,* my bedside film.

Below, right
François Truffaut and Bernadette Lafont in front of the same Center for Juvenile Delinquents seen in *The 400 Blows*

Above, left, and below
An agitated married life: Camille and Clovis Bliss (Bernadette Lafont and Philippe Léotard)

Who are they, those fortunate actors, those lucky gamblers, who come onto the screen balancing "whole cases of clams," as Harpo Marx says in his memoirs? There is Charles Denner who will be a virgin at the start of the story but won't be anymore by the sixth reel; Guy Marchant who will sing his role of crooner from the sticks; Claude Brasseur in a double role of unqualified lawyer and crooked lawyer; Gilberte Géniat in a single role but forever between two wines; Philippe Léotard, her (what else?) unworthy son; Ouvrard who will contribute his eighty-two years and all his teeth (and not a single white hair); Michel Delahaye, the only example of film critic turned actor; André Dussollier, a Conservatoire student with great prospects; and for the first time on the screen, Danièle Girard who manages to get in her three pages of dialogue in sixty-eight seconds; and finally a blonde young girl who had the happy idea of sending her photo to my Films du Carrosse.

Such a Gorgeous Kid Like Me is a film that aims to be funny, so if the public doesn't laugh, that will mean not only failure but also dishonor. The shooting will be done entirely in Béziers, a superb town so far spared by film troupes and, because of that, terrifically hospitable. We laid seige to the city beginning February 7, we invaded it on the 14th, and we'll evacuate it April 16 (unless it "liberates" itself on its own before then). The film will be on view beginning in September 1972, at the very moment when I will perhaps be beginning to prepare a horrendous drama which will prove that life is only a bowl of nuts.

"Pourquoi, Une Belle Fille Comme Moi,"
Le Monde du Spectacle,
February 18, 1972

THE PHILOSOPHY AND CURSES OF CAMILLE

CAMILLE: If I had had a happy childhood, in a happy home with parents who smooch over each other and all like that, well, I wouldn't be here today!

STANISLAS: Mrs. Bliss, I am asking you straight out: did you kill your father?
CAMILLE: That ain't the way to put it: it was a bet on fate!

STANISLAS: You were still a virgin when . . .
CAMILLE: Not really . . . not really . . .
STANISLAS: And your relations with your mother-in-law?
CAMILLE: Old Isobel, she could never make me fit in. And yet, like I told her again and again:"Look, Mama, don't cry like that. You lost a son, you gained a daughter."

CAMILLE: I've always had a real lot of respect for people who can get their names written on walls: I tell myself those types know the real facts of life . . . a gimmick like that, no?

STANISLAS: Your husband was in the hospital . . . You thought about divorcing?
CAMILLE: Look, you don't divorce just like that a dumb ox who's got twenty-seven fractures, no? It's a question of elegance!

ARTHUR: Poor little bird, you believe in God?
CAMILLE: O là là, sure!

CAMILLE: Put yourself in my place. I had four guys on my hands.
STANISLAS: Are you aware, Camille, that you had self-seeking interests in each of them?
CAMILLE: Hey, I should hope so. Go on, I wouldn't have slept with them without no reason. I'm not that type, me.

CAMILLE: It's weird, prison, there are some people who understand it, some who don't. Well, you, now you're like me . . .

Excerpts from the dialogue

Lovers and victims of Camille: Arthur, the Catholic rat exterminator (Charles Denner); Stanislas Previne, the sociologist (André Dussollier); and Maître Murène (Claude Brasseur), the lawyer

SOMETHING WILD PERFORMED IN A PRETTY DRY MANNER

This is my least sentimental film, so the music has to avoid being so, except as concerns Hélène, the separation of Camille and Stanislas in the prison corridor, and, toward the end, Stanislas at Camille's place.

The sonorities should not be warm, but the opposite of warm is not necessarily cold. I think we should aim for something wild performed in a pretty dry manner. You shouldn't let yourself be influenced by the mixing of *Two English Girls,* where I constantly sacrificed the instruments that stood out from the orchestra. I did that because of the annoyance I feel in landscape shots when you can too easily identify the piano or the flute. . . .

But here it's not a matter of landscape but of faces, and we are almost always in action, therefore the importance of considering the whole score like a journey, like a chase, like something in motion that mustn't stop.

If all the music runs along those lines, I would not be absolutely opposed to strange sonorities, the idea for me being to get back to the best moments of *Shoot the Piano Player.*

Notes to Georges Delerue for the music of Such A Gorgeous Kid Like Me, *May 29, 1972*

"I AM" THE TWO CHARACTERS

I don't consider any of my films a special case, not even *Such a Gorgeous Kid Like Me,* which is perhaps the most controlled, coherent, and complementary of them all. I find in it great logic, a real raison d'être. There are errors in it, but I don't at all view this film as a parenthesis or a concession to anything whatsoever. I have never made a film to order, nor a publicity film, nor anything that might have been suggested to me from outside. It is not an absolute rule, but so far all my films were my choices. From that standpoint I consider them all equal, I do not rank them.

I should like you to explain better in what way Such a Gorgeous Kid Like Me *is "complementary" to your other films.*

At the time I made it, it was complementary to *Two English Girls,* which presented romanticism with a certain indulgence. *Such a Gorgeous Kid Like Me* was a takeoff on it. All of a sudden I chose to make fun of myself. People considered the film contemptuous. That's a mistake, because one doesn't run oneself down. The film was made "against me," and that is what people have failed to grasp. The film is ambiguous in the sense in which it is secretly, but not less, autobiographical than my other films. In *Such a Gorgeous Kid* "I am" the two characters, Camille Bliss and the sociologist Stanislas. I make fun of someone who persists in seeing life in a romantic manner, I extend approval to the girl who is a kind of guttersnipe, who has learned to mistrust everyone and to fight for survival. Many people thought I was making fun of intellectuals. I simply gave Dussollier my reactions. He's a character who moves me, but he has to be given a good lesson in living because he doesn't see things from a sufficiently concrete angle. In another way, the film is feminist, but not in the servile manner of the people who would like to be in fashion or follow the "fem-lib" movement.

The failure, to my mind, comes because there are two types of screenplay. There are screenplays that don't fit into genres, classifications; within those, anything goes, as long as it is somewhat consistent. And then there are other screenplays that belong to the cinema of genre, like *Mississippi Mermaid* or *Such a Gorgeous Kid Like Me.* Now, if you do "genre" films you have to respect their laws. In *Such a Gorgeous Kid,* you don't want to approve of all the characters: if one is sympathetic, the other has to be antipathetic. Put another way, if a showing of a "genre" film is stopped midway, you should be able to question the viewers about what they expect now and to recognize that they all expect the same thing. In *Such a Gorgeous Kid* (as in *Mississippi Mermaid*), I shuffle the cards, the public's sympathy wavers, and a certain malaise sets in that prevents laughing or participating.

Interview by Dominique Maillet, Cinématographie, *no. 15, October-November 1975*

1973

DAY FOR NIGHT

I am always returning to the question that has tormented me for thirty years now: is cinema more important than life?

One day, during the shooting of *Jules and Jim,* I was getting a scene together, whispering with the actors Jeanne Moreau, Oskar Werner, and Henri Serre; the time came to go into what we call a "serious rehearsal" and I asked the two men to install themselves in front of a backgammon board while Jeanne Moreau, standing and with a little stick in her hand, spoke the lines agreed on: "Would someone here be willing to scratch my back?" At that moment, we saw entering the field and going toward Jeanne the prop man of the film who, misled by the actress's natural delivery, stepped forward to volunteer to scratch her back. Obviously the whole crew broke up with laughter, and work began again with more harmony because, if it's always good to laugh in life, it's absolutely indispensable in the shooting of a film.

The film within the film (from top to bottom): The technical crew (Jean-François Stévenin, François Truffaut, Nathalie Baye); the actors (Jacqueline Bisset and Jean-Pierre Léaud); the director and his assistant (François Truffaut and Jean-François Stévenin)

Opposite
Julie Baker-Nelson (Pamela in the film within the film) and the director Ferrand (Jacqueline Bisset and François Truffaut)

In every shooting there occur similar incidents, not necessarily funny, some merely strange or even cruel, and sometimes they contrast in their force or crudeness with the banality of the scene you are shooting. At such moments—for example, when it takes no less than two assistants concealed at either side of the bed to hold down the sheets that fly around when a couple of actors are miming physical love—the director can't help but say to himself that the "film of the film" would be a lot more amusing and lively than the film itself.

Everyone who has visited a movie lot for a few hours has felt a kind of unease, the feeling of being in the way and of not understanding what is going on. Having come there with the hope of getting an answer to the question "How do they make a film?" they go away disappointed; and it was of them we were thinking when we—Jean-Louis Richard, Suzanne Schiffman, and I—wrote the screenplay for *Day for Night,* which has as its subject nothing less than the shooting of a film (titled *Introducing Pamela*) from the first day of filming to the last, when the entire crew go their separate ways.

I've been asked a hundred times this year: "Aren't you afraid of ruining the mystery of a craft you're so fond of?" and each time I've replied that an aviator can explain everything he knows about piloting a plane, but he will never succeed in demystifying the intoxication of flight. Filmmaking is a marvelous craft, and the proof is in the fact that, of all those who have the chance to work at it, no one wants to do anything else. Everybody knows the story of that great director of a circus who goes bank-

Julie Baker/Pamela (Jacqueline Bisset): the photographs before her arrival

rupt and ends up grooming an acrobat elephant which slaps him with its trunk and pisses every day in his face. When one of his old friends, dismayed to see him thus fallen and humble, says to him: "You, with your university degrees, your knowledge of bookkeeping and administration, you could get a job anywhere!" he replies: "And give up show business? Never!"

"Pourquoi La Nuit Américaine?" *in first press book*

MY FRIEND JEAN-PIERRE

Jean-Pierre Aumont's gaze turns first of all to the unexpected aspects of life, which makes him one of a family of artists I love enormously, that of the anti-solemn ones: Sacha Guitry, Dauphin, Charles Trenet, Raymond Queneau, Ernst Lubitsch.

Like them, he is gifted with a *malicieux* spirit, not in the French sense, that is, not a scoffer like adolescents who discover that grownup society is made up of puppets who put on serious demeanors.

The cinema has let us look at Jean-Pierre Aumont close-up or in long shot. Now, on the stage of the Théâtre Antoine, we are going to see him move around with that astonishing gait which is his alone, that of a gentleman-burglar who prowls on tiptoe, at night, in a villa on the beach, looking for hearts to steal. At the end of his biography, *Le Soleil et les Ombres,* Jean-Pierre Aumont asks himself if I have as much friendship for him as he has for me. The reply is yes, definitively.

For the Théâtre Antoine, August 1982

FILMS ROLL ON LIKE TRAINS IN THE NIGHT

Why a film on the cinema?

Because it's been in my mind for a long time.

And I feel as if I've waited an enormous time to make it.

The filmmaker's job is a mystery to everybody. We sense it in the questions we're asked and those we have a lot of trouble answering. During the war I asked an adult: "How long does it take to make a film?" And he said to me: "Three months." I learned that what passed across the screen in two hours was shot in three months. I had just found out what people generally know. But within those three months, everything is a mystery.

What is your intention?

I made *Day for Night* like a documentary, and there is very little difference between the shooting I show and that of my films. I set myself very precise limits, I respected the unity of place, time, and action. To show the making of *Introducing Pamela*—the film within the film—I wanted to set out in a quite systematic but plausible manner all the traps that can handicap and menace a successful end to the undertaking.

The set of *Introducing Pamela* constructed in the open air in the Studios de la Victorine, Nice

I wanted also to continue what I had begun in *Stolen Kisses*, that is, I wanted to fight against a tendency in the French film which, since 1960, had more and more concentrated on a single character. In *Day for Night* I tried to have ten characters of equal importance: the prop man and script girl count for as much as the stars. The collective, unanimist aspect of the film expresses nostalgia for the cinema of Prévert.

And isn't there another nostalgia?

There is nostalgia for films that aren't afraid to tell a story, that aren't afraid of melodrama, and that are willing to submit to people's judgment. For me, a storyteller must be willing even to be considered an idiot in the eyes of Paul Valéry's disciples. It's the old business of the good old marquise who goes out at five o'clock and of deciding what you want her to do and to say. *Introducing Pamela* is the story of a young bride who runs off with her father-in-law. I chose that story for its simplicity, because I knew that the viewer would be able to know what was going on at any moment. To be comfortable intellectually, I should have left the subject of *Introducing Pamela* completely in the dark, but I voluntarily took on the middle-class tragedy: it's an example of a cinema of sentiments that I have defended and then practiced and that I will be one of the last to give up.

In Day for Night *you speak also of the demise of a certain kind of film.*

Yes, but with *Introducing Pamela,* I show a more traditional way of filming, more luxurious than in my films, with the exception of *Fahrenheit* which was made in English studios. You know, in art you often go back with a different angle to something you thought gone forever. Look at the baroque exaggeration of Carmelo Bene, the utter sophistication of Werner Schroeter. Once again Dali seems to be right when he says: "Never worry about being modern because, whatever you may do, unfortunately you will be."

My idea was not to tell the whole truth about the cinema, but to say only things that are true. To recount that formidable mobilization that shooting a film involves, that input of feeling that can mess up the private lives of those who take part in a film. For each of us, at that particular moment, it is a privileged period having nothing to do with practical worries, an escape. The crew of a film working outdoors always reminds me of the vacation camps of my childhood.

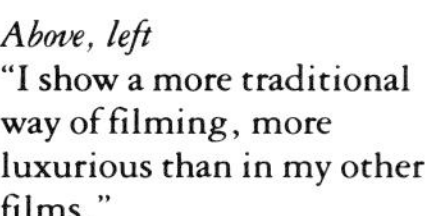

Above, left
"I show a more traditional way of filming, more luxurious than in my other films."

Above, right
The producer and the director: Bertrand and Ferrand (Jean Champion and François Truffaut)

Following pages
A work schedule for *Introducing Pamela*, the film within the film in *Day for Night*

GRAND DECOR . EXT. JOUR — A.-

N° 1 - Tournage scène de la gifle.- La Télévision interviewe Alexandre

Acteurs	Costumes
Alexandre	1
Alphonse	1
Ferrand	prévu
Liliane	prévu
Joëlle	prévu
Bernard	prévu
Odile	prévu

SILHOUETTES : Reporte TV.- 1er Assistant.- Chef Opérateur.- Assistant Cameraman.- Ingénieur du Son.- Perchman.- Femme du régisseur.- Régisseur.-

FIGURATION : 2 machinistes.- 2 électros.- Cameraman TV.- Ingénieur du son TV.- 200 personnes pour circulation sur la place (dont 10 en voitures - 3 agents de police - 15 enfants d'âges divers - 4 garçons de café - 3 coiffeurs).-

VEHICULES : 10 voitures diverses.- 1 moto.- 4 mobylettes.-

ACCESSOIRES : Caméra 16 mm Coutand TV équipée avec Zoom (sans pellicule).- Nagra pour TV, perche et micro TV.- MK 2 avec viseur clair, sans pellicule (voir avec prise de vue).- Nagra, perche et micro pour film (voir avec prise de son).-
Journaux.- Sacs à provisions.- Voitures d'enfants.-
Paquets divers pour figuration.-
Matériel électrique jouant dans le décor (voir avec électriciens).-
Tricot pour femme du régisseur.-
Chaises acteurs (avec leurs noms dans le film).-
Boite maquillage praticable pour Odile.-
Porte-voix pour Assistant.-
Consommations pour café.-
Sacoche et matériel pour la script.-
Lunettes pour la script.-

GRAND DECOR . EXT. JOUR (N° 1 - suite) — B.-

DECORATION : Décor place en état.-
Café avec terrasse.-
Station métro ouverte.-
Boutique coiffure en état.-
Fleuriste.- Kiosque à journaux.-

MAQUILLAGE : Fausses moustaches pour Alexandre.-

MACHINISTES : Travelling.-
2 Grues (dont l'une joue comme accessoire).-

ELECTRICIENS : Matériel électrique jouant en accessoire.-

REGIE : Prévoir deux porte-voix (dont l'un joue comme accessoire).-

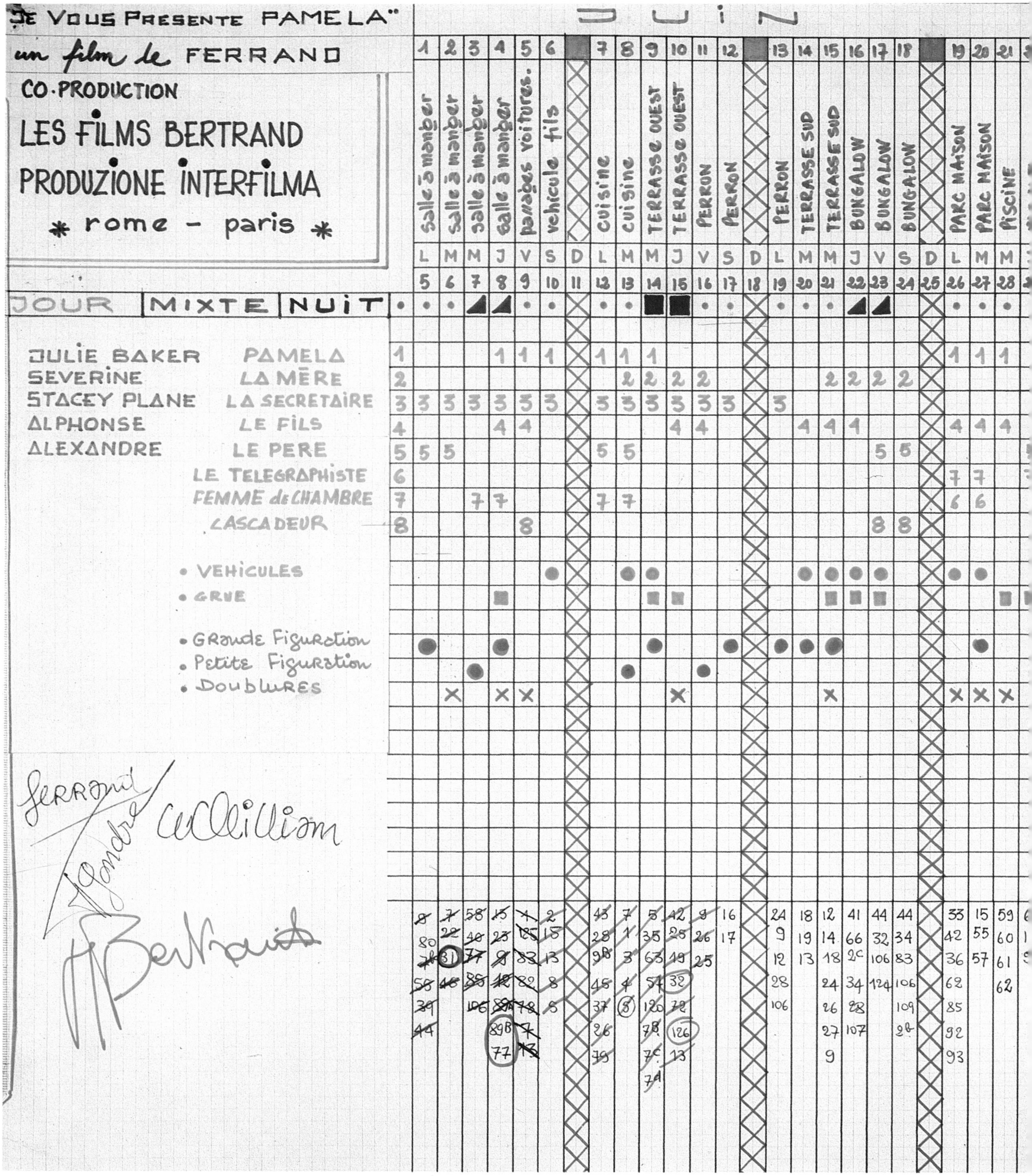

"JE VOUS PRESENTE PAMELA"
un film de FERRAND

CO·PRODUCTION
LES FILMS BERTRAND
PRODUZIONE INTERFILMA
* rome – paris *

JUIN

		1	2	3	4	5	6		7	8	9	10	11	12		13	14	15	16	17	18		19	20	21
		Salle à manger	Salle à manger	Salle à manger	Salle à manger	passages voitures.	vehicule fils	X	Cuisine	Cuisine	TERRASSE OUEST	TERRASSE OUEST	PERRON	PERRON	X	PERRON	TERRASSE SUD	TERRASSE SUD	BUNGALOW	BUNGALOW	BUNGALOW	X	PARC MAISON	PARC MAISON	PISCINE
		L	M	M	J	V	S	D	L	M	M	J	V	S	D	L	M	M	J	V	S	D	L	M	M
		5	6	7	8	9	10	11	12	13	14	15	16	17	18	19	20	21	22	23	24	25	26	27	28
JOUR • MIXTE ◢ NUIT ■	•	•	•	◢	◢	•	•	X	•	•	■	■	•	•	X	•	•	•	◢	◢	•	X	•	•	•
JULIE BAKER — PAMELA	1				1	1	1	X	1	1	1				X							X	1	1	1
SEVERINE — LA MÈRE	2							X		2	2	2	2		X			2	2	2	2	X			
STACEY PLANE — LA SECRETAIRE	3	3	3	3	3	3	3	X	3	3	3	3	3	3	X	3						X			
ALPHONSE — LE FILS	4				4	4		X				4	4		X		4	4	4			X	4	4	4
ALEXANDRE — LE PERE	5	5	5					X	5	5					X					5	5	X			
LE TELEGRAPHISTE	6							X							X							X	7	7	
FEMME de CHAMBRE	7			7	7			X	7	7					X							X	6	6	
CASCADEUR	8					8		X							X					8	8	X			
• VEHICULES							●	X		●	●				X		●	●	●	●		X	●	●	
• GRUE					■			X			■	■			X			■	■	■		X			■
• Grande Figuration		●			●			X			●			●	X	●	●	●				X		●	
• Petite Figuration				●				X		●			●		X							X			
• Doublures			×		×	×		X				×			X			×				X	×	×	×
		8 80 7A 56 39 44	7 22 31 46	58 40 77 85 106	15 23 9 12 89A 89B 77	4 125 83 82 78 7 13	2 15 13 8 5	X	43 28 9B 45 37 26 79	7 1 3 4 5	5 35 63 57 120 7B 7C 7D	42 25 19 32 72 126 13	9 26 25	16 17	X	2A 9 12 28 106	18 19 13	12 14 18 24 26 27 9	41 66 2C 34 28 107	44 32 106 124	44 34 83 106 109 2B	X	33 42 36 62 85 92 93	15 55 57	59 60 61 62

Ferrand
William
Bertrand

JUILLET — AOÛT

N°	Décor	Jour	Date	Symbole	1	2	3	4	5	7	6	8	●	■	●	●	×	Numéros
…3	…MAISON		…0	◢					5						●			2, 2, 0, 5, 9, 6
24	PARC MAISON	S	1	•					5		6				●			20, 107, 85
		D	2															
25	SALON	L	3	•						7		8				●		71, 73
26	SALON	M	4	•					5								×	74, 10, 22, 32
27	SALON	M	5	•		2			5							●	×	21, 22, 41
28	SALON	J	6	•	1	2		4				8				●	×	11, 27
29	PARC MAISON	V	7	■	1	2		4		7	6		●	■			×	29, 30, 10
30	PARC MAISON	S	8	■	1			4		7	6		●		●		×	70, ɩ, 45, 47, 8c
		D	9															
31	TERRASSE OUEST	L	10	•	1							8				●	×	11, 27, 9
32	TERRASSE OUEST	M	11	•	1					7						●	×	3, 32, 34
33	TERRASSE OUEST	M	12	◢	1			4							●			46, 49, 25, 26, 30
34	EXT. AEROPORT	J	13	•					5								×	51, 62, 65
		V	14															
35	EXT. AEROPORT	S	15	•					5			8				●	×	32, 4b, 4c, 30
		D	16															
36	SALON AEROPORT	L	17	•					5						●			52, 38, 30
37	" AEROPORT	M	18	◢		2				7			●					39, 43, 51
38	" AEROPORT	M	19	•		2		4					●		●			48, 50, 6, 20
39	" AEROPORT	J	20	•		2		4					●		●			4, 37
40	EXT. VILLA	V	21	■										■				31, 27, 9, 19
41	EXT. VILLA	S	22	■	1	2		4						■			×	31, 64, 10, 72
		D	23															
42	EXT. VILLA	L	24	•					5			8		■				31, 30, 52
43	EXT. VILLA	M	25	■	1				5				●					31, 40, 61
44	CHAMBRE AL.	M	26	•	1				5			8				●		72, 102, 25, 9
45	CHAMBRE AL.	J	27	◢	1		3			7	6							72, 28, 106
46	CHAMBRE AL.	V	28	•			3											10, 15, 13
47	HOTEL	S	29	•			3									●		10, 17, 19, 18
		D	30															
48	HOTEL	L	31	•			3											10, 126, 74, 32, 36
49	HOTEL	M	1	◢			3							■				0, 74
50	HOTEL	M	2	◢			3								●		×	0
51	RACCORDS	J	3	•		2	3	4		7		8				●	×	
52	RACCORDS	V	4	•		2	3	4		7	6	8	●					
53	RACCORDS	S	5	•		2	3		5		6		●		●		×	
		D	6															

le père :
(Charles Boyer – Louis Jourdan – J. P. Aumont
Hollywood...
l'attente de l'avion
un télégramme : il est heureux. (mandat télégraph.)
choc : c'est un garçon, jeune
à cause de sa problème de fric
x favorable aux essais pour le garçon
* le garçon fait du tennis
* il parle de ses amis de cinéma

le "filleul" :
x le jeu ...
x on lui a proposé des essais
* à la fin il dit oui pour les essais
* il ne regarde jamais une fille
* ~~tennis~~
* archi silencieux et mystérieux.

Lucie-Julie
* elle arrive après quelques jours
aéroport
* mari médecin
* le beurre en motte

la mère :
* elle boit
* la scène de l'empoisonnement
* le placard
* elle rate à cause de V. Felix.

le producteur :
* Lewis Allen – Josef Dorfman..
* le beurre en motte

la secrétaire :
* elle refuse maillot de bain
* la script devine qu'elle est enceinte

le fils :
* il ne s'asseoit jamais autrement que par terre (scène à faire)
* il a casé sa petite amie comme script stagiaire
* amour cirque (meubles cassés...)
* sa petite amie se tire avec le cascadeur
* il n'est plus en état de tourner
* une nuit Julie le console...

Descriptions of the principal characters

In that adventure, which might put one in mind also of the perilous journey of a stagecoach of the Far West, the director himself thinks only of the final destination. The world therefore divides into two for him: what is good for the film and what is bad for the film.

And this time, on the screen, the director is you yourself . . .

His name is Ferrand, and he really is a lot like me. I didn't want to create a character, and you see me at work as if I had been filmed for a television program. There are directors who boast of never going to the movies, but myself, I go all the time. And I am forever marked by the films I discovered before becoming a filmmaker, when I could take them in more fully. If, for example, in the course of *Day for Night* I pay special homage to *Citizen Kane,* it is because that film, released in Paris in July 1946, changed both the cinema and my own life. Through the young actor played by Jean-Pierre Léaud, I am always coming back to the question that has tormented me for thirty years now: is cinema more important than life? That may be scarcely more intelligent than to ask, "Do you like your father better or your mother?" But I think about cinema for so many hours a day, and have for so many years, that I can't stop myself from putting life and the movies in competition. And from reproaching life for not being as well designed, interesting, dense, and intense as the images we organize. "There are no bottlenecks in films," Ferrand says to Jean-Pierre Léaud, "no holes, no dead spots. Films roll on like trains in the night."

Day for Night has a kind of recapitulative character. Even in a comic key, I find myself making fun of my past work. With this film, it's as if I deliberately closed the doors in order to force myself into renewal. I have adapted a lot of American novels because I wanted films with strong situations, because I didn't dare invent death. Now I feel sure enough of myself to do only original screenplays. I should like either to write with actors I like and admire directly in mind or else to write a story for itself but to have it acted by unknowns. I have a strong desire to progress in the direction of truth, plausibility, and purity.

Interview by Yvonne Baby,
Le Monde, *May 18, 1973*

Below, left to right
The film within the film, Julie Baker and Alphonse (Jacqueline Bisset and Jean-Pierre Léaud); glimpsed during the shooting: Alphonse, Alexandre, Julie Baker, and Séverine (Jean-Pierre Léaud, Jean-Pierre Aumont, Jacqueline Bisset, Valentina Cortese); Julie Baker and Dr. Nelson (Jacqueline Bisset and David Markham)

Opposite
"The director himself thinks only of the final destination."

THE STORY OF ADELE H.

1975

Only the realm of feelings engrosses and interests me

It was in 1969 that I first felt I wanted to make a film whose heroine would be Adele Hugo. I had just read in the collection *Bibliothèque Introuvable* (Editions Minard) the biography of Adele as reconstructed by Miss Frances Vernor Guille, professor at Wooster College, Ohio.

While working on the script for *The Wild Child* from Dr. Jean Itard's memoir, we discovered, Jean Gruault and I, the great pleasure to be had from organizing a fictional story on the basis of real events, taking pains to invent nothing and not to alter the truth of the documentary material. First making certain that Jean Gruault shared my enthusiasm, I made contact with Miss Guille, who was enchanted by the project right away, then with Jean Hugo, who showed himself at first reserved and even reticent. That is understandable: the true story of his great-aunt was little known. It brought up a kind of family secret and I think that Jean Hugo was also troubled by the possibility that Victor Hugo himself would be shown

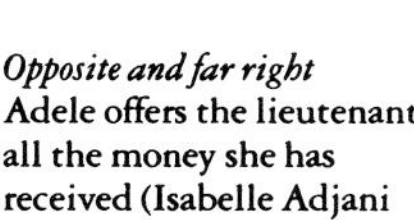

Opposite and far right
Adele offers the lieutenant all the money she has received (Isabelle Adjani and Bruce Robinson)

Love letters without replies: Adele Hugo (Isabelle Adjani)

in the film. I took pains to reassure him, promising that I would spare him the spectacle of a bearded bit-part actor prancing in and announcing: "I am Victor Hugo," and that I even planned to work out a screenplay without ever showing his great-grandfather. I finally asked him to let us draw up a first draft which would be submitted to him in a year's time.

Then I took on three films, but between each shooting I still moved ahead on the script of *Adele*. Our first treatment having won Jean Hugo's approbation, I asked Suzanne Schiffman to join forces with Gruault and me. We had

Adele H. and Lieutenant Pinson (Isabelle Adjani and Bruce Robinson)

"But tell me I can hope . . ."

decided to carry the screenplay right to its end, but we became aware that, if it is difficult to construct a unified plot involving a dozen characters whose actions intersect, it is almost as difficult to write an intimist film putting a single character on screen.

Yet, I believe it was that solitary aspect that attracted me most in this project. Having filmed love stories with two persons and with three persons, I felt as if I were attempting a passionately interesting experiment in tying myself down to a single person devoured by a one-way passion.

If I have to sum up in seven points what attracted me in the story of Adele Hugo, they would be:

1. This girl is alone throughout the story;
2. She is the daughter of the most celebrated man in the world;
3. That man is spoken about but never seen;
4. Adele lives under false identities;
5. Driven by a fixed idea, she pursues an unattainable goal;
6. Not a phrase, not a gesture of Adele's has to do with anything else but her fixed idea;
7. Even if she is fighting a losing battle, Adele shows herself continually active and inventive.

I am not unaware that everything one writes, everything one films, has its significance, but I must confess that, as for me, emotion precedes the general idea and it is most often because of what is written about my work that I discover the subterranean reasons that led me to choose one subject or another.

Letter to Jean Hugo, legal representative of the Hugo heirs

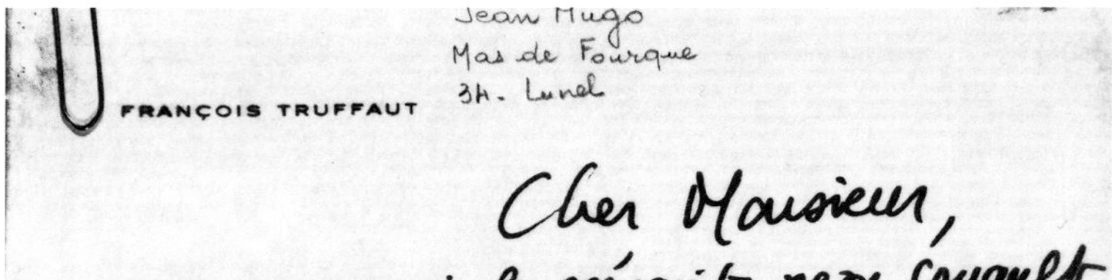

Jean Hugo
Mas de Fourque
34. Lunel

FRANÇOIS TRUFFAUT

Cher Monsieur,

Avec mon ami le scénariste Jean Gruault (nous avons adapté ensemble le roman de Henri Pierre Roché Jules et Jim et le Rapport du Docteur Itard sur L'Enfant Sauvage) j'étudie depuis quelques semaines la possibilité de tirer un film de la biographie d'Adèle Hugo, en particulier du long épisode de son amour pour le lieutenant Pinson.

Je n'ai pas cherché à vous contacter plus tôt car à ce stade, notre travail est expérimental et il nous arrive souvent d'ébaucher des constructions de films auxquels ensuite nous devons renoncer, surtout lorsqu'il s'agit d'histoires réelles, par opposition aux romans.

Mon grand désir eut été de vous atteindre par l'intermédiaire de Louise de Vilmorin que j'aimais beaucoup... hélas.. Puis Me Matarasso s'est offert pour cela mais je lui ai demandé d'attendre un peu car je voulais vraiment vous faire lire un projet cohérent, vous permettant d'émettre une opinion. Entre temps, j'ai rencontré Mrs Frances V. Guille avec qui j'étais en correspondance et elle m'a dit vous avoir déjà parlé de ce projet ; c'est pourquoi j'ai tenu à vous expliquer le côté tardif de ma démarche.

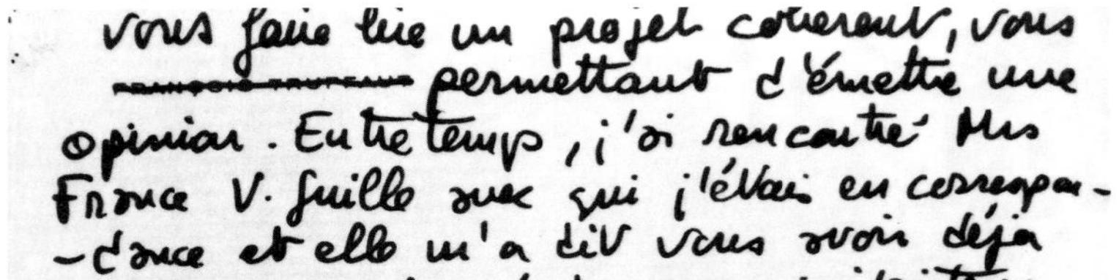

Dans la première quinzaine de février, je pourrai vous soumettre un premier état du scénario en espérant votre accord de principe et naturellement toutes les remarques que vous voudrez formuler sur ce travail.

Pour ce qui regarde les questions morales et légales entre vous-même, Mrs Frances V. Guille et nous, je propose que Maître Matarasso représente nos intérêts respectifs ;

il me reste à vous dire à quel point, Jean Gruault et moi-même nous sommes pris de passion pour Adèle tout au long de notre travail ; en espérant avoir bientôt l'occasion de vous rencontrer, je vous prie, Cher Monsieur, de croire à l'expression de mes sentiments les plus distingués, François Truffaut

François Truffaut and Isabelle Adjani

The years pass, I make good films and bad ones, but all freely chosen, and I am indeed obliged to realize that only the realm of feelings engrosses and interests me.

Working in a more instinctive than intellectual manner, I do not understand what my films mean until two years after their release. This delayed enlightenment constitutes a help rather than a handicap, because it seems to me I just wouldn't have the enthusiasm to go out morning after morning and shoot a film whose entire meaning has been settled in advance. Obviously I am certainly beginning to recognize that I make only films that show what is askew and painful in certain family or love relationships. I am led to go back, for the heart of each film, to the same conflict between definitive feelings and provisional feelings, thus to film always the same heartbreaks. Those interested in that kind of thing—the gentle description of violent emotions—will say that these are all variations on a single theme; those who are bored by such things will say I'm repeating the same drivel.

The Story of Adele H., which resembles a piece of music for a single instrument, does not need long preliminary explanations. Let it be said only that, decidedly incapable of making films "against," I continue to film "for" and that I have the same love for Antoine Doinel, Catherine, Montag, Julie, Muriel Brown, Victor De l'Aveyron, or Adele H.

"Pourquoi Ce Film? Pourquoi Pas," press book of the film, reused for L'Avant-Scène Cinéma, *no. 165, 1976*

I DON'T KNOW ISABELLE ADJANI

I don't know Isabelle Adjani. To praise someone publicly is to wish to influence opinion, if not to create it; it is attempting to convince, to have more or less impact on other people's freedom of judgment. During the shooting of our film I hoped that I would not have to talk about Isabelle Adjani, because I knew it would be impossible to do so in the usual terms and I was not certain I could come up in time with the exact words. And above all, I have no desire to convince whomever it may be of whatever it might be concerning everything that has to do with her.

What has to be judged, because we always end up by judging, is her work and not the commentary I might make on it on any particular day (which would be different from what I would say the day after). I don't know if the word "work" would please Isabelle Adjani, yet it is real work we do, not together but side by side (even if she seems to regret at times that it's not done face to face) and out of which will come a film that I cannot yet describe lucidly.

I do not know Isabelle Adjani.

She is the only actress who made me cry in front of a television screen, and because of that I wanted to film with her right away, in all urgency, because I thought that I could, in filming her, steal precious things from her, like, for example, everything that passes over a body and a face in full transformation. Well then, here I am in Ali Baba's cave going back and forth and catching her glance, which seems to say to me: "That's all that interests you?

That's all you're finding to steal? An oil lamp, a broken rocking chair, a tear, a fluttering of the eyelids, a little glass boat . . . really, that's all?"

I don't know Isabelle Adjani.

During the shooting I watch her acting, I help her as I can, telling her thirty words when she would like a hundred, or saying fifty when one, the right one, would do, because everything is a matter of vocabulary in our bizarre association.

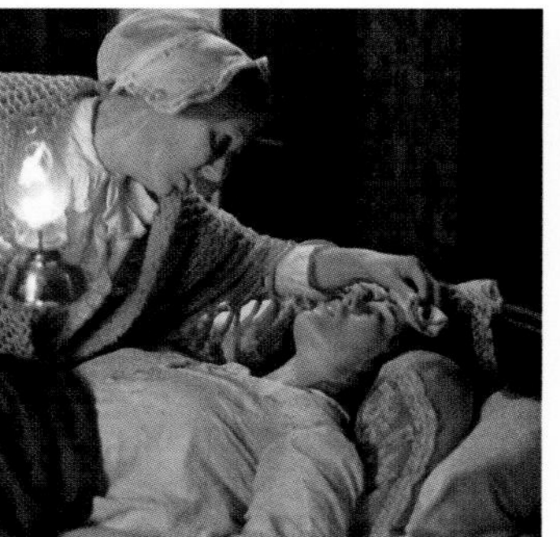

Adele's nightmare: Adele and Mrs. Saunders (Isabelle Adjani and Sylvia Marriott)

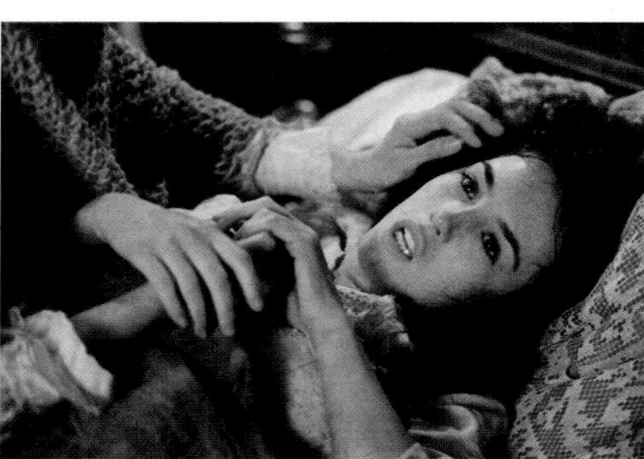

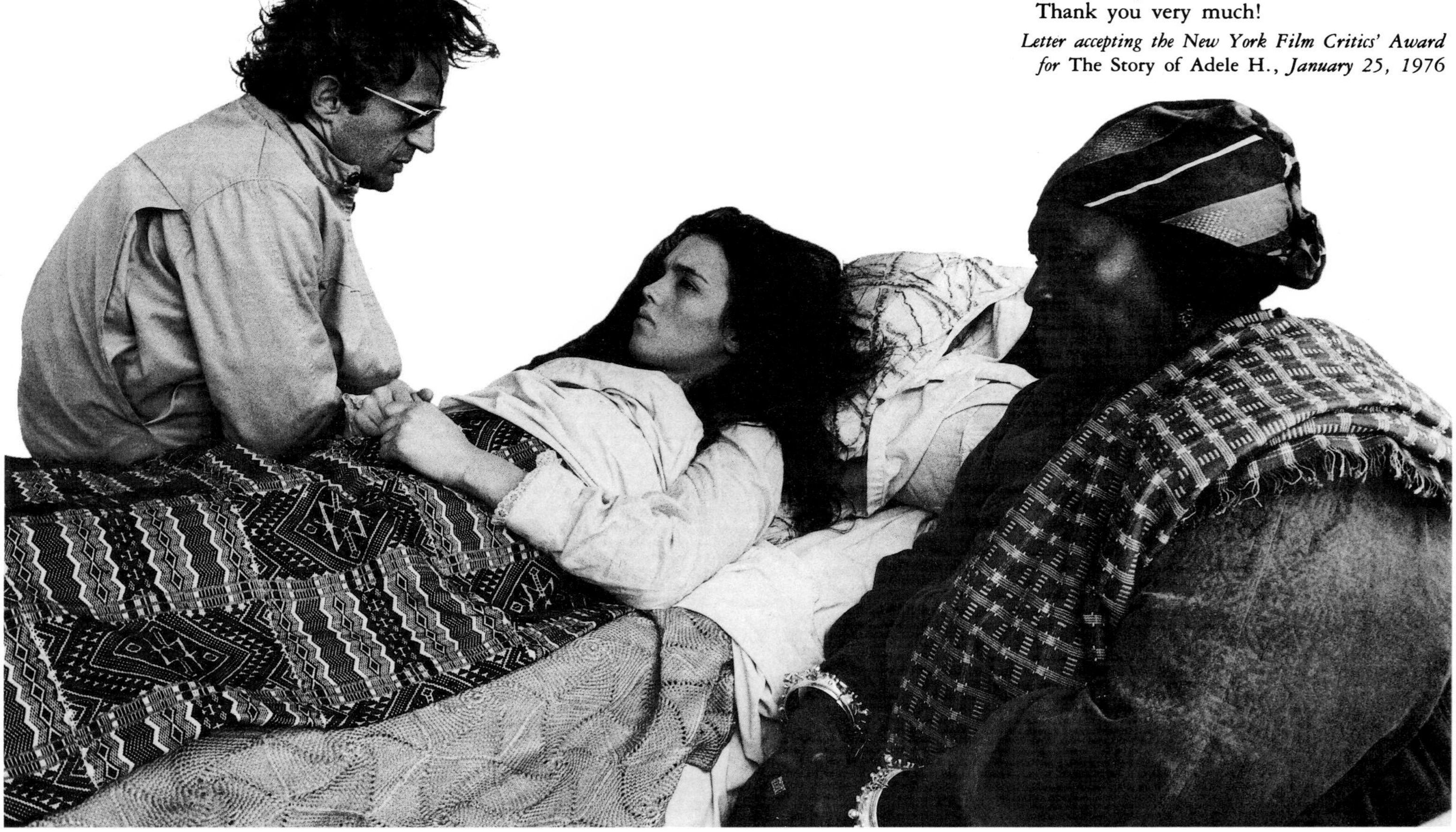

"Films that don't vibrate." François Truffaut and Isabelle Adjani in Barbados

I do not know Isabelle Adjani, yet, evenings, my eyes and my ears are weary from having looked at her too closely and listened to her the whole day long.

I will know Isabelle Adjani in a few weeks, when we will leave each other, that is, when the shooting is over. She will go her way, I don't know where, and every day I will be looking at her at the editing table, in all directions and at all speeds. Then nothing more will escape me, and I will understand everything, belatedly: "There's what should have been done, there's what should have been said, there's what should have been filmed." And thanks to that reawakened dissatisfaction, thanks to that great frustration, I will become eager to begin a new film.

I say sometimes to Isabelle Adjani: "Our life is a wall, each film is a stone." She always gives me the same answer: "That isn't true. Each film is the wall."

In L'Express, *March 3–9, 1975*

FOR SUZANNE SCHIFFMAN

My Dear Ex-colleagues and Friends,

I thank you for having awarded the prize for the best screenplay to *The Story of Adele H.*

It took no fewer than three persons to write that screenplay, and if, concerning myself, I have the duty to be modest, I do not have the right to be so for the two other writers, Jean Gruault and Suzanne Schiffman. That is why I would say that this prize is largely deserved, two thirds of it an any rate.

Suzanne and I have been working together for sixteen years. She has been my script girl from *Shoot the Piano Player* to *Mississippi Mermaid,* my assistant since *The Wild Child,* a job she has combined with that of co-scriptwriter since *Day for Night.*

For many years journalists, principally women journalists, congratulated me for having a woman as my principal collaborator.

But for about two years, the position of Women's Lib has been hardening, the female interviewers' attitude has changed, and the question most often put to me is: "In the credits of all your films we find the name of Suzanne Schiffman. Why is she your assistant, why isn't she the one to make the films?" Well, I am leaving that question for Suzanne to answer today. While I pick up the broom and sweep the offices of the Films du Carrosse, Suzanne is going to Sardi's to drink champagne and accept the prize.

I beg you, dear Ex-colleagues and Friends, explain carefully to Suzanne that if she wants to shoot the films, I would be very happy to become her assistant. I think that that would give me a chance to come drink champagne with you next year!

Thank you very much!

Letter accepting the New York Film Critics' Award for The Story of Adele H., *January 25, 1976*

SMALL CHANGE

1976

It's a matter of filming children because you love them

More than two hundred children's faces pass through this story: a class of thirty-five pupils, a class of twenty-five pupils, a day nursery with forty babies, finally a vacation camp with sixty boys and as many girls!

At the movies one Sunday afternoon

Since it is not easy to present succinctly a unanimist film, I am going to call to my rescue three artists I admire. Victor Hugo with "The Art of Being a Grandfather," Charles Trenet with two hundred and fifty songs admirable for their equilibrium, Ernst Lubitsch indulgent and sly—I see them as three poets who succeeded in retaining the spirit of childhood:

> "Children have the gift of rendering me completely crazy. I adore them and I am an idiot." (Victor Hugo)
>
> "The kids they get bored on Sundays,
> On Sundays the kids get bored." (Charles Trenet)
>
> "A chance for a laugh is never to be sneered at." (Ernst Lubitsch).

These three quotations guided us, Suzanne Schiffman and me, in working out *Small Change,* in the choice of episodes and the way of treating them. What counted was to get laughs, not at the children's expense but "with them," not even at the expense of the adults but "with them," thus the search for a delicate balance between gravity and lightness.

Press book of the film, February 1976; reprinted in the preface to L'Argent de Poche: Ciné-roman, *Paris, Flammarion, 1976*

PEOPLE MAKE USE OF CHILDHOOD, AND I DIDN'T WANT TO DO THAT

"The filmmaker's responsibility is greater when he is filming children."

You have said, I believe, that Small Change *came out of a very old project.*

Oh yes! I sometimes get to the point of asking myself if I'm not *always* filming old projects. Sometimes I can date them with precision. For example, *The Story of Adele H.*, that got started in February-March 1969, when fragments of Adele's story were published. I was immediately interested in getting a film out of it. For the present one, it's more difficult to pin it down because I'd have to go back to the period of *The Mischief Makers.* The first plan for *The Mischief Makers* was to make a film with several stories. I preferred to drop that idea, but I wasn't entirely content with *The Mischief Makers,* and subsequently I built up one episode, which ended up as *The 400 Blows.* After that, I went back several times to the possibility of a film on the different aspects of childhood, but it was especially after having made *Day for Night* that I understood I could do it better than in the form of sketches, by mixing together all the stories and all the characters. *Day for Night* was something of a puzzler on paper as to its construction, but the result was satisfactory: I thought I could fit together my child characters as I had the characters in *Day for Night.*

And then, I personally don't like to make documentaries. I like fiction, I like to work out plots, construct stories, I like to astonish, I like to give pleasure, and all those notions are always valid for me and are close to my heart. Thus I know you can make the public be patient for quite a while, for a half hour of film without really getting into gear with the story. The public is full of patience, so I exploit that patience for a half hour to set up my characters well; but afterwards you have, nevertheless, to set the story in motion, and it doesn't shock me that, little by little, two characters begin to stand out and catch our interest more than the others: actually, they are Patrick and Julien. Let's say that if the others have had two or three scenes, one of which is important, these two little by little become of key importance, they become two threads to be followed. They don't contrast like Crying John and Laughing John, but they are nonetheless two distinct characters. Physically especially, they complemented each other so well. . . . No, I think that's all right.

I think that kind of construction is better, because if I had done the contrary—beginning with two characters and dropping them later for a multitude of characters—I'd have lost the lot. So I preferred the opposite.

But there was also the plan, carried through more or less and for better or worse, which was to cover the entire spread from birth to the age of twelve. Perhaps we should have filmed a birth. I had intended to do so, but it wasn't possible. It is filmed only indirectly, on the teacher's face. The project was to show the ages not usually shown. Usually children aged two and a half are not shown, in any case they're not shown in action. And that's what it was: a little boy and a little girl from birth to the threshold of adolescence.

You have admitted to loving children to the point of becoming "crazy" over them. Doesn't that nonetheless present a certain risk, I mean the risk of

Des enfants pareils

— Le livret de famille 12
— Colonie de vacances et 1er baiser 14
— 2 filles et 2 gars au cinéma 14
— Minûle a fait boum 2 ans
— ~~Le gros méchant loup 2 3 ans~~
— Quand on est mort... (C.V) 4 et 5 ans.
— le bouquet à la mère du copain 14
— le copain qui coupe les cheveux 13
— Harpagon à l'école
+ René-Jean Clot — N.R.F.
+ Saki etc... (cadeaux de Noël) } les cadeaux utiles
+ idem Leacock...

Provisional list of episodes intended for a film about children

being too "nice"? Did you have to react against that?

The only reproach I hear fairly regularly now that the film is out—the fact is, someone began it and a lot of people are taking it up—is the idea that one thing is absent from the film: the cruelty of children.

I thought so, too. The more so since it's present in The Mischief Makers.

Yes, indeed, but in *The Mischief Makers* it shocked me. That's one of the reasons I dropped the idea of going ahead with them. I came to realize that it was very artificial: the children in *The Mischief Makers* were very good when I gave them things to do very much tied up with their daily lives. But when they had to act out a situation, to persecute the pair of lovers, it bothered them and they did it badly. And at that point I said: I'm not making another artificial story with children, I'll start from much more flexible things where I can show their relationships, but I will not again film a story in which children are made use of to demonstrate something. I know the cruelty of children exists; I didn't have to endure it because I was an only child, and I was even then very much drawn to children smaller than me, I always wanted to play, to talk with those children. I believe that people who have brothers and sisters have known much more aggressive relationships. So I didn't myself know children from that angle, and on the other hand I have seen the cruelty of children utilized too often in films or literature in an artificial way, to show the absurdity of war or the cruelty of war, etc. People make use of childhood, and I didn't want to do that. So maybe that's lacking, but I don't regret it.

Was it very difficult to get such a large company of children to act?

It was exhausting, exhausting for the ears above all, because they made a lot of noise. But at the same time you laugh a lot, you get some great surprises, some stronger emotions than when shooting with adults.

The niceness of the film: many people have made that reproach; I think it was to some extent necessary because the kids were always hanging around the camera, wanting to know how it functions; they were very interested in the mechanism. They hung around the sound apparatus, talked with the sound engineer. They came, I let them see the rushes at the cinema in town: I wasn't going to block the doors to keep them from looking at the rushes! They came, I had the editing table there, they looked on while, little by little, our film took shape. Then, little by little, they got so deep into the film that I felt it was becoming a little their film and that I was making it for them. One doesn't say the same thing to children as to adults, you say serious things with a lighter tone or dispassionately, or making things less serious. That was the problem: I wanted all the same to speak of those serious matters, but I wanted the film to please them, to be their film. There you are.

What role did the children's improvisation, or even sheer chance, have?

Oh, it's important, because within the scenes I gave them very little dialogue. I gave them in general the ideas, and they did the rest with their own words. There was no improvisation in the action, because the stories were all there. But, for example, in the scene where the teacher arrives and says: "I have had a child," they asked exactly the questions they wanted. There we functioned like Jean Rouch, the camera first on the children, so they can ask the questions they want to ask, the script girl takes down almost everything said, then camera on the teacher, the children ask more questions offscreen, and they are just about the same, and the teacher replies. There was no written dialogue there. That works very well also because François Stévenin has a very good touch with children.

Interview by Jean Delmas,
Jeune Cinéma, *no. 95, May-June 1976*

"I felt it was becoming a little their film and that I was making it for them."

FILMING WITH CHILDREN IS AS SPECIAL AS FILMING WITH A HELICOPTER

Filming with children is as special as filming with a helicopter. The helicopter kicks up sand. You have to moisten the ground. You figure you're losing time like crazy. And as soon as the camera is in the helicopter, you gain an immense lot of time. You film thirty kilometers in ten minutes. You're in a different universe. That of homing pigeons. With children it's the same. From time to time they refuse to work. You have to allow them time off to play ball. And all of a sudden they give you ten times more than you expected.

Interview by Claude-Marie Tremois, Télérama, *no. 1319, April 23, 1975*

1979, YEAR OF THE MURDERED CHILDREN

If you think about children, the 1970s should be marked with a black stone, and History will not pardon, I hope, the sinister humor that decreed 1979 "Year of the Child," when you can count in the thousands the children dead of hunger or mistreatment in Africa, in Asia, and elsewhere. While French journalists ponder gravely over what our President of the Republic could have done with four or five pillboxes of diamonds, the real questions are not asked: 1. When did the French government learn that a hundred or so children had been massacred at Bangui? 2. What would it have done (or what would it not have done) if Amnesty International had not exposed the matter? 3. Did France drive out Bokassa because he killed those children or only because he got caught?

I can well imagine that a lighter text is expected of me—one more specifically oriented toward the cinema and childhood—but I am not disposed to forget that everything hangs together: weren't there children among the two hundred and fifty spectators in that movie house in Iran where the doors were sealed before starting a fire in the course of the first demonstrations in 1978? Obviously I am not recalling that in order to defend the Shah's regime. For five years in a row I declined, like so many others, of course, the honor of attending the "Cinema and Childhood" festival that took place in Teheran, but saying no all the time to dubious

le decouvre la geographie
Dessin

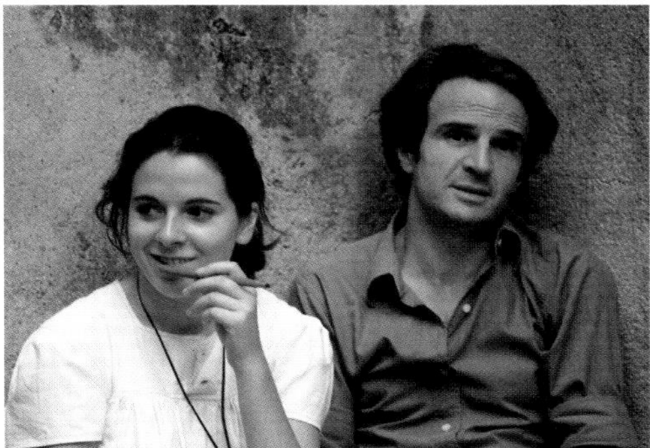

Their first kiss is merely in play

Truffaut with his daughter Laura

"And all of a sudden they give you ten times more than you expected."

propositions does not suffice to spare one the shame: of not protesting more vigorously each time, of being unable to prevent anything, of recognizing that one is of the same species as the executioners and yet impotent. Nor do I ignore the fact that France holds the lamentable European record for the number of maltreated children, since the law against "nonassistance to persons in danger" is never applied.

The Cinema and Childhood? I'm getting to it. It has always irritated me to see the intellectuals expecting that a film in which children take part should express first "the cruelty of children." Children's cruelty is a solid-gold literary theme, but it doesn't exist. When it exists, it is as a caricatural reflection of the cruelty of adults. A child loved, raised, and environed in a normal way feels no desire to martyrize another child or an animal. There are no children who are Nazis, fanatics, terrorists, fascists, there are only children *of* Nazis, *of* fanatics, *of* terrorists, *of* fascists, and because they are children—yes, I come out and say it—because they are children they are innocent. Too bad if I make some of you smile. Like blacks in Hollywood films, children are underrepresented in films compared with the importance they have in our daily lives. As a child growing up in Paris in the neighborhood of Pigalle during the war, I had to suffer from the cruelty of grownups, never of other children, and the love I bear them leads me to show them often in my films, even when the subject does not involve them directly.

The Cinema and Childhood! I suppose that this *Bulletin* will feature all the topics that automatically come to mind: films "for" children, films "with" children, films "with" children intended for adults, films "with" children intended for all audiences. I confess that films belonging to the latter category have my preference, because the divisions between one category of spectators and another are as arbitrary as the laws of the German occupation that classified children into J1, J2, or J3. . . . Let us not forget that Victor Hugo, Alphonse Daudet, Alexandre Dumas, Jules Verne, Hector Malot wrote "for" adults and "for" children.

To finish, I remind you that the filmmaker's responsibility is greater when he is filming children, because the public cannot keep itself from superimposing a symbolic meaning on everything a child does. When we look at a particular child doing something on the screen, we are immediately projected back to our own childhood, and what that child is doing seems to us what childhood as a whole does. That is why I am offended when a filmmaker thinks he can mix a child up in a murder, for example, or in a detective story. A film with children can make do with showing simple happenings, because the drama of childhood is born out of everyday life. Above all, a child must not be used like an actor to whom one hands a text but like a collaborator one asks to bring with him life, plausibility, fantasy.

Finally, contrary to what I read sometimes, here or there, films shouldn't be made with children in order to understand them better. Children should be filmed only because you love them.

Contribution to UNESCO in the name of the Fédération Internationale des Ciné-clubs, Christmas 1979

"The legs of women are the branches of a compass that bestride the terrestrial globe in all senses, giving it its equilibrium and its harmony."

THE MAN WHO LOVED WOMEN

1977

"It appeared that Joey had never had much success with his mother"

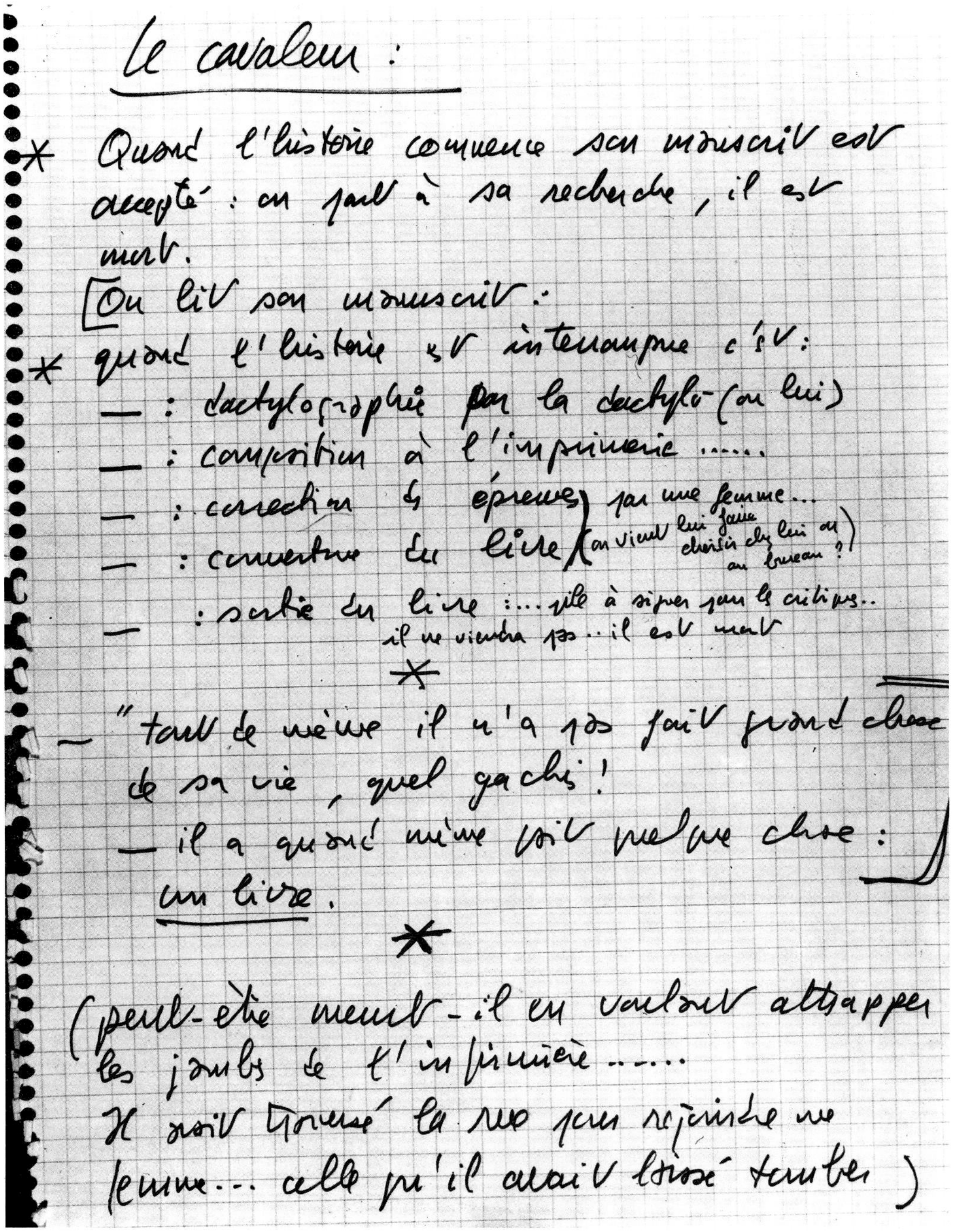

Le cavaleur :

* Quand l'histoire commence son manuscrit est accepté : on part à sa recherche, il est mort.

[On lit son manuscrit :

* quand l'histoire est interrompue c'est :

— : dactylographie par la dactylo (ou lui)

— : composition à l'imprimerie .....

— : correction des épreuves par une femme...

— : couverture du livre (on vient lui faire choisir chez lui ou au bureau ?)

— : sortie du livre :... vite à signer pour les critiques.. il ne viendra pas.. il est mort

*

— "tout de même il n'a pas fait grand chose de sa vie, quel gâchis !

— il a quand même fait quelque chose : un livre.

*

(peut-être meurt-il en voulant attraper les jambes de l'infirmière .....

Il avait trouvé la rue pour rejoindre une femme... celle qu'il avait laissé tomber)

We—Suzanne Schiffman, Michel Fermaud, and I—wrote the screenplay of *The Man Who Loved Women* with Charles Denner in mind and out of admiration for him. I asked Brigitte Fossey, Leslie Caron, Nelly Borgeaud, Geneviève Fontanel, Nathalie Baye, Sabine Glaser, Valérie Bonnier, and numerous good-looking Montpellier girls to be those he has held in his arms. If a sentence can serve as a common denominator for Bertrand's love affairs, it would be that of Bruno Bettelheim in *The Empty Fortress:* "It appeared that Joey had never had much success with his mother."

Foreword to press book, April 1977

LETTERS TO CHARLES DENNER

Paris, May 4, 1976

My dear Charles,

I have to be out of Paris for several weeks, but before leaving I will get to you the first synopsis of our film, *The Man Who Loved Women.*

A more detailed treatment is in the course of being written, and we will get it to you as soon as possible, but if you are impatient to know more, you can contact Suzanne, who will be working with me by correspondence.

As I told you, the entire film will be an extension of the character you played in *The Bride Wore Black,* and moreover it was while watching you play those scenes, while we were shooting, that the first idea came to me for this new film.

With friendly greetings,

Paris, March 29, 1977

My dear Charles,

As you requested, here are a few general statements that may help you in interviews about our film.

I am in favor of avoiding mentioning too often the fact that Bertrand Morane is writing

"Underclothes don't look at us unless we look at them" (from Truffaut's article, "Dessous d'Espoir," of 1955; see page 22).

The unknown woman on the telephone accepts the rendezvous proposed by Bertrand Morane (Charles Denner)

a book, because that would give the public the impression of a literary or intellectual film.

Although the character is very remote from you (and from me), I am mentioning in each interview that we had lunch together eighteen months ago and that I submitted to you the main lines of the film, which was then specially written for you.

Many questions will concern the character. Should he be considered positive or negative? I think the best answer is that given by Brigitte Fossey: "He's simply a man, etc."

There will also be questions having to do with feminism: what will the ladies of the M.L.F. [Mouvement de Libération des Femmes] think, etc? On that point, I favor replying that we haven't tried to soft-soap the M.L.F., but the female characters, numerous and episodic as they are, are strong enough to stand up to Bertrand Morane.

That's all I see for the moment.

Along with this, I am sending a press book, where you will find, slightly rewritten, the text you already know.

It might be good also if you could view the film once again as soon as we have finished the mixing in the week of the 11th to 16th. . . .

To speak like Claude Berri, the opening of the mine is set for April 27.

Good wishes.

THE RISK, CERTAINLY, IS THAT PEOPLE WILL REJECT THE CHARACTER

Is The Man Who Loved Women *an old project?*

Yes. I say that for every new film, but in fact it's almost always true. The idea for this one goes back ten years, to when I first worked with Charles Denner in *The Bride Wore Black:* that's the only part of the film I like. He had a sort of monologue when Jeanne Moreau was posing for him. I very much liked his voice, his way of reciting a text which, without him, would have seemed cynical. I thought at that time that it was he who could best embody a man haunted by women. So we wrote the screenplay with Suzanne Schiffman and Michel Fermaud, thinking constantly of Charles Denner.

For some time now, your films have been taking place in the provinces.

That is not with the aim of showing "France as she is." In the first place, it's to get out of Paris, which is not a favorable site, creatively. In the last film I shot in Paris, *Bed and Board,* the general environment wasn't good, and I have bad memories of it. There is no mobilization of emotions in filming unless you've left your home, family, friends.

"One man's face, the faces of a hundred women"

A great love sacrificed: Véra and Bertrand (Leslie Caron and Charles Denner)

Your character is a collector and writer of memoirs. One can't help thinking of Don Juan and Casanova, even if the reference is brushed aside in the dialogue. What position did you take with regard to those allusions?

I don't know much about the learned studies published on the myth of Don Juan. I proceeded in the spirit of contradiction as I often do: do the contrary of what a Villalonga, a self-satisfied or coxcombish type, would do. I constantly tried to adjust the character to Charles Denner himself. I didn't consider the problem of sympathy. The risk, certainly, is that people will reject the character.

Why do you think he might be rejected?

People might react like the typist in the film. But on the other hand, I knew that with Charles Denner I had not made a mistaken choice. Even if he is sometimes odious, Bertrand retains a great charm. I made a mistake in *The Soft Skin* with that disagreeable character, played by a good actor, who lacks seductiveness, however. I love Lubitsch too much not to regret it. *The Soft Skin* became a disagreeable film in spite of me. Instead of defending the character, I overwhelmed him. With Denner, his timid look and his peaceable shyness win out in any case.

Your character dies in a way on the job, still chasing. Is that the seducer's fate?

It was inevitable. I was working on something mythical. You have to respect the law of the myth. The death scene in a hospital looking at the nurses' legs was already recounted by the character Daniel Boulanger in *Shoot the Piano Player,* telling in a car about his father's death. Here it was visualized. His death is obviously not a punishment. It's a question of logic, like the death of old Grandet: they come to give him last rites, he sees the crucifix, it's gold, it shines, he tries to grab it, and dies. . . .

Is the character an extreme case?

I don't think so, not if you compare him with the statistical confessions of Georges Simenon, who claims to have "known" ten thousand women in his life. Ten thousand, that's a lot of women behind doors, in corridors, or between two typewriters. . . . Denner is a timid little kid compared to him!

Your films more and more show groups: the film crew in Day for Night, *the children in* Small Change, *here Charles Denner's harem.*

First of all, I like the idea that everything connects up with the subject. When you treat a theme, you have to build it up. Here, everything fits in: the woman at the wake-up service, the laundress who has a scrap of ribbon in her hair. . . . In constructed stories there are always some boring scenes, like someone going to the station or taking a taxi. Filming them, you get an impression of a sloppy mess. Here, though, the taxi could be driven by a woman! Everything goes back to the theme; that's very seductive for the mind. I began to represent groups in *Stolen Kisses.* To bring more truth to the screen, the New Wave had ruled out secondary roles. That was an injustice with regard to a certain kind of film, that of Jacques Prévert. Deprived of good second roles, films had become narcissistic. That reflection brought something quantitative into my films, something deliberately worked out in *Stolen Kisses, Day for Night, Small Change.*

As the film goes along, we notice an equivalence between the film and the book written by Denner.

Since *Fahrenheit 451* I tried to show in a film the exact process a book goes through: writing, typing, correction, proof sheets, print. That worked in well with the story here: Denner's disappointment with Geneviève Fontanel gives him the need to lay his life out flat to see it clearly.

Henri-Pierre Roché did that for fifty years: his intense sentimental life and his intimate diary could not exist one without the other. This harping on the book in the film may strike some as naïve, but in life I spend my time encouraging people to write the book they have in their heads.

Interview by Jacques Fieschi,
Cinématographe, *no. 27, May 1977*

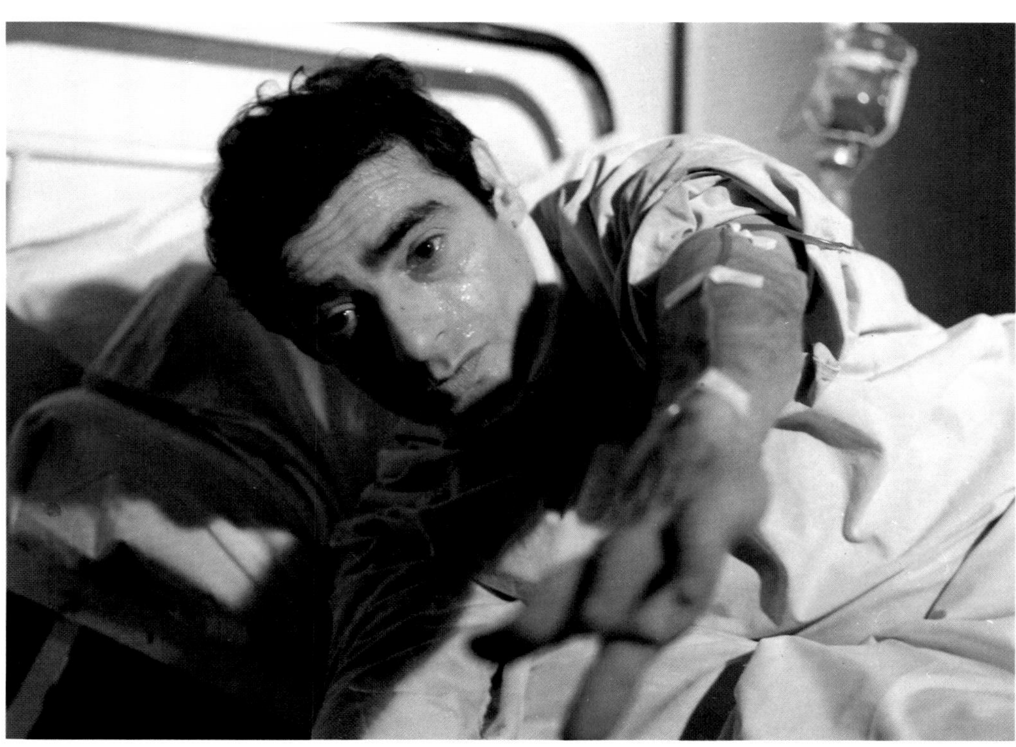

Bertrand Morane, in the hospital, makes one last grab for a nurse

Julien Davenne and the little deaf-mute (François Truffaut and Patrick Maléon)

THE GREEN ROOM

1978

A moment comes when we realize we know more dead people than living

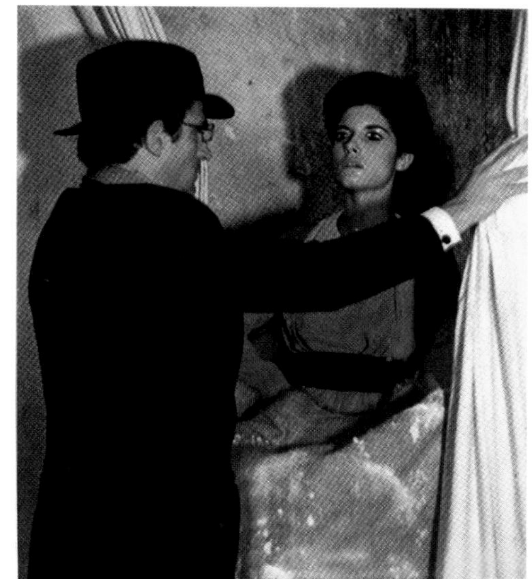

Julien Davenne and the mannequin of Julie (Truffaut and Laurence Ragon)

First page of the first draft of the screenplay for *The Green Room*

- LA DISPARUE -

0 - Generique : les morts de 14-18, la mort en général.

1 - Chez MAZET : DAVENNE chasse un prêtre et console le veuf à sa façon: les morts peuvent continuer à vivre ! Fondu au noir

2 - Salle des ventes : DAVENNE cherche une bague et rencontre CECILIA qui le reconnait - pas lui.

3 - Voiture, nuit - DAVENNE roule.

4 - Maison DAVENNE - GEORGES a réparé l'appareil de projections.

5 - Bureau du GLOBE - DAVENNE refuse de suivre HUMBERT à Paris - il restera pour EUX (les abonnés morts).

6 - Salles des ventes - CECILIA et DAVENNE se sont rencontrés avant la guerre - elle ne l'a pas oublié - La bagùe est retrouvée.

7 - Salle des ventes - C'est Mme RAMBAUD qui achète la bague.

8 - Maison DAVENNE - Mme RAMBAUD remet la bague à DAVENNE qui monte l'escalier- elle répond au téléphone qu'il est absent.

9 - Chambre du haut - DAVENNE rend la bague à JULIE.

10 - Enchainé : tombe de Julie DAVENNE-VALLANCE et cimetière. la musique de la scène précédente continue.

11 - Bureau du GLOBE - MAZET dit à HUMBERT qu'il veut présenter sa nouvelle femme à DAVENNE - celuièci, dissimulé, a tout entendu.

12 - Salle des ventes - DAVENNE confie son indignation à CECILIA - elle plaide pour les vivants.

13 - En voiture : CECILIA pleure puis raconte à DAVENNE la mort de de son père - mais ils ne sont pas pareils - la scène se termine comme une rupture.

14 - BUREAU DU GLOBE - Orage - DAVENNE apprend la mort de Massigny et commence l'article nécrologique.

"It is not because others are dead that our affection for them grows feeble, it is because we ourselves are dying."

Marcel Proust, Albertine disparue

"The flame, among all the objects in the world that give rise to reverie, is one of the greatest producers of images."

Gaston Bachelard, La Flamme d'une chandelle

"Faithful, faithful,
I've remained faithful
To things that don't matter to you."

Charles Trenet, "Fidèle"

Quotations chosen by François Truffaut for the press book of The Green Room

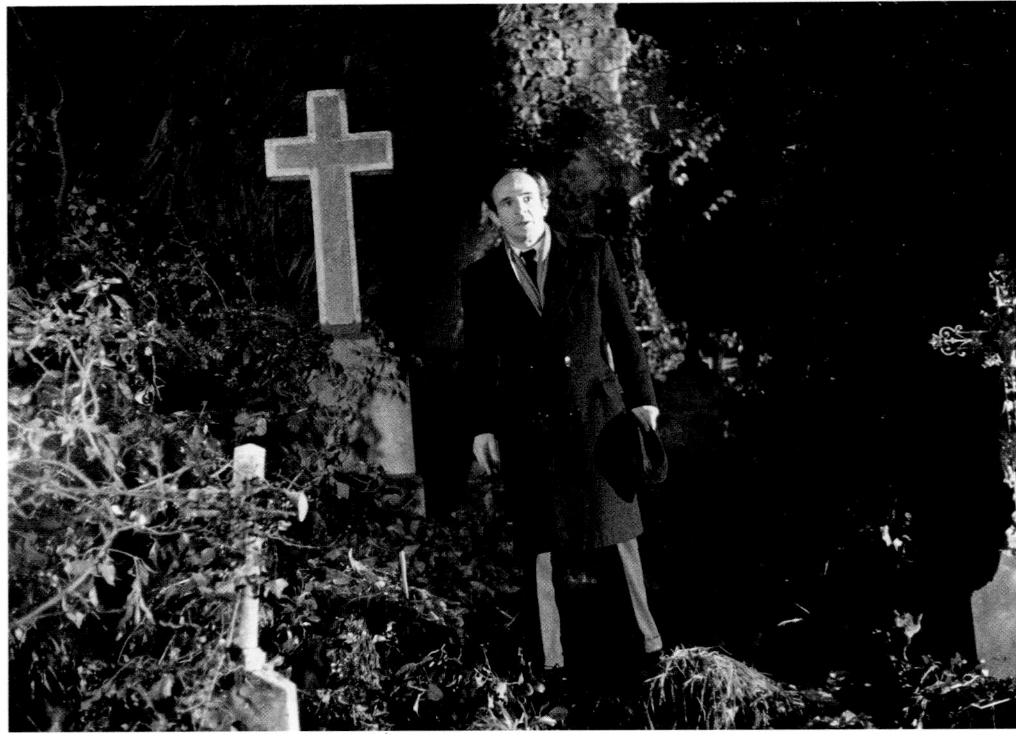

Julien Davenne at Julie's grave: "I was not able to protect you, Julie."

THE GREEN ROOM IS A LOVE STORY

"There is no longer a subscriber at the number you have requested."

Each year we have to cross out names from our address book, and a moment comes when we realize we know more dead people than living.

That observation, simple as *au revoir,* is what dictated to us, Jean Gruault and me, the screenplay of *The Green Room,* which, in the form of a filmed tale, blends together the theme of two short stories by Henry James and biographical notations on that writer's fidelity to the memory of his deceased fiancée.

The film therefore shows how relations develop between two persons who love the dead and respect them, a man and a woman who refuse to forget.

Contrary to what social and religious practices lead one to think, it happens that with certain dead we maintain relations as aggressive and impassioned as with the living.

The vicissitudes of *The Green Room* center about these questions: "Should we forget the dead?" "Does one have the right to remake one's life?" "What would happen if, indifferent to the wear and tear of time, we were to remain attached to the dead by sentiments as vehement as those which bind us to the living?"

The Green Room is a love story, like all the films that Jean Gruault and I have written together. Here, again, it's a matter of showing emotional heartbreaks and also the struggle that goes on in our hearts between passing sentiments and definitive sentiments.

"Pourquoi La Chambre Verte?"
press book of the film, March 1978

THE GREEN ROOM IS LIKE A LETTER WRITTEN BY HAND

Why did you decide to act in The Green Room?

So the film would be more intimate. Charles Denner would have acted it magnificently, but I had just made *The Man Who Loved Women* with him, where he is seen throughout. Besides Denner, I had no other idea. It seemed to me that, if I were to play the role, I would get the same difference as when, doing my correspondence in the office, I dictate certain letters, which are then typed, and I write others by hand. *The Green Room* is like a letter written by hand. If you write by hand it will not be perfect, the writing may perhaps be trembly, but it will be you, your writing. The typewriter is something different. I don't mean any comparison running down actors, because there are Olivettis with marvelous type, Remingtons which have a lot of personality, and Japy portables. Myself, I adore typewriters!

Interview by Danièle Heymann and Catherine Laporte,
L'Express, *March 13, 1978*

At the sculptor's: "Take this money and destroy that thing immediately in my presence."

Julien Davenne and Cécilia Mandel (Truffaut and Nathalie Baye)

Julien Davenne and his housekeeper, Mme Rambaud (Truffaut and Jane Lobre)

Julien Davenne takes down the portraits threatened by the flames

"I don't want to speak with anyone. I don't need anything. . . . "

THE GREEN ROOM IS CONSTRUCTED LIKE A MUSICAL COMEDY WITH NO DANCING AND NO SINGING

"Just one more, just one candle, and the figure will be finished."

Cécilia (Nathalie Baye) and the forest of candles

It's the type of film in which the form is very important. Make one mistake, and the film caves in. Everything has to be thought out, very tight. In fact, the whole film is synchronized to Jaubert's music, the *Concert Flamand,* which we recorded before shooting. The movements of the camera and those of the actors are set to the music. *The Green Room* is constructed like a musical comedy with no dancing and no singing. Ultimately there were three elements to harmonize: James, Almendros's camera work, and Jaubert. It is an anti-Hollywoodian film in the sense that, in Hollywood, they work with great narrative generosity. It is more determinedly European, because it reposes on the classical idea of doing something with almost nothing, with little things that have to be amplified to bring them up to the level of the event. The ideal would be to obtain a film laid out in a single line. But for that, you would have to make a film lasting an hour and ten minutes, like in the first days of the talkies. Today there are too often several films in one.

For me, *The Green Room* belongs to a family of films where one finds *Fahrenheit 451, The Wild Child,* and *Adele H.* The dead in it are like the books in *Fahrenheit,* a great deal of effort goes into making inert things live, the living breathe their own breath into them, their own passions.

Those cemetery scenes, moreover, come from my childhood memories, but I became aware of it only while shooting. I had a paternal grandfather who was a stonecutter. He worked a lot in the cemeteries, and during vacation he often took me along with him. I also went there with my grandmother, whose family had had numerous deaths and who always had many graves to visit. There was a whole hierarchy for her dead. For example, she devoted much more time to the grave of a young girl who died at twenty. I remember that when my grandfather died, she slipped a pair of socks into the coffin because he would be cold.

Interview by Michel Perez,
Le Matin de Paris, *March 29, 1978*

LOVE ON THE RUN

I wanted an ending deliberately, brazenly or, if you wish, desperately HAPPY!

1979

Filming *Love on the Run* in the Gare de Lyon, Paris

Love on the Run *has been announced as the last of the series with Antoine Doinel. Why kill off Doinel just now when he's barely over thirty?*

It's precisely in order not to kill him off that I wanted a happy ending. In general, the endings in the Doinel films were left open. At the end of *The 400 Blows* Antoine was running away from the observation center for juvenile delinquents, we left him at the edge of the sea just as he was turning toward the camera. He placed a question mark before the public which was meant to say: "What have you made of me? What are you going to make out of me? What am I going to become?"

In *Love at Twenty,* which had the structure of a short story, I showed his first disappointment in love: the young student he met at the Jeunesses Musicales, and whom he succeeded in getting close to, ends up considering him a sort of pain-in-the-neck cousin; at the end of the film, a boyfriend comes to call for her and Antoine remains with Colette's parents to watch television after dinner. That was a bitter ending which could make people laugh or could grip their hearts.

The end of *Stolen Kisses* showed that perhaps Antoine would pair up permanently with Claude Jade, but that the couple was already threatened, for example by that man, come out of the blue, who, just as if Doinel didn't exist, makes a declaration of love to Claude Jade right out on the street.

The end of *Bed and Board* showed the couple's temporary reconciliation after many quarrels.

In *Love on the Run,* given the fact that a whole melancholy brew is stirred up (it is practically a filmed biography), I wanted an ending deliberately, brazenly or, if you wish, desperately HAPPY! At the same time it makes it clear that we won't be coming back: the film is "recapitulatory," its ending "conclusive."

Why that recapitulatory aspect and all those flashbacks?

It seems to me that I had to take advantage of a chance that almost no filmmaker has had. When you film a story that dips back into the past, you set yourself the problem of finding a young actor who looks like your adult leading man. When I shot *The Man Who Loved Women* three years ago, in the street in Montpellier I found a little boy who looked like Charles Denner. We jumped on the occasion and had two or three flashbacks of Charles Denner as a child.

But when you have the good luck to have filmed someone at the age of thirteen and a half, nineteen, twenty-four, and twenty-eight and you're going back to him at thirty-three, you've got priceless material in your hands, not too cheerful, because the physical transformation of a person is not necessarily thrilling, but rich nonetheless. I have always felt, when I was filming adolescents, that the filmed material was more precious than that devoted to adults. So here was a chance I was glad to take advantage of: having filmed the same boy at different ages of his life, to go back to him playing the same character and telling a story which permitted him to appear as grown man, adolescent, and little boy.

Did the idea of utilizing flashbacks come to you because the material existed already or because it appeared to you indispensable in the body of the story? Wouldn't it have been possible to imagine Love on the Run *without any flashbacks?*

Yes, but it would have been one more "sequel." I would be lying if I said that Antoine Doinel was successful in his transformation into an adult. He has not become a real adult, he is someone in whom there remains a good deal of childhood. In everyone, a lot of childhood remains, but in him even more. So I wanted to make a kind of mosaic, the story of a life. The Americans, in their films in the past, accustomed us to decidedly more heroic biographies!

I remember a *New Yorker* cartoon in which you saw the staff of a big company gathered around a conference table and alongside was a blackboard on which was written: "The Thrilling Life of?" There was a question mark and all the guys were racking their brains to come up with the name of a likely hero.

In the case of Antoine Doinel, it's not the "thrilling" life, it's not the "prodigious" life, it's just a life plain and simple, that of a human being with his contradictions and insufficiencies. I'm taken to task for it sometimes, but when I have a man as a central character in a film I harp on his weaknesses. I've done it for others than Doinel as well. Aznavour in *Shoot the Piano Player,* Jean Desailly in *The Soft Skin,* Charles Denner in *The Man Who Loved Women,* are not "heroes." The American cinema is magnificent in showing "heroes," but the special calling of the European cinema, it seems to me, is to express the truth, to show people's weaknesses, their contradictions, even their lies. In the case of Antoine Doinel, his lies are of great interest to me. He looks so sincere when he lies that one has the impression that he is the first victim of his lying. I have never seen anyone display so much good faith in lying. Antoine Doinel has the desire to be happy and a sort of impossibility to hold on to happiness when he finds it—or something resembling it. He's a man on the run. He's also a little the man in a hurry, always one jump ahead of himself.

Why did you decide to break off with Antoine Doinel? After all, one can imagine a new Doinel from time to time and—why not?—right up to the age of seventy . . .

The 400 Blows was hailed beyond all my hopes, and at first I didn't want to make a sequel to it, probably because of a puritanical reflex with regard to its success. I think I was wrong, and I've regretted it because I let go by, without filming it, Léaud's physical development between thirteen and nineteen years of age. All the same, when Pierre Roustang, who was producing *Love at Twenty,* proposed I should do the French episode, I felt it would be worthwhile, for a half hour, to go back to the character of Antoine Doinel and to show his first sentimental adventure. In filming *Love at Twenty,* which was a great pleasure as regards both shooting and improvisation, I was sorry it wasn't a full-length film, but that was impossible. Afterwards I kept in mind the idea of making *Stolen Kisses,* which I shot at the start of '68. That was the only time I knew immediately that I would make the sequel. I recall clearly that Henri Langlois, in presenting the film at the Cinémathèque, which had just reopened, said: "Those young ones, you've got to marry them and film what follows." A year and a half later, we undertook *Bed and Board.* After *The 400 Blows,* Jean-Pierre Léaud made films with Cocteau, Duvivier, Godard, Eustache. He became an actor and, because of that, in the interest of his career, I didn't want him to be overly associated with the Antoine Doinel series. Myself I made use of Jean-Pierre at times, aside from Doinel, as in *Two English Girls* or *Day for Night.* Making due allowance, it's the problem Sean Connery ran up against with the character of James Bond.

But this time it's settled: it's really and truly the last Doinel, if only because I gave

Love on the Run the form of a mosaic and patchwork. The fact is, I thought I was done with Doinel after *Bed and Board,* but one day Henning Carlsen, who made a very fine film, *Hunger,* told me something that interested me greatly. In Denmark the movie theaters are "allocated," like state tobacco shops in France. Henning Carlsen inherited the movie theater that Carl Dreyer had had until his death, the Dagmar Theater in Copenhagen. There, Henning Carlsen indulged in the following experiment. He showed all of Doinel in the form of a cycle. At two in the afternoon, *The 400 Blows;* at four-thirty, *Love at Twenty;* at six, *Stolen Kisses;* and at eight, *Bed and Board.* And there were young people there who spent the entire day watching Antoine Doinel growing up, falling in love, and getting older. And it was when he told me that that the idea came to me to make one last "Doinel," which would be *Love on the Run. . . .*

In Love on the Run *there are excerpts manipulated or diverted from their original significance. We can assume, therefore, that a lot of hard work had to go into the editing?*

In reality, out of a length of one hour and thirty-five minutes, there are only eighteen minutes of borrowings from earlier films, but obviously it's a film in which montage is much more important than in a straight narrative like *The Green Room* or *Adele H.* It is certainly the film I spent the most time editing since *Fahrenheit 451,* which was also very much broken up and in which the book burnings were used as flashbacks. The problem in *Love on the Run,* for Martine Barraqué and me, was to homogenize a disparate material, to keep from losing the thread, to avoid disappointing when we come back to the present after a flashback. The more the visual material is disparate, the more the unity of sound has to be preserved. It's the sound that established the bridges. In the screenplay we had of course foreseen the placement and length of the flashbacks, but the editing, which took sixteen weeks, imposed its own laws on us, very curious laws. Let's say that, when there is change of image, there mustn't be change of sound, at any rate the least possible. The flashbacks that begin in the train are particularly dynamic because, when we come back to the present, we are in a train in motion and thus all caught up in something moving ahead. That is the special pleasure we get from those films I call "unrolling films." Everyone knows that a film is an unrolling, unwinding ribbon. Because of that, films taking place entirely in a train, like Hitchcock's *The Lady Vanishes,* or on a raft like Herzog's *Aguirre,* give us a special pleasure because it's cinema to the second power.

Colette in Xavier's bookshop (Jean-Pierre Léaud, Marie-France Pisier, Daniel Mesguich)

Left to right
Truffaut with Claude Jade, with Marie-France Pisier and Jean-Pierre Léaud, with Dani and Claude Jade

Why did you insert flashbacks for the women also, and not only for Doinel?

Well, because it's the principle of the film: everyone tells it all to everyone. That's part of its "manuscript found by a nasty kid" side. It's the principle of a box inside a box inside a box. Doinel doesn't tell about himself with real frankness. He has lied. He has only recounted part of it all to Marie-France in the train. For example, concerning the adventure with Dani, he hasn't told the whole truth, and we'll get to know it only when it's recounted by Claude Jade . . . when she found them in bed, that whole story of the book covered in newspaper. . . . There are deliberately falsified flashbacks, like when Antoine claims that Colette's parents came to live opposite his place while in fact it's he who moved in order to get closer to her. . . . In short, flashback doesn't necessarily mean truth.

Interview by Simon Mizrahi, for the press book of Love on the Run, *1978*

JEAN-PIERRE LÉAUD, HALLUCINATED ACTOR

There are people who love fantasy and others who detest it. Some of those who detest fantasy pretend to love the cinema, but if you question them, you find out that they love most the documentary cinema, the kind as boring as the lectures explorers give at the Salle Pleyel. People who are fond of documentaries occasionally deign to pick themselves up and go to see a fiction film, but you will find that their taste leads them to realistic stories, well defined geographically, historically, sociologically. As if by chance, those stories are most often acted by corpulent actors, who are very reassuring because their weight makes up for the frivolity that, in the public's mind, is associated with the job of acting. No one ever criticizes those hefty good old guys, always believable as bar owners, taxi drivers, deputy mayors. People fanatical for verisimilitude concentrate their criticisms on actors who are scrawny and have hollow cheeks and perpetually mussed hair, Bressonian actors whose introversion makes them express themselves like mournful ventriloquists. Unlike those good old guys scared of nothing, skinny actors dissimulate neither their fear nor a slight tremble in the voice: they are not tamers but untamables. How they must be tempted, those bedside rugs that take themselves to be lions, to bite the ankles of the sleepwalking actors!

I have painted here the portrait of Jean-Pierre Léaud and explained why he doesn't please everyone and why he so hugely pleases those he does please. Jean-Pierre Léaud is an antidocumentary actor: he has only to say "good morning" and we find ourselves tipping over into fiction, not to mention science fiction. Before the war the public, whose ear had not yet become banalized by television, appreciated special actors and singular ways of speaking. They loved Popesco's Romanian accent, Louis Jouvet's asthmatic fits and starts, the hallucinated vehemence of Robert Le Vigan. Hallucinated, the word has come out! Jean-Pierre Léaud, natural son of Goupi Tonkin, also oozes plausibility and verisimilitude, but his realism is that of dreams.

For Studio 43, *February 1983*

Antoine between Liliane and Christine (Dani, Jean-Pierre Léaud, and Claude Jade)

Antoine phones Sabine from the Gare de Lyon

Antoine has written an autobiographical novel, *Les Salades de l'Amour*

(1) Grande lettre à Sabine.

Sabine ma chérie, Sabine que j'aime et qui ne veut plus me voir... Même si tu ne veux pas m'écouter il faut que je te dise que j'ai fait une drôle de rencontre aujourd'hui. J'ai revu Monsieur Lucien, un des amants de ma mère, le principal, l'amant numéro un, le seul peut-être à avoir vraiment compté dans sa vie. Il m'a parlé d'elle d'une façon incroyable : "Ta mère était un petit oiseau" !
un petit oiseau !
C'était à se demander si nous parlions de la même personne !

*

"Pourquoi n'aimes tu pas ta mère

*

retour à J. P. recommençant à écrire : un petit oiseau... C'était à se demander si nous parlions de la même personne !

J. P. s'installe et commence à écrire

image de Sabine en mouvement

J. P.

G. P. écriture

image de M. Lucien (G. P.)

photos d'hommes tombant au sol

G. P. Lucien

G. P. écriture

G. P. J. P. cesse d'écrire et rêvasse

off : "~~??~~ pourquoi n'aimes-tu pas ta mère ?"

~~[illegible] ensemble, avec Martine, [illegible] [illegible] dans la [illegible] 3 plans de [illegible] [illegible] trajets [illegible]~~

G. P. écriture

Antoine (Jean-Pierre Léaud) and Sabine (Dorothée), the girl in the photo

I KNEW WHILE SHOOTING IT THAT I WAS DOING SOMETHING REALLY IDIOTIC

Sometimes I force myself; in the case of *The Bride Wore Black, Bed and Board,* and *Love on the Run,* I laid down certain laws for myself. Henri Langlois, who had loved *Stolen Kisses,* said to me: "Now you have to get Jean-Pierre Léaud and Claude Jade married." Still, maybe it really wasn't so urgent! As for *Love on the Run,* I knew while shooting it that I was doing something really idiotic. I was like a tightrope walker without a rope.

Interview by Serge Daney,
Jean Narboni, and Serge Toubiana,
Cahiers du Cinéma, *no. 315, September 1980*

THIS FILM IS A SWINDLE!

What do you generally expect from the critics?

What touches me sometimes is a phrase that's a bit personal, original. A negative phrase can have the same value as praise. About *Love on the Run,* only a single critic wrote: "This film is a swindle!" He was right. It's a film that depressed me very much, and I realized it reluctantly. If I had been Paramount or M.G.M., I wouldn't have released it.

Interview by Michel Boujut,
Les Nouvelles Littéraires,
no. 2,751, September 18, 1980

With Sabine's photo

THE LAST METRO

1980

Memories of that period came back to me in full force, making me decide to realize my oldest dream

January 21, 1980

My dear friends,

We are going to make a film together. Before beginning, we all have stage fright, that is, our imagination runs away with us and embroiders what is only an abstract worry: it seems to us that everything we have done before will be of no help this time and that the making of *The Last Metro* has in store this or that pernicious difficulty never faced before.

I believe, on the contrary, that *The Last Metro* will be an easy and agreeable film to shoot, as is the case every time the characters are more important than the situations. In short, as I see it, only the celluloid needs to be impressed.

All the same, we must have received a decidedly oppressive education to doubt so systematically our aptitude for one of the rare callings that allows the element of pleasure to occupy first place.

Right now, let's forget stage fright and imagine that we are all as much at ease in *The Last Metro* as fish in water.

We are going to work with the purpose of putting across an interesting and intriguing story. I propose that we keep that story to ourselves and avoid sharing it with journalists. Let's avoid even describing the characters. What goes on in the Théâtre Montmartre, from cellar to attic, concerns only us and . . . the public with which we have an appointment, but only (inevitably) nine months from now.

The camera crew, under the direction of Nestor Almendros, will do its best to get a fine image, evoking with plausibility the time of the Occupation. Let's not let the foolhardy cameras of televised reports convey a muddled impression of our work.

Without offending our comrades of the press and television, without going so far as to buck for the Lemon of the Year prize, let's put off until the fall the so-called promotional activities, to a time when, under firm control, they can be of help in launching the film publicly. Knowing that each of you will be approached separately by the media, I thought it would be easier for you to say no if it is agreed from the start that the set of *The Last Metro* will be closed to journalists.

In protecting our peaceful work, as in centralizing all news releases, we will be helped by the diplomatic talents of our publicity people, Simon Misrahi and Martine Marignac.

And now, may this shooting be fun and let the fun begin.

Letter to the cast of The Last Metro

Lucas Steiner (Heinz Bennent) has Marion Steiner (Catherine Deneuve) read *Les Décombres* by Lucien Rebatet

THE THEATER AND THE OCCUPATION SEEN BY A CHILD

With Catherine Deneuve

The Last Metro is part of a trilogy whose third panel, still to be made, will concern the music hall.

If I have learned anything in the past twenty-five years, it is that it is more difficult to adapt a novel than to write an original screenplay or, more exactly, that I generally make myself understood better by the public when I take off from zero, from the blank page. If I do not regret having made *Fahrenheit 451* (after Bradbury) or *The Bride Wore Black* (after Irish), I prefer *Stolen Kisses* or *Day for Night,* which were born out of a fancy, a desire, often from an image or a memory.

In 1958, writing *The 400 Blows* with Marcel Moussy, I regretted not being able to bring in a thousand details from my adolescence connected with that period of the Occupation, but the budget and the New Wave frame of mind were not compatible with the notion of a "period film." From that standpoint, *Jules and Jim* in 1961 constituted an exception.

It was in 1968, after having made *Stolen Kisses,* that I again felt I wanted to reconstruct that epoch. But at that point I was stopped dead in my enthusiasm by a remarkable film, Marcel Ophuls's *The Sorrow and the Pity,* which, by the use of documents and interviews, mingles past and present with a Proustian felicity. *The Sorrow and the Pity* is certainly not a film of fiction, yet it is not a documentary either but rather an impassioned reflection of such a richness that several viewings do not suffice to exhaust it.

With Gérard Depardieu

Writing the screenplay for *The Last Metro* with Suzanne Schiffman, my intention was to do for the theater what I had done for the cinema in *Day for Night:* the chronicle of a troupe at work, within a framework respecting the unities of place, time, and action. There was a notable difference between the two projects, which is that my acquaintance with the theater is superficial and that, in any case, putting on a play is very much less rich, visually, than shooting a film. At this moment, there comes to mind my friend Jean Aurel's remark after the bitter failure of *The Soft Skin* in 1964 at the Cannes Festival: "You have made a film about adultery and you have failed. You often tell me how you would like to make a film about the Occupation, perhaps you should have situated *The Soft Skin* under the Occupation."

A very good remark, the more so since the Occupation does not constitute a theme in itself but simply a background and, for me who was eight at the start of the war and twelve at the Liberation, a background rich in sensations, emotions, memories.

To suspect, as is sometimes done, that artists haunted by the Occupation are exploiting an ambiguous nostalgia makes no more sense than to reproach John Ford for having devoted two thirds of his output to the conquest of the West or Marcel Proust for having, in his *Recherche,* made numerous references to the Dreyfus Affair.

The war of 1914–18 and the Occupation of 1940–44 have every possibility, in another twenty years, of appearing as the two most thrilling, most romantic periods of the twentieth century, and therefore also the most fascinating and inspiring.

Since the shock of *The Sorrow and the Pity,* ten years have passed and, like everyone, I have seen a dozen films about the Occupation. One struck me as too gloomy, another as too rosy, there was too much sunshine in one, too much modern music in another. In short, I remained with my desire unsatisfied and with a few certainties valid for myself alone: a film about the Occupation should take place almost entirely at night and in closed places, the feel of the

Bernard in Marion's dressing room (Gérard Depardieu and Catherine Deneuve)

Bernard Granger and Marion Steiner (Gérard Depardieu and Catherine Deneuve) on stage

epoch has to be reconstructed by darkness, close confinement, frustration, precariousness, and—the sole luminous element—one should include, in their original recordings, some of the songs heard at the time in the streets and on the radio.

While writing a preface to the first articles of André Bazin for the Collection 10/18, assembled under the title of *Le Cinéma et l'Occupation,* I had to put to work my memories as a young moviegoer, and suddenly memories of that period came back to me in full force, making me decide to realize my oldest dream.

Even if Suzanne and I took off from a blank page, we didn't set sail without a supply of crackers. For months we had been reading a stock of memoirs, ranging from *Ma Vie Privée* by Ginette Leclerc to Jean Marais's *Histoire de Ma Vie* and including the memoirs of Alice Cocéa and Corinne Luchaire, without overlooking the rather more instructive *La Vie Parisienne sous l'Occupation* by Hervé Le Boterf.

I read that during the war fifteen or more theaters in Paris were run by women, actresses or former actresses. My heroine therefore would be a "directress," and I immediately thought of Catherine Deneuve, a thrilling actress I had not used to the best of her possibilities in *Mississippi Mermaid.* I had read that Louis Jouvet, to escape the pressures of German censorship, left Paris at the start of the Occupation for South America. I asked myself what would have happened if, for love of a woman, a Jewish director had pretended to flee France but had remained hidden in the cellar of his theater throughout the war. Invented as it was, the idea was not entirely improbable, because the musician Kosma and the designer Trauner had known that situation, working clandestinely under false names for the films of Marcel Carné, for example. I needed a young fellow, an actor just starting out and torn between his pride in entering a famed theater company and the desire to have a hand in the liberation of his country, as was the case with Louis Jourdan and Jean-Pierre Aumont. It was only after writing the first half hour of the subject that the choice of Gérard Depardieu became inevitable. When we were short on inspiration and could not move our story forward, Suzanne and I would draw up lists of possible actors for such and such a role and, as a rule, that worked as a stimulant. For example, after we had decided that at the end of the film Jean-Loup Cottins, the substitute director, would be arrested in the morning at home by the F.F.I. [the partisan militia], who would take him away in pyjamas and dressing gown (as happened with Sacha Guitry), while trying to think what actor would be most expressive in that short scene, Jean Poiret's face came to mind. In that case, we then went back to our plot to rethink the details of the role in

The substitute director Jean-Loup Cottins (Jean Poiret)

Right
Bernard, Marion, Cottins, and Arlette (Andréa Ferréol) in the restaurant singing "La Prière à Zumba"

order to adjust them to the actor we had in mind. As in *Day for Night,* I felt that a careful distribution of known actors and new faces was necessary in the interest of plausibility. One of the shortest but most interesting roles was that of Daxiat, our only bad character, who could say: "I adore the theater, I live for the theater, but theater people detest me." This character was inspired for us by Alain Laubreaux and also

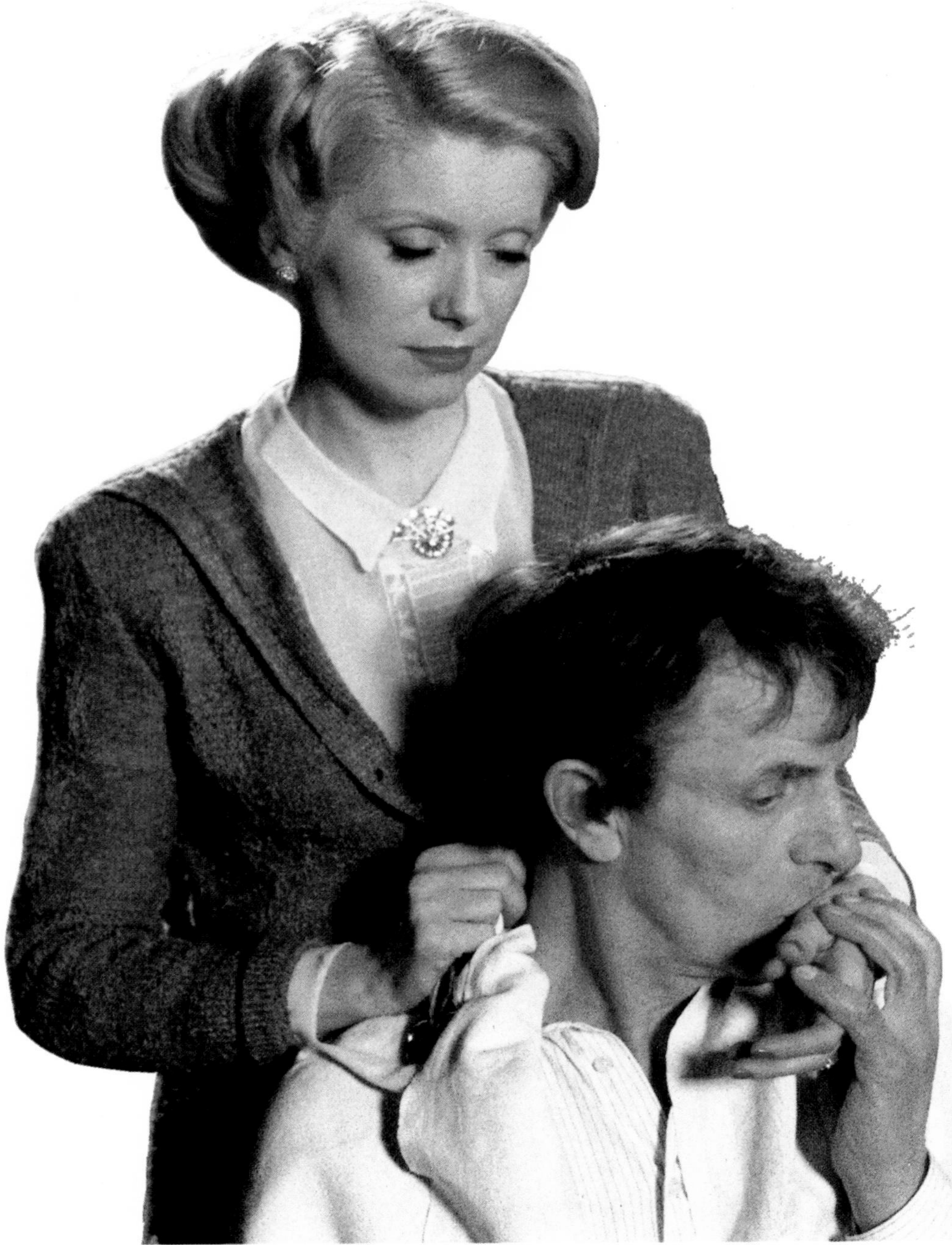

by a talented filmmaker who, in the midst of the fight over the Cinémathèque in 1968, didn't hesitate to pick up his telephone to call a producer hostile to Henri Langlois a "dirty Jew." Daxiat illustrates the irresponsibility of the French extremists who, by their excess of zeal, often did more harm than the Germans. To confide that role to a known actor, even a very talented one, who is seen three or four times a year on the screen would have weakened it. I absolutely wanted to recruit someone of whom people would say after seeing the film, "But who is the guy who plays Daxiat?" So I chose one of my best friends, a former young leading man with Jouvet but now better known as a director and screenwriter, Jean-Louis Richard, who did wonders.

With the work of writing finished, I returned to Paris in September and came to realize that although the screenplay seemed to please each of the actors concerned, it was received very coldly by the distributors and possible backers. The role of Lucas Steiner, a German Jew, would have justified a French and German co-production, but the German distributors didn't like the screenplay and wanted a better known name than Heinz Bennent, whom I was absolutely insistent on. Two of the major French distributors returned the script, one refusing it outright, the other proposing to distribute the film without giving us any money, and I foresaw the moment when I would be forced to announce to the actors that the film would be cancelled or postponed.

A co-producer we had in mind liked the script but disapproved of the choice of Andréa Ferréol for the lesbian wardrobe woman: too improbable. Could I make him understand that it was precisely for that that I chose her, so as to obtain at first an effect of suspense (will Arlette give in to Depardieu's advances?) and then of surprise (Arlette is in love with Catherine)? It is not sufficiently known that the French pro-Nazis who proclaimed their cult of virility (for them, Germany was male and the defeated France female) included Jews and homosexuals in the same hatred. The fascist critics regularly denounced Bataille's "Jewified" theater, Cocteau's "effeminate" theater. I felt that our script had to show that double racism of which Sartre, in *Portrait of the Anti-Semite,* very effectively exposed the obsessional, sexual, and passional aspects.

Was that what, in our screenplay, shocked possible backers or simply the repetition in the dialogue of the word "Jew"? After the first showing, a big boss at Gaumont confided: "The film's not bad and will make its way nicely, but if the word 'Jew' was spoken half as often, that would be all to the good." In reality, I suppose that, since they were merely reading it, the story of *The Last Metro,* deliberately treated as a chronicle of everyday life, seemed to them lacking in dramatic incidents.

Bernard and Marion: "For you it's only your theater that counts!"

Bernard demands that Daxiat apologize to Marion (Gérard Depardieu and Jean-Louis Richard)

In any event, there we were in November 1979, I would have to begin shooting in January 1980, and I could not reasonably justify hiring a set designer, a costume designer, nor even rent a temporarily closed Paris theater, which last was the most serious.

The film was to cost a billion old francs (double my usual productions), and my company, Les Films du Carrosse, had on hand only a third of that sum. Suddenly, thanks to the efforts of Gérard Lebovici, the stalemate was broken. Gaumont agreed to distribute the film, and the television of the First Network, thanks to Jacques Zbinden, would become co-producer for twenty-two percent and would buy in advance the rights to the first run. Finally the S.F.P. [Société Française de Production] lent its services (certain technicians, equipment, and costumes) against ten percent of the film. No question anymore of having specially made costumes or of building sets, we would have to make do with the S.F.P.'s stock of old clothing, and we would fit up a closed-down chocolate factory in Clichy. Later I came to understand that this precariousness, far from harming the film, enhanced its truthfulness.

Arlette (Andréa Ferréol): "It was precisely for that that I chose her" (scene cut in editing)

Three weeks away from shooting, the financing was finally settled, in part at least. When I opened the script to consult or complete it, it pleased me, though without overwhelming me. It corresponded quite well to the rudimentary and intelligent definition John Ford gives of his work: "Filming sympathetic characters plunged into interesting situations." But I hadn't succeeded in making the character of Lucas Steiner speak with the humor and derision I felt indispensable. One evening, at the Théâtre du Gymnase, I saw the superb play *L'Atelier,* both moving and funny, and I immediately got in touch with Jean-Claude Grumberg to ask him to write a sort of additional dialogue designed to give more nuance to the character of Lucas Steiner.

With the screenplay already firmly established, the length estimated at 150 minutes, and shooting about to begin, Jean-Claude Grumberg's freedom to invent was up against a wall, yet his contribution was precious, for example in that scene in the cellar when Lucas puts on a papier-mâché nose and says: "I am trying to feel Jewish. They're very delicate, Jewish roles. If you do just a tiny bit, they say, 'He's exaggerating.' If you put it on a lot, they say, 'He doesn't seem Jewish.' Just what is 'seeming Jewish'?"

Shooting *The Last Metro* was quite pleasant but difficult. I would have been a lot more relaxed if I could have foreseen the success the film would enjoy. After five days of shooting, Suzanne Schiffman, my collaborator from the start, fell ill and had to leave the set for a month. Two days later, Catherine Deneuve had a fall on a staircase, and when she came back to work the doctor forbade her to wear theater costumes (heavily corseted) for another ten days. The working plan had to be changed, the stage scenes put off until later, and the scenes with Catherine in street dress filmed right away, though the necessary sets were still in the making.

What reassured me was to see how very well the actors were fitting into their roles. Working for the first time with Gérard Depardieu, I marveled at the warmth and truthfulness he brought to the role of Bernard.

Jean Poiret's insolent frivolity enchanted me. For the role of a young actress with great ambitions, I engaged the adorable little Sabine of *Jules and Jim.* It was with Heinz Bennent that I worked most, an hour in his dressing room every morning, in order that, as both of us hoped, despite his fine German accent he would speak in the same rhythm as the French actors.

Catherine Deneuve loved this double role of a woman not afraid of appearing antipathetic, cold, and hard in order to protect the man who until then had protected her. In her previous films, to my taste Catherine too often played girls' roles (rather than women's), and that impression was reinforced by her triumphal hairdo

Bernard backstage: "No, not the electrician, the engineer."

public was able to sympathize to such an extent with them, even identifying themselves with this one or that.

When the leading characters in a film are really alive, the situations don't demand an extreme tension, but it's only when the film is shown in public that the author knows if his characters come alive or not. If, as is still done regularly in America, I had arranged two or three previews, I would have kept faith with my original intentions and would certainly have presented the film in a slightly longer version (of which the transcription in *Avant-Scène* remains the only evidence), but doubt led me to deliver a film of 128 minutes (though, for the TV version, my editor Martine Barraqué succeeded in restoring a six-minute scene between a scriptwriter, Monsieur Valentin, and Marion Steiner).

Like babies, films shift around in the belly. As Roger Leenhardt pointed out, "You have the idea for a film, you shoot a second one, and the public gets a third." Today, in 1983, if I have to analyze the good reception *The Last Metro* got, I think that my having filled out the screenplay with details that had struck me in my childhood gave the film an originality of vision it wouldn't have had if it had been conceived by someone older (who

cascading freely over her shoulders. Before shooting I had easily convinced her to look her real age and to wear her hair in a chignon and always rolled up so as to represent not a beautiful girl but a beautiful woman who was responsible and almost authoritarian. Catherine had some misgivings about the scenes on stage. She was the only one in the cast who had never mounted the boards, and she wondered if she would be able to articulate as in the theater, to slow down the flow of words, and to project her voice toward the balcony. She succeeded in all of this perfectly.

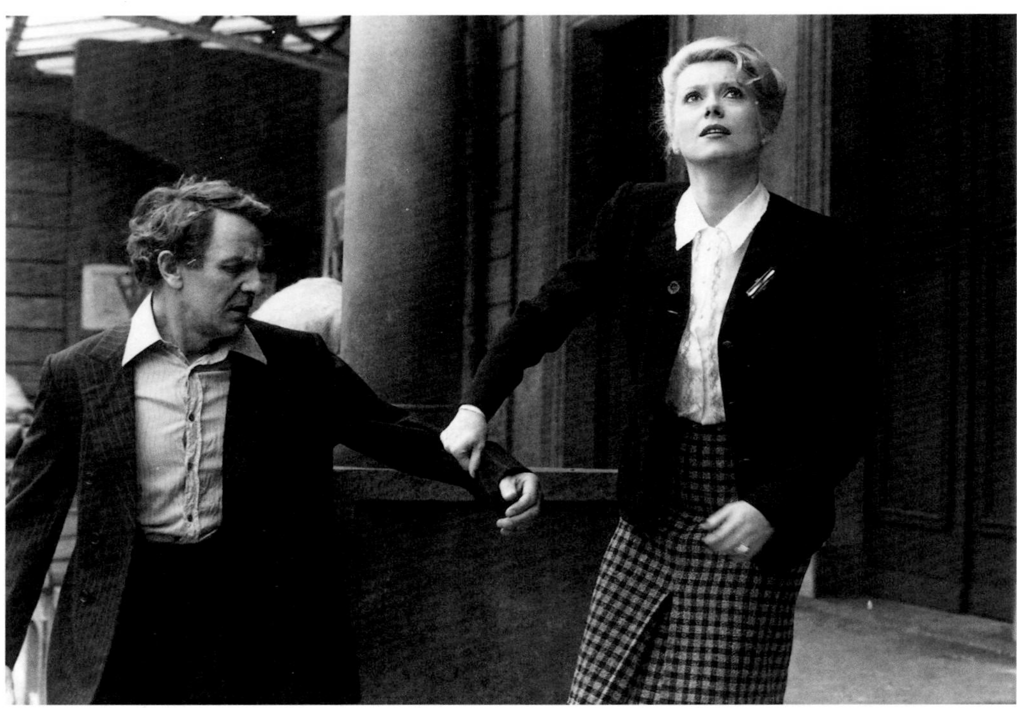

After shooting *The Last Metro,* I was conscious of having made the fictional film with the greatest amount of information about daily life under the Occupation. I knew that viewers of forty-five and more would be concerned with our having got the climate just right, but how to know if young viewers would be interested? Wouldn't they find the incidents in the film too slight and the dramatic vicissitudes too few? I thought: "The American cinema constantly presents characters who carry their action through to its conclusion, and here I am showing only people prevented from realizing their plan and whom circumstances lead to concentrating on survival." On that point, happily, I was wrong, because it is probably thanks to all the obstacles blocking my characters that the would have experienced the Occupation as an adult) or younger (who would have been born during the war or afterward). To illustrate this perfectly obvious truism by an example, I will recall that only children observe a funeral "objectively" and, with a well-dissimulated interest, take note of what does not strike adults as essential: the mourning bands, the silvery letters on the wreaths, the hats, veils, black stockings, Sunday clothes. There you have what *The Last Metro* probably is: the theater and the Occupation seen by a child.

F.T., February 1983

"Pourquoi et Comment Le Dernier Métro,"
in L'Avant-Scène Cinéma,
no. 303–4, March 1984

THE WOMAN NEXT DOOR

"Neither with you nor without you"

1981

Fanny Ardant and Gérard Depardieu: "Here are the lovers I want."

After *The Last Metro,* which brought together six or seven characters of equal importance, I wanted to get back to something disciplined, with a tighter story constructed around a couple. I deliberately kept their respective mates in the background, choosing to play up instead a character acting as confidante who gets the story started and gives it its conclusion: "Neither with you nor without you."

What is *The Woman Next Door* about? Love and, of course, love thwarted, without which there wouldn't be any story. The obstacle between the two lovers here is not the weight of society, it is not the presence of others, nor is it the disparity between the two temperaments but, on the contrary, their resemblances. Both of them are still in the rapturous state of "all or nothing" that had already driven them apart eight years before.

When the accident of moving next door brings them together again, at first Mathilde shows herself reasonable, while Bernard does not succeed in doing so. Then the situation, like the glass cylinder of an hourglass, is turned upside down, and that's the tragedy.

In America, one frequently sees at parties the hostess's former husbands fraternizing agreeably with the new mate. This is rarely so in Europe where, despite the Americanization of life and an increased flexibility in the laws, separations often remain painful across the years. "Do you know what grief is?" Mathilde asks a small boy.

When a love affair ends badly and leaves us torn in little pieces, we feel ourselves "only good to be picked up with a teaspoon." Everything around us seems to have something to

(à relire)

SUR LES RAILS

(projet pour un film Jeanne Moreau-Charles Denner.)

Il est sorti de prison
Il sort d'une dépression nerveuse
Il a connu Jeanne,ils se sont aimés,~~iixiix~~ elle l'a largué; il a craqué.Quelque chose en lui l'a poussé à détruire,il a joué le justicier en tuant un type de grenoble (le docteur machin qui tuait clandestinement des chamois.)

~~x~~ Le film commence en province (sur Charles paumé ou sur Jeanne qui vient là faire je ne sais quoi.)

Au début de l'histoire,dans l'hotel où se trouve Charles. Lorsqu'il aperçoit Jeanne qui vient d'arriver dans cet hotel,il tente de se tirer mais elle le voit;dans un premier temps,il refuse de lui parler;elle insiste,il cède.

On apprend ainsi l'histoire des chamois et de la prison (interdit de séjour).Charles est dans un état épouvan--table,à ramasser à la petite cuiller.Jeanne va s'occu--per de lui et le remettre sur ses rails.

D'abord,elle doit lui faire comprendre qu'il est exclu qu'ils se remettent ensemble :" Notre histoire a eté complète,elle a eu un début,un milieu,une fin et puis j'aime les garçons plus jeunes que moi parceque......"

Malgré ça,malgré le jeune garçon (qu'on entr'aperçoit peut-être) Jeanne prend en main Charles,elle lui esquisse une colonne vertébrale,elle lui montre son amertume,la démonte,elle lui redonne le gout de vivre.

-Pendant deux ans,je ne pouvais pas passer devant notre appartement....Tu sais,cette chanson:"Sans amour on n'est rien du tout" ... les petites pilules pour dormir....Je te jure,Jeanne,je veux absolument m'en sortir,je ne veux pas rester comme ça,j'ai vraiment la volonté de sortir du trou noir (cf.les deux anglaises)

Elle ménage complètement Charles au point peut-ètre de ca--cher le garçon quand il arrive;le garçon ne comprend pas, vaguement jaloux ou simplement un peu humilié;à cause de cela nous avons un épisode plus mouvementé que le reste,au cours duquel Jeanne doit s'activer dans l'hotel,colmater les brèches (un peu comme ~~M~~ le Vice Roi du Pérou,en moins comique mais drole quand mème).

Presque tout se passe dans l'Hotel:un repas dans la cham--bre,un repas dans la salle à manger (commentaires sur les voyageurs,le mystère de toutes ces vies...)

Comme les cuisines du Silence,quelque chose à voir à partir des fenètres (un cinéma de quartier ?) Alors le film serait peut-ètre Paradis Perdu avec souvenir de Jeanne de l'époque "tout le monde pleurait dans la salle,mon père était en permission,beaucoup de soldats,on redoutait une alerte " ou bien c'est Charles qui lui,a le souvenir d'une projection interrompue par une alerte.Donc,ils vont voir le film,acheter les droits de deux passages:la déclaration de guerre et Fernand Gravey dans les tranchées apprennant la mort de Micheline Presle.)

Si on suppose que Charles a tenté de se tuer,utiliser le suicide dans le métro " on m'a dit que j'étais le premier type à rater son suicide dans le métro" . Cela permet des images mentales de Charles sur le quai du métro et surtout des "ponts" sonores trés effectifs:la rame qui arrive et de bons enchainements sur des gros plans de Charles.

Importante l'idée que les tourments moraux se soignent avec la bio-chimie...Mais oui,il y a des petits trucs dans nos cerveaux,des canaux qui creent (ou secrètent) l'eupho--rie ou la déprime.Tout ça c'est une question de circula--tion du sang alors ? Oui,parfaitement.

L'image d'Audiberti:"Faire son devoir,comme un enfant".

Le sens de la vie....L'illusion sociale...il y a des jolies illusions et puis des moches...il faut choisir quelque chose ,un domaine dans lequel on n'agresse personne,on n'emmerde personne...Pense aux chirurgiens qui rafistole les accidentés de la route tous les dimanches soirs...c'est jamais fini... nous on fait des choses dont on voit la fin...On a de la chance...A un garçon d'aujourd'hui qui n'aime rien,qui ne veut rien et qui refuse de vivre,quest-ce qu'on peut dire ? Rien! (A propos des morts sur la route,si la télé le vou--lait vraiment elle ferait diminuer de moitié le nombre d' accidents,en montrant les blessés,les paralysés etc..au lieu de chiffrer les morts...on ne peut pas s'identifier à des morts mais on le peut à des grands blessés) etc...

Sans aucun doute,le film se termine trés optimiste,Charles se rassemble,se réconcilie avec a) la vie b) Jeanne c) son passé -sa mère ? d)avec autrui.

Pour ne pas rester abstrait il faut bien définir la place sociale de chacun.

Une chanson,la chanson tendre " dans la glace,quoiqu'on fasse,tout s'efface..." chantée par Jeanne ? Entendue plusieurs fois.

C'est évidemment un film de dialogue,trés sentimental.

+ une dispute de Charles with someone
+ conduite héroïque de Jeanne.

do with our personal drama. Every movie, every novel—if by chance we're still in a state to watch and to read—seems to paraphrase our lamentable adventure, every song heard on the transistor speaks about us, exposes our mistakes and confirms our humiliation.

Here you have the extreme states of love that I had been wanting to show for some time. Chance had it that one January evening I was present at the meeting of Gérard Depardieu and Fanny Ardant and, seeing them side by side, I said to myself: here are the lovers I want. I hope that the viewer will not be tempted to take sides, to say one is right and the other wrong, but will love both of them as I do.

"Pourquoi La Femme d'à Côté,"
in the press book, 1981

INTRODUCING FANNY ARDANT

Credit for discovering Fanny Ardant goes to Nina Companeez, and the audacity of the choice should not be underestimated. Nina Companeez had written a superb script that would fill five hours, *Les Dames de la Côte,* with very fine roles for Edwige Feuillère, Françoise Fabian, Martine Chevalier, Evelyne Buyle, and she could very well have entrusted the principal role to one of those young actresses you see three or four times a year in films or on television and whose name is already familiar to the men who put up the money. Instead, the director took the risk of installing at the very heart of her story a new face, a new figure, a young woman with great expectations: Fanny Ardant. During the Christmas holidays of 1979, Mademoiselle Companeez knew she had won her bet when, five Saturday evenings in a row, millions of French people demonstrated a fidelity and an enthusiasm for the undertaking and for its leading lady. A new actress made her entry into film, a young and beautiful actress who, for the past five years, had been doing her apprenticeship on the stage, interpreting the finest texts of the French theater: *Polyeucte, Esther, Le Maître de Santiago, Electre, Tête d'Or. . . .* At Christmas 1979, I was within two weeks of beginning the shooting of *The Last Metro,* but without even waiting for the end of the serial *Les Dames de la Côte,* I wanted to interview Fanny Ardant with an eye to a future collaboration. Seeing her on my television screen I had been seduced by her large mouth, her big black eyes, her triangular face, but I immediately recognized and appreciated in Fanny Ardant the qualities I look for most often in the leading characters in my films: vitality, courage, enthusiasm, humor, intensity, but also, on the other side of the scale, a taste for something secret, a shy wildness, a touch of savageness, and, above all, something vibrant.

The accident of moving next door brings together lovers of eight years ago

The shooting of *The Last Metro* was too difficult, too absorbing, to leave me the time to look into a new project, but when, on the evening of the "Césars" in 1980, I had the chance of seeing Fanny Ardant and Gérard Depardieu, side by side, it struck me that there I had a fine film couple, two tall figures, the blond and the brunette, a man apparently simple but complicated, a woman apparently complicated but as simple as "So long." The idea of *The Woman Next Door* was born, was making headway, a new film was taking shape. With my collab-

Sur les Rails, an earlier project already containing certain elements of *The Woman Next Door*

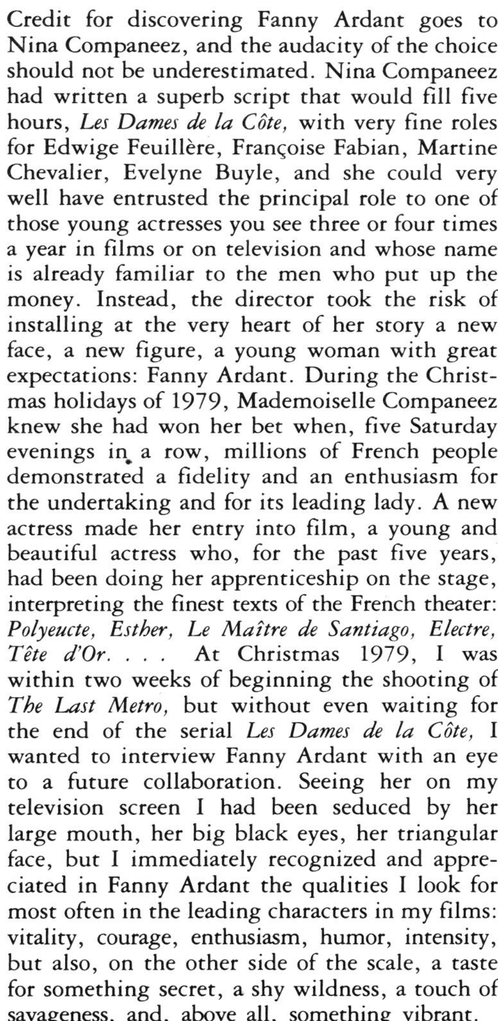

Mathilde (Fanny Ardant) faints in front of the guests

orating scriptwriters, Suzanne Schiffman and Jean Aurel, we began to ask questions. Shall we show our two lovers' meeting? No, their whole story would be in the past. With flashbacks? No, without flashbacks, their dialogue alone would bring back their past, and the rest of the story would be made up of the beautiful but desperate attempt to bring a dead passion back to life.

From the start of shooting, I had the confirmation that our woman next door was the right woman for the situation. After the shooting of the first scene of their new encounter, Gérard Depardieu said to me: "When Fanny looked me in the eyes to say hello, she terrified me and now I can see what we're going to make: a film about a love that strikes fear."

Behavior during shooting varies a great deal from one actress to another. There are those who are afraid and who cover up their fear. There are those who are happy but avoid showing it. Fanny, for her part, is very happy to be acting and never once thinks of concealing it. She gets into a state of concentration quickly before playing serious scenes, without ever resorting to the absurd stratagem of hostility toward the team at work, and as soon as the scene is over, her face lights up, she remains

Bernard and Mme Jouve (Gérard Depardieu and Véronique Silver)

"The rapturous state of all or nothing." Mathilde and Bernard (Fanny Ardant and Gérard Depardieu)

Right
Bernard and his wife, Arlette (Gérard Depardieu and Michèle Baumgartner)

Below, right
Mathilde and her husband, Philippe (Fanny Ardant and Henri Garcin)

silent and lets a smile blossom which seems to say: "I am full, I am filled, I am fulfilled." In 1961, when I was shooting *Jules and Jim* in front of an Alsatian chalet, every day I felt that, thanks to Jeanne Moreau and Oskar Werner, the film would be superior to the screenplay. During *The Woman Next Door,* thanks to Fanny Ardant and Gérard Depardieu, I had the same impression, that of doing a good job, something more than a job: a film.

Unifrance Film, *December 1981*

A HAPPY ENDING IS NOT NECESSARILY A HAPPY END

The structure of *The Woman Next Door* had existed within me for years. What blocked me from going ahead with it was the symmetry of the characters I had imagined. There were two couples: a foursome. I believe, rightly or wrongly, that a story should have an odd number of characters.

Then I remembered a woman I had met fifteen years before. She had told me her life story, in a neighborhood in old Nice, while I was trying to rent a tuxedo so I could go hear

Charles Trenet at the Casino. That's how Madame Jouve came into being, the fifth character in *The Woman Next Door.*

In Europe we have a deep feeling for the metaphysical side of life. Unlike in the United States, we know that social ambition is absurd. So we find it easier to make stories of love, passion, obsession, what I call "to-the-bitter-end" stories, which soon enough end in death.

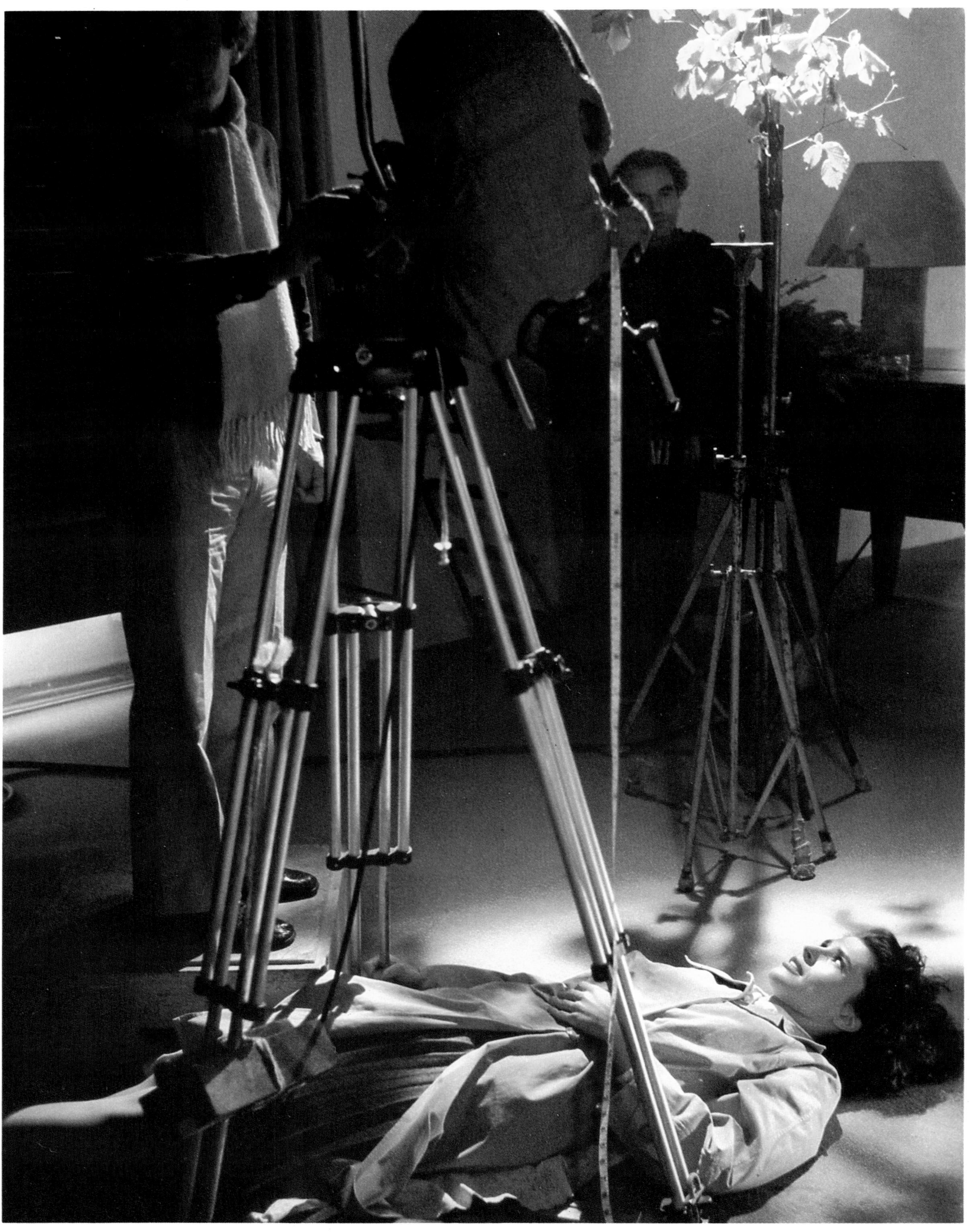

The final scene: *opposite*, filming the scene; *this page*, the death

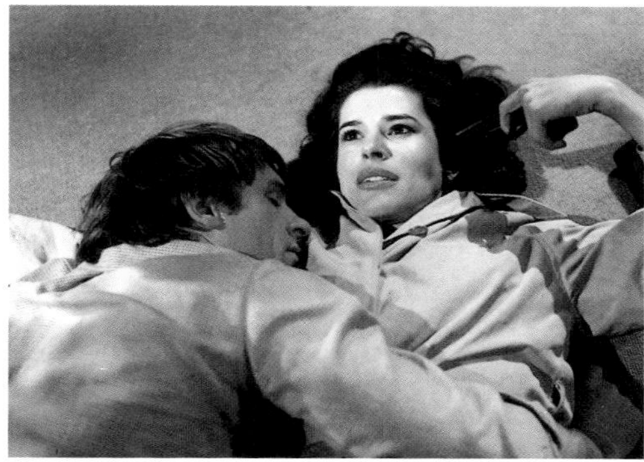

In times past, the happy ending was the wedding. Yet Sacha Guitry used to say: "A comedy that ends in a wedding, that's a tragedy that's beginning." For me, a happy ending is not necessarily a happy end. In *The Soft Skin,* I had asked Nelly Benedetti, when she had just killed her husband, to smile very slightly. I wanted to show that this woman had been delivered of her torment. Free, in spite of the years of prison ahead of her.

In *The Story of Adele H.,* when Isabelle Adjani in the Barbados Islands passes by without recognizing the man she has been pursuing for years, that is for me a happy ending: Adele has gone to the limit of her passion.

I am very open to the idea of an exalted ending, and death can be exalted, as in *The Woman Next Door.*

Interview by Pierre Murat,
Télérama, *no. 1,655, September 30, 1981*

I THOUGHT OF THE SONGS OF PIAF

I couldn't manage to strike the right note. And then I thought of the songs of Piaf, which are passion in a pure state, with a touch of grandiloquent madness. Those songs gave me the idea of the key character in *The Woman Next Door,* the owner of the tennis court who lost a leg throwing herself out of a window in the desperation of love: she would reveal the mad love between Gérard Depardieu and Fanny Ardant.

I also understood that this film would function better if I opened it on a shot of an ambulance. From the start, the grave tone was struck. . . .

Interview by Luc Honorez,
Le Soir, *June 18–19, 1983*

1983

CONFIDENTIALLY YOURS!

We feel repugnance at inventing death, but we love to stage it

Good or bad, an original screenplay is generally logical, and one sees scenes taking place on the screen whose justification seems self-evident. Contrariwise, adaptations of novels most often give a strange result, and I'm not using "strange" here in a complimentary sense. The adapter-director retains scenes from the novel for a variety of reasons: those that seem to him indispensable for understanding the story, those that he has a tremendous wish to visualize. Along the way, he has gotten rid of what he judges useless or unrewarding. In the course of this arbitrary operation, often carried out by a number of people, the initial logic of the whole subject gets lost, and nine times out of ten you end up with a film on the screen whose material is lacking in harmony. Scenes very often don't have the same value for the person who filmed them as for those who watch them. All filmmakers who tackle the material of the crime story feel that inconsistency, but they persist—we persist—because one finds in that literature the strong liquor that the cinema, for as long as it has existed, has needed. We feel repugnance at inventing death, but we love to stage it. The crime-story writer supplies the corpses, the director does the rest, for better or worse.

This year my choice went to *Vivement Dimanche!* by Charles Williams, because that novel describes an investigation carried out by a woman, an everyday woman, a secretary. Dissatisfied with *The Bride Wore Black,* which I adapted from William Irish in 1967 and which was too colorful, too sunny, I chose to shoot *Confidentially Yours!* almost entirely at night, in the rain, and above all in black and white. The material is that of the detective play, the tone is rather euphoric, the experiment was interesting, I'll know this autumn if it succeeded.

"Pourquoi Vivement Dimanche!"
first press book, March 1983

The secretary conducts the investigation (Fanny Ardant)

Opposite
Julien Vercel and Barbara Becker (Jean-Louis Trintignant and Fanny Ardant)

Truffaut with Fanny Ardant and Jean-Louis Trintignant

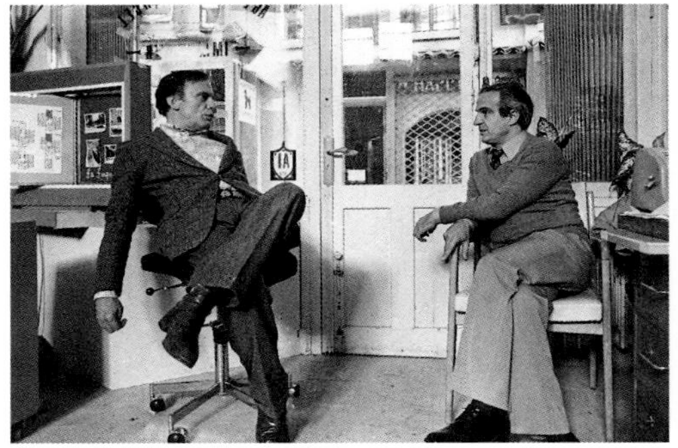

Truffaut with Jean-Louis Trintignant

Julien Vercel discovers the corpse of his wife, Marie-Christine (Jean-Louis Trintignant and Caroline Sihol)

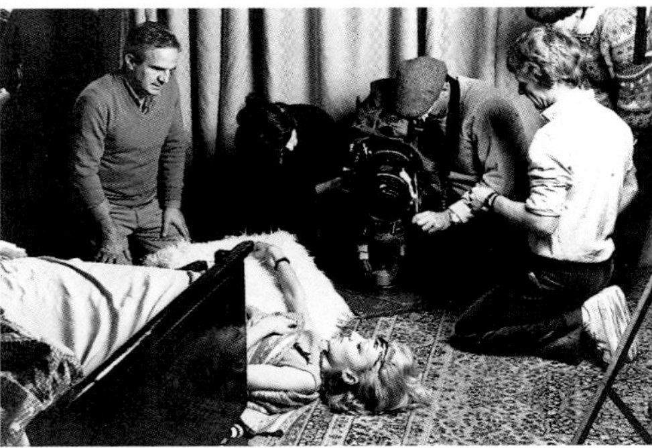

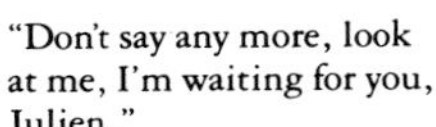

"Don't say any more, look at me, I'm waiting for you, Julien."

LETTER TO JEAN-LOUIS TRINTIGNANT

July 9, 1982

My dear Jean-Louis,

This film, *Confidentially Yours!,* will tell the story of a secretary conducting an amateur investigation in order to clear her boss, wrongly accused of several murders. Fanny Ardant will play the role of the secretary, and I am proposing that you play her boss, Julien Vercel, director of a real estate agency in a town like Hyères or Sète. Nestor Almendros will be the chief cameraman of this black-and-white film, of which we may shoot certain scenes at the Victorine, which will therefore be our headquarters. The shooting should begin at the start of November and extend over about eight weeks.

What more can I say to you, dear Jean-Louis? You have in your hands the thirteenth treatment, and there will be one or two more aiming to improve the story and the roles, but that will mean an increase in degree rather than a change in nature. The story being what it is, the roles being what they are, we have to get onto the screen some humor and some charm, all our hard work having to remain invisible.

If you say to me: "Dear François, as I told you in Pézenas, I would like very much to work with you, but I prefer to wait for a role more

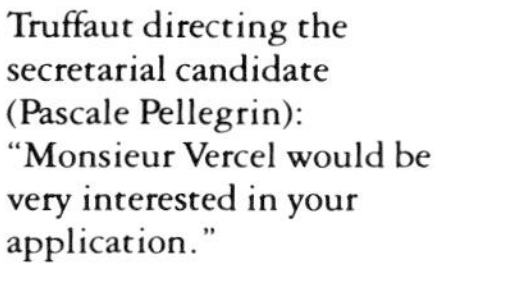

Truffaut directing the secretarial candidate (Pascale Pellegrin): "Monsieur Vercel would be very interested in your application."

this or more that," I will understand you very well and on both sides it will be only a pleasure deferred.

On the other hand, if you break this role in as one does a pair of shoes, you won't have foot trouble, because we will adopt a supple way of working, moccasin-style.

When you have read the script, I propose that you phone me at Rochegude (very close to Bollène) or come to lunch at three turns of the wheel from your place, I believe.

Friendly greetings.

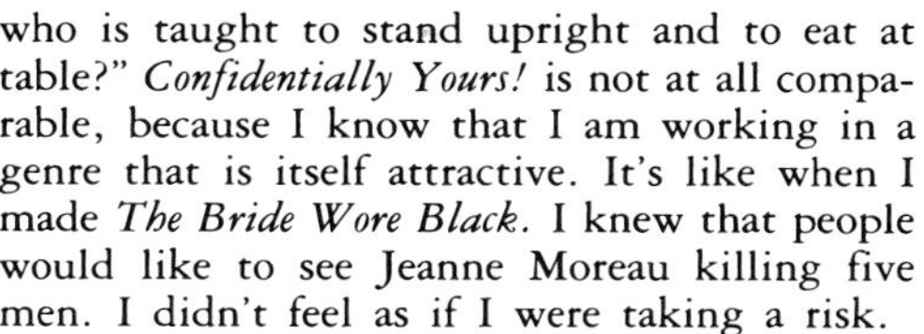

who is taught to stand upright and to eat at table?" *Confidentially Yours!* is not at all comparable, because I know that I am working in a genre that is itself attractive. It's like when I made *The Bride Wore Black.* I knew that people would like to see Jeanne Moreau killing five men. I didn't feel as if I were taking a risk.

Confidentially Yours! is the same thing, but there is also an experimental aspect: mixing a thriller and a comedy about a couple. I wanted to see if all of it could be mixed in a single film. And also to present Fanny Ardant—who has pretty much a romantic and lyrical reputation—as the heroine of a comedy, a little on the style of Katharine Hepburn. For that, the character has to speak very fast, trespass on the dialogue of others, remain very courageous, very animated. Let her make gaffes and, at the same time, succeed in an almost impossible undertaking. It's difficult, and I worked longer on this film, ten times longer, than on *The Woman Next Door.*

On the set: Fanny Ardant, Suzanne Schiffman, Jean-Louis Trintignant, François Truffaut

CRIME FILMS GAIN BY BEING IN BLACK AND WHITE

Every film is a wager. In *Adele H.,* the wager was: "Can a story be made without showing the partner?" Remaining solely on the face of one woman? *Adele H.* is an hour-and-a-half closeup on Isabelle Adjani. Practically nothing else took place in the film.

The wager of *The Wild Child:* "Can you interest people in a little boy found in the forest

As is stated after the film credits, any coincidence between this film and persons once existing would be fortuitous or involuntary. It is not a provocation. The idea came to me during a session of rushes of *The Woman Next Door.* A night scene was being shown in which Fanny Ardant prowls through the house wearing a raincoat. Someone remarked: "It's a real crime-story feeling." And indeed, Fanny Ardant looked like the heroine of a murder story.

To refresh myself from *The Woman Next Door,* I decided to make a film with Fanny Ardant, utilizing her as heroine in a murder story. I then reread certain books, among them those by Charles Williams because they often have the best female characters. I finally chose *Vivement Dimanche!,* which contained a lot of comic elements. That story would also permit me to combine two kinds of cinema: a detective film in which an ordinary person conducts the investigation (as it happens, a secretary who wants

The detective (Georges Koulouris): "During the twenty-five years I've been doing this work, if there's one thing I'm sure of it's that it's never their lovers who have women tailed but their husbands."

A film resembling a B-movie: Fanny Ardant

Julien Vercel and Jacques Massoulier (Jean-Louis Trintignant and Jean-Pierre Kalfon)

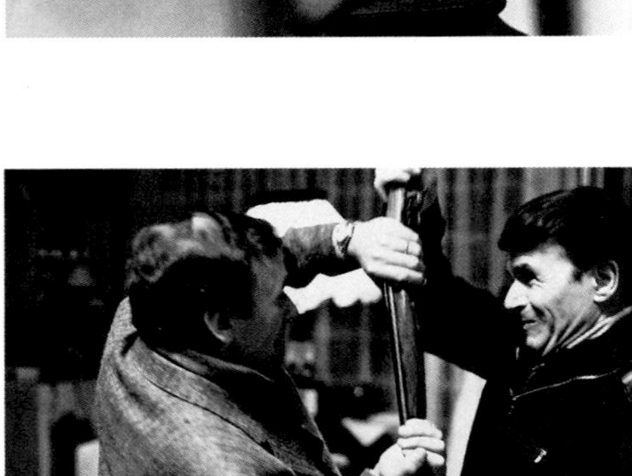

to clear her boss) and then an almost conjugal comedy in which a couple never stop arguing.

And, certainly, those arguments make the public want to see the two characters finally get together. As for the choice of black and white, it was clear to me that the thriller is a genre that should have stuck to black and white. As much as one sees color contributing to a Western, to a musical comedy, to the same extent crime films gain by being in black and white.

There was also on my part some small polemical intention, the desire to prevent black and white from disappearing. Nowadays, if you make Polaroid photos, you can no longer find black-and-white Polaroid film. If a young filmmaker wants to make a film in super 8, he can no longer get film in black and white: super 8 comes only in color. This is dangerous escalation. It will end up with a monopoly of color.

I said to myself: "We'll see if black and white can be put across for a medium-budget film." It was an experiment, and when Gérard Lebovici asked me: "Are you willing to co-produce it with the TV?" I thought we'd get turned down. Just the same, we tried the experiment. The project was proposed to the Second Network. And there I had a happy surprise: Pierre Desgraupes accepted in spite of the black and white. . . .

This creates a precedent. No one can tell

us now that it's at the demand of television that films are in color. The invasion by color is more bound up with a kind of unwritten law which is dictatorial but which is tacitly accepted. Because, in reality, when you get right down to it, you find that the foreign buyers buy the film nonetheless. *Confidentially Yours!* has even already been sold for worldwide distribution in cassette.

For *Confidentially Yours!* I asked Nestor Almendros to film very rapidly. At the start he was shocked: "I don't understand why you're in such a hurry. You made money from *The Last Metro.*"

It was not to make economies. But to make a film that resembles a B-grade film, you have to devote little time to each shot; if not the actors will simply demobilize. So we made this film in seven and a half weeks. We could have made it in ten weeks, but I preferred to maintain that breathless, somewhat feverish tone. For me that's part of the genre. . .

Curiously, this type of film counts very much on the public's complicity. Every time you are in too improbable situations, you have to add very real details in order to lend believability to what is impossible. You can't make totally plausible films. They would be boring. But you are obliged to give useless explanations to justify things.

I take off from the principle that people want the film to function. Things are put over if you use authority. For example, *Confidentially Yours!* is played very fast. There's no time to analyze it. There's a kind of intoxication. During the shooting, you have to be alert to the moments that call for emphasizing realism and those where you just want to distract the public's attention. The stories are always implausible, but that doesn't matter if sheer pleasure wins out. Pleasure has to weigh more than analysis.

Maybe later, at home, when you think

Barbara (Fanny Ardant) on the track of the criminal

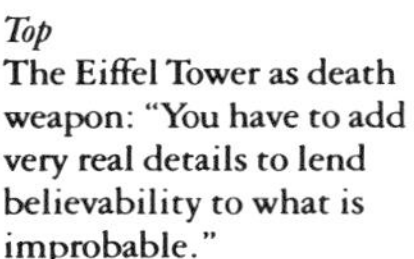

Top
The Eiffel Tower as death weapon: "You have to add very real details to lend believability to what is improbable."

"Love, sentiments, and *tutti quanti*"

over the essentials of the film you say to yourself: "But, after all, he only had to go to the police, or she didn't have to launch that investigation on her own." But it's too late. What really counts is if you enjoy it in the theater, watching the film with others. I prefer to think that there is a complicity on the public's part. Lubitsch, for example, gets a lot of fun out of making the public believe it has guessed what's going to happen next. And at the end of the scene: surprise! Something else happens. It's a game.

A screenplay is not made like a poem. You make a screenplay saying to yourself incessantly: "At that particular moment, what are people believing?" They believe such and such. So we're going to goad them on from that side. The public constantly has its part in your work.

Sometimes you bowl the public over highhandedly, at other times you take it along with you or, on the contrary, surprise it. For example, the two scenes in the police station had me scared. They're very conventional interrogation scenes. I tried to insert unexpected things after them. In the first, it's an Albanian refugee asking for political asylum. In the second, it's the police superintendent who pours himself a glass of water in a perfectly ordinary manner, and suddenly the tap explodes and the police station is drenched. Such things are a big help to me. They get laughs and act as a sort of safety valve. But above all they help people believe what is said just before and just after.

Interview by Paul Ceuzin and Gilles Costaz,
Le Matin de Paris, *August 8, 1983*

"Mixing a thriller and a comedy about a couple." François Truffaut and Fanny Ardant

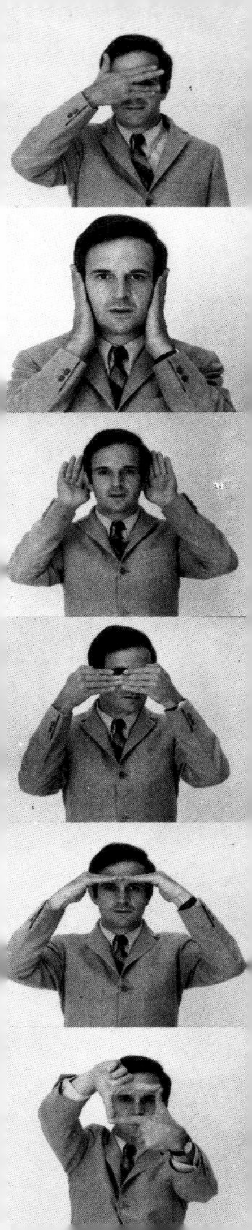

CINEMA ACCORDING TO TRUFFAUT

THEORY
PRACTICE

THEORY

"To be madly ambitious and madly sincere"

WE HAVE TO FILM OTHER THINGS, IN ANOTHER SPIRIT

For there to be a true changing of the guard, with new blood coming in, the young filmmakers must make up their minds not to tread in the footprints of the "old" cinema. What they mustn't do is make films costing fifty million that ape the luxury and the stupidity of the grand productions. Nor is it a matter of making crime films with half as many gangsters, half as many cops, in shabby settings and with twice as many revolvers in compensation.

We have to film other things, in another spirit. We've got to get out of the overexpensive studios (they're nothing but noisy slums anyway, unhealthy and poorly equipped) and invade the beaches in the sun where no filmmaker (except Vadim) has dared to plant his camera. Sunshine costs less than klieg lights and generators. We should do our shooting in the streets and even in real apartments. Instead of, like Clouzot, spreading artificial dirt over the sets and sticking five hangdog spies in front of them, we have to film more substantial stories in front of walls that are dirty for real. If the young director has to direct a love scene, instead of having his interpreters recite stupid dialogue by Charles Spaak he should think back to the conversation he had with his wife the night before or—why not?—let his actors find for themselves the words they're accustomed to saying.

"Truth pays off." Shooting *The Soft Skin*

The young director must not say to himself: "I'm going to try to get my foot into this redoubtable industry by making a compromise between what the producer wants and what I want, by pretending to cook up for him the comedy or detective film he expects but sticking in my own little ideas," etc., because with that reasoning you're lost in advance. You need to say to yourself: "I'm going to knock off for them something so sincere that it will be howling with truth and of a formidable force; I'm going to prove to them that truth pays off in hard cash and that my truth is the only truth." I mean, the young director must be convinced that he should not work *against* the producers nor *against* the public but that he has to convince them, bowl them over, seduce them, put them in his pocket. You have to be desperately ambitious and desperately sincere, if the enthusiasm you felt while shooting is to communicate itself in the showing and win over the public. The starting point must be the principle that any constraint you accept gets you only aridity and insipidity, whereas if you love what you film, the public too will probably love it.

But isn't all that obvious?

"30 Jeunes Metteurs en Scène en 1958: Relève. Non. Un Faux Problème," Arts, *1958*

THE OLD AND THE NEW

Once, during a conversation, you spoke of how you were reproached for your moderation, your "classicism," with respect to certain aesthetic developments that have come about in the cinema in the last few years. What do you think about that?

I certainly intend to remain outside those aesthetic developments, because I absolutely cannot do anything I don't feel deep down. Up to now, I have had the luck to film only projects that interested me and to do them with a free hand. I think you're lost once you begin to undertake something that doesn't resemble you; in any case, I myself would be. I have the reputation of liking many different films, and actually, a little like Rivette, I can understand all sorts of films and like them, films that most often have nothing to do with what I would myself like to do. But what I don't like are films of simulation; I detest snobbism profoundly and its twin brother, bluff, and that extends from *Modesty Blaise* to *Trans-Europe Express* and includes *Polly Maggoo, Anna, Help!, Pussy Cat, Privilege, Dragées au Poivre, A Coeur Joie,* the Westerns by Mekas, everything that gives the impression of teeming with ideas when there isn't even one, everything that parodies, everything that counts on playing it smart by bowling people over with crosscutting, zoom, and fast motion. That is miserable filmmaking because the director, in his readiness to sow confusion, hopes to escape serious critical judgment. The motto of those simulators could be the phrase in Cocteau's *Thomas the Impostor:* "Since this disorder is getting out of hand, let's pretend to be its organizer."

Interview by Jean-Louis Comolli and Jean Narboni, Cahiers du Cinéma, *no. 190, May 1967*

Opposite
On the set of *Fahrenheit 451*

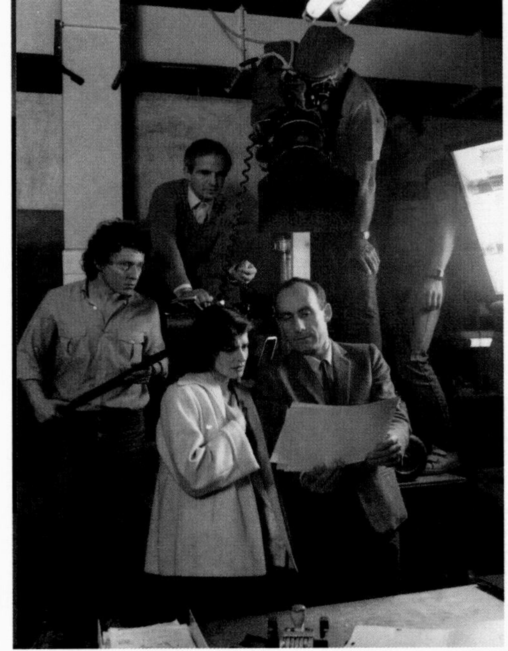

"Incidents and false leads." On the set of *Confidentially Yours!* in 1983, with Fanny Ardant

I AM CERTAINLY NOT AN INNOVATOR

From the beginning I said right out loud that I was not an innovator, but that was maybe a means of protecting myself because, ever since *The 400 Blows* was shown at Cannes, people have said: "But there's nothing new in it!" in part, I suppose, by comparison with *Hiroshima Mon Amour*. When *The 400 Blows* was attacked with "it's just Pagnol," because of the theme of bastardy, or "it's just Dickens," or then again "it's straight melodrama," I took none of those propositions to be a put-down. I contented myself with quoting the old saying: "He who hears only one thing hears only one sound," but adding that, if people will let me do so, I propose to contribute my own little "ring."

No, I am certainly not an innovator, because I belong to the last squad to believe in the notions of characters, situations, progression, incidents, false leads: in a word, the whole show.

It is not given to many film directors to be innovators. Griffith invented the concept of matching successive shots on the same axis as the preceding shot, and his disciples John Ford and Howard Hawks perfected that way of telling a story. Hitchcock virtually invented the subjective mise-en-scène and matching shots taken at ninety degrees from one another. Orson Welles invented movements using oblique angles. Today a great visualizer like Fellini invents, but his invention takes place in *front* of the camera. Shooting *Fahrenheit 451,* I felt my limitations on the visual side; there was too much of a disparity between the originality of the theme and the banality of the treatment, and I understood then that my true path lay in character films. What did John Ford say? "I film sympathetic characters in interesting situations."

Interview by Serge Daney, Jean Narboni, and Serge Toubiana, Cahiers du Cinéma, *no. 316, October 1980*

I WORK FOR THE PUBLIC OF THE CINÉAC-SAINT-LAZARE

Because I think a lot about the public, I work for the public of the Cinéac-Saint-Lazare, for the viewer who pops in to watch a bit of the film distractedly before catching his train. I'd like my films to be like a circus performance . . . I never show two elephant acts in succession. After the elephant the juggler, after the juggler the bears . . . I even arrange an entr'acte toward the sixth reel because people get tired, nervous. With the seventh reel, I take them back in hand and try to end with whatever I've got that's best. I would like people to hiss the sequences that don't come off and applaud those that please them. Considering that people lock themselves up in the dark to see my films, I never fail at the end of a film to take them out into nature, to the seashore or into the snow, to get myself pardoned.

I have fabricated entirely naïve laws for myself, and I try to improve them from film to film. If you wish, it's a cinema of compromises in the sense that I constantly keep the public in mind, but it is not a cinema of concessions because I never do a comic effect if it hasn't made me laugh first, nor a sad effect that doesn't move me.

I believe it is necessary to keep the public in mind. I no longer believe in that idea which fascinated me in the past, according to which there are no problems with the public: "If something pleases me, I know it will please the public." That's not true, it's more complicated than that, and nowadays I even hold the opposite. I believe that an idea that pleases an artist will by definition displease the public. Why? Because the artist is someone *outside* society and addresses himself *to* society. So what it amounts to is imposing your own originality on people and not falling in with their banality. Yes, you really have to say things as they are. It's a work of conviction, and the whole undertaking becomes a match with people.

Cited by Claude de Givray, Cinéma et Télé-Cinéma, *no. 341, October 1966*

THERE IS A NEW CINEMA AND I AM NOT PART OF IT

There is a new cinema and I am not part of it, that's clear.

And yet, the New Wave . . .

The New Wave was a historical phenomenon, it had no aesthetic program. I still feel myself loyal to it, if only because it is still much under attack; but not to the new cinema, no, not really, even if it interests me as spectator.

And as regards Godard, who seems rather to stand as godfather for this new cinema, do you feel yourself further from him than ten years ago?

Certainly. To the extent that there is anything to the Godard-Picasso parallel, I feel myself in the situation of a figurative painter who resolutely continues to be figurative while hoping that that kind of painting will not disappear entirely. Moreover, my favorite painter is Balthus. Four years ago, I hesitated between doing a short on Balthus's paintings or writing my book of conversations with Hitchcock. I gave up on the Balthus film because the Ektachromes were too unfaithful to the original canvases.

Ultimately one makes the films one can love as a viewer. The cinema helped me endure life when I was an adolescent, it pleased me as an escape. That escape could work only through identification. I had a horror of costume films, for instance. Well, as a filmmaker I make the films I saw when I was thirteen, fourteen years old, that's to say, with people in the wrong, weak, all fouled up, hiding out, always keeping aloof from groups, films with which it is easy to identify and which drag you into a kind of escapism that is nonetheless quite close to real life. I forbid myself pure comedy because there you can't forget that you are a spectator, and also purely tragic films because that would be too much of a stylization of life; I forbid myself gangster films, films about the Resistance, any heroic film, any prestigious character, any satirical or historical film, and I work with what remains, with films about love. There again it's not simple, because I don't want to film naked bodies, nor embraces, nor kisses, only stories about feelings. So there is love and also children: I've got three projects with children.

Interview by Pierre Ajame,
Le Nouvel Adam, *no. 19, February 1968*

"To work with real-life material." With Jean-Pierre Léaud during the filming of *Bed and Board* in 1970

GODARD HAS PULVERIZED THE SYSTEM

Jean-Luc Godard is not alone in filming as he breathes, but he's the one who breathes best. He is rapid like Rossellini, wickedly witty like Sacha Guitry, musical like Orson Welles, simple like Pagnol, hurt like Nicholas Ray, effective like Hitchcock, deep, deep, deep like Ingmar Bergman, and insolent like nobody else.

Even Godard haters, seated in the dark before one of his films, well, even if they don't understand a thing, I guarantee they don't miss a thing. By that I mean that if, in the same way the French Radio takes surveys to determine how large a public listens to its broadcasts, you could measure the intensity in a theater during the showing of a film by Jean-Luc Godard, you would see that he knows how to make himself heard and watched like nobody else.

He has killed off, all by himself, the two or three worst things I know about the public: polite indifference, vague interest, amused condescension. His authority, since that's what we're talking about, is such that one could use the word good-luck charm or infallibility jinx. Is Jean-Luc Godard going to become more popular than the pope and so just a little less than the Beatles? That's possible.

Professor Chiarini has declared: "There is the cinema BEFORE Godard and AFTER Godard." That's true, and the years that pass confirm us in the certainty that *Breathless* (1960) will have marked a turning point in the history of cinema as decisive as *Citizen Kane* in 1940. Godard has pulverized the system. He has thrown the cinema for a loop, just like Picasso in painting, and, like him, has made everything possible.

"La Savate et la Finance, ou Deux ou Trois Choses Que Je Sais de Lui," preface to "Deux ou Trois Choses Que Je Sais D'Elle," L'Avant-Scène Cinéma, *no. 70, May 1967*

"If the beauty of a literary work is in its prose, nothing prevents that prose from being heard in the cinema." With Jean-Pierre Léaud, Stacey Tendeter, and Kika Markham during the filming of *Two English Girls* in 1971

I NEED TO IDENTIFY

I have become aware of a peculiarity that sets me apart from the average run of viewers. It is that I identify with the weak characters and never with the strong ones. That explains why I didn't like the films with Errol Flynn, the Tarzan films. I couldn't identify with strength. I'll go further: if you have a character who is beyond reproach, who is goodness itself, and another who is not beyond reproach, and who represents everything bad, I identify even with the character who represents evil. I can't say where that comes from. I really ought to psychoanalyze myself, but that . . .

I detested Jules Verne, I detested children's books. When I read *Madame Bovary,* I identified completely with Mme Bovary. She was a woman who was having problems in love; that was maybe a little early for me, but just the same it interested me. I don't ever think of filming anything too remote from the way I am. I need to identify, to say to myself that I have been in such circumstances or I could be in such circumstances. I need that criterion in order to work. I work a great deal with real-life material, but it's a material 20 percent autobiographical, 20 percent taken from the newspapers, 20 percent taken from the lives of people I know around me, 20 percent pure fiction. The share left for pure fiction is slight, because I prefer taking off from things in the newspapers or that have happened to me or that have been told to me by people I know. I like to have verification from life.

Interview by Jean-Pierre Chartier, "Cinéastes de Notre Temps," French radio, December 2, 1965

THE CINEMA IS A PROSE ART

For me, the cinema is a prose art. Definitely. It involves filming beauty but without appearing to or without making a fuss over it. I believe that, enormously, and that's why I can't nibble at Antonioni's hook: too indecent. Poetry exasperates me, and when people send me poems in letters I chuck them right into the garbage can. I love poetic prose, Cocteau, Audiberti, Genet, and Queneau, but only prose. I love the cinema because it is prosaic, it's an indirect art, not confessional, it conceals as much as it reveals. The filmmakers I like have in common a modesty, a discretion, which makes them much like each other on that point at least: Buñuel who refuses to shoot two takes, Welles who foreshortens "beautiful" views until they become illegible, Bergman and Godard who work at high speed in order to make things seem less important, Rohmer who imitates the documentary, Hitchcock who is so emotional that he pretends to be thinking only of the money, Renoir who pretends to be relying on chance—all of them instinctively reject the poetic attitude.

To finish with modernity, I don't know if I'm reactionary but I don't go along with the critical tendency that consists in saying: "After such and such a film we can never again put up with seeing well-made stories," etc. As much as I like new films like *Two or Three Things, L'Homme N'Est Pas un Oiseau, La Barrière,* and others, I believe that if *The Magnificent Ambersons, The Golden Coach,* or *Red River* were to come out now, in '67, they would be the best films of the year. That's why I'm determined to continue the same cinema, which consists either in telling a story or in pretending to tell a story—it's the same thing. Deep down, I am not modern, and if I pretended to be, it would be artificial. In any case, I wouldn't be satisfied and that's reason enough not to do so.

Interview by Jean-Louis Comolli and Jean Narboni,
Cahiers du Cinéma, *no. 190, May 1967*

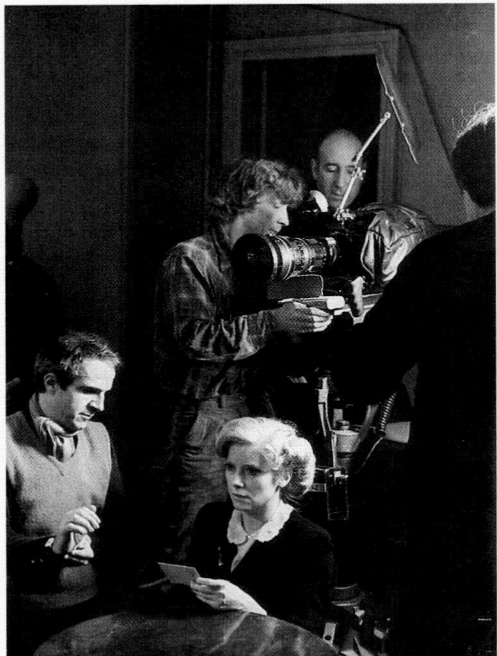

"The cinema would do better imitating popular imagery." Catherine Deneuve and, at the camera, Nestor Almendros on the set of *The Last Metro*

"Notice" in the first edition (1966) of *Le Cinéma selon Hitchcock*

Pourquoi Hitchcock apparait-il dans tous ses films ? — Quel rapport y a-t-il entre le sexe et les menottes ? — Connaissez-vous l'Understatement ? — Quelle est la différence entre surprise et suspense ? — Avez-vous déjà vu un Mac Guffin ? — Préférez-vous une tranche de vie ou une tranche de gâteau ? — Qu'est-ce qu'ils ont en Suisse ? — Les acteurs sont-ils du bétail ? — Hitchcock est-il un sophistiqué barbare ? — Pratiquez-vous le Run for Cover ? — Qu'est-ce qu'un Hareng rouge ?

Vous trouverez les réponses précises à toutes ces questions angoissantes dans:
le Cinéma Selon Hitchcock
par François Truffaut - Editions Robert Laffont.

PROPAGANDA FILMS AFFECT ONLY PEOPLE ALREADY CONVINCED

What do you think of "committed" films, placed at the service of an ideology?

I think that if you really want to influence the life of your contemporaries—for their good, moreover—you have to give up cinema in favor of political action if that's what you believe in. But in films, I don't think so: that takes fifth place, sixth place. . . . The film can only shake you up violently while it's being shown. Maybe there's an exception in *Z*. I think that that's one of the rare cases where a film was able to trouble people in the opposed camp, and I have the impression that that film influenced the "no" on the referendum. Because as a rule, propaganda films affect only people already convinced. The others just don't go. The true militants are against *Z*, but I think that's absurd because it's the only film of the Left which has been seen by a clientele of the Right.

Interview by Anne Gallois,
Témoignage Chrétien, *January 8, 1970*

Soldiers—it's demoralizing just to film them, simply seeing them all with the same helmets: that bores me to hell in advance, enormously. Look, the very idea of a guy who walks into another guy's place and salutes and clicks his heels, all that stuff . . . No, really . . .

Interview by Pierre Billard, Christiane Collange, and Claude Veillot,
L'Express, *May 20, 1968*

Do you feel yourself close to the Godard of today?

For the present, no, because he has virtually abandoned cinema. He is making a militant's cinema. Until May he was in the vanguard and was foreseeing things, then the "events" came along and proved him right, which must have troubled him a lot and led him to abandon cinema in the traditional form of fiction. Because he needs to be ahead of things, and for once reality was ahead of him. He has placed his talent at the service of the revolution because he believes in it. I also don't think anything can be done with our society, but I don't like any society, any country, I can't like anyone who gives orders to others. It's another form of anarchism, but very peaceable.

Interview by Anne Gallois,
Témoignage Chrétien, *January 8, 1970*

THE CINEMA SHOULD NOT COMPETE WITH THE PLASTIC ARTS

In certain respects the cinema is a plastic art, but I don't believe it should compete with the plastic arts. To make Vermeers on the screen, like Feyder, to my mind that is of absolutely no interest. The cinema would do better to imitate popular imagery.

Certain Japanese films achieve that: you have a night scene, the lake all brilliant, the moon reflected, a woman in a white dress goes by, etc. You find that also in *The Birds*. There you have an ideal cinema: you film during the day what you dreamed at night and you dream ideal things: moon, night, everything that defies the laws of optics, the possibilities of film, of gelatine.

Hitchcock not only loves cinema, he loves film itself, frame after frame, and with him there is no longer any problem of what to shoot. When he begins a film he has twelve hundred drawings already done, and they have to be reproduced faithfully whatever you may have to do to achieve that. This is not a matter of renouncing the visual idea. It is a cinema I find extremely complete because it is just as experimental as McLaren's tiny four-minute films, as Trnka's researches, and as universal as *Ben Hur*. In Hitchcock's work there is abstraction, there is concreteness, there is absolutely everything. It is always of great beauty.

Interview by Pierre Billard,
Cinéma 64, *no. 89*

WORKS OF ENTERTAINMENT

. . . the ignoble opposition between "works of reflection" and "works of entertainment," as if the three hundred novels of Simenon, Charles Trenet's five hundred songs, the plays and films of Sacha Guitry were not there precisely to prove that works that are genuinely entertaining provide matter for reflection.

Preface to Sacha Guitry, Le Cinéma et Moi, *Paris, Ramsay, 1977*

I MUST NOT DO ANYTHING BY CONSTRAINING MYSELF

Listen, the only thing I can believe in is Gide's "Doubt everything, but do not doubt yourself": in no case should one force oneself. To force oneself for exterior reasons, or to keep in line with the times, or to respond to what is expected of you, I don't think you should do that, even if you have to disappoint people. If I do not feel myself truly in my time, if it does not interest me, if I do not understand it well, if I believe that I do not feel myself part of it, there is no reason to force myself. I must not do anything by constraining myself.

That is the very essence of art. But can one make a film only for oneself? Do you do that?

At the outset, yes, I make it for myself, for my pleasure. Afterwards, as I get further along with the preparations, I do my very best to make it comprehensible to everyone, clear, logical, but without ceasing to please myself. And in the shooting, once more, I feel that the film again becomes very personal.

Interview by Pierre Billard, Christiane Collange, and Claude Veillot,
L'Express, *May 20, 1968*

THE FILMS THAT DON'T VIBRATE

When I was a critic, I thought that a film, to be successful, had to express simultaneously an idea of the world and an idea of the cinema.

Overleaf
"In *Close Encounters* I never had the impression of playing a role, only of lending my carnal envelope." With Steven Spielberg, summer 1976

The Rules of the Game or *Citizen Kane* fits that definition very well. Today I want a film I watch to express either the joy of making cinema or the anguish of making cinema, and I am not interested in everything between the two, that is, in all the films that don't vibrate.

Interview by Anne de Gasperi, concerning The Story of Adele H., *in* Le Quotidien de Paris, *May 2, 1975*

I WANT VERY MUCH TO FILM PAROXYSMS

I need to see strong subjects confirmed by reality or simply by a work of fiction, but an admirable fiction like *Jules et Jim.* Likewise Nabokov's *Kamera Obskura,* if I film it some day, it's a novel full of excess and paroxysms.

I want very much to film paroxysms, which contradicts my realistic temperament, but I want nevertheless to satisfy that desire, without which I'd be making the same film every year.

Interview by Pierre Billard, Cinéma 64, *no. 86*

"The films that don't vibrate." During the filming of *Two English Girls,* 1971. *Above:* With Stacey Tendeter and Jean-Pierre Léaud; *below:* with Jean-Pierre Léaud in the grotto scene

THE BEAUTY OF A FILM LIES IN ITS LOGIC

You prefer working in the third person; do you prefer that others work in the third person?

Oh no! I don't ask anyone to work in the same way I do. I am irritated when I hear someone say, "In films you have to do it that way." That's not true. One has the right to be one's own cameraman or to ignore the laws of optics, one has the right to tell about oneself or not to tell, to do eight hundred takes or only a hundred, to be your own scriptwriter or not, to hire stars or unknowns, you even have the right, when it comes down to it, not to show up at the shooting: one has *all* the rights. Every affirmation in that domain is a roundabout way of saying, "I am the only one and the others don't even exist." The beauty of a film lies in its logic, and it is certainly obvious that Orson Welles's logic is not Bresson's.

It is certain that I don't have a very strict idea of cinema if I can admire Carl Dreyer as much as Alfred Hitchcock. I admire all the "interesting" filmmakers except Antonioni: that's the only injustice I permit myself! Obviously I feel more at ease in the tracks of the scriptwriting directors, Lubitsch, Renoir, Buñuel, Bergman, Wilder, Rossellini, Hawks, than in those of the "art directors" Eisenstein, Dreyer, Visconti, Orson Welles, Sternberg. . . .

Interview by Pierre Ajame, Le Nouvel Adam, *no. 19, February 1968*

My favorite film director is certainly Eric Rohmer because he is right now the most logical, the most firm in his intentions, and the most decisive in his execution. He has perfected, with his series of *Moral Tales,* a way of "suspending dialogue" which is very powerful. The success of *My Night at Maud's,* not in France alone but everywhere, is the most moral cinema event there can be, because if four fifths of films deal with love, one realizes that *My Night at Maud's* is one of the first devoted to the importance of marriage, to the importance of the choice of a woman for life: seeing *My Night at Maud's,* you discover to your amazement that this theme, so essential and universal, has practically never been treated. Among "ourselves," by which I mean the old hands of *Cahiers du Cinéma,* we have known for twenty years, since his 16-mm films (*Kreutzer Sonata, Bérénice,* etc.), that Rohmer was the strongest among us and our master, but he remained an éminence grise. I am glad and proud that Rohmer is now recognized and appreciated in New York as well as in Stockholm and in Paris.

Interview by Claude-Marie Trémois, Télérama, *December 11, 1971*

WE HAVE ALL ENDED UP ADOPTING BAZIN'S MAYONNAISE THEORY

When I was twenty I reproached André Bazin for considering films like mayonnaises that take or don't take. I used to say to him: "Don't you see that all of Hawks's films are good and all of Huston's are bad?" a roughshod formula that later, when I had become in my turn a film critic, I forced myself to refine somewhat, thus: "The least good film of Hawks is more interesting than the best film of Huston." Here you will have recognized the main idea behind the "*auteur* theory," launched by the *Cahiers du Cinéma,* which is forgotten nowadays in France but is often debated in the American magazines by movie fans.

Today many of the Hawksians and Hustonians have become directors. I don't know what one group or the other thinks of the "*auteur* theory," but I am sure we have all ended up adopting Bazin's mayonnaise theory because the practice of cinema has taught us a certain number of things:

It demands as much effort to make a bad film as a good one;
Our most sincere film can look like a practical joke;
The one we do most casually may end up going around the world;
An idiotic but energetic film can be better cinema than an intelligent but flabby film;
The result is rarely proportionate to the effort put into it.

Success on the screen does not necessarily result from our brain's good functioning but from the harmony between preexisting elements of which we were not even aware: the happy blend of the subject chosen and our deeper nature, the unpredictable coincidence between our personal preoccupations at that point in our life and those of the public at that point in current events.

Preface, Les Films de Ma Vie

Seriously, I find that I have to admit that a negative criticism by Philippe Collin or Pauline Kael has stirred up profounder ideas than a rave review by X or Y. When you start out, you may need to feel yourself esteemed, but with

"Is Hitchcock a sophisticated barbarian?"

Notes in the margin of the script of *L'Agence Magic,* by Claude de Givray and Bernard Revon, which Truffaut planned to film after *Small Change*

the years you prefer to be liked. Among the negative articles I make a great distinction between "Alas, it's bad" and "Wow, it's bad": you sense this very well between the lines.

Interview by Serge Daney, Jean Narboni, and Serge Toubiana, Cahiers du Cinéma, *no. 315, September 1980*

I AM A DIRECTOR WITHOUT THEORIES

In your book of conversations with Hitchcock, you recalled his famous formula: "Certain films are slices of life, mine are slices of cake." Yours are slices of what?

I don't like to be the man of compromises, but ultimately I'm for life and for the cake. Obviously Hitchcock said that against neorealism, because he is very angry at the idea of taking just anybody from the street and having him act out ordinary situations. If that's all, he says, you only need to open a window to get yourself paid, and when Hitchcock says that, I think he's right. But when Bresson explains that he doesn't use actors and explains why with splendid theories, then I find he's not wrong either. If I, Truffaut, am a director without theories, it's because I find that all theories are good.

Hitchcock and Bresson are both right?

They're right, but they're right only for themselves. Where I am not in agreement is when Bresson goes so far as to condemn Hitchcock in the name of his theories, and vice versa.

Interview by Pierre Billard, Christiane Collange, and Claude Veillot, L'Express, *May 20, 1968*

ANYBODY CAN BECOME A MOVIE CRITIC

Anybody can become a movie critic; they won't demand of the candidate a tenth of the knowledge required from a literary, music, or art critic. A director in our time must accept the idea that his work will on occasion be judged by someone who will never have seen a film of Murnau's.

Preface, Les Films de Ma Vie

On ne doit pas écrire une scène pour caser une idée mais caser 6 idées dans une (longue) scène.

Vous manquez de confiance :
— dans le public
— dans vos personnages
— dans l'histoire
— en vous

Relisez les grandes choses : Marius - Fanny - Scènes de la vie conjugale - la Strada - le Visage - le Carrosse d'or - Baby Doll

PRACTICE

PROJECTS

I HAVE ALWAYS HAD MANY IRONS IN THE FIRE AT ONCE

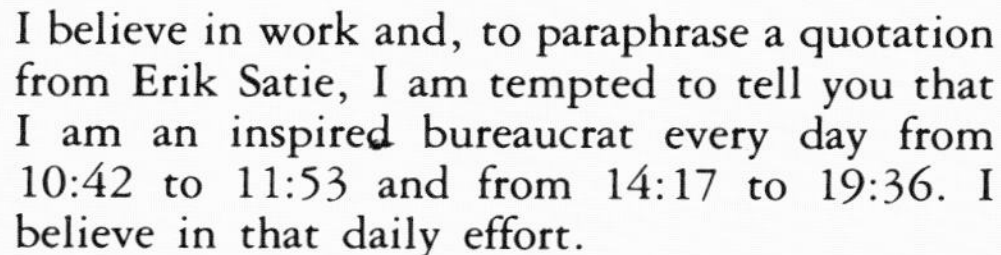

I believe in work and, to paraphrase a quotation from Erik Satie, I am tempted to tell you that I am an inspired bureaucrat every day from 10:42 to 11:53 and from 14:17 to 19:36. I believe in that daily effort.

I have always had many irons in the fire at once, and I believe there exists a secret bond between the number three and myself. With *The 400 Blows* I already had two other films in mind: *Shoot the Piano Player* (which I had proposed to Pierre Braunberger) and *Jules and Jim.* I didn't know if I would be accepted as a filmmaker, but I already knew my second film and also the third.

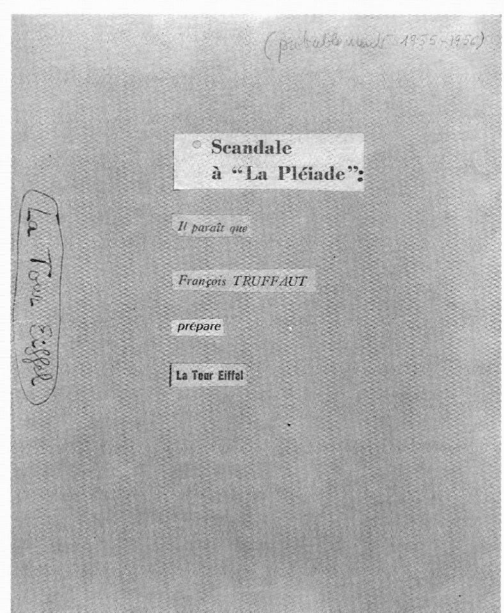

Collage by François Truffaut for the short film *La Tour Eiffel*

Between *The Soft Skin* and *Fahrenheit 451* I had to wait three years before finding a producer. That was a very painful period of distress and frustration but one which made me determined to speed up the rhythm of filming and, above all, never to go back and question the choice of a film as I had just been doing for certain projects.

It may seem stupid to decide never to have doubts about a subject, but I believe that all film projects have their advantages and drawbacks. Every made-up story supposes a certain naïveté. What counts is the enthusiasm that an idea, a story, arouses in you. You should never throw into question that initial impact, even if you endure doubts and anxieties as time goes on.

Since that decision, I make a film a year. That may seem a lot, but I have known too many directors who have suffered periods of physical cave-in or who lost the confidence of the industry just when they were seized with a frenzy of work. Being in good health, I consider that if I obtain backing for a film, even a difficult one, I have to make that film.

Unifrance Film, *1977*

THE UNREALIZED PROJECTS

1957: *LA TOUR EIFFEL* (THE EIFFEL TOWER)

Eiffel (Gustave), French engineer, born in Dijon (1832–1923). He constructed numerous metal bridges and the tower on the Champ-de-Mars.

Eiffel (Tower), iron tower 300 meters [984 feet] high erected on the Champ-de-Mars in Paris in 1889 by the engineer Eiffel.

La Tour Eiffel, twenty-five-minute film in 16-mm Kodachrome, conceived for large screen.
Director: François Truffaut.
Screenplay and commentary: Robert Lachenay (with the collaboration of Jean Giraudoux).
Chief cameraman: Charles Bitsch.
Interpreter: Jean-Claude Brialy (the Peasant in Paris).

1/BEFORE THE CREDITS:

The entrance to the slaughterhouse on Rue Vaugirard held in a broad shot.

With a heavy, rocking gait, a peasant enters the camera field from the right, leading an enormous recalcitrant cow by a rope.

The man and the animal pass in front of the camera, enter the slaughterhouse courtyard, and disappear behind a wall screen left.

For a few seconds the shot remains empty, then the man comes out, alone, counting a wad of bills. He walks toward the camera until he is framed in closeup, and his blissful face is raised while his gaze passes above the camera to lose itself in the distance, behind the houses, and comes to rest on a vague piece of metal seen above a roof.

At that point it will be clear that our peasant has decided to visit the Eiffel Tower before returning to his village.

CREDITS, during which shots dissolving in and out show us the peasant strutting comically through Paris.

2/FIRST PART:

From the Place de l'Alma, the Champs-Elysées, Montmartre, La Motte-Piquet, from wherever he goes, the peasant catches sight of the Tower, its point, the third storey, perching high above the rooftops, more or less close or more or less distant, never entirely different nor ever quite the same, inaccessible, ungraspable, tantalizing. Our man, at 100 meters [328 feet] from the Champ-de-Mars, finally thinks he's "got" the Eiffel Tower. He rushes ahead and comes smack up against the end of a blind alley. Retracing his steps, he almost gets himself run over by a sports car, a convertible, driven by a young girl who never stops smiling, someone out of a Giraudoux novel, who seeing him half in tears on the sidewalk invites him to get in the car, consoles him by making him laugh, and finally drives him to the Eiffel Tower.

3/SECOND PART:

The history of the tower told by the girl, Juliette. Visit; ascension. In the elevator and at every storey, lovers. Gags involving tourists, children, snapshot cameras . . . Little by little, almost imperceptibly, the peasant becomes

Edgar Poe

Robert Lachenay .... le Scarabée d'or
Marcel Ophuls .... la Barrique d'Amontillado
Michel Varesano .... Ligeia

Jean Luc Godard .... le portrait ovale

Fr. Truffaut .... le démon de la perversité

Eric Rohmer .... Bérénice

— Claude Chabrol (Stéphane Audran)
— Claude de Givray
— Georges Franju
— Paul Gegauff .... le démon de la perversité
— Resnais — Demy —

Notes for a film with episodes after Edgar Allan Poe, about 1960

During the filming of *Bed and Board* in 1970: "We are made for being happy in our work, in our work in the cinema" (from *Day for Night*).

transformed. His beret, pulled down to his eyebrows at the start of the film, gradually climbs higher and higher until it disappears into the air, while Juliette tries to hold back the man, who wants to chase it right up to the top of the tower. From up there, the peasant discovers Paris, a Paris Parisian to its fingertips, that of Giraudoux *(Prière sur la Tour Eiffel)*. He discovers the capital of France and, while we're at it, France itself.

When they come down, the two of them obviously in love, they form the most Parisian of couples: she, ever more smiling, and he, freshly shaved, elegant, totally transformed, spiritual: Adam 1957 arm in arm with Eternal Eve.

THE END.

1959: *TEMPS CHAUD* (HOT WEATHER)

When I got married, I had just filmed *The Mischief Makers* and I was to do my first full-length feature for Braunberger, *Temps Chaud.* Fearing it would be too much like *And God Created Woman,* I wanted to replace it with *The 400 Blows,* but Braunberger refused, so then I filmed *The 400 Blows* for my father-in-law, who was very satisfied with it. After that, obviously, Braunberger let me replace *Temps Chaud* with *Shoot the Piano Player!*

Interview by Pierre Ajame, Le Nouvel Adam, *no. 19, February 1968*

Can you tell us about Temps Chaud, *the film you're preparing at the moment?*

No, because I'm not making it. I've dropped that project.

May we know about your other projects, then?

Yes, I should like to make a film about friendship with Charles Aznavour. That, for the moment, is my only project.

Interview by Pierre Wildenstein, Télé-Ciné, *no. 84, July 1959*

1960: *BLEU D'OUTRE-TOMBE* (SPECIAL DELIVERY FROM THE BEYOND)

Paris, March 31, 1960

Dear Sir,

I am very sorry to inform you that the realization of *Bleu d'Outre-tombe* is being put off to next year.

My present film will not really be finished before the end of May, and since we were to begin *Bleu* at the start of July, a month of preparation would simply not be enough to choose the actors, make trial runs, and familiarize myself with a screenplay that I know even less for not having had a hand in it. I take in things slowly, and to proceed in this manner would amount to doing bad work.

I will not film *Bleu d'Outre-tombe* until I know all its speeches by heart and am sure of the ten or twelve actors selected.

If you are willing, we can see each other about adopting new working methods.

With my regrets, please believe, dear Sir, in my gratitude and my sincere good wishes.

Letter to René-Jean Clot

1964: *LES TROIS FACES* (THE THREE FACES)

July 17, 1964

Dear Madam,

I suppose that Dino has told you that I am giving up filming one of the sketches in your first film.

At the moment I have many personal and professional worries, and it was scarcely reasonable for me to run away from them by throwing myself into an unexpected and not well-defined piece of work.

I generally work quite rapidly but after having thought about each film for a very long time. I was a little frightened by the early date for shooting and by the difficulty of finding a suitable story.

I should have been very happy to work with you, and I am very touched that the idea of this collaboration was acceptable to you.

I very much liked the test you submitted to for Dino, and I am certain that you are right to envisage a career as a movie actress.

This first film will be very important for you, and I hope it will bring you every satisfaction. I very much liked your book, *Ma Vie,* and I was very happy to make your acquaintance.

I wish you every happiness and happiness in general.

Letter to Princess Soraya

1965: *BONNIE AND CLYDE*

Paris, June 18, 1965

Dear Friend,

I received your telegram and thank you for it. But before accepting your invitation to come to New York and discuss *Bonnie and Clyde,* I should like to submit to you a few points of importance for me.

The fact is, the successive delays in *Fahrenheit 451* are causing me many worries, and to all those troubles are added grave difficulties with the film *Mata-Hari,* of which I am one of the producers.

That is why your proposition concerning *Bonnie and Clyde* comes at a very good moment, on condition, as I told you, that shooting can begin this summer.

As it happens, the screenplay is sufficiently in shape, the choice of locations practically already made. The preparation of the film should be easy and rapid.

Excuse me if I speak immediately of money, but it seems to be called for at this point.

For making *Bonnie and Clyde,* I would want a salary of $80,000 advanced against 10 percent of the producer's net receipts.

The second point of my letter concerns Helen Scott, whom I should like to have as my personal assistant and who I hope will be formally hired right from the day when I myself am and until the film is finished. She should have the same salary as that settled on for her collaboration on *Fahrenheit 451*.

The third point concerns the role of Bonnie, which I should like to assign to my friend Alexandra Stewart, with whom I have long wanted to make a film. To me, she corresponds perfectly to the character. She is English Canadian, fully bilingual, and takes on any accent whatsoever with great facility.

I am confident of her as an actress and as a friend, and it would mean for me, in addition to Helen, another reassuring presence, because I want very much, for my first film in English, to be surrounded in the affair by people easy to get along with and who will have confidence in me, whether they be technicians or actors.

If you are in agreement on these three points, I can come to New York whenever you wish to discuss the other important points which are:

a) the male lead: I think the role could be proposed to Terence Stamp, whom I admire very much and who hopes to play Montag in *Fahrenheit 451*. But I won't speak of this with him before having your opinion on this point, and besides, because he is very particular about his career, it is possible that he may want to do *Fahrenheit* and not *Bonnie and Clyde*. This is a question mark;

b) the choice of *chef-opérateur*—cameraman, who should be someone very pleasant and modern because, apart from myself, the rapidity of shooting will depend essentially on him. It is not necessary that he speak French, but it is necessary that he be competent, sympathetic, speedy, modern, and favorable to what you people call "The New Wave";

c) David Newman and Robert Benton. I would be very happy to go over the screenplay with them carefully before shooting, and if they themselves could follow the shooting it would be very good in case we might want to change little things along the way.

There you are!

If you have ideas about actors for the film, I suggest you send me photos as soon as possible. In any case, we can talk about that in New York where, as I have said to you, I am ready to go at your call.

Hoping to hear from you, I send you friendliest greetings.

Letter to Norton Jones

1965: *NIGHTFALL*

Paris, April 8, 1965

My dear Don,

In the next letter I will tell you in detail the situation with *Fahrenheit 451*, in which Sam Spiegel is now interested (you know the advantages and drawbacks of a proposition coming from him), and with the Hitchcock book which is being finished at this moment.

I am writing you today to ask you to secure the film rights for a novel by David Goodis, *Nightfall*, of which I would like to make a short film either before or after *Fahrenheit 451*.

At the time I asked you to negotiate the rights to *The Bride Wore Black* I had to send you the duplicate of the contract for the purchase of the rights to *Down There (Shoot the Piano Player)*.

I hope we will have better luck with *Nightfall* than with *The Bride Wore Black*, and the experience with *Shoot the Piano Player* fortifies that hope.

Since it involves David Goodis (author of *Shoot the Piano Player*), the publisher and David Goodis are likely to think it involves a film to be made by me. So it is preferable not to hide the fact from them, but to call to their attention that it will be a "B Picture." Despite its good reputation in New York, *Shoot the Piano Player* was not a success!

There you are, dear Don.

We hope the conditions will be reasonable, that is, between four and eight thousand dollars.

Above all, I hope the rights are free and I await a telegram from you on that point.

With all my friendly greetings.

Letter to Don Congdon

1968: PROJECT FOR A FILM ABOUT FRANÇOISE DORLÉAC

On June 27 Françoise Dorléac died, victim of a car accident. For the general public it was dismaying news, a news item so much the crueler since it had to do with a very beautiful girl of twenty-five, an actress who was appreciated but had not had the time to become a star.

For all those who really knew her, Françoise Dorléac represented much more. She was a personality such as one rarely encounters in a lifetime. . . .

We will try to make Françoise Dorléac better known and loved by making a montage of her best scenes in *Mensonges, Les Loups dans la Bergerie, La Fille aux Yeux d'Or, Les Portes Claquent, Ce Soir ou Jamais, La Gamberge, Le Jeu de la Vérité, Tout l'Or du Monde, Arsène Lupin, L'Homme de Rio, Genghis Khan, La Chasse à l'Homme, The Soft Skin, Where the Spies Are, Cul de Sac,* and *Les Demoiselles de Rochefort*.

Between these excerpts from films will be inserted interviews, statements by Françoise Dorléac, photos, and various documents.

I propose to carry out this undertaking with the collaboration of my script girl, Suzanne Schiffman, and the television journalist Philippe Labro, if he will accept. He knew Françoise Dorléac well and devoted to her a few stunning minutes in a short film commissioned by Unifrance.

No one wishes to make money out of this film—whose cost it is difficult to estimate at the moment—but we think it should be finished for June 27, 1968, and distributed via the television stations and the noncommercial networks: film clubs, etc.

A twenty-minute version might make a short to be exploited in the normal fashion.

April 2, 1968

1976: *L'AGENCE MAGIC*

1983: *LA PETITE VOLEUSE* (THE LITTLE THIEF)

la couleur de Virginie, oui c'est très important, mais mal montré, trop direct, trop simple, trop banal... * le public ne doit pas toujours découvrir les choses en même temps que les personnages, c'est trop simple, pas intrigant, pas excitant!

Notes in the margin of the script of *L'Agence Magic*

PRODUCTION

THE PRODUCER'S JOB DOESN'T INTEREST ME

I am a producer because, that way, people annoy me less, and then I need an office. Everything is sacrificed to the cinema: if I pick out a car it will be a car in which film equipment can be stowed, etc. Everything that permits me to make films is good, period. The only thing important is working.

What exactly is your activity as producer?

It only backs up my activity as director. With my organization, Les Films du Carrosse, named in homage to Jean Renoir's *The Golden Coach,* we work as independent producers. I put my salary on the scale, I contribute the screenplay, all of it giving me a 50 percent right in the film, and therefore artistic control, therefore independence. If it's too big a film, then it's more difficult. That's what happened to me with *Fahrenheit 451,* where the amount I could contribute was pitiful with respect to the cost of the film.

And your activity as producer for films made by others?

I was co-producer for Jean-Louis Richard's *Mata-Hari,* Claude de Givray's *Tire-au-Flanc,* Rivette's *Paris Belongs to Us,* Cocteau's *Testament of Orpheus,* and for Godard's *Two or Three Things I Know About Her.* In general, it's friendship that makes me decide to get involved, because the producer's job doesn't interest me.

Interview by Pierre Ajame,
Le Nouvel Adam, *no. 19, February 1968*

Filming *Small Change* in 1976: "It's a different way of working, you need patience."

YOUTH IS BLESSED

Twenty years ago, in *Paris-Presse,* I was struck by Juliette Gréco's assertion: "Mademoiselle Sylvie Vartan and I do not practice the same profession." That seemed to me the height of the ridiculous, above all coming from someone well established as compared with a newcomer. . . .

As much as by Juliette Greco's statement, I was impressed by that of Bernanos in *Le Journal d'un Curé de Campagne:* "I understood that youth is blessed, that it is a risk that has to be run, and that the risk itself is blessed." That prodigious sentence had its effect on me, I am deeply marked by it, it is magical and true, it influences me even in the field of production. For example, if I don't like to make my financiers lose money, when the financiers are younger than I the idea becomes unbearable to me. I feel as if I were swindling them. This will soon create problems for me, because I work more and more with people who are younger.

Interview by Serge Daney, Jean Narboni, and Serge Toubiana,
Cahiers du Cinéma, *no. 315, September 1980*

WRITING

NOWADAYS WHEN YOU TELL A STORY YOU ARE JUDGED BY THAT STORY

I cannot belong to a group. I don't want to speak badly of intellectuals, but I am a filmmaker for a normal public, I like to tell stories that everybody understands. I would hate it if, leaving my films, there were only ten people who understood and who would be obliged to explain to the others, because I like what is simple, I like normal stories. There is even an element of melodrama in my films. Only, contrary to you who say to yourselves, "That's comfortable," one can say, "That's courageous," because there is a horrendous fear of melodrama: today no one any longer dares to say he loves Dickens or *Les Misérables.* . . .

In the mere fact of telling a story I find there is a certain courage nowadays, because people have become more and more articulate, more and more intelligent, more and more skeptical. There have been thousands of films, thousands of screenplays, and today when you tell a story you are judged by that story. In *Day for Night* I assure you that many directors would have chosen the solution of rendering *Introducing Pamela* incomprehensible. That would have been very easy, and people would have said: "Oh, yes, he's a guy who's making a poetic film about his life." All right, I opted for a melodrama, the story of a girl who runs off with her father-in-law. I had it told three times so people would know what it's about, and I am willing for people to judge by that story—and they certainly haven't failed to do so. Someone has written: "The film within a film is a stupidity." All right, I've run that risk—because I knew that that's what would be said—but it was indispensable to do so. In fact, to make a comedy film, the film within the film had to be a drama, and for every scene to be interesting to look at, it had to fit nicely into a story easy to summarize which was told right at the start, so that every scene would come across.

Interview by Etienne Ballerini, Alain Thery, Roger Carrache, Bernard Oheix,
Jeune Cinéma, *no. 77, March 1974*

WORKING OUT THE SCREENPLAY

How do you go about working out your screenplays?

I myself have never worked alone, and I find questions of vanity stupid in the cinema. What should count all the time is the result, and if, to make a good film, eight people are needed to work on the screenplay, I will work with eight people, and because I consider that everyone should get credit for his work, I will list all eight in the credits. People who, in order to remain the sole authors of their film, work all by themselves when they're really not equipped to do so, are wrong because that is absurd. But it is obvious that a film is a one-

"I am one hundred percent in favor of romance in films." With Isabelle Adjani during the filming of *The Story of Adele H.*

"The whole thing is to find the right collaborator." The director and his script girl (Truffaut and Nathalie Baye) in *Day for Night*

Overleaf
"The strongest influence." Interviewing Hitchcock with Helen Scott as assistant

man job when it comes to the shooting, because everything happens between "camera!" and "cut!" and because the decisions that have to be made all day long are one-man decisions.

In Day for Night *there is talk of the fellow scriptwriters but we don't see them.*

Yes, it works out that way, that's to show the isolation in which the director finds himself. But then too I think that, all the same, one has friends, people who think like you and who can help you, most of all when it comes to comedy. It's obvious that with three of you in a room for a month and a half you will find more gags and ideas than if you're alone. I am aware of a very great difference in richness between the films Bresson has made entirely on his own and those he made "with" Bernanos, Cocteau, Giraudoux. So I work with friends I choose on the basis of the screenplay. If it's a job that calls for a lot of documentation, books to be read, research to be done, I will do it with Gruault; if on the contrary it's a job demanding much rigor in construction, I will do it with Jean-Louis Richard; I now work even more with Suzanne Schiffman, who used to be a script girl and has become my assistant. The whole thing is to find the right collaborator and not to be pressured by dates: there are a lot of films that aren't good simply because it had been decided to shoot on such and such a date, because the contracts were signed, because the actors were hired, and then two weeks before, you realize that the script is bad and you say to yourself: "We'll work it out somehow." There again, there are people who can scrape through, but there are others who can't, so it's best to push ahead on a script until you're satisfied with it and only afterwards begin shooting.

How do you go about your literary adaptations? Because, for example, in Two English Girls *there are often pages of the book annotated. . . .*

Yes, but it was only for the credits that I had the book photographed. Ultimately adaptations are more difficult than original scripts. At the start, one feels that it's easier, but afterwards difficulties arise; I know that now. In the new period I am entering, I am going to try to do original screenplays, because I realize, with the passing of time, that I have made myself understood better with *The 400 Blows, Stolen Kisses,* or *Day for Night* than with *Mississippi Mermaid, Two English Girls,* or *The Bride Wore Black.* Adaptations bring something a little mysterious to the final result, they give the impression that it takes place in a country that doesn't exist or in some pretty weird fashion. Often they are American stories transposed, and because I don't really want to transpose them to France I end up with a kind of imaginary country. Then too, the choice one makes of scenes to be retained is obviously arbitrary, and because scenes referring to scenes one has cut always remain on the screen, the film becomes too mysterious. I know that people know very well what to think when they come out of one of my films for which I've done the script from A to Z, whereas they are always disconcerted when it's one of my adaptations of novels. That confusion, I believe, is what encourages me to try to do original screenplays.

Interview by Etienne Ballerini, Alain Thery, Roger Carrache, Bernard Oheix, Jeune Cinéma, *no. 77, March 1974*

THE INFLUENCE OF ERNST LUBITSCH

You don't choose influences, they just come to you. Seeing old films again, I began to love those by Lubitsch, and I believe that that is the strongest influence I have undergone recently. From Hitchcock I took lessons in effectiveness, in simplification, the aim being to reinforce the visual value of a film. With Lubitsch I am now attracted by work on the screenplay: how to mistreat it so as to make it more interesting, how to recount things by ricochets, in a roundabout manner.

Interview by Jean-Pierre Chartier, "Cinéastes de Notre Temps," O.R.T.F. (French radio), 1970

ADAPTATIONS

When I was a critic, I was pretty violent against the adaptations by Aurenche and Bost, because the adaptations by Aurenche and Bost consisted in taking a novel like *Le Diable au Corps,* like *Le Rouge et le Noir,* and saying: "We've got an hour and a half, we'll make twenty-eight scenes," and then they made twenty-eight scenes. Ultimately that pretty much came down to transforming novels into plays, but when the essential is in the prose or poetry, as in *Le Diable au Corps,* which is full of extraordinary images, at that particular moment I found the book really distorted. In point of fact, the formula that seemed good to me and which had already been tried out by Melville and Cocteau in *Les Enfants Terribles,* consisted instead of a kind of filmed reading, in which scenes constructed not like theater scenes but like scenes played, with dialogue, alternate with the outright narrative, the commentary.

Interview by Jean-Pierre Chartier, "Cinéastes de Notre Temps," O.R.T.F. (French radio), December 2, 1965

DIALOGUE

When people talk about films, they underestimate the importance of the words, and I understand Astruc very well when he films *The Pit and the Pendulum* "first of all" to let Baudelaire's text be heard. With the visual side of a film, you manage a partial satisfaction, perhaps in the best of cases 70 or 80 percent of what you dreamed. With dialogue, you can hit 100 percent. In *The Soft Skin,* for example, I am 60 percent content with the images but 100 percent with the words spoken. I believe they entirely fill the bill. Even if people don't like the film, I know that it hits the right note, and I would not say the same of *Fahrenheit 451*, where my frustration lay precisely in that. Basically I came to cinema via the dialogues, I learned them by heart. I know perfectly that of *Le Corbeau,* all of Prévert's and all of Renoir's. It was later that I heard about "mise-en-scène" from Rivette. My nature was to get myself so drunk on films that I got to know the sound track by heart, both dialogue and music. That is why I never go along with the opponents of

dubbing. I can recite *Johnny Guitar,* which probably has a greater importance in my life than in that of its author, Nicholas Ray. Well, I almost prefer the dubbed version of *Johnny Guitar* to its original version, and I can even say that certain things in the *Piano Player,* for example, are influenced by the tone of the dubbing in *Johnny Guitar:* "Jouez-nous quelque chose, Monsieur Guitare. . . . "

Interview by Jean-Louis Comolli and Jean Narboni, Cahiers du Cinéma, *no. 190, May 1967*

Doesn't the often very distinctive character of your dialogues correspond to an increasing importance of the book?

Yes, I'm going to have to stop that. Moreover that omnipresence of the book is becoming just too clear to everybody. My friend Helen Scott, who does my American subtitling, often grumbles about the dialogues: "You call that dialogue?" she says to me, "Myself, I call it a series of declarations!" *Love on the Run* nonetheless got her approval, I don't know why.

Sometimes you really do lay it on. To make Charles Denner (who has just been woken up) say things like: "What duplicity, what a crude trick . . . "

Yes, yes . . . [laughter].

You are in favor of highly written dialogues, a little in the manner of the prewar dialogue writers.

Yes. Rohmer proceeds in that way, but Rivette not so much. . . . He dreams that the actors will say what they wish, whether they hit on it or don't hit on it; Pialat likewise. Those are directors who expect a lot of the actor. Myself, I am very fond of actors, but I have told myself once and for all that the text put in their hands is better than the one they invent. You know, a mistake was made at the start of the New Wave, calling the characters by the actors' first names, that was an affectation practiced at the outset and which I consider a mistake. I did it myself in *The Mischief Makers.* Actors need to *play* someone else.

Interview by Philippe Carcassone, Michel Devillers, and Jacques Fieschi, Cinématographe, *February 1979*

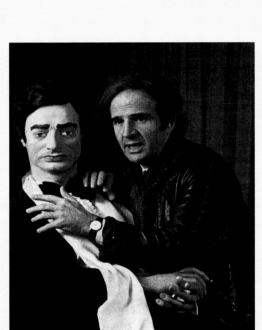

"I myself visualize certain passages of the film and not others." With the mannequin of Charles Denner for *The Man Who Loved Women*

ONCE THE THEME IS CHOSEN, THE SCRIPT ALMOST WRITES ITSELF

My work, come to think about it, does seem often to consist of filming scenes I've experienced myself that I want to bring back, scenes I'd like to live through and scenes I'd be afraid to live or relive. With that system, which is worth what it's worth, once the theme is chosen, the script almost writes itself, and I don't fuss too much over whatever significance comes out of it.

A film like Chaplin's *The Kid* brings together everything I love: laughter, tears, dancing, food, survival, the apprenticeship of the street, and even what is called nowadays "the quest for identity."

Interview by Serge Daney, Jean Narboni, and Serge Toubiana, Cahiers du Cinéma, *no. 316, October 1980*

I CAN'T GET AWAY FROM WRITING

I can't get away from writing. In all my films there are people who send each other letters, a young girl who writes in her diary. Nor can I move from one place to another without explaining it on a map. That is simply not done anymore, but it's in my character: to leave even one person uninformed distresses me. The taste for writing has been pursuing me ever since I concerned myself as a critic with the form of the screenplay. I didn't think I would become a filmmaker but, rather, a scriptwriter.

Interview by Anne de Gasperi, Le Quotidien de Paris, *May 2, 1975*

THE CHARACTERS

The idea is not to show characters and say: "Here's how my characters are and to hell with you"; the idea is, "Here is how my characters are, I ask you to understand them." I think there was a moment in my life when I hesitated between the desire to become a novelist and the desire to become an attorney, so there was already the idea of convincing, yes, I do like the idea of convincing people.

Interview by Aline Desjardins, Radio-Canada, 1971

CUTTING

As regards shots, takes, their succession, do you do that work in editing, or do you already have precise ideas when shooting?

There are directors who visualize everything in shooting. I myself visualize certain passages of the film but not others. I think that I take off instead from this idea: there is always a part that you visualize a lot and that is often disappointing, whereas things you didn't have the foggiest notion about can become very beautiful, and that happens often.

But anyway I don't plan the cutting beforehand, because it's really when I see the actors playing the scene that I decide if I will make a single long take or if, on the contrary, there will have to be several. A directorial idea has to be really very strong to exist on the day before filming. That happens to me sometimes, I can't at the moment think of any precise examples, but there is always at least once in every film an effect that I foresaw for the mise-en-scène. Thus there was an effect I liked a lot in *Bed and Board:* when Jean-Pierre Léaud has a fling with a Japanese girl, his wife knows about it, and when he comes home he opens the door and there is his wife in the back of the apartment dressed in Japanese fashion. I knew that people would laugh, but then I make him come forward into the room and I do a tracking shot of her, and when we get a very close shot we see that there is a tear on her cheek, and the laughter stops short, people are ashamed of having laughed. It was something I had foreseen entirely, as to how to do it and the effects to be obtained, because I knew that once the girl was dressed in Japanese fashion, the scene could not be good if she were to keep on, if she served his dinner. . . . I knew that anything that could be invented would be inferior to the effect of seeing her. So I knew we had to finish with the moment we see her, but I was looking for a final "effect," and I thought that that tear would be the strong point, because it would make a kind of completely unexpected surprise. And that worked out very well, I think. Things like that are a little experimental on my part, it's thinking back a little to Lubitsch that brings them up: "What do people expect? Give them what they expect and then give them the opposite of what they expect at the same time." You see? Sure, that's toying with people, but it amuses me a lot, it pleases me.

"Adaptations lend something mysterious to the final result." Working on *Mississippi Mermaid* with Catherine Deneuve

Interview by Etienne Ballerini, Alain Thery, Roger Carrache, Bernard Oheix,
Jeune Cinéma, *no. 77, March 1974*

IMPROVISATION

Do you change many things, in the course of shooting, with respect to what you have written?

That is very variable; I changed a great deal for my first three films and very little for *The Soft Skin*. But I consider that the others hadn't been worked on enough. It seems to me that, filmed very faithfully, the screenplay of *The 400 Blows* would have presented grave drawbacks. That of *Shoot the Piano Player* and that of *Jules and Jim* likewise. Improvisation on the set was really and truly necessary.

Not because of external constraints?

Not at all, no. One sees the characters come to life and one recognizes that the film is going off in this or that unforeseen direction, so one has to compensate. I am often guided by the idea of "compensation." The film is going to become too "this," so let's compensate with "that." It's a matter of balancing the pans of the scale. A sequence risks becoming indelicate, let's give it some gravity; a sequence is becoming too solemn, introduce three gags, etc. In *The Soft Skin* such problems were solved at the script stage. Improvisation was used for the character of the airline hostess: that role was feeble in the script, it lacked reality. I had picked out that job of airline hostess solely because I had wanted to film an aviation setting and, to tell the truth, in the script there was no such character. I was embarrassed to have the young actress who would play it read the script, because she could only be disappointed reading it. I warned her and I told her also that along the way we would work together, we would make a real effort to build a character and to give it reality. Little by little, without adding a single scene, simply by making the ends of scenes a little different, by tacking on a phrase or a look here and there, I think the character became interesting.

Filming *Confidentially Yours!* (Truffaut, then Fanny Ardant)

Interview by Pierre Billard,
Cinéma 64, *no. 87*

ACTORS

WORKING WITH ACTORS

But are those scripts very detailed?

No . . . they are precise in construction and in general have very little dialogue because I'm very fond of making up dialogues in the course of shooting, when I've come to know my actors better. I can follow better what the film is becoming from the way the actors react. For almost all the films, I do just that. All the same, there is the drawback of making scenes a little too short during the filming, because it happens that one says to oneself: "If we shoot more than two pages, the actor will not be able to remember it all," and so one makes scenes a little short.

In *Day for Night* there were many actors I didn't know; I knew them from having seen them in other films, but for example Jacqueline Bisset, I had to wait to learn what her French vocabulary was like; likewise Jean-Pierre Aumont, I had never filmed with him, nor Valentina Cortese. So I discovered them in the course of shooting and with that as a basis, wrote their texts every Sunday for the next week on the set.

It is important to know an actor?

Ah, I think yes. When you know him well you can write for him. In fact, you get to know an actor well only at the editing table, by looking at him there: you begin to discern his strong points, his weak points, and then, if you work with him another time, it seems to me that you can write better for him because you know the things he will act very well. In *Day for Night* there is a scene where, after Jacqueline Bisset leaves the room where she has spent the night with him, Jean-Pierre Léaud picks up the phone and calls her husband, Dr. Nelson. That's a scene I would certainly not write for an actor I didn't know, but it goes so well with the idea of Jean-Pierre Léaud, with what one has seen him do in other films, with what he's like a little in life too, that the scene simply forced itself on me and no sooner did the idea strike me than I found it highly amusing and wrote it. So I am sure that you don't write the same thing for people you know and for those you don't know.

Interview by Etienne Ballerini, Alain Thery, Roger Carrache, Bernard Oheix,
Jeune Cinéma, *no. 77, March 1974*

DIRECTING ACTORS

You like to distinguish between "working with the actors" and "directing actors," the latter a term you don't much like.

That is an expression invented and propagated by the *Cahiers du Cinéma* ten years ago. There is direction of actors when there is "transformation" of actors, for instance what Jean-Louis Barrault does in Renoir's *Le Testament du Docteur Cordelier,* that is to say, when you change even the way someone walks or when you make him dance his role rather than act it. For my part, I consider that I have *never* directed an actor: I simply switched him on to the things I like, that's to say that I prevented him from looking satisfied with himself, I prevented him from appearing too clever or bombastic or whatever I might think to his disadvantage; in short, I've kept him on rails that are my own but which were not necessarily indicated in the script. That's all, that's what I've done with Jean-Pierre Léaud, with Aznavour, Marie Dubois, Françoise Dorléac, Jeanne Moreau. . . .

Do you have the impression of remaining faithful to the same type of actor?

Not for the women. But for the men, there is a point in common, which is fragility; I can't film with someone who looks too sure of himself, who would be arrogant or even a brute, a force of nature.

Interview by Pierre Ajame,
Le Nouvel Adam,
no. 19, February 1968

Filming *The Man Who Loved Women* in 1976, with Brigitte Fossey

PERSONAL EXPERIENCE

And you, at what point did you want to be an actor?

I don't consider myself an actor, just an interpreter on occasion. When I was filming *Fahrenheit 451* in London the actors had doubles who took their places while the lighting was being set, and I became aware that the doubles, accustomed to the English cinema with fixed shots, didn't like to move around inside a set. Because I often set up sequence shots with Nicholas Roeg, I took Oskar Werner's place several times and I became aware that, facing the camera, the inspiration for the staging is quite different. That is what made me decide to play the role of Dr. Itard in *The Wild Child,* to take the child in hand more completely, and to impersonate absolute neutrality. Same exercise in *Day for Night,* where I circulate in the midst of the actors instead of making signs to them from a distance.

In *Close Encounters,* where I should have felt myself at last truly an actor, I never had the impression of playing a role, only of lending my carnal envelope. Spielberg had shown me the two thousand sketches of his storyboard, so I knew that what he was after was a grand cartoon strip and that I could put back in my suitcase the book by Stanislavsky that I had bought for the occasion. I wanted to be the ideal actor, the one who never asks questions, I wanted Spielberg not to have any worries because of me. For certain scenes the camera movements were computer-controlled in order to guarantee the precision of later special effects, and so we could verify the result immediately on television screens. Then I looked at my image and told myself it would be more pleasing if I opened my arms a little to make the silhouette sharper. *That* was a real pleasure.

Interview by Serge Daney,
Jean Narboni, and Serge Toubiana,
Cahiers du Cinéma, *no. 316, October 1980*

With Nestor Almendros, chief cameraman for *The Wild Child, Bed and Board, Two English Girls, The Story of Adele H.*, and four of Truffaut's last five films

I DISCOVERED A REAL PLEASURE AS AN ACTOR

Why did Spielberg select you? Why did you accept?

Spielberg had decided that the O.V.N.I. specialist would be a European. To give extra weight to his character he wanted a nonactor. He had seen me in *The Wild Child* and in *Day for Night,* and the plausibility of my two characters decided him. In film today, that notion of plausibility of the characters is more important than in the past.

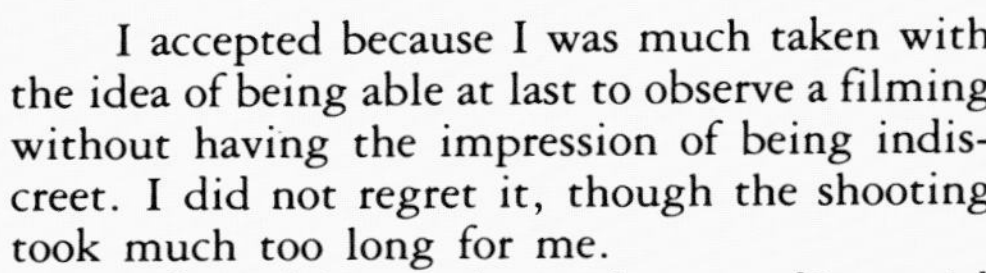

I accepted because I was much taken with the idea of being able at last to observe a filming without having the impression of being indiscreet. I did not regret it, though the shooting took much too long for me.

What did you learn from working with Spielberg?

Mobilizing a crew of two hundred and fifty, Spielberg's cinema had nothing in common with the cinema I make. Moreover, *Close Encounters,* being above all a film with trick photography, I *learned* nothing on the technical plane that really concerned me.

On the human plane, on the contrary, I discovered the world of actors and that behind-the-scenes world I suspected but did not really know. I lived that family life common to all filmings, with the backstage intrigues kept hidden from the director. I learned to know the universe of the makeup people, dressers, hairdressers . . . , that life where more time is spent in the dressing rooms than on the set. During all that time I kept thinking about *Day for Night,* which that experience would certainly have enriched.

Did you have the impression, as an actor, of making progress?

I had warned Spielberg: "I will be a neutral actor, I am only capable of being myself, don't ask me to laugh or cry on command like a professional actor." Spielberg had accepted that limitation, but several times during the shooting he made me surpass myself. He directed me so as to make me come out of myself. Thanks to that, I discovered a real pleasure as an actor. I behaved like every actor in the world who, as soon as the take has been shot, turns to the director to find out if he is satisfied. And every time I achieved the result Spielberg expected, I was content, as is every actor.

Has that made you want to interpret other roles in films you would not yourself direct?

No, I now feel that I no longer have any wish to act in films other than my own.

Has this experience with Spielberg influenced the way you now work with actors?

I believe that it has in fact led me to have more patience with the actors. I think I can help them better, speak with them. . . .

You are in any case writing a book about actors? What is its theme?

It's a book about the way actors behave and feel. About that mixture of pleasure and anxiety that goes along with that profession, where ultimately the percentage of pleasure is extremely small compared with the moments of misgivings. I felt the urge to write when I observed certain reactions common to all actors.

Unifrance Film, *no. 19, 1977*

TECHNICAL MATTERS

I DON'T LIKE STUDIO SETS; THE FACT IS, THEY SCARE ME

I have never dealt with the movie set because I have always filmed in genuine settings. Anyway it's extraordinary, one is only afraid of what one doesn't know. For nothing in the world will Autant-Lara film in genuine settings, and he claims he doesn't like them; that's not true, he's afraid. Myself, I say: I don't like studio sets; the fact is, they scare me. One pretends. I'm afraid, he's afraid, everybody's afraid.

To my mind, one of the advantages of the genuine setting is that there are not thirty-six places in which to plant the camera: the choice is very limited. You're there, in a particular room, a particular action is called for. Thus, the apartment where Jean-Pierre Léaud lived with his family was tiny; you would never dare construct something like it in the studio. In genuine settings you're obliged to simplify; there is no longer anything but the image, and it's a little as if you were snapping photographs.

Interview by Gilbert Salachas,
Télé-Ciné, *no. 94, March 1961*

COLOR HAS DONE ALMOST AS MUCH HARM TO THE CINEMA AS TELEVISION

I think that color has done almost as much harm to the cinema as television. One has to fight against too great a realism in films; if not, there is no art. At the start of the New Wave, in order to exist, we had to bring things down to the minimum, to go back to silent films, and they were dubbed later. At a second phase we arrived at direct sound, and then on top of that came color, and people forgot to analyze the phenomenon. From the moment that a film is in color, that it is shot in the street, nowadays, with the sun and the shadows and the dialogue covered by the noise of motor bikes, well, it's no longer cinema. It's not art, it's boring. When all films were in black and white, very few were ugly, even when they didn't aspire to be artistic. Now ugliness prevails. Eight films in ten are as boring to look at as a traffic jam in the street.

Yet you don't film in black and white?

Because I can't do otherwise. Whatever the film, it is anticipated that one day it will go on television, which only buys color. . . .

Interview by Danièle Heymann and Catherine Laporte,
L'Express, *March 13, 1978*

"For the men, there is a point in common, which is fragility." With Gérard Depardieu, filming *The Woman Next Door*

THE IMPORTANCE OF TECHNIQUE

Do you think that poor continuity, shaky dolly shots are things of no importance, technical weaknesses to be corrected little by little, or would you, like others, be tempted to turn them into a system?

Everything depends on what you consider important. For my part, I am only bothered by what I'm responsible for. If an actor acts badly, it's my fault: I should have noticed it while shooting, guided him, repeated the take. . . . If the film comes back from the laboratory scratched, that's not my fault. It's my work that is important. In any case, after eight days of showing, the film will be scratched, so I don't even redo that take. A traveling shot trembles, that's of no importance. What is, is knowing whether the traveling shot was necessary, whether it looks good, what it brings to the film. If it's trembly, that's just too bad.

Interview by Gilbert Salachas,
Télé-Ciné, *no. 94, March 1961*

I BELIEVE THAT A FILM IMPOSES ON US A FORMAL AND MORAL APPROACH THAT WILL GUIDE EVERYTHING THROUGHOUT THE FILMING

I believe that a film imposes on us a formal and moral approach that will guide everything throughout the filming. That commitment can concern an actor's work: you know you won't get a single smile out of him in the entire film (Montgomery Clift in *I Confess*), that he'll wear a hat even in bed or in the bathtub (Michel Piccoli in *Contempt*), perhaps that he will never be seen walking or ever sitting down. . . . It can affect the camera: there will be not one single traveling shot (Eisenstein) or sixty moving sequence shots in a row (*The Long March*), etc.

Are there such preconceived approaches at the start of your films?

In *The 400 Blows,* obviously Jean-Pierre Léaud had to be prevented from smiling, the opposite of the sanctimonious adolescent in *Louisiana Story* who still galls me today because it's so obvious that he's playing for the camera. You don't smile when you're alone. In *Shoot the Piano Player,* every scene had to be ended in a spirit opposed to its opening: more than a *parti pris,* that was a sort of wager, an experiment. In *Jules and Jim,* things had to be kept strict, the moralizing side of Roché had to be preserved; therefore the actors always had to act against the situation, and nature constantly had to be fitted in—and the environment—whence all those 360-degree panoramas. No question of showing the chalet without showing the meadow, and the meadow without the forest. On the other hand, *The Soft Skin* being surgical, panoramas had to be ruled out, the camera didn't have the right to promenade around. Critics said: he has changed style. No, I had changed subject.

And for Fahrenheit?

There it was a matter of making a film that would be an object. As in *Piano Player,* we were going back to childhood: tin soldiers, snow, toy fire station, flames. . . . The subject of *Fahrenheit,* the love of books, is so positive that there wasn't even any question of my "treating" it but simply of illustrating it. Some people expected a film à la Richard Brooks; that's good too, but it's not my nature. In *The Bride Wore Black,* my initial *parti pris* concerned Jeanne Moreau's acting. In *Jules and Jim,* I had her "open out" to counteract the morose style, the sulky intellectual side she had shown in *Moderato* and *La Notte.* But since *Jules and Jim* they've made her laugh and smile a lot in her films, so this time we'll head in another direction: no laughter, no smiles, no sulkiness nor bitter pouting but an absolute neutrality, the gaze neither open nor closed but normal. . . . I am going to ask her to act without coquetry, like a man, a man thinking about a job to be done; basically she will have only to look at Coutard, whose face is generally without expression, tranquil and competent.

Interview by Jean-Louis Comolli and Jean Narboni,
Cahiers du Cinéma, *no. 190, May 1967*

François and Laura Truffaut with Bernard Herrmann during the mixing of *The Bride Wore Black* in 1967

MUSIC

PEOPLE WHO MAKE DO WITHOUT MUSIC ARE VERY STRONG

I utilize music in the traditional way. Nowadays it's disappearing from films: that's a good thing, and I find that people who make do without music are very strong. You have Buñuel, Bresson, Rohmer, Bergman, four who have practically no music in their films or very little; for my part I can't do that, because I have stories that take place over a very long time. I think it's possible when you have a story complete in itself and very brief. I always need music to go from one place in time to another. In *Day for Night,* I used it solely for the scenes at work because I felt that the true subject was work and that, in the moments when work was no longer shown as realistic but as narrative, as frequentative, the work itself had to be glorified at those moments. It was the subject: the idea that all those people you see are stronger when at work. And I asked Delerue to make a somewhat Vivaldian music because what was needed was a music that soared and at the same time was light, but also a music that would glorify.

But other times it's a different utilization. In *Such a Gorgeous Kid Like Me,* I asked him for the same kind of music as in a Hitchcock movie, music as reinforcement, music that sets up an urgency, that says: "Look out, there we have to go real fast! Careful, what's going to happen there?" It was a very utilitarian music, and he had a lot of trouble writing it because it wasn't in his nature, but it came out very well, it was very good.

It must be difficult to collaborate with a musician on the music for a film, no?

If you know each other well, if he knows cinema, it's all right because you can find a vocabulary. If he doesn't know cinema and if you yourself don't know music, it's a dialogue between deaf men. Without considering, too, that he'll play us something on the piano and, one bright day, when we get to recording, there will be fifty instruments and it won't be at all what we heard on the piano: so there are surprises and it's all very delicate.

Have you had surprises of that sort?

Oh, that's happened to me, yes. I had a very good collaboration with Duhamel for *Stolen Kisses* and then we didn't get along well on *Mississippi Mermaid* and *Bed and Board.*

Interview by Etienne Ballerini, Alain Thery, Roger Carrache, Bernard Oheix,
Jeune Cinéma, *no. 77, March 1974*

Ferrand and Stacey (François Truffaut and Alexandra Stewart) editing *Introducing Pamela* (in *Day for Night*)

EDITING

TO MISTREAT THE FILM, TO KNOCK IT ABOUT

I began to get really interested in editing with *Shoot the Piano Player,* because it was a pretty special film in which there was a great deal of improvisation. At the end of shooting, after the first rough cut, it gave the impression of being unusable, because of a too jerky story, especially compared with that of *The 400 Blows,* which was simple and in a straight line. I spent several months on the editing of *Shoot the Piano Player,* I came to think of it as passionately interesting work, and for the first time I began to mistreat the film, to knock it about. In that work there was also influence from *Breathless,* finished a few months earlier and whose editing had been quite revolutionary, really free.

In *Jules and Jim,* editing likewise plays an important part because there were many improvised scenes that could be placed here or there; I had thought up many short skits for the chalet scenes, and with the script girl we classified them as scenes of happiness, scenes of unhappiness. The editing of *Jules and Jim* consisted in finding a kind of equilibrium: will this bit of film go better after a scene of happiness or after a scene of unhappiness? That was another work, special, exhilarating.

Interview by Pierre Billard,
Cinéma 64, *no. 87*

I get to understand certain things only at the editing table: in *Day for Night,* for example, important decisions were made rather late. So when you see Jean-Pierre Léaud firing several shots one after the other at Jean-Pierre Aumont, that came out of the montage because normally there was only one take but here, because we shot the scene six times, I realized that we needed this sort of ballet at the end and I mounted all the gunshots one after the other. Editing is a very creative period because, as a rule, you can't afford to blunder. A film can get ruined in the editing, but generally you do it a lot of good. One of the montages I regret is that of *Two English Girls* because I edited it as if the film had turned out really well. I did an optimistic montage that I regretted later, because the film was too long. And I likewise regretted not having been as strict and severe as in other montages: it should have had two more months' work, tightening, etc.

Interview by Etienne Ballerini, Alain Thery, Roger Carrache, Bernard Oheix,
Jeune Cinéma, *no. 77, March 1974*

MISE-EN-SCÈNE

THE PROGRESS ONE MAKES

One thing I'm sure of is that the progress one makes has almost no importance on the artistic, aesthetic plane. It's important for oneself, because one gets the impression of having acquired terrific know-how. You know how to simplify,

"The proof by camera." With Jérome Zucca (The Amateur Filmmaker) during the filming of *Such a Gorgeous Kid Like Me*

build, rip out three pages of screenplay, and replace them with one sentence. You have the impression of progressing, but it is illusory and, if you happen to see again a film you made when starting out, you realize that the best of you was in it and that the slight enrichment that came afterwards is nothing special compared with the initial richness. I really believe that.

Interview by Jean-Pierre Chartier,
"Cinéastes de Notre Temps,"
French radio, June 20, 1970

THE SCREEN REFLECTS WHAT TOOK PLACE BETWEEN "CAMERA!" AND "CUT!"

Do you consider yourself the sole author of your films, as a painter is of his pictures, or do you have the feeling that it's a collective creation and even perhaps spontaneous?

I don't believe much in collective creation. Of course the people you surround yourself with are very important, as are the actors, but to the extent that you are responsible for choosing them, those people also resemble you. To have chosen them is a matter of your own personality. So I believe, and will always believe, that the director is completely responsible, because the screen reflects what took place between "Camera!" and "Cut!" All cinema is just that, that interval that may last fifteen seconds and during which the director is on his own to reflect, to judge if the take is empty, if it's full, if it's rich, if it's stupid: entirely alone in taking initiatives. Even if the dialogue is bad and is not the director's work, it is he who is responsible for it, because that proves he doesn't know how to judge the quality of dialogue.

When you learn that So-and-So is going to make a film, it's a big mystery. You say to yourself: "Well, well, what can the likes of him do?" and when you see the film: "It's extraordinary how that's just like him," when the fact is you couldn't have even guessed what it would be.

Interview by Pierre Loubière and Gilbert Salachas,
Télé-Ciné, *no. 160, March 1970*

"Is the cinema superior to life?" Filming *The Last Metro*

DIRECTION, WHAT EXACTLY IS IT?

My favorite filmmakers are all scriptwriting directors, because direction, what exactly is it? It is "the totality of decisions taken" in the course of preparation, of shooting, and of finishing up the picture. I believe that all the choices offered to the director—choice of scenario, of cuts, of locations, of actors, of collaborators, of angles, of lenses, of takes to be printed, of noises, of music—are for him to decide, and what is called direction is obviously the common course toward which tend the thousands of decisions taken during those six, nine, twelve, or sixteen months of work. That is why the "partial" directors, those who concern themselves with only a single phase of work, even when talented, interest me less than Bergman, Buñuel, Hitchcock, Welles, who *are* their films in every respect.

Interview by Jean-Louis Comolli and Jean Narboni,
Cahiers du Cinéma, *no. 190, May 1967*

Toujours des scènes trop courte, flashes, scénette, ça manque de poids, de force, d'importance.

Il faut tenir le public assis, la bouche ouverte

Notes in the margin of the script of *L'Agence Magic*

VIVIANE finit de se rhabiller et laisse entendre qu'elle devra s'acheter une conduite parce que : ''ces parcours ne sont plus de son âge''.

SYLVIE n'est pas dupe, VIVIANE adore ça.

Ce bloc 39 → 43 semble être
la première chose qui fonctionne
bien, n'ayez pas peur de préciser,
dilater. Généralement vos scènes
sont trop courts, comme des
flashs.
Pour créer des personnages héroïques
Pagnol, Fellini, Bergman n'ont pas
peur des <u>scènes longues</u>. Une scène
ne doit pas être une scenette. Elle
peut constituer un petit film à elle
seule avec un mouvement en 3
temps, début, milieu, fin;

CHRONOLOGY

1932 February 6: birth of François Truffaut, only child of Roland Truffaut, architect-decorator, and Jeanine de Montferrand, secretary for the magazine *L'Illustration.* The Truffaut family lives in the Pigalle district, Rue Henri-Monnier, and François attends the kindergarten on Rue Clauzel and later the Lycée Rollin.

1940 December 13: first-run release in Paris of Abel Gance's *Paradis Perdu,* the first film François Truffaut would remember.

1946 First jobs.

1947 Founds a film club, the Cercle Cinémane, in the Latin Quarter.
Meets André Bazin.
Escapades and delinquency; consigned to the center for observation of juvenile delinquents at Villejuif.

1948 André Bazin puts him to work at a cultural organization, Travail et Culture.

1950 First articles for the *Bulletin du Ciné-club* of the Latin Quarter, *La Gazette du Cinéma,* and *Elle.*

1951 Enlists in the army without waiting to be called up. Sent to Germany. Deserts. Military prison. André Bazin comes to his rescue. Released from military service for medical reasons. Lives with the Bazins.

1953 Returns to Paris. Works a few months in the film department of the Ministry of Agriculture.
The *Cahiers du Cinéma* (no. 21, March 1953) publishes its first article by François Truffaut (on David Miller's *Le Masque Arraché*).
Film reviewing becomes Truffaut's chief activity.

1954 Writes for *Arts, Cahiers du Cinéma, La Parisienne.*
Announces his personal critical positions ("Une Certaine Tendance du Cinéma Français," *Cahiers du Cinéma,* no. 31).
Makes his first short film, in 16-mm and silent, *Une Visite.*
Writes a first screen treatment for Godard's *Breathless.*

1955 Publishes a short story, "Antoine et l'Orpheline," in *La Parisienne* (first appearance of the character Antoine Doinel).
First conversations with Alfred Hitchcock, in Paris, for the *Cahiers du Cinéma.*

1956 Projects assistant to Roberto Rossellini.

1957 Founds his own production company, Les Films du Carrosse.
August: begins shooting *The Mischief Makers.*
October 29: marries Madeleine Morgenstern.

1958 Spring: films *Une Histoire d'Eau.*
November 10: begins filming *The 400 Blows.*
November 11: death of André Bazin.

1959 January 22: birth of Laura Truffaut.
November 30: begins filming *Shoot the Piano Player.*

1960 Is one of the signers of the Manifesto of the 121, an antimilitarist, anticolonialist declaration.
He co-produces Cocteau's *Testament of Orpheus.*

1961 April 10: begins filming *Jules and Jim.*
June 29: birth of Ewa Truffaut.
November: films *Antoine and Colette.*

1963 Screenplay, dialogue, and co-production of Jean-Louis Richard's *Mata-Hari.*
October 21: begins filming *The Soft Skin.*

1965 December 2: first broadcast of the radio series "Cinéastes de Notre Temps" devoted to him.

1966 January 12: begins filming *Fahrenheit 451.*
Publishes *Le Cinéma selon Hitchcock.*

1967 May 16: begins filming *The Bride Wore Black.*

1968 February 5: begins filming *Stolen Kisses.*
The Langlois Affair: he is active in the committee to defend the Cinémathèque Française against government interference.
December 2: begins filming *Mississippi Mermaid.*

1969 July 7: begins filming *The Wild Child.*

1970 January 21: begins filming *Bed and Board.*
Publishes *Les Aventures d'Antoine Doinel.*

1971 April 21: begins filming *Two English Girls.*
Publication, through his initiative, of André Bazin's *Jean Renoir.*

1972 February 14: begins filming *Such a Gorgeous Kid Like Me.*
September 25: begins filming *Day for Night.*

1973 *Day for Night* wins Oscar for best foreign film.

1975 January 8: begins filming *The Story of Adele H.*
July 17: begins filming *Small Change.*
Publishes *Les Films de Ma Vie.*

1976 October 19: begins filming *The Man Who Loved Women.*
Publishes *L'Argent de Poche* as the book of the film *Small Change.*

1977 Acts in Steven Spielberg's *Close Encounters of the Third Kind.*
Publishes the book of *The Man Who Loved Women.*
October 11: begins filming *The Green Room.*

1978 May 29: begins filming *Love on the Run.*

1979 October: accepts the presidency of the International Federation of Film Clubs.

1980 January 28: begins filming *The Last Metro.*

1981 April 1: begins filming *The Woman Next Door.*

1982 November 4: begins filming *Confidentially Yours!*

1983 September 28: birth of Joséphine Truffaut.

1984 October 21: death of François Truffaut in Neuilly.

FILMOGRAPHY

1954 Une Visite

Script: François Truffaut. Photography: Jacques Rivette. Assistant Director and Producer: Robert Lachenay. Editor: Alain Resnais. 16-mm film, black and white. Running time: 7 minutes 40 seconds.
Actors: Laura Mauri, Jean-José Richer, Francis Cognany, Florence Doniol-Valcroze.

1957 The Mischief Makers (Les Mistons)

Script, adaptation, and dialogue: François Truffaut, based on a short story in "Virginales" by Maurice Pons (Julliard). Music: Maurice Le Roux. Narrator: Michel François. Director of Photography: Jean Malige. Assistant Directors: Claude de Givray and Alain Jeannel. Editor: Cécile Decugis. Production Company: Les Films du Carrosse. 16-mm film, black and white. Running time: 23 minutes. Distributor: Les Films de la Pléiade.
Actors: Bernadette Lafont, Gérard Blain, and les Mistons.

1958 Histoire d'Eau

Directors: François Truffaut and Jean-Luc Godard. Director of Photography: Michel Latouche. Editor: Jean-Luc Godard. Producer: Pierre Braunberger. 16-mm film, black and white. Running time: 18 minutes. Distributor: Les Films de la Pléiade.
Actors: Jean-Claude Brialy, Caroline Dim.

1959 The 400 Blows (Les Quatre Cents Coups)

Original script: François Truffaut. Adaptation and dialogue: François Truffaut and Marcel Moussy. Music: Jean Constantin. Director of Photography: Henri Decae. First Assistant Director: Philippe de Broca. Art Director: Bernard Evein. Editor: Marie-Josèphe Yoyotte. Production Company: Les Films du Carrosse, SEDIF. Process: Dyaliscope. 35-mm film, black and white. Running time: 93 minutes. Distributors: Cocinor (France), Zenith (U.S.A.).
This film is dedicated to André Bazin.
Actors: Jean-Pierre Léaud (Antoine Doinel), Albert Rémy (the stepfather), Claire Maurier (the mother), Patrick Auffay (René Bigey), Georges Flamant (M. Bigey), Yvonne Claudie (Mme Bigey), Robert Beauvais (school director), Pierre Repp (the English teacher), Guy Decomble (teacher), Claude Monsard (judge), Henri Virlojeux (night watchman), Richard Kanayan (Abbou), Jeanne Moreau (young woman with dog), Jean Douchet (the lover), Jean-Claude Brialy, Christian Brocard, Bouchon, Marius Laurey, Luc Andrieux, Jacques Monod, Jacques Demy, François Truffaut, and the children: Daniel Couturier, François Nocher, Renaud Fontanarosa, Michel Girard, Serge Moati, Bernard Abbou, Jean-François Bergouignan, Michel Lesignor.

1960 Shoot the Piano Player (Tirez sur le Pianiste)

Script and adaptation: François Truffaut and Marcel Moussy. Dialogue: François Truffaut, based on the novel *Down There* by David Goodis (Gallimard). Music: Georges Delerue. Songs: "Framboise," written and sung by Boby Lapointe; "Dialogue d'Amoureaux," by Félix Leclerc, sung by Félix Leclerc and Lucienne Vernay. Director of Photography: Raoul Coutard. Art Director: Jacques Mély. Editors: Cécile Decugis and Claudine Bouché. Producer: Pierre Braunberger. Production Company: Les Films de la Pléiade. Process: Dyaliscope. 35-mm film, black and white. Running time: 85 minutes. Distributors: Cocinor (France), Astor (U.S.A.).
Actors: Charles Aznavour (Charlie Kohler), Marie Dubois (Léna), Nicole Berger (Théréso), Michèle Mercier (Clarisse), Catherine Lutz (Mammy), Albert Rémy (Chico), Claude Mansard (Momo), Daniel Boulanger (Ernest), Serge Davri (Plyne), Jean-Jacques Aslanian (Richard), Alex Joffé (stranger), Boby Lapointe (singer), Claude Heymann (impresario), Richard Kanayan (little Fido), Alice Sapritch (the concierge).

1962 Jules and Jim (Jules et Jim)

Script, adaptation, and dialogue: François Truffaut and Jean Gruault, based on the novel *Jules et Jim* by Henri-Pierre Roché (Gallimard). Narrator: Michel Subor. Music: Georges Delerue. Song: "Le Tourbillon" by Bassiak (Serge Rezvani), sung by Jeanne Moreau. Director of Photography: Raoul Coutard. Art Director: Fred Capel. Editor: Claudine Bouché. Production Company: Les Films du Carrosse, SEDIF. Process: Franscope. 35-mm film, black and white. Running time: 100 minutes. Distributors: CINEDIS (France), Janus Films (U.S.A.).
Actors: Jeanne Moreau (Catherine), Oskar Werner (Jules), Henri Serre (Jim), Marie Dubois (Thérèse), Boris Bassiak (Albert), Danielle Bassiak (Albert's friend), Sabine Haudepin (Sabine), Vanna Urbino (Gilberte), Anny Nelsen (Lucie), Bernard Largemains (Merlin), Dominique Lacarrière (one of the women), Jean-Louis Richard (customer in café), Elen Bober (Mathilde), Christiane Wagner.

1962 Antoine and Colette (Antoine et Colette)

First sketch of the film *L'Amour à Vingt Ans (Love at Twenty)*, made up of five episodes directed by François Truffaut (France), Renzo Rossellini (Italy), Marcel Ophuls (Germany), Andrzej Wajda (Poland), Shintaro Ishihara (Japan). Original script: François Truffaut. Music: Georges Delerue. Narrator: Henri Serre. Director of Photography: Raoul Coutard. Photographic links between sketches: Henri Cartier-Bresson, filmed by Jean Aurel. Editor: Claudine Bouché. Production Company: for the French sketch, Ulysse Production, reprinted by Les Films du Carrosse. Process: Cinemascope. 35-mm film, black and white. Running time of French sketch: 29 minutes (total running time: 120 minutes). Distributors: Twentieth Century Fox (France), Embassy (U.S.A.).
Actors: Jean-Pierre Léaud (Antoine Doinel), Marie-France Pisier (Colette), Patrick Auffay (René), Rosy Varte (Colette's mother), François Darbon (Colette's stepfather), Jean-François Adam (Albert Tazzi).

1964 The Soft Skin (La Peau Douce)

Original script: François Truffaut and Jean-Louis Richard. Dialogue: François Truffaut. Music: Georges Delerue, Haydn. Director of Photography: Raoul Coutard. Editor: Claudine Bouché. Assistant Editor: Lila Biro. Production Company: Les Films du Carrosse, SEDIF. Aspect ratio: 1:66. 35-mm film, black and white. Running time: 116 minutes. Distributors: Athos Films (France), Cinema V (U.S.A.).
Actors: Françoise Dorléac (Nicole), Jean Desailly (Pierre Lachenay), Nelly Benedetti (Franca), Daniel Ceccaldi (Clément), Jean Lanier (Michel), Paule Emanuèle (Odile), Sabine Haudepin (Sabine), Laurence Badie (Ingrid), Gérard Poirot (Franck), Dominique Lacarrière (Pierre's secretary), Carnéro (the Lisbon organizer), Georges de Givray (Nicole's father), Charles Lavialle (night porter at Hôtel Michelet), Mme Harlaut (Mme Leloix), Olivia Poli (Mme Bontemps), Catherine Duport (young girl at Rheims), Philippe Dumat (cinema manager at Rheims), Thérésa Renouard (cashier), Maurice Garrel (bookseller), Brigitte Zhendre-Laforest (linen delivery woman), Pierre Risch (canon).

1966 Fahrenheit 451

Script: François Truffaut, Jean-Louis Richard; additional dialogue: David Rudkin, Helen Scott, based on the novel *Fahrenheit 451* by Ray Bradbury (Denoël). Music: Bernard Herrmann. Director of Photography: Nicholas Roeg. Editor: Thom Noble. Production Company: Lewis M. Allen, Vineyard Films Ltd. Process: Technicolor. 35-mm color film. Running time: 113 minutes. Distributor: Universal (France and U.S.A.).
Actors: Julie Christie (Linda Montag and Clarisse), Oskar Werner (Montag), Cyril Cusack (the Captain), Anton Diffring (Fabian), Jeremy Spenser (the man with the apple), Ann Bell (Doris), Caroline Hunt (Helen), Gillian Lewis (TV announcer), Anna Palk (Jackie), Roma Milne (neighbor), Arthur Cox (1st male nurse), Eric Mason (2nd male nurse), Noel Davis (1st TV announcer), Donald Pickering (2nd TV announcer), Michael Mundell (Stoneman), Chris Williams (Black), Gillian Aldam (Judoka woman), Edward Kaye (Judoka man), Mark Lester (1st small boy), Kevin Elder (2nd small boy), Joan Francis (bar telephone operator), Tom Watson (sergeant instructor), Bee Duffell (the book-woman), and the book-men: Alex Scott *(The Life of Henry Brulard)*, Dennis Gilmore *(The Martian Chronicles)*, Fred Cox (Pride), Frank Cox (Prejudice), Michael Balfour (Machiavelli's *The Prince*), Judith Drynan *(Plato's Dialogues)*, David Glover *(The Pickwick Papers)*, Yvonne Blake *(The Jewish Question)*, John Rae *(The Weir of Hermiston)*, Earl Younger (nephew of *The Weir of Hermiston*).

1967 The Bride Wore Black (La Mariée Etait en Noir)

Script, adaptation, and dialogue: François Truffaut and Jean-Louis Richard, based on the novel *The Bride Wore Black* by William Irish (Presses de la Cité). Music: Bernard Herrmann. Director of Photography: Raoul Coutard. Art Director: Pierre Guffroy. Editor: Claudine Bouché. Assistant Editor: Yann Dedet. Production Company: Les Films du Carrosse/Les Productions Artistes Associés (Paris); Dino de Laurentiis Cinematografica (Rome). Aspect ratio: 1:66. Process: Eastmancolor. 35-mm color film. Running time: 107 minutes. Distributors: United Artists (France), MGM/UA (U.S.A.).
Actors: Jeanne Moreau (Julie Kohler), Claude Rich (Bliss), Jean-Claude Brialy (Corey), Michel Bouquet (Coral), Michel Lonsdale (Morane), Charles Denner (Fergus), Daniel Boulanger (Delvaux), Serge Rousseau (David), Christophe Bruno (Cookie), Alexandra Stewart (Mlle Becker), Jacques Robiolles (Charlie), Luce Fabiole (Julie's mother), Sylvine Delannoy (Mme Morane), Jacqueline Rouillard (maid), Van Doude (inspector), Paul Pavel (mechanic), Gilles Quéant (examining magistrate), Frédérique and Renaud Fontanarosa (musicians), Elisabeth Rey (Julie as a child), Jean-Pierre Rey (David as a child), Dominique Robier (Sabine, Julie's niece), Michèle Viborel (Gilberte, Bliss' fiancée), Michèle Montfort (Fergus' model), Daniel Pommereulle (Fergus' friend).

1968 Stolen Kisses (Baisers Volés)

Original script: François Truffaut, Claude de Givray, Bernard Revon. Music: Antoine Duhamel. Song: "Que Reste-t-il de Nos Amours?" written and sung by Charles Trenet. Director of Photography: Denys Clerval. Sound: René Levert. Art Director: Claude Pignot. Editor: Agnès Guillemot. Assistant Editor: Yann Dedet. Production Company: Les Films du Carrosse, Les Productions Artistes Associés. Process: 35-mm Eastmancolor. Running time: 90 minutes. Distributors: United Artists (France), Almi (U.S.A.).
This film is dedicated to Henri Langlois' Cinémathèque.
Actors: Jean-Pierre Léaud (Antoine Doinel), Claude Jade (Christine), Daniel Ceccaldi (M. Darbon), Claire Duhamel (Mme Darbon), Delphine Seyrig (Fabienne Tabard), Michel Lonsdale (M. Tabard), André Falcon (M. Blady), Harry Max (M. Henri), Catherine Lutz (Mme Catherine), Christine Pellé (the secretary), Marie-France Pisier (Colette Tazzi), Jacques Robiolles (unemployed television writer), Serge Rousseau (the stranger), François Darbon (sargeant-major), Paul Pavel (Julien), Simono (M. Albani), Jacques Delord (the magician), Jacques Rispal (M. Colin), Martine Brochard (Mme Colin), Robert Cambourakis (Mme Colin's lover), and at the Darbon Garage: Marcel Mercier and Joseph Mériau.

1969 Mississippi Mermaid (La Sirène du Mississippi)

Script, adaptation, and dialogue: François Truffaut, based on the novel *Waltz into Darkness* by William Irish (Gallimard). Music: Antoine Duhamel. Director of Photography: Denys Clerval. Sound: René Levert. Art Director: Claude Pignot. Editor: Agnès Guillemot. Assistant Editor: Yann Dedet. Production Company: Les Films du Carrosse, Les Productions Artistes Associés (Paris); Produzioni As-

sociate Delphos (Rome). Process: Eastmancolor, Dyaliscope. 35-mm color film. Running time: 120 minutes. Distributor: United Artists (France), MGM/UA (U.S.A.).
This film is dedicated to Jean Renoir.
Actors: Catherine Deneuve (Julie/Marion), Jean-Paul Belmondo (Louis Mahé), Michel Bouquet (Comolli), Nelly Borgeaud (Berthe Roussel and, in the photograph, Julie Roussel), Marcel Berbert (Jardine), Roland Thénot (Richard).

1970 The Wild Child (L'Enfant Sauvage)

Script, adaptation, and dialogue: François Truffaut and Jean Gruault, based on *Mémoire et Rapport sur Victor de l'Aveyron* by Jean Itard (1806). Music: Antonio Vivaldi. Musical Direction: Antoine Duhamel. Director of Photography: Nestor Almendros. Sound: René Levert. Art Director: Jean Mandaroux. Costumes: Gitt Magrini. Editor: Agnès Guillemot. Assistant Editor: Yann Dedet. Production Company: Les Films du Carrosse, Les Productions Artistes Associés. Aspect ratio: 1:33. 35-mm film, black and white. Running time: 83 minutes. Distributor: United Artists (France), MGM/UA (U.S.A.).
This film is dedicated to Jean-Pierre Léaud.
Actors: Jean-Pierre Cargol (Victor de l'Aveyron), François Truffaut (Dr. Jean Itard), Françoise Seigner (Mme Guérin), Jean Dasté (Philippe Pinel), Paul Villié (old Rémy), Pierre Fabre (orderly), Claude Miller (M. Lémeri), Annie Miller (Mme Lémeri), Nathan Miller (the Lémeri baby), Mathieu Schiffman (Mathieu), René Levert (Gendarme), Jean Mandaroux (Jean Itard's doctor), Jean Gruault (visitor at Institute), Robert Cambourakis, Gitt Magrini, Jean-François Stévenin (peasants in the chicken-stealing scene), and the children at the farm: Laura and Ewa Truffaut, Guillaume Schiffman, Frédérique and Eric Dolbert, Tounet Cargol, Dominique Levert, Mlle Théaudière.

1970 Bed and Board (Domicile Conjugal)

Script: François Truffaut, Claude de Givray, Bernard Revon. Music: Antoine Duhamel. Director of Photography: Nestor Almendros. Sound: René Levert. Art Director: Jean Mandaroux. Editor: Agnès Guillemot. Assistant Editor: Yann Dedet. Production Company: Les Films du Carrosse, Valoria Films (Paris); Fida Cinematografica (Rome). Process: Eastmancolor. 35-mm color film. Running time: 100 minutes. Distributors: Valoria Films (France), Columbia (U.S.A.).
Actors: Jean-Pierre Léaud (Antoine Doinel), Claude Jade (Christine Doinel), Daniel Ceccaldi (Lucien Darbon), Claire Duhamel (Mme Darbon), Hiroko Berghauer (Kyoko), Barbara Laage (Monique), Sylvana Blasi (tenor's wife), Daniel Boulanger (tenor), Claude Véga (the strangler), Bill Kearns (the American boss), Yvon Lec (traffic warden), Jacques Jouanneau (Césarin), Pierre Maguelon (bistro customer), Danièle Gérard (bistro waitress), Marie Irakane (concierge), Ernest Menzer (little man), Jacques Rispal (old solitary), Guy Piérauld (SOS chum), Marcel Mercier and Joseph Mériau (people in courtyard), Pierre Fabre (the sneerer), Christian de Tilière (the backer), Marcel Berbert, Nicole Félix, and Jérôme Richard (employees in American company), Marianne Piketti (violin pupil), Annick Asty (violin pupil's mother), Jacques Robiolles (the sponger), Ada Lonati (Mme Claude), Nobuko Maki (Kyoko's friend), Iska Khan (Kyoko's father), Ryu Nakamura (Japanese secretary), Jacques Cottin (Monsieur Hulot), Marie Dedieu (Marie), little Christophe Vesque, Mlle Irakane, Frédérique Dolbert, and Mlle Barbault (the newborn Alphonse Doinel).

1971 Two English Girls (Les Deux Anglaises et le Continent)

Script, adaptation, and dialogue: François Truffaut, Jean Gruault, based on the novel *Les Deux Anglaises et le Continent* by Henri-Pierre Roché (Gallimard). Music: Georges Delerue. Narrator: François Truffaut. Director of Photography: Nestor Almendros. Sound: René Levert. Art Director: Michel de Broin. Costumes: Gitt Magrini. Editor: Yann Dedet. Assistant Editor: Martine Barraqué. Production Company: Les Films du Carrosse, Cinétel. Aspect ratio: 1:66. Process: Eastmancolor. 35-mm color film. Running time: 132 minutes. Distributor: Valoria Films (France), Janus Films (U.S.A.).
Actors: Jean-Pierre Léaud (Claude Roc), Kika Markham (Anne), Stacey Tendeter (Muriel), Sylvia Marriott (Mrs. Brown), Marie Mansart (Claire Roc), Philippe Léotard (Diurka), Irène Tune (Ruta, photographer and painter), Annie Miller (Monique de Montferrand), Jane Lobre (concierge), Marie Irakane (Claire and Claude Roc's maid), Georges Delerue (businessman), Marcel Berbert (art dealer), David Markham (palmist), Jean-Claude Dolbert (policeman), Christine Pellé (secretary), Anne Levaslot (Muriel as a child), Sophie Jeanne (her friend Clarisse), René Gaillard (taxi driver), Sophie Baker (friend in café), Laura and Ewa Truffaut, Mathieu and Guillaume Schiffman (the children near the seesaw), Mark Peterson (Mr. Flint).

1972 Such a Gorgeous Kid Like Me (Une Belle Fille Comme Moi)

Script, adaptation, and dialogue: François Truffaut, Jean-Loup Dabadie, based on the novel *Such a Gorgeous Kid Like Me* by Henry Farrell (Gallimard). Music: Georges Delerue. Director of Photography: Pierre-William Glenn. Art Director: Jean-Pierre Kohut-Svelko. Editor: Yann Dedet. Assistant Editor: Martine Barraqué. Production Company: Les Films du Carrosse, Columbia. Aspect ratio: 1:33. Process: Eastmancolor, Panavision. 35-mm color film. Running time: 98 minutes. Distributor: Columbia.
Actors: Bernadette Lafont (Camille Bliss), Claude Brasseur (M. Murène), Charles Denner (Arthur, the exterminator), Guy Marchand (Sam Golden, the singer), André Dussollier (Stanislas Previne, the sociologist), Philippe Léotard (Clovis Bliss, the husband), Anne Kreis (Hélène, the secretary), Gilberte Géniat (Isobel Bliss, the mother-in-law), Danièle Girard (the real Florence Golden), Martine Ferrière (prison secretary), Michel Delahaye (M. Marchal, the faithful friend), Annick Fougerie (schoolmistress), Gaston Ouvrard (old prison warder), Jacob Weizbluth (Alphonse, the mute).

1973 Day for Night (La Nuit Américaine)

Original script and dialogue: François Truffaut, Jean-Louis Richard, Suzanne Schiffman. Music: Georges Delerue. Director of Photography: Pierre-William Glenn. Sound: René Levert. Art Director: Damien Lanfranchi. Editor: Yann Dedet. Assistant Editor: Martine Barraqué. Production Company: Les Films du Carrosse, P.E.C.F. (Paris); P.I.C. (Rome). Aspect ratio: 1:66. Process: Eastmancolor, Panavision. 35-mm color film. Running time: 115 minutes. Distributors: Columbia-Warner (France), Warner Bros. (U.S.A.).
This film is dedicated to Dorothy and Lillian Gish.
Actors: François Truffaut (Ferrand, the director), Jacqueline Bisset (Julie Baker-Nelson–Pamela), Valentina Cortese (Séverine), Alexandra Stewart (Stacey), Jean-Pierre Aumont (Alexandre), Jean-Pierre Léaud (Alphonse), Jean Champion (Bertrand, the producer), Nathalie Baye (Joëlle, script girl), Dani (assistant script trainee), Bernard Menez (Bernard, the property man), Nike Arrighi (Odile, the make-up artist), Gaston Joly (Gaston Lajoie, the assistant director), Maurice Séveno (TV reporter), David Markham (Dr. Nelson, Julie's husband), Zénaïde Rossi (the assistant director's wife), Christophe Vesque (little boy with cane), Henry Graham, Graham Greene, and Marcel Berbert (English insurers), Marc Bayle and Xavier Saint-Macary. Some technicians, machinists, and electricians appearing as themselves: Jean-François Stévenin, Pierre Zucca, Yann Dedet, etc.

1975 The Story of Adele H. (L'Histoire d'Adèle H.)

Original script and dialogue: François Truffaut, Jean Gruault, Suzanne Schiffman, with the collaboration of Frances Vernor Guille, who published "Le Journal d'Adèle Hugo" (Minard "Lettres Modernes"). English adaptation: Jan Dowson. Music: Maurice Jaubert. Director of Photography: Nestor Almendros. Sound: Jean-Pierre Ruh. Art Director: Jean-Pierre Kohut-Svelko. Editor: Yann Dedet. Assistant Editor: Martine Barraqué. Production Company: Les Films du Carrosse, Les Productions Artistes Associés. Aspect ratio: 1:66. Process: Eastmancolor, Panavision. 35-mm color film. Running time: 96 minutes. Distributor: Les Artistes Associés (France), New World Pictures (U.S.A.).
Actors: Isabelle Adjani (Adèle Hugo), Bruce Robinson (Lieutenant Pinson), Sylvia Marriott (Mrs. Saunders), Reuben Dorey (Mr. Saunders), Joseph Blatchley (bookseller), Mr. White (Colonel), Carl Hathwell (Pinson's orderly), Ivry Gitlis (magician-mesmerizer), Sir Cecil de Sausmarez (M. Lenoir, notary), Sir Raymond Falla (Judge Johnstone), Roger Martin (Dr. Murdock), Madame Louise (Madame Baa), Jean-Pierre Leursse (copyist), Louise Bourdet (Victor Hugo's servant), Clive Gillingham (Keaton, bank clerk), François Truffaut (officer), Ralph Williams (Canadian), Thi Loan N'Guyen (the Chinese woman), Edward J. Jackson (O'Brien), Aurelia Mansion (widow with dog), David Foote (David as a young man), Jacques Fréjabue (cabinetmaker), Chantal Durpoix (young prostitute), Geoffrey Crook (George, the Johnstone valet).

1976 Small Change (L'Argent de Poche)

Original script: François Truffaut, Suzanne Schiffman. Music: "Les Enfants S'Ennuient le Dimanche," written and sung by Charles Trenet. Director of Photography: Pierre-William Glenn. Sound: Michel Laurent. Art Director: Jean-Pierre Kohut-Svelko. Editor: Yann Dedet. Assistant Editor: Martine Barraqué. Production Company: Les Films du Carrosse, Les Productions Artistes Associés. Aspect ratio: 1:66. Process: Eastmancolor, Panavision. 35-mm color film. Running time: 104 minutes. Distributor: Les Artistes Associés (France), New World Pictures (U.S.A.).
Actors: The children: Geory Desmouceaux (Patrick Desmouceaux), Philippe Goldmann (Julien Leclou), Claudio and Franck Deluca (Mathieu and Franck Deluca), Richard Golfier (himself), Laurent Devlaeminck (Laurent Riffle), Bruno Staab (Bruno Rouillard), Sébastien Marc (Oscar), Sylvie Grézel (Sylvie), Pascale Bruchon (Martine), Corinne Boucart (Corinne), Ewa Truffaut (Patricia), and Little Grégory (himself); Francis Devlaeminck (M. Riffle, hairdresser and Laurent's father), Tania Torrens (Nadine Riffle, hairdresser), Jean-Marie Carayon (the commissioner, Sylvie's father), Kathy Carayon (commissioner's wife), Paul Heyraud (M. Deluca), Christine Pellé (Mme Leclou, Julien's mother), Jane Lobre (Julien's grandmother), Nicole Félix (Gregory's mother), Virginie Thévenet (Lydie Richet), Jean-François Stévenin (Jean-François Richet, schoolteacher), René Barnérias (M. Desmouceaux, Patrick's father), Christian Lentretien (M. Golfier, Richard's father), Laura Truffaut (Madeleine Doinel, Oscar's mother), Jean-François Gondre (Oscar's father), Chantal Mercier (Chantal Petit, schoolteacher), Marcel Berbert (school principal), Vincent Touly (concierge), Yvon Boutina (Oscar as an adult), Annie Chevaldonné (nurse), Michel Dissart (M. Lomay, the policeman).

1977 The Man Who Loved Women (L'Homme Qui Aimait les Femmes)

Original script and dialogue: François Truffaut, Michel Fermaud, Suzanne Schiffman. Music: Maurice Jaubert. Director of Photography: Nestor Almendros. Sound: Michel Laurent. Art Director: Jean-Pierre Kohut-Svelko. Production Company: Les Films du Carrosse, Les Productions Artistes Associés. Aspect ratio: 1:66. Process: Eastmancolor. 35-mm color film. Running time: 118 minutes. Distributors: Les Artistes Associés (France), Cinema V (U.S.A.).
Actors: Charles Denner (Bertrand Morane), Brigitte Fossey (Geneviève Bigey, editor), Nelly Borgeaud (Delphine Grezel), Geneviève Fontanel (Hélène, lingerie saleswoman), Nathalie Baye (Martine Desdoits), Sabine Glaser (Bernadette, "Midi Car" employee), Valérie Bonnier (Fabienne, the embrasure woman), Martine Chassaing (Denise, engineer at the Institut de Mécanique des Fluides), Roselyne Puyo (Nicole, movie usherette), Anna Perrier (Uta, babysitter), Monique Dury (Mme Duteil, home typist), Nella Barbier (Liliane, waitress at Karateka Restaurant), Frédérique Jamet (Juliette), Marie-Jeanne Montfajon (Christine Morane, Bertrand's mother), and Leslie Caron (Véra, the ghost), Roger Leenhardt (M. Bétany, editor), Henri Agel and Henri-Jean Servat (readers), little Michel Marti (Bertrand as an adolescent), Christian Lentretien (inspector), Rico Lopez (practical joker in restaurant), Carmen Sardà-Canovas (laundress), Philippe Lièvre (Bertrand's colleague), Marcel Berbert (surgeon, Delphine's husband), Michel Laurent, Pierre Gompertz, Roland Thénot (naval officers), Josiane Couëdel (operator), Valérie Pêcheur (young woman from the cemetery in tennis outfit), Anne Bataille (young woman in the fringed dress), Ghylaine Dumas (second employee of "Midi Car"), Jean-Louis Povéda (printer), Thi Loan N'Guyen (Chinese woman), Suzanne Schiffman (lady with baby on Mme Duteil's staircase).

1978 The Green Room (La Chambre Verte)

Script and dialogue: François Truffaut, Jean Gruault, based on themes by Henry James. Music: Maurice Jaubert. Director of Photography: Nestor Almendros. Sound: Michel Laurent. Art Director: Jean-Pierre Kohut-Svelko. Costumes: Monique Drury and Christian Gasc. Editor: Martine Barraqué. Production Company: Les Films du Carrosse, Les Productions Artistes Associés. Aspect ratio: 1:66. Process: Eastmancolor. 35-mm color film. Running time: 94 minutes. Distributors: Les Artistes Associés (France), New World Pictures (U.S.A.).
Actors: François Truffaut (Julien Davenne), Nathalie Baye (Cécilia Mandel), Jean Dasté (Bernard Humbert, editor of *The Globe*), Jean-Pierre Moulin (Gérard Mazet), Antoine Vitez (bishop's secretary), Jane Lobre (Mme Rambaud, the governess), Patrick Maléon (Georges as a boy), Jean-Pierre

Ducos (priest in the mortuary), Annie Miller (Geneviève Mazet), Nathan Miller (her son), Marie Jaoul (Yvonne Mazet), Monique Dury (Monique, secretary at *The Globe*), Laurence Ragon (Julie Davenne, in the photos and model), Marcel Berbert (Dr. Jardine), Guy d'Ablon (wax-dummy maker), Thi Loan N'Guyen (apprentice artisan), Christian Lentretien (speaker at cemetery), Henri Bienvenu (Gustave, auctioneer), Alphonse Simon (one-legged man at *The Globe*), Anna Paniez (Anna, little girl at piano), Serge Rousseau (Paul Massigny in photo), Carmen Sardà-Canovas (woman with rosary), Jean-Claude Gasché (policeman), Martine Barraqué (nurse at auction room), Jean-Pierre Kohut-Svelko (cripple at auction room), Josiane Couëdel (nurse at cemetery), Roland Thénot (cripple at cemetery), Gérard Bougeant (cemetery guard).

1979 Love on the Run (L'Amour en Fuite)

Original script and dialogue: François Truffaut, Marie-France Pisier, Jean Aurel, Suzanne Schiffman. Music: Georges Delerue. Song: "L'Amour en Fuite," words by Alain Souchon, music by Laurent Voulzy, sung by Alain Souchon. Director of Photography: Nestor Almendros. Sound: Michel Laurent. Art Director: Jean-Pierre Kohut-Svelko. Editor: Martine Barraqué. Production Company: Les Films du Carrosse. Aspect ratio: 1:66. Process: Eastmancolor. 35-mm film, color and black and white. Running time: 94 minutes. Distributor: A.M.L.F. (France), New World Pictures (U.S.A.).
Actors: Jean-Pierre Léaud (Antoine Doinel), Marie-France Pisier (Colette), Claude Jade (Christine), Dani (Liliane), Dorothée (Sabine), Rosy Varte (Colette's mother), Marie Henriau (divorce judge), Daniel Mesguich (Xavier, bookseller), Julien Bertheau (M. Lucien), Jean-Pierre Ducos (Christine's lawyer), Pierre Dios (M. Renard), Alain Ollivier (judge in Aix), Monique Dury (Mme Ida), Emmanuel Clot (Emmanuel, friend at printing press), Christian Lentretien (pick-up on train), Roland Thénot (angry telephone operator), Julien Dubois (Alphonse Doinel), Alexandre Janssen (child in dining car).

1980 The Last Metro (Le Dernier Métro)

Script: François Truffaut, Suzanne Schiffman. Dialogue: François Truffaut, Suzanne Schiffman, Jean-Claude Grumberg. Music: Georges Delerue. Director of Photography: Nestor Almendros. Sound: Michel Laurent. Art Director: Jean-Pierre Kohut-Svelko. Costumes: Lisèle Roos. Editor: Martine Barraqué. Production Company: Les Films du Carrosse, SEDIF, TF 1, SFP. Aspect ratio: 1:66. Process: Fujicolor. 35-mm color film. Running time: 128 minutes. Distributors: Gaumont (France), MGM/UA (U.S.A.).
Actors: Catherine Deneuve (Marion Steiner), Gérard Depardieu (Bernard Granger), Jean Poiret (Jean-Loup Cottins), Heinz Bennent (Lucas Steiner), Andréa Ferréol (Arlette Guillaume), Paulette Dubost (Germaine Fabre), Sabine Haudepin (Nadine Marsac), Jean-Louis Richard (Daxiat), Maurice Risch (Raymond, the stage manager), Marcel Berbert (Merlin), Richard Bohringer (Gestapo officer), Jean-Pierre Klein (Christian Léglise), Martine Simonet (Martine, the thief), and little Franck Pasquier, Rénata, Jean-José Richer, Laszlo Szabo, Hénia Ziv, Jessica Zucman, Alain Rasma, René Dupré, Pierre Belot, Christian Baltauss, Alexandre Aumond, Marie-Dominique Henry, Jacob Weizbluth, Rose Thierry, Philippe Vesque, and the children's choir of the Abbey.

1981 The Woman Next Door (La Femme d'à Côté)

Original script: François Truffaut, Suzanne Schiffman, Jean Aurel. Music: Georges Delerue. Director of Photography: William Lubtchansky. Sound: Michel Laurent. Art Director: Jean-Pierre Kohut-Svelko. Editor: Martine Barraqué. Production Company: Les Films du Carrosse, TF 1, Films Production. Aspect ratio: 1:66. Process: Fujicolor. 35-mm color film. Running time: 106 minutes. Distributors: Gaumont (France), MGM/United Artists (U.S.A.).
Actors: Gérard Depardieu (Bernard Coudray), Fanny Ardant (Mathilde Bauchard), Henri Garcin (Philippe Bauchard), Michèle Baumgartner (Arlette Coudray), Véronique Silver (Mme Jouve), Roger Van Hool (Roland Duguet), Philippe Morier-Genoud (psychoanalyst), Roland Thénot (real-estate agent), Jacques Preisach and Catherine Crassac (couple on hotel staircase), and little Olivier Becquaert.

1983 Confidentially Yours! (Vivement Dimanche!)

Script, adaptation, and dialogue: François Truffaut, Suzanne Schiffman, Jean Aurel, based on the novel *The Long Saturday Night* by Charles Williams (Gallimard "Carré Noir"). Music: Georges Delerue. Director of Photography: Nestor Almendros. Sound: Pierre Gamet. Art Director: Hilton McConnico. Editor: Martine Barraqué. Production Company: Les Films du Carrosse, Films A2, Soprofilms. Process: Kodak. 35-mm film, black and white. Running time: 111 minutes. Distributors: A.A.A. (France), Spectrafilm (U.S.A.).
Actors: Fanny Ardant (Barbara Becker), Jean-Louis Trintignant (Julien Vercel), Philippe Laudenbach (M. Clément), Caroline Sihol (Marie-Christine Vercel), Philippe Morier-Genoud (Superintendent Santelli), Xavier Saint-Macary (Bertrand Fabre, photographer), Jean-Pierre Kalfon (Jacques Massoulier), Anik Belaubre (cashier at the Eden), Jean-Louis Richard (Louison), Yann Dedet ("Angel Face"), Nicole Félix (scarred woman), Georges Koulouris (Detective Lablache), Roland Thénot (Policeman Jambrau), Pierre Gare (Inspector Poivert), Jean-Pierre Kohut-Svelko (rowdy Slav), Pascale Pellegrin (secretarial candidate), Jacques Vidal (the King), Alain Gambin (theater director), Pascal Deux (Santelli's sidekick), Franckie Diago (employee at detective agency), Isabelle Binet and Josiane Couëdel (M. Clément's secretaries), Hilton McConnico (prostitute's client), Marie-Aimée Debril and Christianne Marmande (dog-groomers), the dog Golaud, Thi Loan N'Guyen (Chinese woman at the commissioner's office), Jacques Gaillard (man on the bike), Martine Barraqué (passerby with newspaper), Rosine Robiolle (commissioner's secretary), Armand Barbault (passerby with prostitute), and Michel Aubossu, Paulina Aubret, Dany Castaing, Michel Grisoni, Pierrette Monticelli.

(The complete text of this filmography was formulated from *Cahiers du Cinéma* by Josiane Couëdel and Marc Chevrie for *Le Roman de François Truffaut.*)

BIBLIOGRAPHY

WRITINGS BY TRUFFAUT

Le Cinéma selon Hitchcock, Paris: Laffort, 1966. Rev. Eng. ed., *Hitchcock.* In collaboration with Helen G. Scott, New York: Simon & Schuster, 1984.

"Journal of *Fahrenheit 451,*" *Cahiers du Cinéma* (Eng.) no. 5 (Feb.–July 1966), pp. 1–23. Kay Mander and R. K. Neilson Baxter, translators.

Gheur, Bernard. *Le Testament d'un Cancre.* Foreword by Truffaut. Paris: A. Michel, 1970.

Dreyer, Carl Theodor. *Jesus.* New York: Dial, 1972. Includes tribute to Dreyer by Truffaut.

Truffaut, François, et al. *La Politique des Auteurs.* Paris: Champ libre, 1972. See also: John Hess (below).

Bazin, André. *Jean Renoir.* Edited and with an introduction by Truffaut. W. W. Halsey II and William H. Simon, translators. New York: Simon & Schuster, 1973.

——— and Eric Rohmer. *Charlie Chaplin.* Foreword by Truffaut. Paris: Du Cerf, 1973.

"Truffaut on Bogart," *Saturday Review Arts* no. 1 (Mar. 1973), pp. 31–32.

"La Nuit Américaine" et le Journal de Tournage de "Fahrenheit 451." Cinéma 2000. Paris: Seghers, 1974.

Renoir, Jean. *La Grande Illusion.* Foreword by Truffaut. Paris: Balland, 1974.

Bazin, André. *Le Cinéma de la Cruauté.* Foreword by Truffaut. Paris: Flammarion, 1975.

Les Films de Ma Vie, Paris: Flammarion, 1975. Eng. ed., trans. by Leonard Mayhew, New York: Simon & Schuster, 1978.

Small Change: A Film Novel. Anselm Hollo, translator. New York: Random House, 1976.

L'Homme Qui Aimait les Femmes. Paris: Flammarion, 1977.

Guitry, Sacha. *Le Cinéma et Moi.* Foreword by Truffaut. Paris: Ramsay, 1977.

"Children Are Born Actors," *UNESCO Courier* no. 32 (May 1979), pp. 13–14.

"Hitchcock–His True Power Is Emotion," *New York Times,* Mar. 4, 1979, section 2, pp. 1, 19.

Almendros, Nestor. *Un Homme à la Caméra.* Foreword by Truffaut. Paris: Hatier, 1979.

Andrew, Dudley. *André Bazin.* Foreword by Truffaut. New York: Oxford, 1978.

Bazin, André. *French Cinema of the Occupation and Resistance: The Birth of a Critical Esthetic.* Collected and with an introduction by François Truffaut. Stanley Hochman, translator. New York: Ungar, 1981.

"Slow Trade: The Declining Years of Alfred Hitchcock" [with interview], *American Film* no. 10 (Nov. 1984), pp. 40–47.

SCREENPLAYS FOR FILMS BY TRUFFAUT

The 400 Blows. In collaboration with Marcel Moussy. David Denby, ed. New York: Grove, 1969.

"Les Mistons," *L'Avant-Scène* no. 4 (1961).

"Une Histoire d'Eau," *L'Avant-Scène* no. 7 (1961).

Jules and Jim. Lorrimer Classic Screenplay Series. Nicholas Fry, translator. New York: Simon & Schuster, 1968.

"La Peau Douce," *L'Avant-Scène* no. 48 (1965).

"Fahrenheit 451," *L'Avant-Scène* no. 64 (1966).

The Wild Child. Linda Lewin and Christine Leméry, translators. New York: Washington Square Press, 1973.

The Adventures of Antoine Doinel: Four Autobiographical Screenplays [containing *The 400 Blows, Antoine and Colette, Stolen Kisses, Bed and Board*]. Helen G. Scott, translator. New York: Simon & Schuster, 1971.

"Les Deux Anglaises et le Continent," *L'Avant-Scène* no. 121 (1972).

Day for Night. Sam Flores, translator. New York: Grove, 1975.

The Story of Adele H. Helen G. Scott, translator. New York: Grove, 1976.

"La Chambre Verte," *L'Avant-Scène* no. 215 (1978).

"Le Dernier Métro–Une Visite," *L'Avant-Scène* nos. 303–4 (1983).

SCREENPLAYS FOR FILMS BY OTHERS

Breathless by Jean-Luc Godard, 1960 (after a synopsis drawn up by Truffaut in 1955). Truffaut's original screenplay published in *L'Avant-Scène* no. 79 (1968).

Charlotte et Son Jules by Jean-Luc Godard, 1961. Truffaut worked on dialogue, not credited.

Tire-au-Flanc by Claude de Givray, 1962. Truffaut co-author of screenplay.

Une Grosse Tête by Claude de Givray, 1963. Truffaut co-author of screenplay and dialogue, not credited.

Mata-Hari, Agent H-21 by Jean-Louis Richard, 1965. Truffaut co-author of screenplay.

INTERVIEWS

"On Film: Truffaut Interview," *New Yorker,* Feb. 20, 1960, pp. 36–37.

Marcorelles, L. "Interview with Truffaut," *Sight & Sound* vol. 31, no. 1 (Winter 1961–62), pp. 35–37.

Franchi, R. M., and Marshall Lewis. "Conversations with François Truffaut," *New York Film Bulletin* no. 3, issue 44 (1962), pp. 16–24.

"François Truffaut," *Film Quarterly* vol. 17, no. 1 (Fall 1963), pp. 3–13.

Samuels, C. T. "Talking with Truffaut," *American Scholar* no. 40 (Summer 1971), pp. 482–86.

Gow, G. "Intensification," *Films and Filming* vol. 43, no. 10 (July 1972), pp. 18–22.

Rosenthal, S. "Truffaut Interview," *Focus on Film* no. 16 (Autumn 1973), pp. 6–7.

Mallow, S. "A Portrait of François Truffaut," *Filmmakers Newsletter* vol. 7, no. 2 (Dec. 1973), pp. 22–27.

Higham, C. "François Truffaut," *Action* vol. 9, no. 1 (Jan.–Feb. 1974), pp. 20–25.

Dudinsky, Donna. " . . . François Truffaut . . . ," *Take One* vol. 4, no. 2 (Mar. 1974), pp. 8–10.

Adair, G. *"Adele H.," Sight & Sound* vol. 44, no. 3 (Summer 1975), p. 156.

"Dialogue on Film: François Truffaut and Jeanne Moreau," *American Film* vol. 1, no. 7 (May 1976), pp. 33–48.

McBride, J., and T. McCarthy. "Kid Stuff: François Truffaut Interviewed," *Film Comment* vol. 12, no. 5 (Sept.–Oct. 1976), pp. 42–45.

Allen, Don. "Truffaut Twenty Years After," *Sight & Sound* vol. 48, no. 4 (Autumn 1979), pp. 224–28.

Lawson, S. "Truffaut at Mid-Career," *Saturday Review* no. 9 (Jan. 1982), pp. 42–45.

Josselin, J.-F., and J.-P. Enthoven. "Truffaut Views Truffaut," *World Press Review* no. 30 (Oct. 1983), p. 58.

"Truffaut," *Film Comment* no. 21 (Jan.–Feb. 1985), pp. 33–53.

Yakir, D. "Looking Back," *Film Comment* no. 21 (Jan.–Feb. 1985), pp. 48–53.

ON TRUFFAUT

Affron, Mirella J., and E. Rubinstein, eds. *The Last Metro: François Truffaut, Director.* Rutgers Films in Print Series. New Brunswick, N.J.: Rutgers, 1985.

Allen, Don. *Finally Truffaut: A Film-by-Film Guide to the Master Filmmaker's Legacy.* New York: Beaufort, 1985.

Braudy, Leo, ed. *Focus on "Shoot the Piano Player."* Englewood Cliffs, N.J.: Prentice-Hall, 1972.

Coffey, Barbara. "Art and Film in François Truffaut's *Jules and Jim* and *Two English Girls,*" *Film Heritage* vol. 9, no. 3 (Spring 1974), pp. 1–11.

Crisp, C. G. *François Truffaut.* New York: Praeger, 1972.

Gerlach, J. "Truffaut and Itard: *The Wild Child,*" *Film Heritage* vol. 7, no. 3 (Spring 1972), pp. 1–9.

Hess, John. "La Politique des Auteurs." Part 1: "World View as Aesthetic"; part 2: "Truffaut's Manifesto," *Jump Cut* 1 (May–June 1974), pp. 19–22, and *Jump Cut* 2 (July–Aug. 1974), pp. 20–22.

Insdorf, Annette. *François Truffaut.* Twayne's Theatrical Arts Series. Boston: G. K. Hall, Twayne Publishers, 1978.

Jebb, J. "Truffaut: The Educated Heart," *Sight & Sound* vol. 16, no. 3 (Summer 1972), pp. 144–45.

Kinder, Marsha, and Beverle Houston. "Truffaut's Gorgeous Killers," *Film Quarterly* vol. 27, no. 2 (Winter 1973), pp. 2–10.

Klein, Michael. "*The Story of Adele H.:* The Twilight of Romanticism," *Jump Cut* nos. 10–11 (Summer 1976), pp. 13–15.

———. "Truffaut's Sanctuary: The Green Room," *Film Quarterly* vol. 34, no. 1 (Fall 1980), pp. 15–20.

Mambrino, J. "La Chambre Verte," *L'Avant-Scène Cinéma* no. 215 (Nov. 1, 1978), pp. 3–22, 41–51.

Mast, Gerald. "From *The 400 Blows* to *Small Change:* Truffaut's Progress," *The New Republic* no. 14 (Apr. 2, 1977), pp. 23–25.

Monaco, James. *The Films of François Truffaut.* New York: New School for Social Research Monograph, Zoetrope One, 1974.

———. *The New Wave: Truffaut, Godard, Chabrol, Rohmer, Rivette.* New York: Oxford, 1976.

Petrie, Graham. *The Cinema of François Truffaut.* The International Film Guide Series. New York: A. S. Barnes, 1970.

Le Roman de François Truffaut. Paris: Cahiers du Cinéma–Editions de l'Etoile, 1985.

Shatnoff, Judith. "François Truffaut—The Anarchist Imagination," *Film Quarterly* no. 3 (Spring 1963), pp. 3–11.

Thiher, Allen. "The Existential Play in Truffaut's Early Films," *Literature Film Quarterly* no. 3, pp. 183–97.

François Truffaut: An American Film Institute Seminar on His Work. Beverly Hills, Cal., 1977.

Wall, James McKendree. *Three European Directors: Truffaut, Fellini, Buñuel.* Grand Rapids, Mich.: Eerdmans, 1973.

Walz, Eugene P. *François Truffaut: A Guide to References and Resources.* Boston: G. K. Hall, 1982. With extensive bibliography.

SPECIAL ISSUES

New York Film Bulletin no. 3, issue 44 (1962).

Cinématographe no. 15 (Oct.–Nov. 1975).

L'Avant-Scène Cinéma nos. 303–4 (Mar. 1–15, 1983).

Cinématographe (Dec. 1984).

Cinéma 84 (Dec. 1984).

FRANÇOIS TRUFFAUT, ACTOR

Le Coup du Berger by Jacques Rivette, 1957

The 400 Blows, 1959

Tire-au-Flanc by Claude de Givray, 1962

The Wild Child, 1970

Day for Night, 1973

The Story of Adele H., 1975

Small Change, 1976

Close Encounters of the Third Kind by Steven Spielberg, 1977

The Man Who Loved Women, 1977

The Green Room, 1978

FRANÇOIS TRUFFAUT, PRODUCER OR CO-PRODUCER

Paris Belongs to Us by Jacques Rivette, 1959

The Testament of Orpheus by Jean Cocteau, 1959

Le Scarabée d'Or by Robert Lachenay (C.M.), 1960

Anna la Bonne by Claude Jutra (C.M.), 1961

La Fin du Voyage by Michel Varesano (C.M.), 1961

Tire-au-Flanc, 1961

Mata-Hari, Agent H-21 by Jean-Louis Richard, 1965

Two or Three Things I Know About Her by Jean-Luc Godard, 1967

L'Enfance Nue by Maurice Pialat, 1968

My Night at Maud's by Eric Rohmer, 1969

La Faute de l'Abbé Mouret by Georges Franju, 1970

Les Lolos de Lola by Bernard Dubois, 1976

Ce Gamin-là by Renaud Victor, 1977

Le Beau Mariage by Eric Rohmer, 1982

INDEX

Page numbers in *italic* type indicate illustrations; those in **bold**, the major discussion of a Truffaut film.

TRANSLATIONS OF ILLUSTRATED DOCUMENTS

PAGE 21

THE RULES OF THE GAME

For those who consider *The Rules of the Game* the greatest film in the history of the cinema, the uncut showing of Renoir's masterpiece at the Ciné-Club du Quartier Latin was an event. We knew *The Rules of the Game* only in a version more or less slashed up according to the movie houses where it was only too rarely seen.

This print included thirteen scenes or sequences and four shots that no longer figure in the commercial versions.

At the opening of the film, after André Jurieu has expressed his disappointment at the microphone, the girl announcer says, "But we have right here an engineer from the Baudron plant . . . " In this version we see and hear the engineer. A scene in which Dalio crawls on his belly in front of his servants to recover from under a sofa the spring of one of his mechanical gadgets, a scene missing as a rule, is very significant. A third scene shows us the guests in a corridor noisily returning to their rooms. It is followed by another in which Octave and Jurieu talk things over in the room they share. Numerous additional gunshots and the death of the little rabbit that twitches its tail in a final spasm, a scene famous for its meaningfulness but also for its ritual absence. Two intimate scenes make clear the exact relationships between Octave and Lisette on the one hand and Jurieu and Jackie on the other. The scene that is most important and necessary for a proper understanding of how the film works out is the scene in the hothouse. Octave proposes that Christine leave with him, then having gone to fetch their coats, he lets himself be convinced by Lisette, and it is precisely at that moment that Jurieu pops up.

Very moving also, Lisette's farewell to Octave and Marceau after André's death, followed by Dalio's speech, which is longer in this print.

Finally masters and servants merge in shadows on the wall, while the film ends with the theme by Mozart with which it began.

Thanks to those thirteen scenes, thanks to Renoir, it was a very fine evening.

FRANÇOIS TRUFFAUT

PAGE 22

HOPEFUL UNDERWEAR

[The title of Truffaut's first piece of "fancy writing," *Dessous d'espoir,* is probably meant as a characteristic cinematic pun on the French title, *Deux Sous d'Espoir,* of Renato Castellani's 1952 Italian neo-realist film, *Due Soldi di Speranza.* (Translator's note)]

Two editors-in-chief take up most of my in-between time. One is to be visited at the Etoile and the other at Saint-Philippe-du-Roule. Driven from pillar to post by the caprices of the news of the day, I have made the Champs-Elysées my personal fief and, if I am not out hunting there, I look and I see.

Once stone and bronze (those of our childhood years), our age will be that of transparency. I am leaving aside plates, dustpans, glass walls and, I give you fair warning, clothespins, and am concerning myself with a single item of clothing, and feminine at that.

It all began with silk stockings. Bravo. Then a long silence before recent days, a decade maybe, when it hit underclothing. Decent women, subject to the law of opacity, could no longer, nylon-slipped and held up likewise in the bosom region, walk through the apartment to greet guests arriving too early or to box the children's ears without putting on a dress. The slip in its turn has become translucid, while waiting to disappear altogether if parish priests in the provinces and the rigors of winter did not ensure its remaining as is.

So far, nothing against it; appearances being saved, underclothes don't look at us unless we look at them.

Where the affair turns serious, where a cry of alarm is in order, is when transparency hits outer clothing, accessories in particular. Nylon gloves are disgusting and turn the hand into a fan of stingily decorated condoms. Two cents of thought, Mesdames: are you going to put your billets-doux in a plexiglass handbag? Let us return to the intimates.

It was the old gals who began it, slatterns from way back. As if a third chin wasn't enough, and also the rolls of fat around the waist (I'll skip the thighs, which offer themselves to our view when they are no longer fit to be seen), we have had to look without laughing at enormous breasts collapsing behind a lacy mauve opacity. The young ones—where do they keep their heads?—in their turn had to get into the act. That virgins should wear stockings was already shocking to me, because they are the sign of feminine mystery, instruments of seduction after virginity has been lost.

1. Mademoiselle X . . . , aged 18, you are ridiculous with:

a) your transparent white blouse . . .

b) . . . which lets us see your transparent slip . . .

c) . . . beneath which I distinguish a transparent brassiere.

Impolite female! You think yourself sheltered behind three windows, frosted as they may be? The time will come when crude fellows with their dirty-minded looks will pierce that triple opacity. You are—whether you wish it or not—a young girl out of Baudelaire!

2. Madame Y . . . , aged 30 (she says), you are no less ridiculous with:

a) your transparent pink blouse . . .

b) . . . under which there is *no slip at all* but . . .

c) . . . a brassiere in black satin!

And if you cross your legs—that type always crosses them—I'll see what? A petticoat you pinch in at the waist hoping people will think you Juliet's age instead of Lady Macbeth's. Pretty soon we'll be seeing transparent girls at their first communion, brides even—fine weddings, those!

Stockings, on the initiative of M. Christian Dior, have lost their seam: *Dior Stockings, Invisible but Present.* There we are. Does anyone remember that before the dictatorship of nylon, at the time when silk didn't cost more than butter today, they invented the liquid stocking? Good-looking blondes smeared their legs with a bronzish dye that imitated a luxurious suntan in winter, very expensive stockings in summer. And more than one—the French woman is nothing if not resourceful—more than one got a black crayon and she, or her lover, contrived to draw the seam from the heel right up to, on my word, a little above the buttocks. For the uninitiated, undressing proved difficult to manage. In short, and according to Christian

Dior: if you're not wearing stockings pretend you are, and if you are pretend you're not.

I will be accused of generalizing, and I will be told about women who have not submitted to transparency: colored rough cloth, hobbled skirt. That kind I make out to be shameless in their own fashion, without underthings outside and outside things inside, all topsy-turvy. Under an armor-plated rig like that, the cloth takes the exact shape of the flesh it contains, it's impossible to slip in even the shadow of your hand, and that's so much better for your morals. Underneath those tight skirts, those bodices heaving but only with merriment, there is really nothing at all, no lingerie? What then is that Sunday eroticism that ignores the subtle ploys by which the experienced eye learns just the right angles that will reveal behind the brassiere the matter, color, even the very life of that bosom? The face can feign, modesty be false, virtue be simulated, but the brassiere doesn't lie. Sharp angles, learned on the spur of the moment when an arm is raised to fix a curl. Designs in diagonal, panty hems revealed in walking, your pride and your humility thereby made known to all. Under the pretext of legs crossed or uncrossed, the pretty lace of a slip ravishes us. And the complicated seams and joins, idyllic interlacing strapwork, the mysterious bond that holds together all those little diamond-shaped bits of silk, what is it? Now it is stupidly made public by the detestable transparent bodice, and ridiculous as men's garters, for our part we prefer to divine it by chance, knowledge gained over a long stretch being its own best reward.

On the Champs-Elysées a pretty tourist was questioning a policeman about the route to take. Her white skirt was so thin that in spite of the sun—or thanks to it?—everyone was ogling two rock-firm thighs with no slip to make an obstacle to their sweaty coexistence. Hoping she might turn into the Passage du Lido, I rushed in there, foreseeing the view I could get in that shaded spot. The beautiful foreigner did just what I hoped, the sun did exactly the job of the spotlight-behind-girl-in-nightgown in a sexy film. My only regret was that I was not alone in enjoying a show for which, nevertheless, I had myself arranged the mise-en-scène.

* * *

Tomorrow we'll be having women covered with cellophane like jars of jam. We can size them up before buying, though the right to touch will have to wait until our grandchildren's time.

Like Grimm's fairy-tale king, victim of his crafty tailor, tomorrow's woman will be able to promenade down the Champs-Elysées naked to the bone, make the Unknown Soldier burst into flame all over again, and hear people whisper along her way: Isn't nylon becoming!

FRANÇOIS TRUFFAUT

PAGE 24

LITTLE PERSONAL DIARY OF THE CINEMA

by François Truffaut

Tuesday, June 1st

1:00 P.M. I accompany Bazin and his parrot to the Gare de Lyon. They are going to Tourrette-sur-Loup, near Venice, to rest up from three months' hard work at Sao Paulo and Cannes. Madame, Bébé, and Pluto have gone by car. As for the crocodile, it has been entrusted to the Musée des Colonies.

9:00 P.M. Buñuel shows a few friends and some friends of his friends one of his latest films, *Robinson Crusoe,* in which the author of *El* tries his hand at color for the first time. (Cameraman Alex Philippe.) Good film, excellent Technicolor.

Wednesday, June 2nd

6:00 P.M. Cocktail party at the Vendôme for the premiere of *El.* I am always very bored at that type of affair where everyone gives me the impression of being drunk . . . except myself. A fat woman grabs Buñuel by the neck—to his utter confusion—and howls to everyone around: "He's a genius! He's a genius!" There is no doubt something of genius in this film *(El)* whose key phrase may well turn out to be: "The happiness of fools exasperates me."

Thursday, June 3rd

News that will please some people: *Notorious* and *Rebecca* are going to be rereleased by Columbia.

Friday, June 4th

Audiberti's very fine novel *Les Jardins et les Fleuves* is dedicated *"to Molière, to Chaplin, to Jouvet."* There is quite a lot about the cinema in it. A book to read.

Jacques Flaud has announced the results of statistics undertaken very recently and having to do with the indifference of moviegoers:

1. Out of 100 French, 64 go to the movies and 36 no longer go, of whom 30 used to go before the war and 6 have never gone.

2. Out of 100 French who go to the movies, 80 deliberately pick out the program to see.

3. Out of 100 French who go to the movies, 80 go in company (how many of those in "merry company"? That's what statistics in their numerical rigor don't say.).

I must confess my indifference toward that balance sheet, which does look pretty pessimistic. All I see is that Autant-Lara makes four films one after the other, Becker two; that Gance is going to make a film after a twelve years' silence; color is becoming common; true or false, quality is paying at this moment, and I claim that everything is going fine in the best of cinema worlds.

11:00 A.M. With Doniol we meet Buñuel at the Sélect on the Champs-Elysées. A survey I am making among certain filmmakers leads me to ask an indiscreet question about films that would be impossible to propose because impossible to film. "I can tell it to you," Buñuel said to us, "because I know that I will never be able to film it. It would be a quite realistic film but whose characters would behave exactly like insects: the heroine like the bee, the priest like the beetle, etc. It would be a film about instinct." To Doniol, who questioned him about *El,* he declared: "We laughed a lot shooting *El,* we never stopped laughing." Which is to be put alongside Renoir's dictum: "You have to amuse yourself making films, that's very important."

Saturday, June 5th

Alfred the Great has arrived on the Côte d'Azur where for three days now he has been shooting his new film, *To Catch a Thief,* with Cary Grant, Grace Kelly, Charles Vanel, Brigitte Auber, Roland Lessafre, Georgette Anys, Jean Martinelli, Michel Piccoli, René Blancard, Jean Hebey, Dominique Davray, and Gérard Buhr. In Vistavision.

Jean de Létraz is dead. I have always thought that he would have been the best French screenwriter. Let me explain. His plays are often disgusting, sometimes crude and always vulgar. Listening to them, laughter froze in the throat, you came away humiliated and disappointed, but the plot construction, the dovetailing of situations, in a word the workmanship, were beyond reproach. I am convinced that, patched together by him, the screenplays of *Thérèse Raquin, Les Orgueilleux, La Minute de Vérité,* etc., would have lost some of their arbitrariness and above all their awkwardness. That is my opinion . . .

PAGE 28

FILM DIRECTOR SEEKS 5 BOYS 11 TO 14 YEARS OLD TO ACT IN *THE MISCHIEF MAKERS* CONTACT *MIDI LIBRE*

After Henri-Georges Clouzot, Robert Hossein, and a few others, François Truffaut, filmmaker, has chosen the Gard region as the setting for the film he is going to make: "Before going to Cannes, where I will report on the festival for various Paris periodicals (the weekly *Arts* among others), I visited this Département and it was a revelation to me," he declared. "At Saint-André-de-Valborgne I admired the ruggedness, the wild beauty of nature in the Cévennes. At Nîmes I appreciated the splendor of a city that has not only beautiful monuments but also a 'style,' a soul.

"That was more than enough to convince me to come here to carry through a project I place great stock in, my film *The Mischief Makers."*

The Mischief Makers: a promising title for what it implies of irreverent spirit, good-natured banter, picturesqueness; a "catchy" title. But not only a title, a subject as well, and of the best: "I have adapted—very freely as concerns the incidents but very faithfully, I hope, as regards the spirit—an excellent short story by Maurice Rons [sic]. The script is as simple as possible: two lovers would enjoy the sweetest of idylls if five adolescents, unconsciously smitten with the pretty girl, did not turn up, jealous, to act as spoil-sports to all the billing and cooing. That's all."

That's all, and that should suffice to offer a talented filmmaker material for a short film (about 20 minutes) based entirely on nuances, on subtle psychological touches.

As for talent, if François Truffaut has as much of it as a filmmaker as he does as a film critic that will be quite enough for one to be sure that his film will prove a success. In fact, he is considered in Paris to be the most representative, the harshest, the most "committed" of the cinema journalists of the "young school," less respectful of the canons of a traditional aesthetic than of the new tendencies which are as much condemned by the stick-in-the-muds as they are championed by the *enfants terribles* of the Seventh Art. Soft talking, the art of running with the hare and hunting with the hounds are not in his character of executioner of high-class (?) film creations. Which means that his frankness in speaking has earned him not a few enmities in the studios and that his first try at filmmaking is being kept under close watch by his adversaries who will not let any occasion pass, good or bad as it may be, to pay him back in his own coin and with interest.

But François Truffaut has confidence, confidence in himself without braggadocio but also without false modesty, confidence also in his crew who are entirely devoted to his cause: the two stars are Bernadette Lafont and Gérard Blain, juvenile leads of already proven aptitude, and the chief cameraman is our friend Jean Malige of Nîmes, now returned here after having made on his own a humorous short film in color about Palavas-les-Flots, *I'll Send You Postcards,* and a Provençal Christmas tale, *Nicholas the Shepherd.*

"All I'm lacking is 'the mischief makers,'" François Truffaut stated, which is to say that all boys between 11 and 14 years old who will present themselves tomorrow at 4:00 P.M. in the lobby of *Midi Libre,* Boulevard Amiral-Courbet, to contact Truffaut and his co-workers will be welcome. The only abilities required: to be photogenic in a way that accords with the roles that will be assigned to them, quite apart from any acting ability. Attention all amateurs.

PAGE 35

TWO DISTRIBUTORS OF *LA CAUSE DU PEUPLE* RUN IN

Arrested Saturday afternoon in Rue de la Charbonnière, Paris, while selling No. 25 of *La Cause du Peuple,* Mlle Nicole Prunier, aged 21, student in psychology, and M. Patrick Weiss, aged 19, student in history, were brought before M. Leloir, examining magistrate of the Court of Internal Security, who charged them with maintaining or reconstituting a disbanded group. After both designated Maître Revon as defense attorney, they were jailed, the girl student at La Roquette, her comrade at the Santé.

It should be remembered that the same day these young people were arrested, M. Jean-Paul Sartre, Mme Simone de Beauvoir, and M. François Truffaut had been able to sell *La Cause du Peuple* in another neighborhood of the capital without being disturbed (*Le Monde,* June 23).

PAGE 53

VIRGINALS

. . . lovers our surveillance. We could no longer count on chance encounters but had to organize a scrupulously careful network of information. Each of us in turn was assigned to stand guard either in front of the Jouves' villa or at the entrance to the Student Union. Our shadowing service was then carried on throughout the city. Never could Yvette go to the five-and-ten, never could Etienne cut a course without its being carefully recorded in our pocket notebooks. Every week we compared our observations and, in a large notebook, set down the presumed way our two suspects used their time. To fill in the blanks, we took pleasure in imagining horrors:

"Tuesday 14, 7:30 P.M. Y. not back. Obviously will be sleeping at E.'s."

"Saturday 28, 9:00 A.M. E. went out alone on his bicycle. Make inquiries at the River Police."

Thursday mornings they used to play tennis on a large grassy court shaded by sycamore trees. We all gathered behind the fence around the court. What brought us there on those sunny mornings while the balls shot back and forth on the [hard, hot] gravel? Love of the sport? Or the short pleated skirt, the naked legs of Yvette? When she bent down to pick up a ball, we poked each other with our elbows. If one flew over the fence and rolled in the grass at our feet, it was no use for Etienne to call out, as was the custom on the courts, "Ball, please!" Not one of us budged. But let Yvette come up to us, sweating a little, a little out of breath under her cotton sweater, and if, through the fence, she said to us with her fancy voice, smiling, simply, "If you please," we knocked each other over like puppies to get the ball and send it back to her. It was Etienne who thanked us. Furious, we turned our backs, swearing never to be seen on the court again. The following Thursday we were all there.

Two or three times we succeeded in surprising them at the movies. The films they chose were not very interesting to us. American stars kissed each other right on the mouth in them. But from the back of the dark auditorium we never lost sight, not for a second, of the couple we detested, while dreading and hoping for, both at once, the slightest sign of improper behavior. When, all unaware, Etienne's face drew tenderly close to Yvette's, there was always one of us to yell out, *"A la tienne, Etienne!"* [Here's to you, Etienne!], and all of us roared with laughter, not caring about.

PAGE 57 (LEFT)

Antoine Runs Away
The Four Hundred Blows
The Four Thursdays
The Awkward Age
~~The Children of Paris~~
The Forgotten Children
~~The Vagabonds of Paris~~
The Little Pals
Vagrancy
The Vagabonds
The Vagabond Children
Down with School
The Evil Geniuses

The Wild Ducks
—Report-Card Children
—The Runaways—
—Adventures Playing Hookey
The Dupes — The Little Soldiers

PAGE 57 (CENTER)

Paris, October 20, 1958

Monsieur P. Léaud
12, avenue George V
Paris 8e

Monsieur,

I have decided to entrust an important role in *The 400 Blows* to your son Jean-Pierre, without yet knowing which.

I should like to have him go through several scenes in the film, this time without camera, on

THURSDAY, OCTOBER 23, 1958, AT 3:00 P.M.
in my home: 27, rue Saint-Ferdinand, Paris 17e.

Métro: ARGENTINE or TERMES
Building D—6th floor to the left coming out of the elevator.

Your son Jean-Pierre struck me as very intelligent and sufficiently precocious that the few weeks during which we will make him miss school should not constitute an insurmountable handicap for his standing at school.

With my thanks, believe me yours very truly,

François TRUFFAUT

PAGES 58–60

ANTOINE AND THE ORPHAN GIRL

Antoine loved the half light. Waking up, it makes us mistake old objects for new toys. When the curtains are drawn back and the shutters opened, the imposture stands exposed. That new toy was the old candlestick, that suit of armor your woolen trousers.

To be the son of a woman who admires Alfred de Vigny is not easy. It was criminal to fall ill, no coughing allowed. With his hand over his mouth to choke back a cough, Antoine used to hear his mother bellow: *"Suffer and die without speaking!"* In the bathtub she would cry out through the door: *"I love the majesty of human sufferings!"*

Cloistered in his room, called the back room because it was at the end of the apartment and the sun scarcely ever reached it, Antoine preferred to prolong his night until evening. That is why Antoine never stopped dreaming.

Awake, he still slept.

To act while sleeping is somnambulism. Antoine preserved his childhood, intact, well beyond the proper time.

Little children charm one. Big children are a bother and an embarrassment.

Antoine obeyed the mysterious and absurd disciplines which, by dint of respect and patience, childhood carries to the point of a rite. Balancing forks and knives on a glass topped by a cork; holding a nail right in the flame of a candle until there is an intolerable burn. The meal finished, a rigorously quartered banana peel in the plate quickly became a starfish made of sponge-cloth or, turned over, a devil-fish with a woman's skin.

You will understand Antoine if I show you him at the bathing beach.

He believed himself to be as incapable of swimming as of writing a letter or driving a car. The determination to do-like-the-others drove him into the water. He next went through the right motions for swimming, then, astonished to have in fact swum, he asked himself: "Can I stand up?" The interrogation became so imperious that he placed himself upright: his feet didn't touch bottom; so he gave up, and his gestures became those of someone who just dozes off.

That's how Antoine was fished out of a Center for the observation of juvenile delinquents, then out of the army, where he had signed on well before being called up, under the impression that sleepwalkers became officers. Accustomed to miracles, he did not thank those who saved him: it was natural.

* * *

One day Antoine's mother died.

That day Antoine turned twenty.

That death was the death of the wolf, and the silence that disinfected the house made it uninhabitable.

Antoine had never made use of anything

that belonged to him. As far back as his memory could stretch, he had lived in other people's homes, smoking their cigarettes, wearing their clothes.

Making love with other men's women, it had never dawned on him that he could have one of his own. You could have made him crack up laughing by suggesting that some day he might have children.

Working in ways impenetrable to man, fate made Antoine meet, leaving a concert of Italian music, a pink and blonde young girl: Henriette was twenty, lived alone, and had no lover.

Long silence broken by maxims about the bankruptcy of the arts in the twentieth century turned an astonished Antoine into that charming girl's lover.

They set themselves up in the apartment whose furniture had been sold by Antoine's father, an explorer of faraway places, to finance an expedition. A few beds and settees had been left behind and broke up the bareness of the nine rooms.

Antoine and Henriette loved each other in an empty theater. Neither day nor night existed for them any longer, they set the alarm clock for every two hours to make love.

Have I made it clear that with Henriette Antoine was not having his first affair?

Afflicted with an insignificant appearance, he possessed not a single moral quality but quite a few of those charms which young girls poke fun at but which easily win the favors of women whose familiarity with men has made them less demanding and at the same time rather more so.

Antoine, you can imagine, had no illusions about his forced conquests. He was not duped by those new and eternal Bovarys. They offered him entertainment and not pleasure.

The inconstancy of those women, their indecency, their immodesty, in short their lack of restraint, wounded his modesty, which was considerable.

It was only with Henriette that he knew happiness: with Henriette he would come to know later that there is no such thing as love, that there are only obstacles to love.

To deserve that happiness more, it was only fitting and proper, thought Antoine, to break off his current affairs. He therefore wrote two letters, of which this was the first:

Madame,
After Monsieur your husband afforded me the honor of introducing me to you, you afforded me that of wishing to be my mother, then my sister; upon fuller acquaintance, we thought we were good friends, you became my mistress. I propose today that you become once again the wife of your husband because I confess I am a little tired of being your subject and the running mate to that decent man Gérard.

I caress your children and pose my lips on your fingertips.

ANTOINE

and the second:

Dear friend,
It will soon be six months that you have been letting me hope you would become my mistress, then making me cool my heels waiting it out on the pretext that "we are of the race of those who esteem each other and not of those who go to bed."

So let us separate "good friends." I regret only your stubbornness in desiring to be loved not for yourself but for what there is in you that belongs to others: your conversation.

Friendly greetings,

ANTOINE

* * *

Antoine loved to watch Henriette sleeping. Her eyelids in repose took on a sadness that Antoine did not know in her. Henriette was pure even in her sleep, dreams were something unknown to her.

At the end of five or six weeks they were short of money. Antoine got the idea of borrowing from his grandfather. But there had to be a pretext. That's where Henriette came in. It was important that appearances be kept up and propriety observed. Antoine would introduce Henriette as his fiancée.

The grandparents lived in J.; they went there by train.

Antoine had a passion for trains, but on condition that he travel alone. He knew the value of smiles at the door of a compartment, stowing away the suitcases, the casual contact with faces passing down the corridor. He dreamed of international expresses, of people going off for the snow, of pegged pants stretched taut, of white pullovers. He was ravished, too, at the sight of a garter belt hanging loose, twisted stockings put back in line, a skirt stretched over the knee, kisses blown through windows.

Wrapped up in his disappointment to be traveling only to the suburbs, he neglected Henriette somewhat, but when he realized it his attention became the keener and he grew ever more tender.

They finally arrived at the grandparents' house. The grandmother was a dry old thing. One day when she was weeping in the cemetery, her face had gone stiff and her tears hardened like tallow from a candle; her face was a snapshot of tears and, along with that, nasty, like those who know what it is to suffer more than is right for a woman. Making up the worst to say about everyone, sometimes she hit the mark, which is the secret of intuition in people in the provinces. Grandfather stuck to his principles: he complimented the bride-to-be. He thought it fitting to tell them all about his own engagement, and once he worked up steam on those memories which the grandmother shrugged her shoulders at, there was no stopping him.

Henriette used to come downstairs humming the old folksong, "My father gave me a husband." That song, which Antoine had known since childhood, struck him now as terrifying, monstrous. "My Lord, what a man, what a tiny man, my Lord, that man how tiny he is!" That little man who disappeared in the young woman's bed had to be, could only be, he thought, the Devil.

The piano: a method teaches you how to put your fingers on the keys; the best one—German—teaches you how to lift them off. Thus, for a woman, there are a hundred ways to undress. One of them is a sure sign of innocence: Henriette undressed as one peels a fruit. Silk undies thrown on the chair, skirts stepped out of. Women who are guilty only know how to get dressed.

Antoine helped Henriette dress. He loved to button her up on the side rather than in front or behind. Hips are a spot rarer than bust or neck, and Antoine never failed, before buttoning her dress, to run his hand over her belly, feeling it through her slip. His indiscreet hand, a thief's hand, came back empty: a thief who would return things stolen, would buckle bracelets, steal only what he had permission to steal.

Removing the hair from Henriette's legs was another ceremony with unchangeable rites. Antoine would place his left arm along Henriette's calf, the hand making a shell over one knee. With the other hand he would apply a small black oval, turning it around on itself. The depilated leg was white and Henriette happy. Lavender water was applied before she slipped into her stockings again.

For women, stockings are only one accessory among others. In Antoine's eyes they were the sign of woman's mystery. It seemed to him that stockings were the real way to know that mystery, and it irritated him that virgins wore them.

Henriette's family was calling her home to the provinces. An old aunt had died. Antoine and Henriette talked it over: she would be gone eight days in all. He accompanied her to the station. He was jealous that she was going away and not he. Jealous also of a gentleman whose thick eyebrows shot up when he understood that Antoine, who was putting the luggage up on the rack, was going to leave Henriette alone with him in the compartment. Henriette pretended not to notice anything and promised to write often.

* * *

Antoine had little desire to go home. He had got out of the habit of living alone. He resigned himself to hanging about in Pigalle. It was evening.

Pigalle is the center, the center because there the extremes meet.

Unwilling to return to the empty apartment, Antoine took a room for one night in a hotel not far from Place Pigalle. It was a long time before he fell asleep.

Hotels are temples of love. When children are dreaming, husbands snoring, good women sighing, when apartment buildings go to sleep, hotels become beehives where smocked towels come and go, brought along with sweet messages by discreet, see-nothing, diligent maids who pad silently down the corridors on rubber-soled shoes, nurses in a hospital where scarcely anything is cured except the maladies of love.

Dimmed, the electricity does its day's work and only goes off when it's time for embracing.

Thick curtains let through just enough of a slit of light to intrigue the nocturnal stroller. He imagines ideal couplings, his favorite actor and actress, in color and with all shapes visible, billets-doux slipped under doors, bellhops bribed.

Tomorrow the disreputable hotels will sleep with one eye open to admit illicit loves, the kind broken off by a dictated letter, a wedding ring removed, reproaches, questions of money, little veils that mask no more than blushes, little veils that refuse to be accomplices, little veils that only multiply the shame.

Guilty loves made and unmade by day.

Hotels have an extreme share in the love that makes the world go around.

When dawn broke, Antoine left the room like a solitary thief.

He went home and threw himself on the bed fully dressed.

A few days went by that he filled with loitering around milk bars and movie houses. One film enchanted him. An American actress came and went without opening her mouth but parading a superb bust put on exhibition by one blouse after the other. He went back the next day to see the film again and counted fourteen different blouses plus one dress. A third visit inspired him to an article in which he pointed out that, unlike Egyptian graven images that show women with the face and limbs in profile and the bust front-view, this actress exhibited herself with face front-view and bust in profile. He described in detail the blouses and the material they were made of. He submitted the article to a movie magazine.

In a bar on the Champs-Elysées Antoine ran into a friend, René, whom he had lost sight of since Henriette was filling his life. René was a big fellow with emaciated features and a staccato way of speaking. His mistress, an American whose husband was always preoccupied with business, had just left him for a big blond guy with Slavic charm. They chattered away like the two bachelors they were, swore a mutual vow not to separate until each had found a girl to move in with, and slandered women because that's the way to console yourself. Women are so harebrained, don't they hang their little panties out the window to dry? Old maids talk about their colic; married women guffaw at dirty stories. Pregnant? Even in public conveyances they exhibit themselves with happy faces lost in bliss and well and truly satisfied. The two friends agreed that one's merit in being virtuous is measured by one's possibility of not being; that knowing how to make love is knowing the right moment to take off your tie. They made fun of people who make love on Saturday night because Sunday is a day off, and of women who make love like they make breakfast: out of duty.

Finally both of them praised to the skies the fantasies and refinements that fools put under the heading of vices, and the man who invents them, they agreed, is a poet.

Then came the day when Antoine counted on receiving a letter from Henriette. She had left no address to which he could write, promising to write first. The letter box remained empty.

The next morning Antoine, certain there would be a letter, rushed into the concierge's lodge. There was only an advertisement. He forgot about mail in the afternoon and only remembered it the next morning, happy at the thought that now his chances were doubled. Alas! nothing yet. Then he resigned himself to wishing that no letter would come, and since nothing did come he pretended to wish that it would come just to mix things up more. A grain of sand blocks the machinery, several grains cancel each other out, and then it was the day Henriette was due back. Antoine thought that she hadn't wanted to write so as to make him want her even more and that her return would be a so much greater joy. He would disarm her by beating her at her game: he inquired about the time of the train and went to wait for her at the station. Vainly; she didn't turn up.

From that point on resentment settled into Antoine's heart, resentment that he had to transform into sadness, bad humor into chagrin, jealousy into a stomachache.

Once again he came home alone but this time there was a letter. Henriette wrote that her aunt's death posed problems she could not settle except by prolonging her visit another week. She spoke also about the weather they were having, which was bad, about new material she had bought, and about a cousin whose acquaintance she had made. She did not make excuses for not writing earlier. That and the frivolousness of her letter turned Antoine sour, and he decided to make her wait a few days for an answer. As better proof that he missed Henriette, he made a great disorder in the apartment without knowing that order and disorder are one and the same. Henriette, a month later, married her cousin; Antoine heard nothing more about her and forgot her.

FRANÇOIS TRUFFAUT

PAGE 61 (LEFT)

Production LES FILMS DU CARROSSE
10, rue Hamelin, Paris 16e
Tel: KLE 54-60–Ext. 62

Film: THE 400 BLOWS

CALL SHEET

MONDAY, NOVEMBER 10, 1958

1st day of shooting

SCHEDULE: 9 A.M.–6 P.M. (1 hour for lunch)

RENDEZVOUS: 9 A.M., 82, rue Mercadet, Paris 18e, 6th floor at rear of court

Setting: Loinod flat. Daytime.

Nos. to be shot: 18–34–79

in reserve: 52–53

Actors	Roles	Costumes	Ready for shooting
Claire MAURIER	Gilberte Loinod	0–1–apron coat I	9:00
Albert REMY	Julien Loinod	0	9:00
Jean-Pierre LEAUD	Antoine Loinod	0–2	9:00
Daniel COUTURIER	Bertrand Mauricet	arranged	10:00

Props

Antoine's bed, practicable (dyed sheets)
Antoine's schoolbag—*Le Parisien*
1 pair of socks with holes. Hot coffee—bowl—bread—butter—spoon
dirty shirt—fog light—practicable schoolbag—radio
parents' bed, practicable—1 tub—bath towels—soap—sponge

CAMERAMEN—ELECTRICIANS

Meet at 8:00

PAGE 61 (CENTER)

PRODUCTION REPORT

MONDAY 10 NOVEMBER 1958–1st day of shooting 9:00 A.M.–6:00 P.M.

Building 82, rue Mercadet, Paris 18e–6th floor at rear of court

Setting: Julien Loinod's flat

8:00	—Installation and transport of material to the 6th floor
9:00–9:30	—Setting up for sequence 18
9:30	—Rehearsal with the actors—lines drawn—lighting equipment set up
10:30	—Continuation of lighting adjustment
11:00	—Runthrough with lighting—with actors
11:30	—Shooting of 18/1—sound check
11:40	—End of sequence 18/1 Setting changed to kitchen—18/2—adjustment
12:00	—Leave for lunch
1:15	—Return to adjusting equipment in kitchen—continuation
1:25	—Rehearsal with actors
1:35	—Shooting of 18/2

1:50	—End of sequence—sound only and preparation of reverse shot
2:00	—Rehearsal of 18/3—adjustment continued
2:25	—Rehearsal of action
2:35	—Shooting of 18/3
3:00	—End of sequence 18/3—closeup on Antoine
3:20	—Shooting of 18/4
3:25	—End of sequence 18/4 Change of camera axis and of sequence—preparation of 34^{A}
4:15	—End of sequence 34^{A1}—and setup for closeup shot
4:35	—Rehearsal of 34^{A2}
4:45	—Shooting of 34^{A2} (loops break on camera a 2nd time)
4:50	—End of sequence 34^{A2} Camera axis changed for 34^{A3}
5:15	—Shooting sequence 34^{A3}
5:20	—End of sequence 34^{A3} Preparation of sequence 34^{A4} Rail set up—lighting adjustment
5:50	—Continuation of lighting adjustment—fuses blow on the entire floor Notification of electricity department obligatory Rehearsal of action for tomorrow
6:00	—End of shooting

PAGE 62

REMARKS CONCERNING THE SCRIPT

1) The behavior of Antoine's parents and more generally of all the adults implicated in this film is to be nuanced, clarified, humanized in the next treatment.
2) The initial idea of the revelation of his "bastardy" is to be dropped as too obvious, in favor of this which is more visual: Antoine, playing hookey, runs into his mother arm in arm with a man. Since she says nothing about it that evening at home, he imagines a total complicity and, on that basis, a systematic impunity which is quickly given the lie by the facts. His mother will be present at the school when he is slapped by his father. This letdown constitutes a motivation powerful enough to bring about his first attempt to run away.
3) Certain little gags or quick scenes have scarcely any connection with the plot properly speaking. The effort will be made to preserve them but integrated more skillfully into the action in such a way as to paint a picture of childhood in general: joyous, sad, persecuted, spoiled. Thus there will intervene, periodically, little girls and little boys of different ages.
4) The ending is not definitive but its principle must be assured: freedom but shadowed over, a just revolt only half recompensed . . . No doubt that a better final contrivance remains to be found.

PAGE 64

THE 400 BLOWS

First treatment

We make out a child's body under the sheets on a divan that blocks the narrow entrance of a tiny apartment; a few strands of hair can perhaps be seen on the pillow; dim light. We hear doors banging; a good-looking young woman comes in and wakes Antoine brusquely. She grabs hold of the quilt, covers, and sheets, and shakes them violently: "Let's go, boy, get up and get a move on, please." We see Antoine making a pretense of a toilette, dressing, folding back his divan-bed, taking down the milk pitcher and rushing out at a run. We find him again in the street, running from one shop to another; he is soon back with milk, bread, and the newspaper. Since he slips in quietly, he waits in the front hall until his parents have stopped arguing in the bedroom; listening hard he can make out that they are talking about him, about maybe shipping him off to boarding school if it's not too expensive. Footsteps heard, Antoine pretends to be doing nothing in particular; his mother enters: "Ah, you're here?"

Very rapid breakfast, general bad humor. Antoine asks his father for some money to pay the school canteen for the week: "Ask your mother!" The mother: "Ah, pardon me, I don't have any money, not I!" New fight between father and mother at Antoine's expense. Finally the father gives Antoine some money: "In exchange you will take this registered letter to the post office." Antoine replies that he is already late. The father: "It's not because you turn up late now and then that you get zeroes in deportment every week, I don't think?" Then

1: Interior of classroom. Daylight

The credits superimposed on a desk

2: The desk top lifts up, a pupil takes out a photo of a starlet in a bathing suit. The photo circulates from desk to desk, which lets us glimpse the apparently studious appearance of the class: pupils who chew their penholder or bite their tongue as if in deep concentration. The teacher keeps an eye on them.

COMMENTARY. The paradise lost of childhood is an invention of elderly gentlemen. How can we believe in it at eighteen when the memory of the awkward age remains as present as a sore itch? Will they never have enough of reproaching us with not sitting still and with all sorts of devilment? At home as at school our thirteenth year seems to drag on forever. Antoine Loinod remembers it all very well: for him it was the age of injustice.

The photo has reached Antoine who proceeds to draw mustaches on it.

Teacher. Loinod! Bring me what you have there.

Antoine gets up reluctantly.

Teacher. Ah! That's a fine business! (Still looking at the photo) Go stand in the corner! (Putting the photo in his pocket) Obviously that's more than enough to flunk you on. (He looks at his watch and addresses the entire class):

Teacher. A minute to go!

The Class. Awww!

Teacher. Silence!

PAGE 66

Antoine (willful). No.

Mother. That means your father and I will probably no longer have the right to take you back home if we wish to. That means you're all set for the apprenticeship Center. Oh! You wanted to ruin your life. You'll see how hard iron bars are.

101 EXIT OF THE CENTER—DAYLIGHT—STREETS

The "juvenile delinquents" all lined up go off to the stadium singing a marching song (to be found with Constantin; if necessary they won't really sing but we will hear the song on the sound track). Two monitors keep them in line.

102 TOWN STADIUM—DAYLIGHT

A soccer match. A few plays. The ball flies out of bounds and out the stadium exit. A boy runs to get the ball, Antoine shoves the boy out of his way: Leave it to me and get back. The other boy makes no move to stop him. They exchange looks. Antoine throws the ball and runs off full speed. (Music from here without interruption to the words THE END.)

103 ENVIRONS OF TOWN STADIUM—DAYLIGHT

Antoine makes off through the hedges. We hear a whistle being blown and cries of pursuit. According to the layout of the site, Antoine's successful escape will be made logical, pursued by a single monitor, the other having to control the rest of the band.

104 VARIOUS

Succession of landscapes. Antoine still running, more and more out of breath. The panorama becomes in turn flat, rolling, hilly, monotonous, bleak, picturesque. Rapid shots, rapid dissolves.

105 A COUNTRY ROAD—INN DOOR—LATE AFTERNOON

Antoine goes up to a truck and reads on the rear license plate: Fourcroy sur Mer. He goes all around the truck, no one at the wheel; he climbs in the back and lies down on some tarpaulins. The truck takes off.

106 INTERIOR OF THE TRUCK—DAYLIGHT

Antoine catches sight of something that might be the sea. The truck is in fact on a road along the sea, disappearing and reappearing in turn. At a turn, when the driver slows down, Antoine jumps from the moving truck and takes a bad tumble.

107 ON THE BEACH—DAYLIGHT

It is low tide. Antoine comes forward, running, then walks very slowly toward the fine line of the waves. He will stop only when the foam wets the soles of his shoes. He lifts one leg delicately, bends the other, draws back, moves forward and draws back again, bends down to pick up a shell.

108 The last image of this sequence, Antoine at the edge of the sea, becomes frozen and very slowly dissolves into another in movement: Antoine and Robert walking in the streets of Paris (we will already have had this image of them cutting school). This image in turn freezes, reminding us that it is taken by a street photographer, while we hear the last phrases of commentary: "That's how I received a card from Fourcroy sur Mer where I succeeded in joining Antoine . . . How are we doing? Very well, thanks . . . and you? We are free and far indeed from the torments of adolescence, yet when we walk down the street we cannot help but regard as our accomplices the successors of our thirteenth year who are starting on their own FOUR HUNDRED BLOWS!

THE END

PAGE 72

JULES AND JIM PARIS

1—EXTERIOR—NIGHT—STAIRCASES AND STREETS

Jules and Jim strolling while chatting

COMMENTARY:
(underlined each time)

It was around 1907.

The short and round Jules, a foreigner in Paris, had asked the tall and slender Jim, whom he hardly knew, to get him into the Quat-z'Arts ball, and Jim had gotten him a ticket and had taken him to the costumer's. While Jules was gently rummaging through the material and choosing a simple slave costume, Jim's friendship for Jules was born. It grew during the ball, where Jules was tranquil, with eyes round as globes, full of good humor and tenderness.

Jules and Jim saw each other every day. Each taught the other, until late at night, his language and his literature. They showed each other their poems, and they translated them together. They chatted, without haste, and neither had ever found such an attentive listener. The regular customers of the bar were soon attributing to them, though they were unaware of it, dubious morals.

PAGE 77

Paris, December 22, 1961

Monsieur Oscar WERNER
Triesen
Liechtenstein

My dear Oscar,

First of all let me thank you for the superb theatrical calendar which I indeed received and for the big two-volume book I have not yet had time to read.

The film is finished and the first previews are generally very enthusiastic (and 100 percent enthusiastic about you). In short, all goes fairly well despite a few difficulties with the censor.

Jeanne, who has spent twenty-four hours in Paris, would be very happy, as would I, if you could come to the premier of the film on Tuesday, January 23 (by coincidence, Jeanne's birthday).

I, too, am astonished at the behavior of the BETA-Film Company which had at the outset agreed that the dubbing would be supervised by Marcel Ophuls and then, indirectly, has very recently pushed him out. In what concerns you, I know that they are hesitant, and that at times they bring up your Austrian accent (which is stupid considering the nationality of the character in the film), at times the financial penalties you are demanding from them.

In any case, a few weeks ago I informed them by letter that I would present the film in Germany only:

1) if you yourself did the dubbing for Jules;

2) if Marcel Ophuls selected and directed the other actors;

3) if the title remained *Jules and Jim*.

Since we have sold the film outright for Germany, they would be the only victims if the sabotage of the German version harms the film commercially.

At last hearing I was told that they would settle for the title *Jules, Jim, and Catherine,* which certainly is better than *Oh You, Adorable Witch*.

I am going to send them one last letter tomorrow, after which I am dropping any idea of having a say in this version.

Let me hear from you quickly about the premier of the film in Paris on January 23rd.

PAGE 78

EXTERIOR—DAYTIME —PERE LACHAISE

The crematory at Père Lachaise

COMMENTARY. The bodies were found caught up in the bushes of a small island covered over by the flood.

Jules accompanied them to the cemetery.

Procedure for the ceremony

a) the hearse draws up to the crematory oven
b) Jules enters the enclosure
c) the 2 corpses go up in flames
d) emergence of the iron conveyor—Catherine's skeleton in white powder
e) the ashes are gathered in the urns which are then sealed

All this quite rapidly. (The gestures dissolve into each other)

COMMENTARY. He saw again the Catherine at the start of it all, who had not yet tasted blood, the vivacious Catherine who won races by taking 'off on *Two!* Generous, irresistible Catherine. Catherine severe, Catherine-Alexandre, Catherine dial-of-a-compass

Catherine's face at different moments of the film superimposed. Perhaps the face of Sabine screwing up her eyes like her mother.

COMMENTARY. The ashes were gathered in the urns, and set into a case that was then sealed.

On his own, Jules would have mingled them. Catherine had always wanted hers cast into the wind from the top of a hill. But it was not permitted.

THE END

PAGE 80

ANTOINE'S PASSION (a short)

Antoine Doinel, as was to be expected, would fall passionately in love at the first opportunity.

He is now sixteen. His adolescent troublemaking has carried him to a juvenile court. Having escaped from a Center for the Observation of Juvenile Delinquents, he was caught five days later and transferred to a more heavily guarded Center. Because the resident female psychologist took an interest in his case, he was finally given parole. His parents were stripped of their rights.

Antoine has a room in town, near the Place de Clichy. He is a warehouse employee for a record store and has become a music fanatic. He has taken a subscription to the Jeunesses Musicales de France and doesn't miss a single concert of introduction to classical music. He often goes out with his old school friend, René Bigey. When they aren't talking about high fidelity and stereophonics, they talk about the girls they have known, know and will know.

It is at a Berlioz recital that Antoine falls madly in love with a young girl, Colette, who is there, that Sunday morning at the Théâtre du Châtelet, a few rows in front of him. He follows her with his eyes as they leave; she greets her girlfriends.

Antoine notices her at other concerts and succeeds, one day, in sitting next to her and making her acquaintance.

On another occasion, he manages to see her home. Through his employers, Antoine sometimes gets tickets to major concerts (not open to the Jeunesses Musicales), thanks to which he is able to go out alone with Colette.

He learns in bits and pieces that she is the daughter of a Polish woman, that her father is dead, but that her stepfather, a very nice man, owns a garage near the Gare Saint-Lazare. Her mother owns a small fabric store beneath the apartment.

Colette tends to discourage Antoine's amorous transports, but he pays little attention to this: Under the pretext of returning borrowed books, he goes to Colette's. She isn't there, but her mother receives him. She is very pretty and speaks with a strong accent.

The next day, Colette will say to Antoine: "My mother found you very romantic."

Later, Colette's mother will say in a more familiar way: "Your hair, how long are you going to let it grow?"

In short, Antoine, ever obstinate, having noticed a little hotel opposite the shop, moves into it.

Antoine, who watches all of Colette's comings and goings from his bedroom window, has been completely accepted by the parents of the young girl, to the point of eating there sometimes in her absence. The point of this sketch is the following: Antoine, wanting to get closer to his idol, has become a member of the family, therefore a wet blanket, and our story ends one night when Antoine dines at Colette's parents' house.

A boy comes to take Liliane [Colette] to the movies and Antoine stays with the parents to watch television.

François Truffaut

PAGE 81

The role of Colette, the heroine beside Jean-Pierre Léaud in the French sketch *Love at Twenty,* is still not cast.

We are therefore looking for not a small young woman but a small young girl aged fourteen at least and fifteen and a half at most, the important thing being that she look exactly fifteen.

She should not be saucy, nor piquant, nor dainty, nor seductive, nor showy, nor sexy but, instead, simple, well brought up, fresh, pretty, and at one and the same time a little serious and quite merry. Of medium build, she can have hair of any color so long as it is natural and she will be, if possible, witty, music-loving, and of a good average culture.

PAGE 82

The Mother: What is it?
Colette: It's a real procession.

Colette gets up to open the door while the others look in that direction. She returns with a young man slightly older than Antoine.

Colette: Maman, I'd like you to meet Albert. I've already spoken to you about him. This is Antoine, you know him already, I think.
Albert: Sure, I've seen you around . . . Hi!

Colette: Just a minute, Albert. I'll get my coat.
The Mother: (to her husband) Give me a cigarette, please.
Colette: O.K. All set! I'm ready. Let's get out of here. Bye!

And Colette leaves with her chum, while Antoine remains at the table with the parents. Father and Mother look with embarrassment at each other.

Stepfather: Good. Well, how about seeing the program . . .

All three settle themselves in front of the television where the Master of Ceremonies of the musical evening, Bernard Gavoty, appears.

END

PAGE 84

THE NEWS ITEM THAT WAS THE BASIS FOR TRUFFAUT'S FILM "THE SOFT SKIN" IS MENTIONED BEFORE THE ASSIZES OF THE SEINE

PARIS—Mr. Buisse, the examining magistrate at the Seine tribunal, signed yesterday an order returning Nicole Gérard, 41, murderer of her husband, Dr. Guy Gérard, to the Seine Court of Assizes.

On June 26, 1963, in the restaurant "le Petit Chevreau," located in the rue de la Huchette, Nicole Gérard killed her husband with two bullets from a buckshot gun; one struck the doctor in the right shoulder, the other in the right temple.

This event inspired the screenwriter François Truffaut to produce the film "The Soft Skin," acted by Françoise Dorleac and Jean Dessailly [sic].

Here, it concerned an additional drama in the life of a young woman who was thrice divorced and had survived two suicide attempts.

In 1948, she had already tried to commit suicide because a doctor in the military had refused to marry her.

Her marriage to Guy Gérard dated from 1951. Three years previously, these two young people had met one evening in Paris and from this liaison, a son, Frank, had been born in 1950.

In order to legitimize the child, Dr. Gérard had decided to marry his mistress the following year. But no longer feeling any affection for his wife, he soon began to hate her and the difficulties of life together separated them still further.

One incident followed the next, degenerating into scenes of violence.

In 1959, fed up with this life, the doctor abandoned the conjugal home, leaving the child and the apartment to his wife. He also left her a monthly allowance of 1,400 francs.

For Nicole Gérard, who continued to love her husband, the situation was desperate. She tried to commit suicide by taking Phenergan tablets, but she was saved "in extremis," as was little Frank who had followed his mother's example.

After this drama, Dr. Gérard took custody of his son and tried to forget the past. He became engaged to a young girl whom he promised to marry as soon as his divorce was finalized.

A Long Crisis

In June 1962, the divorce was granted in his favor, but Nicole Gérard appealed the decision.

However, she did not wait for the result of the appeal and, one year later, desperate at having lost her son, she made her fatal decision. To the police who arrested her, she explained that she wanted revenge for all the miseries her husband had subjected her to.

The report of the expert psychiatrists notes that "the act of which she is accused is typically a reaction of passion motivated by rancor and the fear of another failure. It is the end result of a long crisis of tension fed by numerous incidents, as the only way out from a veritable dead end . . . "

Nicole Gérard will be defended before the jury by the lawyer Germaine Sénéchal. The lawyer, Jacqueline Trouvat, for her part, will help the sister of the victim, Madame Ribac, who is bringing the civil action.

L'ESPOIR—NICE—27 JULY 1965

PAGE 89

RESTAURANT INTERIOR

Franca enters. A waiter recognizes her: "Good afternoon, Mrs. Lachenay."
—She moves into the dining room and we precede her, close-up, dolly out. She looks straight ahead.
—She sees: Pierre reading and smoking.
—Dolly in, subjective camera, toward Pierre.
—Back to Franca who walks forward.
—Pierre raises his head and sees Franca. He is surprised.
—Franca looks at him and puts her hand in the right pocket of her raincoat.
—Pierre gestures slightly with his hand and perhaps even hints at a smile.
—Franca pulls the photographs from her raincoat pocket and throws them all in front of her, as though into Pierre's face.
—Pierre sees the photos fluttering in front of him.
—Franca opens her raincoat and seizes the rifle.
—Pierre sees the rifle and rises.
—Franca, the rifle at waist level, fires without aiming.
—Pierre collapses.
—Franca looks at Pierre.
—He falls between the table and the seat.
—General view of the restaurant. People stand up.
—Focus again on Franca, who lets the rifle fall and sits on a chair. "Off," one vaguely hears: "Call a doctor, the police . . . "
—In close-up, Franca, who is taking deep breaths and blowing the air out as though she were emerging from water. A great relief. "Off," one hears the owner dialing the police from the bar telephone.

PAGE 91

FAHRENHEIT 451

NOTE CONCERNING THE POST-SYNCHRONIZATION OF MONTAG'S ROLE

Independently of questions of the quality of the synchronism, the English pronunciation for this role, and the possible variants in the vocabulary, all of which are beyond the scope of my competence and for which I rely completely on Norman Wanstall and Helen Scott, I should like Oscar Werner to improve seven scenes in the film:

Nos. 21 to 27: Montag's first scene, going home and seeing Linda. In this scene, Montag speaks too loudly. Although he is somewhat distant from Linda, he must not convey the impression of hostility, but of normal life.

No. 70: The day after Linda's fainting spell. Same criticism, but more serious this time, because Montag has to force Linda to remember what happened the night before, but without hostility—more of a weary tone, or else there will be a complete contradiction of the intention.

No. 79: For the first time, Montag reads a book, at night, in front of the television. Indeed, he must read like a child who is beginning to learn, since it's . . .

PAGE 95

REREAD THE SCRIPT TO:

1. condense the dialogue to the maximum; replace it by the visual—dryness for characters [illegible]
2. to invent and fit in Science-Fiction details. IBM machines.
3. to study the development of the characters, one by one.
4. to verify the principle: *daily scene* in an *unusual context* and *unusual scene* in a *realistic setting.*
5. suspense and amount of the purely visual. Try to expand.
7. attitude of the public before or after each scene: the feelings, emotions, the responses to the eternal question: *"And afterwards?"*
8. questions of "viewpoint."
9. to fit in the generalities and details omitted in the course of drafting.
10. the concept of the book as *object.*
11. to pay attention (and with Coutard) to everything that can be filmed—a) speeded up b) in slow motion c) in reverse d) in reverse played in reverse.
12. to assess everything that is *seen* and *said* on television or *only that which is said.*
13. to fit in a few funny details in order to lighten tension.
14. to closely connect the scenes (hook or link).
15. from the point of Montag, Aznave (Does he *act?* does he *love* Clarisse.)

PAGE 105

Madame D.: Look who's here! . . .
Monsieur D.: What a treat . . . It's a pleasure to see you after all this time . . . You're on leave?
Antoine: No, no, I'm discharged, my enlistment's been cancelled . . .
Madame D.: Have you eaten?
Antoine: Oh, yes. Don't disturb yourselves for me . . .
Monsieur: No, I'm sure you haven't had supper . . . Sit down.
Madame: Christine will be so sorry. She isn't home.
Monsieur: H'm . . . At least you're not sick . . . They gave you a temporary discharge?

PAGE 118

MY DEAR FRANÇOIS
I HAVE PREVIEWED L'ENFANT SAUVAGE WHICH I FIND MAGNIFICENT I BEG YOU PLEASE SEND ME THE AUTO-

GRAPH OF THE ACTOR WHO PLAYS THE DOCTOR HE IS FORMIDABLE I WANT THAT AUTOGRAPH FOR ALMA HITCHCOCK HER EYES WERE SWIMMING IN TEARS THIS FILM SHE SAYS IS THE BEST OF ALL THOSE BY TRUFFAUT PROFOUND AFFECTION

HITCHCOCK

PAGE 119

"DOMICILE CONJUGAL"

Notes (dictated by F.T.) to be used in working out the first script of *Domicile Conjugal* (attention Claude de Givray and Bernard Revon).

1st Act—*They are married!*

1/ We will avoid an exposition in the traditional sense of the word, that is to say, documentary and antidramatic. We will try instead to inform the public in an amusing manner:

a) that Antoine is married;
b) that his work consists in dyeing flowers.

2/ Christine gives violin lessons either at the pupil's home or at hers (it's not a matter of choosing but of profiting from the advantages of both situations if we need to).

PAGE 125

"Come quickly. Perhaps you will still find the child." Was that *perhaps* a threat? It cut down further what little strength he had left. He could not leave on no more than a *perhaps*.

Everything between them was in eclipse.

*There was talk of Kathe coming to Paris, to rejoin him in his own home, but his mother, knowing all, disapproved of their life and did not conceal it. He feared their contact. Kathe would be hurt to the quick. Jim mentioned a nearby hotel for her first days in Paris. She interpreted that very badly.

They ran the risk of passing each other en route.

Jules was offering to remarry Kathe and to bring up the child.

"Ah," thought Jim, "it's fine to want to rediscover the laws of mankind, but how good and helpful it must be just to go along with the existing rules!"

Worn out by these alternations of heaven and hell before its birth, the tiny child died at a third of its prenatal life.

This was announced to Jim by a note from Jules—and Kathe henceforth desired only silence between them.

Thus, the two of them, they had created nothing.

Jim was still intrigued by this sudden impregnation, and he questioned his doctor, who told him: "It can happen that a well-matched and passionate couple may not have a child for a long time—and that they have one all of a sudden if, as consequence of some circumstance or other, a quarrel perhaps, the woman remained frigid for once."

Their last night! Light broke on Jim. For the first time he really believed Kathe.

He thought: "We toyed with the sources of life. We turned them into combat weapons. She sterilizes us and rolls us along in her wave."

He would know the details if some day Jules would be willing to speak.

He convinced himself little by little that the misfortune would have been avoided if Kathe and he had belonged to the same stock and the same religion.

When it came down to it, they spoke to each other only in translation. Words had absolutely not the same meaning for the two of them—not even gestures. In the moments of great disorder when their love was breaking up, they no longer had any common base. Their notions of order, of authority, of the role of the man and the woman, differed.

They had been foolhardy, they had wanted to build a bridge between people, they had done well—but they had kept their pride, they had not been apostles . . . Perhaps their son would have been one?

Not that Kathe and Jules were of the same stock. Kathe was pure Germanic through and through, a "fighting hen." Jules was a Jew who, except for a few great friends, in general steered clear of Jews.

Six months went by. Jim had regained his strength. He was working in his Paris.

In June, Jules let him know that he had remarried Kathe.

And so their home was not falling to pieces. Kathe was remaining with Jules, far from Albert! Jim sent congratulations.

In August he had occasion to go to their capital, where they were living now.

He wrote to Jules, asking if he could see him. Jules replied yes—but that Kathe preferred not to meet him.

Jim found that natural.

*Claude's mother or the mother of the two girls

PAGE 131

WHY SUCH A GORGEOUS KID LIKE ME

by François Truffaut

When I met Bernadette Lafont we were under the Fourth Republic but I saw right away that she was an aristocrat. She was posing at the time for sweater ads and she accepted the idea that we would make our debuts together, she in front of the camera and I behind; the film was called *The Mischief Makers* and when it appeared on the screen we were in the Fifth Republic. In *The Mischief Makers* Bernadette in flowing skirt bicycled across the Gard Département, and it was such a pleasure to watch her pedaling away like that across the countryside that I could not bring myself to say, "Cut!"

After that, Bernadette and I had children, separately, made full-length films separately, and when she finally returned to live in Paris I looked at her and thought, "What beautiful movies we could have made together!"

In the crime story series a book was published titled *Such a Gorgeous Kid Like Me* by Henry Farrell; I read it, collapsing with laughter at every page, and I lent it to Jean-Loup Dabadie and asked him, "What actress does the heroine of this book remind you of?" Jean-Loup Dabadie replied, "At every page I thought of Bernadette Lafont!"

For a long time I have been convinced that Bernadette Lafont is an aristocrat and that this aristocrat is at the same time the most sexually arousing actress in French cinema.

Even if you asked her to be vulgar she couldn't manage it; she can say everything, she can do everything, she has the class of a Michel Simon or of a Charles Laughton. I am quite sure that they are her favorite actors.

PAGE 137

FULL SET. EXTERIOR LOCATION. DAY
No. 1—Film of slap scene.—Television interviews Alexandre

Actors	Costumes
Alexandre	1
Alphonse	1
Ferrand	arranged
Liliane	arranged
Joëlle	arranged
Bernard	arranged
Odile	arranged

SPECIAL EXTRAS: Remote TV.—First Assistant.—Head Cameraman.—Assistant Cameraman.—Sound Engineer.—Boom Operator.—Wife of Assistant Director.—Assistant Director.
EXTRAS: 2 stagehands.—2 electricians.—TV Cameraman.—TV Sound Engineer.—200 people to move around the square (of which 10 in cars—3 policemen—15 children of various ages—4 waiters—3 hairdressers).
VEHICLES: 10 different cars.—1 motorcycle.—4 motorbikes.
PROPS: 16mm Coutand TV equipped with Zoom (without film).—TV Nagra, boom and TV microphone.—MK2 with clear viewfinder, without film (see when shooting).—Nagra, boom and microphone for film (see when recording).—Newspapers.—Bags of provisions.—Baby carriage.—Various parcels for the extras.—Electrical equipment figuring on the set (see with electricians).—Sweater for assistant director's wife.—Actors' chairs (with their film names).—Movable make-up box for Odile.—Megaphone for Assistant.—Beverages for café.—Bag and material for script assistant.—Glasses for script assistant.
FULL SET. EXT. DAY. (No. 1 cont'd)
SETS: Square set ready.—Café with terrace.—Open Métro station.—Hairdresser's parlor ready.—Flowershop.—Newspaper stand.
MAKE-UP: False moustache for Alexandre.
STAGEHANDS: Traveling platform.
2 boom dollies (one of which figures as a prop).
ELECTRICIANS: Electrical equipment figuring as props.
STAGE DIRECTION: Arrange 2 megaphones (one of which figures as a prop).

PAGE 140

The father—(Charles Boyer—Louis Jourdan—J.-P. Aumont—Hollywood . . . the wait for the airplane—a telegram: he is happy (telegraph money order)—shock: it's a boy, player—because of his money problems—favorable to the tryouts for the boy—the boy plays tennis—he speaks of his cinema deaths

The "godson"—the game . . . it has been proposed that he try out—finally he says he will try out—he never looks at a girl—arch-silent and mysterious

Lucie-Julie—she arrives after some days—airport—husband a doctor—pats of butter

The mother—she drinks—the scene of the poisoning—the placard—she fumes because of M. Félix

The producer—Lewis Allen-Javal Dorfman—pats of butter

The secretary—she refuses bathing suit—the script girl guesses she is pregnant

The son—he never sits down except on the ground (scene to be done) he has got his girlfriend a job as script girl—wild passion (furniture smashed up) his girlfriend takes off with the stunt man—he is no longer in a state to act—one night Julie consoles him . . .

PAGE 144

Jean Hugo
Mas de Fourque
34 Lunel

Dear Sir,

My friend the scriptwriter Jean Gruault (together we adapted Henri-Pierre Roché's novel Jules and Jim and the Report of Doctor Itard on The Wild Child) and I have been thinking for several weeks of making a movie about the life of Adèle Hugo, specifically the long episode of her love for Lieutenant Pinson. I haven't tried to reach you sooner because, at this stage, our work is experimental and we often rough out a draft which we then reject, above all when it's a question of real stories as opposed to fiction.

My great hope had been to reach you through the intermediary of Louise de Vilmorin whom I very much loved . . . alas . . . then Maître Matarasso offered to contact you but I asked him to wait a little because I really wanted you to read a coherent project, allowing you to give an opinion. Meanwhile, I met Mrs. France V. Guille with whom I have corresponded and she explained that you had already spoken about this project; which is why I wished to explain to you the lateness of my request.

During the first half of February, I could submit a first draft of the screenplay in hopes of getting your agreement in principle and, of course, any comments you wish to make on the work.

As far as any moral and legal questions between you, Mrs. France V. Guille and ourselves are concerned, I suggest that Maître Matarasso could represent our respective interests.

Finally, I would like you to know how very much Jean Gruault and I myself have been taken with Adèle throughout our work; and in hopes of soon having an occasion to meet you, please accept, Dear Sir, the expression of my most distinguished sentiments,

François Truffaut

PAGE 150

Kids like these

The family identity card	12
At camp and first kiss	14
2 boys and 2 girls at the movies	14
Minûle falls down	2 years
When you are dead . . . (c.v.)	4 and 5 years
The bouquet to the pal's mother	14
The pal who cuts his hair	13
Harpagon at the school	

+René-Jean Clot—N.R.F.
+Saki etc. (Christmas presents) useful
+idem Leackok presents

PAGE 155

The Skirt-Chaser

*When the story begins his manuscript is accepted; they go to find him; he is dead. They read his manuscript:

*When the story is interrupted it is:
——— : typed up by the typist (or by him)
——— : set up at the printers'
——— : proofs corrected by a woman . . .
——— : jacket designed (they come to look for him at home or at the office)
——— : book comes out . . . pile to be signed for the critics . . . he will not turn up . . . he is dead

*

——— : All the same, he didn't make much of his life. What a mess!
——— : Still and all, he did do something: *a book.*

*

(perhaps he dies making a grab at the nurse's legs . . .
He had crossed the street to catch up with a woman . . . the one he had dropped)

PAGE 159

THE DEPARTED

0—Generic: The dead of 14–18, death in general.
1—At MAZET: DAVENNE chases away a priest and consoles the widower in his own way: the dead can continue to live! Fade out.
2—Auction room: DAVENNE looks for a ring and meets CECILIA who recognizes him, but not he her.
3—Car. Night. DAVENNE drives.
4—The house of DAVENNE: George has repaired the projector.
5—Office of the GLOBE—DAVENNE refuses to follow Humbert to Paris—he will stay for THEM (the dead subscribers).
6—Auction room: CECILIA and DAVENNE had met before the war—she hasn't forgotten him—the ring is found again.
7—Auction room:—It's Madame Rambaud who buys the ring.
8—The house of DAVENNE—Madame Rambaud gives the ring to DAVENNE who goes up the staircase—she answers the telephone and says he is out.
9—Room upstairs—DAVENNE gives the ring back to JULIE.
10—Lap dissolve: Tomb of Julie DAVENNE-VALLANCE and the cemetery. Music from the previous scene continues.
11—Office of the GLOBE—MAZET tells Humbert that he wants to introduce his new wife to DAVENNE—the latter, hiding, has overheard everything.
12—Auction room—DAVENNE confides his indignation to CECILIA—she pleads for the living.
13—In the car: CECILIA cries, then tells DAVENNE about the death of her father—but they are not the same—the scene ends with a breakup.
14—Office of the GLOBE—Storm—DAVENNE learns of the death of Massigny and begins to write the obituary.

PAGE 170

(first column)
(1) Grand letter to Sabine

Sabine, my dear, Sabine whom I love and who doesn't want to see me anymore . . . *Even if you don't want to listen to me I must tell you that I had an odd encounter today.* I ran into Monsieur Lucien, one of my mother's lovers, the main one, Lover Number One, the only one perhaps to have really counted in her life. He spoke to me about her in an incredible manner: "Your mother was a little bird"! A little bird? It was enough to make me wonder if we were talking about the same person!

"Why don't you love your mother?"

Back to J.-P. beginning to write again: A little bird . . . It was enough to make me wonder if we were talking about the same person!

(second column)

J.-P. settles down and begins to write
Image of Sabine in movement over J.-P.
closeup of writing
image of M. Lucien (closeup)
photos of men falling on the ground
closeup Lucien
closeup of writing
closeup of J.-P. who stops writing and dreams, "Why don't you love your mother?"
closeup of writing

PAGE 182

BACK ON THE RIGHT TRACK (to reread)

(project for a film with Jeanne Moreau and Charles Denner)

He has gotten out of prison

He is getting over a nervous breakdown

He knew Jeanne, they loved each other, she threw him over, he cracked up. Something in him drove him to destroy, he acted as judge and jury and killed a man from Grenoble (Dr. X. who clandestinely killed chamois).

The film begins in the provinces (with Charles in a bad way or with Jeanne who has come there to do something or other, I don't know what). The story begins in the hotel where Charles is staying. When he sees Jeanne who has just arrived in the hotel, he tries to get away but she sees him. At first he refuses to speak to her, she insists, he gives in.

We learn in this way the story of the chamois and the jail term (forbidden to live in certain places). Charles is in a frightful state, a mess needing straightening out. Jeanne is going to concern herself with him and put him back on the right track.

From the start she has to make him understand that it is out of the question for them to get back together: "Our story was complete, it had a beginning, middle, and end, and anyway I love fellows younger than myself because . . . " Despite that, despite her current young fellow (whom we perhaps catch a glimpse of), Jeanne takes Charles in hand, she makes him straighten up, she shows him his bitterness and then takes it to pieces, she gives him back a taste for living.

"For two years I couldn't walk past our apartment . . . You know that song, 'Without love you're just nothing at all' . . . The little pills for sleeping . . . I swear to you, Jeanne, I really and truly do want to get out of myself, I don't want to remain like this, I really have the will to pull myself out of the black hole" (cf. Two English Girls).

She handles Charles as gently as possible, to the point perhaps of hiding her young man when he turns up. The young man doesn't understand, is vaguely jealous or simply a little humiliated; because of this, we have one episode with more action than the rest, in the course of which Jeanne has to bestir herself in the hotel to straighten things out (a little like the Viceroy of Peru, but less comical though still somewhat droll).

Almost everything takes place in the hotel: a meal in the room, a meal in the dining room (comments about the travelers, the mystery of all those lives . . .)

Like the kitchens of Silence, something to see from the windows (a neighborhood movie theater?). Then the film could be *Paradis Perdu* with Jeanne remembering back when "everybody was weeping in the theater, my father was on leave, a lot of soldiers, we were afraid there would be an air raid warning," or else it is Charles who remembers a showing interrupted by an alert. So they go to see the film. (Buy the rights to two passages: the declaration of war, and Fernand Gravey in the trenches learning about Micheline Presle's death.)

If we suppose that Charles has tried to kill himself, make use of suicide in the Métro: "They told me I was the first guy ever to fail at suicide in the Métro." This makes possible mental images of Charles on the Métro platform and above all very effective sound "bridges": the train arriving and good dissolves into closeups of Charles.

Make much of the idea that moral torments can be treated by biochemical means . . . But yes, there are little gadgets in our brains, canals that create (or secrete) euphoria or depression. That's all only a question of blood circulation, then? Yes, of course.

Audiberti's image: "To do one's duty, like a child."

The meaning of life . . . The social illusion . . . There are real nice illusions and also rotten ones . . . One has to pick out something, a domain in which you don't act aggressively against anyone, you don't step on anyone's toes . . . Think about the surgeons who patch up the accident cases on the roads every Sunday evening . . . There's no end to it . . . We ourselves do things we can see an end to . . . We're lucky . . . What can you say to a fellow today who loves nothing, who wants nothing, and who refuses to live? Nothing! (On the subject of the dead on the highways, if the TV really wanted to it could reduce the number of accidents by showing the injured, the paralyzed, etc. . . . instead of giving the number of dead . . . You can't identify yourself with the dead but you can with people gravely injured) etc. . . .

Without a doubt the film ends very optimistically, Charles pulls himself together, reconciles himself with a) life, b) Jeanne, c) his past—his mother?, d) other people.

In order not to be abstract, the social position of everyone must be well defined.

A song, the tender song "In the glass, whatever may pass, everything fades . . ." sung by Jeanne. Heard several times.

Obviously a dialogue film, very sentimental.

+Charles has a fight *with someone* [in English in original].
+Jeanne's heroic behavior.

PAGE 202

Why does Hitchcock appear in all his films?—What is the connection between the sex organ and handcuffs?—Are you acquainted with the *Understatement* [in English]?—What is the difference between surprise and suspense?—Have you ever seen a MacGuffin?—Do you prefer a slice of life or a slice of cake?—What's going on in Switzerland?—Are actors livestock?—Is Hitchcock a barbarian sophisticate?—Do you practice the *run for cover* [in English]?—What is a red herring?

You will find precise answers to all these agonizing questions in: *Le Cinéma Selon Hitchcock* by François Truffaut, Editions Robert Laffont.

PAGE 206

A scene should not be written to make a place for an idea, but 6 ideas should be given their place in one (long) scene.

You lack confidence:
— in the public
— in your characters
— in the story
— in yourselves

Read again the great things: Marius—Fanny—Scènes de la Vie Conjugale—La Strada—Le Visage—Le Carrosse d'Or—Baby Doll

PAGE 207

Scandal at La Pléiade: It appears that François TRUFFAUT is preparing La Tour Eiffel

PAGE 208

Edgar POE

Robert Lachenay .... The Gold Bug
Marcel Ophuls ..... The Cask of Amontillado
Michel Varesano .... Ligeia
Jean-Luc Godard .... The Oval Portrait
Fr. Truffaut .... The Demon of Perversity
Eric Rohmer .... Berenice
—Claude Chabrol (Stéphane Audran)
—Claude de Givray
—Georges Franju
—Paul Gegauff .... The Demon of Perversity
—Resnais—Demy—

PAGE 209

Viviane's sorrow. Yes, it is very important but badly shown, too direct, too simple, too banal . . .

The public should not always discover things *at the same time* as the characters. That's too simple, not intriguing, not exciting!

PAGE 219

always scenes that are too short, flashes, scenettes, that lacks weight, force, importance. You have to keep the public in their seats, mouths open.

PAGE 220

VIVIANE finishes putting on her clothes and lets it be understood that she really ought to change her life because: "That street stuff doesn't go with my age any more."

SYLVIE is not fooled, VIVIANE adores it.

This section 39–43 seems to be the first thing that functions well. Don't be afraid of pinning down, of expanding. Generally your scenes are too short, like quick turns.

In order to create *heroic* characters Pagnol, Fellini, Bergman are not afraid of *long scenes*. A scene should not be a scenette. It can constitute a little film in itself with one movement in 3 phrases: beginning, middle, end.

PHOTOGRAPH CREDITS

The photographs and documents illustrating this book come, for the most part, from Les Films du Carrosse, from the personal collection of Dominique Rabourdin, and from:
L'Avant-Scène Cinéma: pages 51, 52, 55, 179.
G. Botti/Kippa: pages 36, 37.
Patrick Brion: pages 35, 38, 94, 95.
Les Cahiers du Cinéma: page 198.
Cinéma (and the F.F.C.C.): pages 53, 54, 74, 109, 110.
Jean Dousset: page 218.
Gamma: pages 31, 32, 106, 206.
Philippe Halsman: page 212.
Christophe L.: pages 97, 98, 99, 100, 101, 108, 109, 110, 111, 135, 147, 153, 154, 156, 158, 161, 200, 219.
Alain Pelé: pages 199, 204/205.
Sygma: cover and pages 189, 190, 191, 217, 225.
Pierre Zucca: pages 8, 48, 196, 219.

ACKNOWLEDGMENTS

This book would not exist without the journalists and editors who gave us permission to reproduce François Truffaut's texts and conversations. We thank Pierre Ajame, Guy Allombert, Janick Arbois-Chartier, *L'Avant-Scène Cinéma*, Yvonne Baby, Jeanine Bazin, Raymond Bellour, Pierre Billard, Michel Boujut, Christian Bourgois, Guy Braucourt, *Les Cahiers du Cinéma*, Paul Ceuzin, *Cinéma*, *Cinéma Pratique*, *Cinématographe* (and Olivier Dazat), *La Cinématographie Française*, Christiane Collange, Gilles Costaz, *Encre*, *L'Express*, La Fédération Française des Ciné-clubs, Jacques Fieschi, Editions Flammarion, Anne Gallois, Anne de Gasperi, Claude de Givray, *Jeune Cinéma*, Editions Robert Laffont, Gérard Langlois, Editions Lemeac, Pierre Loubière, Dominique Maillet, Michel Mardore, *Le Matin de Paris*, *Le Mercure de France*, Jean Michaud, Simon Misrahi, *Le Monde*, Pierre Murat, Jean Narboni, Michel Perez, *Le Point*, Jérôme Prieur and the I.N.A., *Le Quotidien de Paris*, Editions Ramsay, Ruta Sadoul, Gilbert Salachas, *Télérama*, *Témoignage Chrétien*, Pascal Thomas, Serge Toubiana, Claude-Marie Trémois, *Unifrance Films*, Claude Veillot, Pierre Wildenstein.

For their thoughtfulness and help, I also thank Claude Basnier, Yves Boisset, Josiane Couëdel, Christophe L., Alain Pelé, Bernard Revon, Guy Teisseire, and Pierre Zucca.

And, without Claude Beylie, Philippe Collin, François Dalemont, Catherine Fel, Les Films du Carrosse (Lucette de Givray, Monique Holveck, and Madame Madeleine Morgenstern know how much I owe them!), Bénédicte Frot, Odile and Alain Gauvreau, Joël Magny, Benoît Nacci, Aube Rabourdin (who let me see certain films again), Elizabeth Rabourdin, and Nata Ramtazzo, this book would certainly not be what it is.

I should have liked to have shown it to François Truffaut.

Cet ouvrage a été achevé d'imprimer le 3 avril 1987
sur les presses de Maury-Imprimeur S.A. à Malesherbes.
Photogravure : Nuances graphic à Montrouge.
Composition : Composetting à Paris.

ISBN 2.85108.415.1 - ISSN 0768/6196
Dépôt légal 36 - janvier 1986 - 34.0547.9
Imprimé en France

VIVEMENT DIMANCHE !

Un film de FRANÇOIS TRUFFAUT

Production : LES FILMS DU CARROSSE
5 rue Robert-Estienne
75008 PARIS

tél. : 256 12.73
359 18.74

1982

	1	2	3	4	5	6	7	8	9	10	11	12	13	14	15	16	17	18
MOIS	NOVEMBRE																	
SEMAINES	1							2							3			
TOURNAGE	X			1	2	3	X	4	5	6	X	7	8	X	9	10	11	12
JOUR	L	M	M	J	V	S	D	L	M	M	J	V	S	D	L	M	M	J
DATE	1	2	3	4	5	6	7	8	9	10	11	12	13	14	15	16	17	18
DECORS	FÉRIÉ	VOYAGE	VOYAGE	Rue petite ville. Ext. "Ange Rouge" Nice.	Hôtel Garibaldi. Façade. Hall. Chambre.	Hôtel Garibaldi. Ascenseur. Couloir.	X	Arrêt car. Téléphone (Courses). Sorties ville	Agence Lablache.	Immeuble "Provençal". Kiosque. Rues.	FÉRIÉ	Palier. Escalier. Façade avocat.	Bureau avocat.	X	Cabine de projection. Rue cinéma.	Rue cinéma. Rue Petite ville.	Rue "Ange Rouge".	Rue "Ange Rouge".
JOUR / NUIT / MIXTE				Mixte	Mixte	Jour		Nuit	Mixte	Jour		Jour	Jour		Mixte	Mixte	Mixte	Mixte
NUMEROS DES SEQUENCES				0, 24	25, 26, 29	27, 28		31, (80), 82	30, (86)	59, 60, 6, (80)		38, 39, 87	36, (37), 64, 87		43, 42, 44	78, (51), 4	45, 46, (47)	65

Nombre de cachets	ACTEURS	ROLES	N°	1	2	3	4	5	6	7	8	9	10	11	12	13	14	15	16	17	18
33	Fanny ARDANT	BARBARA BECKER	1				1	1	1		1	1	1		1	1		1	1	1	1
3	Jean-Louis TRINTIGNANT	JULIEN VERCEL	2																		
1	Serge ROUSSEAU	MAITRE CLEMENT	3												3	3					
10	Philippe MORIER-GENOUD	COMMISSAIRE SANTELLI	4																4		
4	Xavier SAINT-MACARY	BERTRAND FABRE	5										5								
6	Jean-Pierre KALFON	ABBÉ MASSOULIER	6																		
6	ANIK BELAUBRE	CAISSIÈRE CINEMA	7													7		7	7	7	
6	Jean-Louis RICHARD	LOUISON	8				8	(8)										8	(8)	8	
3	Yann DEDET	FACE D'ANGE	9																		
3	CAROLINE SIHOL	MARIE-CHRISTINE VERCEL	10																		
4	Nicole FÉLIX	LA BALAFREE	11																	11	11
1	GEORGES KOULOURIS	MONSIEUR LABLACHE	12									12									
3	R. THENOT	JAMBRAU	13												13				13		
3		TROUPE THEATRE	14																		
3	ALAIN GEMBIN	METTEUR EN SCENE	15																		
1		GLADYS	16																		16
2		LES PROSTITUEES	17																	17	17
2	ISA RAMBAUD	LA FEMME DE MENAGE	18																		
2	CASTEL CASTI	CHAUFFEUR DE TAXI - NICE	19				19	19													
2	Pierre GARE	DETECTIVE POIVERT	20				(20)	20				20									
2	Roberte BOREL	CLIENTE AGENCE IMMOBILIERE	21																		
1	Isabelle BINET	SECRETAIRES AVOCAT (2)	22													22					
1	J.P. KOHUT	NOCEUR SLAVE	23						23												
2	GERARD BABOULIN	PROJECTIONNISTE CINEMA	24															24	24		
1	PAUL STEIGER	RECEPTIONNISTE HOTEL	25					25													
1		CHEF-RECEPTIONNISTE HOTEL	26					26													
1	DANY CASTAING	FEMME DE CHAMBRE HOTEL	27						27												